"Those of us now engaged as teaching artists and co-learners have the joyful responsibility to begin reimagining the future of actor training in this country, which includes centering the lived experiences and stories of our students who identify as members of historically marginalized communities. *Latinx Actor Training* is an invaluable resource for all theatre practitioners who seek to bring their full, authentic selves to their creative work. This book inspires a genuine sense of hope that, in art as in politics, intentionally making space for diverse voices to lead the conversation will result in greater liberation for *all of us*."

**Walton Wilson**, *Professor in the Practice,*
*Acting Program David Geffen School of Drama at Yale*

"I wish I'd had a resource like this to ground me and guide me. If we want a robust field full of voces artísticas in all their multifangled complexity, essays like these will help pave the way."

**Quiara Alegría Hudes**, *Pulitzer Prize-winning playwright and writer of* In the Heights

# LATINX ACTOR TRAINING

*Latinx Actor Training* presents essays and pioneering research from leading Latinx practitioners and scholars in the United States to examine the history and future of Latino/a/x/e actor training practices and approaches.

Born out of the urgent need to address the inequities in academia and the industry as Latinx representation on stage and screen remains disproportionately low despite population growth; this book seeks to reimagine and restructure the practice of actor training by inviting deep investigation into heritage and identity practices. *Latinx Actor Training* features contributions covering current and historical acting methodologies, principles, and training, explorations of linguistic identity, casting considerations, and culturally inclusive practices that aim to empower a new generation of Latinx actors and to assist the educators who are entrusted with their training.

This book is dedicated to creating career success and championing positive narratives to combat pervasive and damaging stereotypes. *Latinx Actor Training* offers culturally inclusive pedagogies that will be invaluable for students, practitioners, and scholars interested in the intersections of Latinx *herencia* (heritage), identity, and actor training.

**Cynthia Santos DeCure** is a bilingual actor, and voice, speech, dialect coach specializing in culturally inclusive pedagogies in actor training, accents, and dialects. She is an Associate Professor Adjunct of Acting at David Geffen School of Drama at Yale University, certified as Associate Teacher of Fitzmaurice Voicework® and teacher of Knight-Thompson Speechwork. A member of SAG/AFTRA and AEA with over 30 years of acting experience, Cynthia has an M.F.A. in Acting from CSULA and a B.A. in Acting from University of Southern California. She is co-editor of the award-winning anthology *Scenes for Latinx Actors*.

**Micha Espinosa** is an international teaching artist, activist, and voice/performance specialist in culturally inclusive pedagogies. She is a Professor at Arizona State University School (ASU) in the School of Music, Dance, and Theatre, affiliate faculty with ASU's School of Transborder Studies & the Sidney Poitier New American Film School (30 year member of SAG-AFTRA), Artistic Director of Fitzmaurice Voicework® (FV®), and Lead Teacher trainer for the FV® Teacher Certification. Micha is also a core member of the performance art collective La Pocha Nostra and the award-winning editor of *Monologues for Latino Actors* and co-editor of *Scenes for Latinx Actors*.

# LATINX ACTOR TRAINING

*Edited by Cynthia Santos DeCure and Micha Espinosa*

NEW YORK AND LONDON

Designed cover image: Leigh Busby

(Nefesh Cordero Pino in a scene from *BODAS DE SANGRE/BLOOD WEDDING* adapted by Tatiana Pandiani and Cynthia Santos DeCure at David Geffen School of Drama at Yale, with costume design by Travis Chinick.)

First published 2023
by Routledge
605 Third Avenue, New York, NY 10158

and by Routledge
4 Park Square, Milton Park, Abingdon, Oxon, OX14 4RN

*Routledge is an imprint of the Taylor & Francis Group, an informa business*

© 2023 Taylor & Francis

The right of Cynthia Santos DeCure and Micha Espinosa to be identified as the authors of the editorial material, and of the authors for their individual chapters, has been asserted in accordance with sections 77 and 78 of the Copyright, Designs and Patents Act 1988.

All rights reserved. No part of this book may be reprinted or reproduced or utilised in any form or by any electronic, mechanical, or other means, now known or hereafter invented, including photocopying and recording, or in any information storage or retrieval system, without permission in writing from the publishers.

*Trademark notice*: Product or corporate names may be trademarks or registered trademarks, and are used only for identification and explanation without intent to infringe.

*Library of Congress Cataloging-in-Publication Data*
Names: Santos DeCure, Cynthia, editor. | Espinosa, Micha, editor.
Title: Latinx actor training / edited by Cynthia Santos DeCure and
    Micha Espinosa.
Description: New York : Routledge, 2023. | Includes bibliographical
    references and index.
Identifiers: LCCN 2022044718 (print) | LCCN 2022044719 (ebook) |
    ISBN 9780367898595 (hardback) | ISBN 9780367898601 (paperback) |
    ISBN 9781003021520 (ebook)
Subjects: LCSH: Acting. | Hispanic American actors.
Classification: LCC PN2061 .L375 2023 (print) | LCC PN2061 (ebook) |
    DDC 792.02/80809730468—dc23/eng/20221129
LC record available at https://lccn.loc.gov/2022044718
LC ebook record available at https://lccn.loc.gov/2022044719

ISBN: 978-0-367-89859-5 (hbk)
ISBN: 978-0-367-89860-1 (pbk)
ISBN: 978-1-003-02152-0 (ebk)

DOI: 10.4324/9781003021520

Typeset in Bembo
by Apex CoVantage, LLC

*For our students and Latinx community*

# CONTENTS

Contributor Biographies *xii*
Acknowledgments *xvi*
Foreword *xviii*

    Introduction 1
    *Cynthia Santos DeCure and Micha Espinosa*

## PART 1
## History and Theory                       5

1  Ancestral Echoes: Excavating Latinx Histories
   in Actor Training                                     7
   *Chantal Rodriguez*

2  Diane Rodríguez's Acting Activism               28
   *Marci R. McMahon*

3  "Let Me Define Myself": An Interview With Puerto
   Rican *teatrera* Rosa Luisa Márquez               42
   *Priscilla Meléndez and Aníbal González*

4  Actor Training With Global Perspectives: A Historical
   Narrative of the Only Spanish-Language Theatre
   Conservatory in the United States                  50
   *Joann Yarrow*

x Contents

  5  Dr. Alma Martinez: A Narrative Toward Becoming
a Chicanx Actor    60
*Alma Martinez*

  6  Performance for Innocents: Live Art Pedagogy for Rebel
Artists With Guillermo Gómez-Peña and Luz Oropeza    73
*Paloma Martínez-Cruz*

  7  Confessions of a Racial Nomad: Indigenous-Mestizx
Ethnicity in the World of Eurocentric Performance Practices    82
*Saúl García-López aka La Saula*

## PART 2
## Acting    95

  8  The Complexity and Poetry of Latinx Identity and Actor
Training, a Narrative    97
*Micha Espinosa*

  9  From Method to Mythic: Why Latinx? Why Mythic?
How Mythic? Why Now?    110
*Marissa Chibás*

10  The Latinx Actor's Linguistic Identity: Preserving Our
Culture in Speech Training    117
*Cynthia Santos DeCure*

11  Accent and Dialect Training for the Latinx Actor    132
*Cynthia Santos DeCure*

12  Freeing the Bilingual Voice: Thoughts on Adapting the
Linklater Method Into Spanish    145
*Antonio Ocampo-Guzman*

13  Toward a Latinx-Driven Physical Theatre Pedagogy:
Acrobatic Theatre for Social Change    153
*CarlosAlexis Cruz*

14  Experiences in Working With Shakespeare in Adaptation,
Shakespeare in Spanish and Bilingual Heightened Text    164
*Cynthia Santos DeCure and Micha Espinosa*

| 15 | Navigating the Musical Theatre Industry for Latinx Actors<br>*Julio Agustin* | 176 |
|---|---|---|
| 16 | School of Autodidacts<br>*Mónica Sánchez* | 183 |
| 17 | The Five Elements<br>*Caridad Svich* | 192 |
| 18 | Afro-Latinas in Conversation: Interview With Debra Ann Byrd, Founder of Harlem Shakespeare and Creator of Becoming Othello<br>*Christin Eve Cato* | 200 |
| 19 | On Latinx Casting: Interview With Peter Murrieta, Emmy Award-Winning Writer and Producer<br>*Micha Espinosa* | 208 |
| 20 | Championing Unheard Voices: Developing the Civic Voice Through Story<br>*Michelle Lopez-Rios* | 221 |
| 21 | Theatre Where You Are<br>*Emilio Rodriguez* | 228 |
| 22 | Strategies for Directing Latinx Plays<br>*Jerry Ruiz* | 235 |
| 23 | Teaching Acting Using the Four Agreements as a Framework for Self-Acceptance and Cultural Connection<br>*Christina Marín* | 243 |
| 24 | Performance of Identity—A Practice<br>*Marie Ramirez Downing* | 255 |
| 25 | Fitzmaurice Voicework® as a Contemplative Practice and a Decolonizing Agent in Actor Training<br>*Lorenzo González Fontes* | 262 |

*Bendiciones* 273
*Index* 274

# CONTRIBUTOR BIOGRAPHIES

**Julio Agustin** is an Associate Professor and Director of Music Theatre at Elon University. His Broadway credits include *Chicago, Fosse, Bells Are Ringing, and Women on the Verge of a Nervous Breakdown*. He is a nominated director-choreographer: The Geva, Theatre Under the Stars, Hangar, New Haarlem Arts. His refereed articles: *Theatre Topics, SDC Journal*. Author: *The Professional Actor's Handbook: From Casting Call to Curtain Call*.

**Christin Eve Cato** is Playwright and Performing Artist from the Bronx. She holds an M.F.A. in Playwriting from Indiana University and completed her B.A. degree at Fordham University. Cato is also a graduate of Fiorello H. LaGuardia High School for Music and Art and the Performing Arts. Her work can be found on New Play Exchange. www.christinevecato.com

**Marissa Chibás** is a Cuban American writer, award winning filmmaker, actor, and #1 new release author on Amazon for her book, *Mythic Imagination and the Actor*. Her solo show, *Daughter of a Cuban Revolutionary*, toured the United States, Europe, and Mexico. Marissa is Director of Duende CalArts and a Sundance Fellow.

**CarlosAlexis Cruz** is Producing Artistic Director of the Nouveau Sud Circus project, a circus for social change company in service of intercultural and cross-cultural communication in the urban region of Charlotte, North Carolina. Cruz is an Associate Professor of Physical Theatre and the Diversity Coordinator for the College of Arts + Architecture at the University of North Carolina at Charlotte.

Contributor Biographies **xiii**

**Cynthia Santos DeCure** is an Associate Professor Adjunct of Acting at David Geffen School of Drama at Yale University. She is a bilingual actor member of SAG/AFTRA, AEA, and voice, speech, dialect coach certified in Knight-Thompson Speechwork and Associate Teacher of Fitzmaurice Voicework®, specializing in culturally inclusive pedagogies in actor training, accents, and dialects; M.F.A. in acting from CSULA; B.A. in acting from University of Southern California; Co-editor: award-winning *Scenes for Latinx Actors*.

**Marie Ramirez Downing** is an Assistant Professor of Theatre Arts at Sonoma State University. She has an M.F.A. in Acting from The Theatre School at DePaul University and B.A. in Theatre Arts, Acting from California State University, Fresno. She is a Designated Linklater Voice Teacher.

**Micha Espinosa** is a Professor at Arizona State University (B.F.A., Stephens College; M.F.A. Acting, U.C. San Diego). She is an International teaching artist, Activist, and Voice specialist in culturally inclusive pedagogies; Artistic Director of Fitzmaurice Voicework® (FV®), trainer for the FV® Teacher Certification; award-winning editor of *Monologues for Latino Actors* & Co-editor, *Scenes for Latinx Actors*.

**Lorenzo González Fontes** is a Theatre performer, Director, and Educator. He is an Associate Professor at Naropa University. He received his M.F.A. from the Professional Theatre Training Program (PTTP) at the University of Delaware, and is Associate Teacher of Fitzmaurice Voicework®.

**Saúl García-López aka La Saula** is a Professor of Performance at the Norwegian Theatre Academy, and Co-artistic Director of La Pocha Nostra. Saul is Co-author of the book *La Pocha Nostra: A Handbook for the Rebel Artist in a Post-Democratic Society*. His work focuses on performance pedagogy, indigeneity, gender, and decolonial theory.

**Aníbal González** is a Professor of Modern Latin American Literature at Yale University. A Guggenheim fellow, he has authored seven books of literary criticism. His most recent are *Love and Politics in the Contemporary Spanish American Novel* and *In Search of the Sacred Book: Religion and the Contemporary Latin American Novel*.

**Jorge A. Huerta**, Ph.D., is Chancellor's Associates Professor of Theatre *Emeritus* at the University of California, San Diego, California, the United States. He has directed in regional theaters throughout the United States and is a leading authority on contemporary Chicanx and Latinx theatre. He published the first book about Chicano theater, *Chicano Theater: Themes and Forms* (Bilingual press 1982) and *Chicano Drama: Performance, Society and Myth* (Cambridge 2000); as well as many articles in journals, anthologies and has edited three collections of plays.

**Michelle Lopez-Rios** is an Associate teacher of Fitzmaurice Voicework® and Co-founder of the Royal Mexican Players. As a director, teaching artist, and activist, she has explored voices with many community organizations, professional performers, and students. She is an Associate Professor of Voice at The Theatre School at DePaul University.

**Christina Marín**, PhD is currently the Program Director for Theatre & Film at Phoenix College in Phoenix, Arizona. She is a Bilingual actor and Director and has worked at La Universidad de Antioquia in Medellín, Colombia; New York University, and Emerson College in Boston.

**Alma Martinez**, PhD is an Associate Professor, Department of Theatre at the University of La Verne and Emerita Faculty, Theatre and Dance Department, at UC Santa Cruz. Her publications and research examine the interstices of Chicanx/Latinx and Latin American political theatre. A prolific actor, she is a member of SAG AFTRA, AEA, SDC, and the Academy of Motion Picture Arts & Sciences.

**Paloma Martínez-Cruz** teaches Latinx Cultural Studies at The Ohio State University. She is Author of *Food Fight! Millennial Mestizaje Meets the Culinary Marketplace* (2019) and Editor of *A Handbook for the Rebel Artist in a Post-Democratic Society* (2021). She is a core member of La Pocha Nostra and directs Onda Latina Ohio.

**Marci R. McMahon**, Professor at The University of Texas Rio Grande Valley, has over 20 years of experience leveraging her voice as an advocate for Latinx stories in curriculum and on theater stages. She is the author of *Domestic Negotiations: Gender, Nation, and Self-Fashioning in US Mexicana and Chicana Literature and Art* (Rutgers University Press, 2013).

**Priscilla Meléndez** is a Professor of Hispanic Studies at Trinity College in Hartford. She is a specialist in Spanish American theatre and the author of *La dramaturgia hispanoamericana contemporánea: Teatralidad y autoconciencia*, *The Politics of Farce in Contemporary Spanish American Theater*, and *Asaltos al escenario: Humor, género e historia en el teatro de Sabina Berman* (Forthcoming). She earned her B.A. in Hispanic Studies from the University of Puerto Rico and received her Ph.D. from Cornell University.

**Antonio Ocampo-Guzman** is an Associate Professor and Chair of the Department of Theatre at Northeastern University and President-VASTA (2022–2024). Antonio is trained with Teatro Libre in his native Bogotá, Colombia, and has an M.F.A. in Directing and a Graduate Diploma in Voice from York University, Toronto. He is Designated Linklater Teacher and is the author of *La Liberación de la Voz Natural: El Método Linklater* (UNAM, 2010).

**Chantal Rodriguez** is Associate Dean of David Geffen School of Drama at Yale University, and Associate Professor Adjunct in the School's Dramaturgy and Dramatic Criticism Program. Chantal holds a Ph.D. in Theater and Performance Studies from UCLA and a B.A. in Theatre and Spanish Studies from Santa Clara University.

**Emilio Rodriguez** is recipient of a Kresge Detroit Artist Award, a National Association for Latino Arts and Culture Catalyst for Change Grant and the Victor Bumbalo/Robert Chesley LGBT Playwriting Award. He has taught at Michigan Actors Studio, Kalamazoo College and currently teaches at the University of Michigan.

**Jerry Ruiz** is an Assistant Professor of Directing at Texas State. His directing credits include the world premieres of *Fade* and *Mala Hierba* by Tanya Saracho (DCPA, Second Stage); *Twelfth Night* (Old Globe, PlayMakers); *Basilica* by Mando Alvarado; (Rattlestick Playwrights Theater) and *Enfrascada* by Tanya Saracho (Clubbed Thumb). M.F.A., UC San Diego; B.A., Harvard University.

**Mónica Sánchez** is an Actor, Playwright, and Educator, originally from New Mexico. She is an Assistant Professor of Playwriting and Performance at Colorado College. As a theatre maker, Mónica continues striving to understand, to translate, and to transform the metaphor of the world through the world of metaphor. www.dramatista.com.

**Caridad Svich's** recognitions include an OBIE for Lifetime Achievement, Ellen Stewart Career Achievement Award from ATHE, and a Visiting Research Fellowship at Royal Central School of Speech and Drama. She is Editor at *Contemporary Theatre Review*. She is published by Intellect, Routledge, Manchester University Press and Methuen Drama, the United Kingdom.

**Joann Maria Yarrow** is a professional director and producer with 35 years of experience collaborating with creative teams globally. She is Director for Community Engagement and Education at Syracuse Stage. She was Artistic Director of Teatro Prometeo, co-founded A Laboratory for Actor Training with Vernice Miller, and worked for Hal Prince on seven Broadway productions.

# ACKNOWLEDGMENTS

We thank our ancestors.

During the course of writing this book we experienced the loss of our parents and family members.

Cynthia thanks the late Ray Santos, who offered years of counsel and modeling of how to be an artist. Thank you to the late Rosemary DeCuir, for her generous spirit and enthusiasm to always keep going. Thank you to the late Mary Louise Espinosa, who was an inspiration to all who knew her and will be forever missed, and the late Marco Espinosa, whose service to others will always make him a veteran for veterans.

Micha would like to thank the late Manuel Gregorio Espinosa, who taught her how to sing and dance and to not be afraid of love.

To those still with us:

Cynthia thanks her mother and step-father Maria del Carmen Santos and JR Rodriguez, *por su amor y apoyo*. Micha thanks her *hermanas,* Cha Cha Mosseso and Darel Whitman for the late night conversations.

We thank the many friends and colleagues who supported us in challenging times, especially Tiffany Lopez, Chantal Rodriguez and Jorge Huerta.

To Stacy Walker, thank you for your unwavering faith, and Lucia Accorsi, for your patience and guidance toward the completion of this book. We thank Kevin G. Little for his sage advice, and Martha Baker for her clarity and humor.

Cynthia would like to thank her husband, John DeCure, for his extraordinary listening and loving support. Micha would like to thank her friends Steve Mena, Lissa Tyler Renaud, Mark Plutowski, and Gordon Freeman for always being willing to chat about an idea or offer support when needed.

We would also like to thank Arizona State University (ASU), Herberger Institute for Design and the Arts for officially supporting this work. Principally, we thank Dean Steven Tepper, Senior Associate Dean Sandy Stauffer, Director Heather Landes, and Business Manager Shauna Allison, who helped us manage the Herberger Institute Research-Building Investment (HIRBI) Award. Cynthia offers special thanks to David Geffen Yale School of Drama acting chairs, Walton Wilson and Tamilla Woodard. We are forever grateful to our talented contributors for their remarkable dedication to the advancement of the field.

To the next generation:

We thank our children: Colin, Aidan, and Ethan DeCure, and Kai Espinosa-Golinski. We are grateful for all for your patience during the many hours that your *mamis* were occupied during the crafting of this book. We hope that our commitment to the craft will inspire you to invest in your artistry and community.

Lastly, thank you to our students who are paving the way.

# FOREWORD

This book could not have been written during the 1960s, when Chicano and Latino theatre movements were developing across the country. However, as Professor Chantal Rodriguez points out in Chapter 1, those movements did not emerge in a vacuum; theatrical performances have been a part of Spanish-speaking and Indigenous cultures of *las Américas* for centuries. However, after the arrival of the Spanish colonizers, those theatricals were performed in Spanish and did not attract the attention of English language theatre producers or scholars until the late 1960s. As the first Chicano to earn a doctorate in Dramatic Art in 1974, my path was clear: to teach at a research university, develop courses in Chicano theatre, and direct plays, while most importantly documenting the evolution of Chicano theatre *as it was happening*. Initially, my focus was on Chicano theatre but as this volume reveals, the movement became multicultural and Pan-American. Today, the popular term is Latinx, the new iteration of these multiple identifiers.

One of the joys of reading the chapters in this book is the way in which the authors all speak of *Familia*, a family of scholars and artists who have made a life in the theatre, sometimes against all odds. Few of the contributors to this collection were already performing, directing, or producing Latinx theatre when I started my academic career in 1970. Indeed, some of the contributors were not yet born. Other contributors have trajectories that began in the 1970s and their narratives are distinct, as pioneers who paved the way for the current generation. Although I do not know some of the more recent contributors, their essays make me want to learn more about each and every one of them. So prepare yourself for honesty, sincerity and passion above all, passion with a purpose.

This volume represents the incredible intellectual and artistic growth in the field of Latinx theatre performance and training. Most of us have heard the following exclamation from a non-Latinx: "You Latins are *SO* passionate!" Although this sounds very stereotypical, it usually comes from a well-meaning person, sometimes as a microaggression. So what did the contributors in this volume do? Through a variety of actions, they turned and continue to turn their passions into a purpose with every character they interpret or create on the stage or the page. Another through line is the process of collaboration that infuses so many of these essays. Many of these contributors know one another; some met when they began their journeys and the idea of training became more than a dream, as possibilities opened up from coast to coast and on the island of Puerto Rico.

In the mid-1970s, when I first joined the American Educational Theatre Association, the predecessor to what became the Association for Theatre in Higher Education (ATHE), I was the only Chicano at the annual conferences. As the name indicates, ATHE is an international organization for theatre artists, educators, and scholars to share their work through papers, workshops, publications, etc. I also started attending the American Society for Theatre Research (ASTR) conferences in the same period. Again, I was the only Chicano, speaking for theatre that came from Chicanas and Chicanos. As the lone Chicano at these conferences, I was often asked to speak for "my people," as if we were a monolithic group. Each essay relates, quite vividly, some of the distinctions between Latinxs. But be aware that much has changed since the early period.

As the field of Latinx theatre continued to grow and evolve, the idea of professionalism was taking hold. The mainstream (read: white, male) artistic directors' indifference to plays by or about the Latinxs began to change when Joseph Papp of the New York Shakespeare Festival produced Miguel Piñero's *Short Eyes* on Broadway in 1974 and the Center Theatre Group and Teatro Campesino co-produced Luis Valdez's *Zoot Suit* in Los Angeles and New York City in 1978–1979.[1] Motivated by the critical and financial success of these plays and *Zoot Suit*'s record-breaking run in Los Angeles, some non-profit mainstream theatre companies began to show an interest in what Latinos were writing and began to solicit their plays. Some of us decided to "play in the Big House." This practice can be termed either "mainstreaming" or "infiltrating," depending upon one's point of view as well as the results of such alliances. The cultural map was expanding to include plays about the Chicano, Puerto Rican, and Cuban communities of the country, slowly exposing non-Latino audiences to these little-known populations, some of whom could trace their "American" ancestry back centuries.

I call the 1980s the beginning of the professional stage of Latinx theatre. Instrumental to that development, the Ford Foundation began to bolster what was then being called Hispanic-American theatre in the United States and Puerto Rico. One of the most important initiatives of this effort was a fully funded "National Hispanic Theater Conference" in San Antonio, Texas, in 1986. That meeting brought together theatre artists, directors, producers, and funders to discuss the state of "Hispanic-American" theatre. One hundred thirty representatives of the leading and emerging theatre groups from across the country and Puerto Rico attended the San Antonio meeting. There were keynote speakers, panels, workshops, performances, and other activities that ushered in the next phase of Latinx theatre in this country. Actor training was among the major topics.

Prior to the 1986 conference in San Antonio, the Chicano *teatros* were performing mainly to their respective communities from California to the mid-west, while the Puerto Rican and Cuban groups in the Northeast and South Florida also played to their particular audiences. I observed that there was no love lost between the conservative Cubans and the more progressive Chicanos and "Nuyoricans" (Puerto Ricans living in the boroughs of New York), who shared leftist politics. But this two-day gathering demonstrated how much the participants had in common. Alliances were formed, connections were made, and everybody returned to their respective communities and companies with renewed enthusiasm. This was a major step in bringing the Four Corners (including the "southeast corner" of Puerto Rico) together, reviving an important Indigenous relationship with "*La Tierra, Nuestra Madre*" (Mother Earth).

When the Ford Foundation published a report on the state of Hispanic theatre in the mainland and Puerto Rico in 1988, it was clear that there were a number of Latinx theatre companies that were artistically sound but financially in trouble.[2] In response, the Theatre Program of the Ford Foundation began to offer grants to *teatros* to enhance their fiscal management. The Director of the Theatre Program asked if I would moderate two meetings of the 12 leading companies and I gladly agreed. The first meeting was held in San Juan Bautista, California, December 5–7, 1986, and the second meeting was held in San Juan Puerto Rico, June 12–17, 1987. The main topic of discussion would center on "Artistic Direction in Hispanic-American Theatre." These historic meetings were attended by "The Founders," leaders in the field, individuals who had begun their trajectories in the 1960s.[3] They will all be mentioned in this book.

Alongside the noble efforts aimed at Hispanic theaters, the Ford Foundation also began to pump funds into mainstream theaters for their "Hispanic Projects." Theaters across the country vied for these dollars as well as for major funding from the Rockefeller Foundation and the Lila Wallace Reader's Digest Fund, among others. As you read these chapters, you will note that several people in this book participated in many of the projects across the country. These projects became important development tools for Latino playwrights and theatre artists across the country. As a participant in many of these initiatives, as a director or an observer, I noted that as the years passed, the quality of acting was improving. Two of the most important projects were INTAR's Hispanic Playwright-in-Residence Laboratory, run by the late Maria Irene Fornés, and the South Coast Repertory's "Hispanic Playwright's Project."[4]

Language was a major concern for *teatros* across the country. Companies like *Repertorio Español* and *Thalía* in Manhattan, and Miami's *Teatro Avante* were producing their works in Spanish only, while INTAR (International Artists Relations) was producing Latin American plays in English only. The Puerto Rican Traveling Theatre began by taking plays to the people, performing outdoors; the other groups were performing indoors, to a more educated and affluent audience base, eager to see their plays in the language of the homeland.[5]

Language has always been a consideration for Latinx writers and artists if they want to reach the working-class communities, who are generally native Spanish speakers and/or recent emigres from south of the border. In the earliest stages of Chicano and Nuyorican theatre, the *actos* (brief, satiric sketches) or plays were generally bilingual. You will read about the use of "code-switching" in this book. The earliest plays reflected how many Latinx families communicated in a combination of English and Spanish. This was prevalent in the Nuyorican communities of Manhattan. The Puerto Rican Traveling Theatre performed in both languages with plays by contemporary Nuyorican or Puerto Rican playwrights as well as Spanish plays from a variety of countries. Another New York company, the *Repertorio Español* (Spanish Repertory), performed Spanish Golden Age classics, in the original verse. In terms of the Cuban or Cuban-American theaters, the language was generally Spanish, often in classical text or contemporary plays from Cuba, also, of course, *en español*.

Language is one of the most obvious topics that these contributors share. As you will read, language can be a challenge for an actor who learned to speak English as a second language and wants to perform "mainstream" plays, which call for a standard American accent, or a third-generation Latinx who self-identifies as Latinx but who does not speak Spanish. Being told by a non-Latinx person that "you're different" is almost a universal for Latinxs. Or the more common question from a non-Latinx person is "Where are you from?"

What these chapters confirm is that Latinx actors of all backgrounds and language proficiencies have to work hard to achieve their goals as artists, as teachers, and as spokespeople for their communities. Sometimes, a Latinx actor who is fluent in both Spanish and English will perform in the same play, changing languages from one performance to another. You will read how this issue is or is not addressed in reference to Latinx actors. Some of the authors are native-born Spanish speakers while others' first language is English. Further, there are degrees of language abilities as well as differences in *what* Spanish is required in a play, depending upon the actor's background and training. Having directed plays with the same cast in both languages, the majority of actors have told me they prefer the play *en español*. Of course, both Spanish and English are beautiful languages but there is something about performing in Spanish, especially for the Spanish speakers in the audience whose appreciation for the language is palpable.

In the early period there were very few Latinx plays in print and few critical studies of the field *in English* because the majority of scholars writing about theatre from *Las Americas* were Spanish literature professors, publishing in Spanish or Portuguese. Further, those professors wrote about the *text*, generally, not the *acting*, unless they had witnessed the play in either Latin America or the United States. But eventually, English-speaking theatre scholars began to pay attention to live theatre from Latinx playwrights. We now have so many books, anthologies of critical essays, and articles about all aspects of Latinx theatre published in a variety of scholarly journals—not to mention plays—that we cannot teach them all in a year, which is another reason why this book is so important to the field. Professors Santos DeCure and Espinosa are leaders in the field of training professional and graduate student actors in acting, voice, speech, and dialects. Their journeys, like so many of the contributors, began as actors on stage, television, and film. And like almost all of the contributors, their early experiences as students were difficult, as marginalized or ignored in the classrooms or auditions. Now they, and the contributors to this unique volume, are the mentors bringing to the world of theatre studies this, the first book of its kind in Latinx actor training.

The chapters in this collection are varied, including contributions by actor practitioners, movement practitioners, producers, scholars, performance theorists, directors, and playwrights. The format includes round-table discussions as well as interviews. All of the essays are written from the heart, eager to share their journeys. The contributors had wonderful teachers and not-so-wonderful teachers and directors but their foci are always on the positive. It is important to recognize where the contributors are coming from, both literally and figuratively. In the early period, the three major Latinx groups in the United States had roots in Mexico, Puerto Rico, or Cuba. By the turn of the 21st century, we began to see plays by Dominicans, Salvadorians, and combinations of Latinx cultures, including Afro-Latinxs, finally coming to the fore as representatives of the African diaspora in *Las Americas*—and many whose backgrounds are bi-cultural or multi-cultural.

For years, producers and directors, as well as university theatre professors, would say "There are no Hispanic plays" or "There are no Hispanic actors." That was then, this is now. And the list does not include the number of plays that have been published since Luis Valdez's first play *The Shrunken Head of Pancho Villa* was first produced in 1974. As the field evolved from performance-centered to plot and character-driven plays, Latinx playwrights were writing plays that challenged the actors. Most importantly, the characters in these plays were no longer stereotypes and if they were, it was for a reason.

In conclusion, I think the underlying message in this collection is that the Latinx actor often stands apart, in the wings, as it were, hoping to be noticed. Some of the contributors learned by what we used to call, "OJT," that is, "on the job training." They learned by doing as well as by observing. They also learned by "infiltrating" theatre departments and regional theaters, as this volume attests. The authors in this book represent some of the people who have built communities of actors, playwrights, directors, designers, and producers who know the distinctions, sometimes subtle, at other times, stark, between the cultures represented in this collection and beyond. This long-awaited anthology centering the Latinx actor will inspire more serious examinations of this kind: actor training that is inclusive of all communities and cultures that represent the many faces of the United States.

*Jorge A. Huerta, Ph.D.,*

## Notes

1. *Zoot Suit* was produced on Broadway in 1979 but closed after a five-week run due to mostly negative reviews. See Broyles-Gonzalez, Chapter 4, for an excellent discussion of the evolution of *Zoot Suit* during this period. What is important to note here is the fact that although the play did not fare well on Broadway, the Los Angeles run lasted 11 months, longer than any other professional platy in Los Angeles at the time.
2. The Ford Foundation commissioned an assessment of Hispanic Theatre in 1986–1987. See Joanne Pottlitzer's monograph "Hispanic Theater in the United States and Puerto Rico." A Ford Foundation report, 1988. ISBN 0–916584-33-X.
3. The following founders have since passed: Rene Buch, (*Repertorio Español, NYC*), Miriam Colon (Puerto Rican Traveling Theatre, NYC), Max Ferra (INTAR NYC), and Carmen Zapata (Bilingual Foundation of the Arts, Los Angeles, California). Other participants who are no longer with us are Tony Curiel (Teatro Campesino) and Ruben Sierra (The Group Theatre, Seattle, Washington).
4. The South Coast Repertory's Hispanic Playwrights Project was initiated under the direction of José Cruz González and later guided by Juliette Carrillo. Among the more prominent "Projects" were Teatro Meta, Old Globe Theatre, San Diego, California; Latino Theatre Initiative, Center Theatre Group, Los Angeles; Latino Theatre Lab, Los Angeles Theatre Center; New York Shakespeare Festival, "*Festival Latino*;" Hispanic Playwright's Project, South Coast Repertory, Costa Mesa, California. Of these, none exist today. The only project that still exists is the San Diego Rep's, "*Teatro Sin Fronteras*."
5. For an analysis and history of INTAR, the Puerto Rican Traveling Theatre and *Repertorio Español,* see Elisa de la Roche, *¡Teatro Hispano! Three Major New York Companies, Garland*, 1995.

# INTRODUCTION

*Cynthia Santos DeCure and Micha Espinosa*

In 2010, Ellen Margolis and Lissa Tyler Renaud, in their book *The Politics of Actor Training*, highlighted the need to create scholarship that analyzes policies, practices, theory, and pedagogy of the 21st-century American actor training. The essay "Identity Politics and the Training of the Latino Actors"[1] illuminated the challenges Latinx actors encounter when training, including the systemic erasure of language and identity, which lead to diminishing pathways of success and visibility. Our book, *Latinx Actor Training*, continues the long-needed conversation to ameliorate the ongoing struggles and develop pathways for success.

This book was born out of the urgent need to address the inequities in training that we experienced and witnessed in academia and the industry. We are actresses-scholars, *madres*, and *teatristas* who met over a decade ago and bonded when we saw our students perpetually measured by Eurocentric values. We have developed a lasting collaboration as colleagues in the field and allies in the struggle for social justice for Latinx actors and narratives. To that end, we work from an anti-racist ethos and commit to a hemispheric awareness and the centering of people of the Global Majority/BIPOC[2] as we seek to realign actor training to have a more diverse and global perspective. This book seeks to re-imagine and restructure the practice of actor training by inviting culturally inclusive forms and deep investigation into heritage and identity practices.

We acknowledge that we are not alone in this struggle, and several scholars and artists have forged pathways for change, such as the published scholarship by *Black Acting Methods*, *Intercultural Acting and Performance Training*, and *A Korean Approach to Actor Training*, among others. Their work along with that of We See You White American Theatre, and many more social justice warriors, continues to shed light on the disadvantages that BIPOC actors face. Acting is action, and we offer this book as a collective call to action.

DOI: 10.4324/9781003021520-1

This book is needed today more than ever. Latinx representation on stage and screen has remained disproportionately low despite the population growth. In the United States, Latinx actors are underrepresented on screen, accounting for an average of 6 percent of roles in television and film,[3] and on stage less than 4 percent,[4] even though we comprise 62.1 million,[5] or 18.5 percent, of the nation's population and are projected to reach 106 million by 2050.[6] The vicious cycle of these continuing low numbers is disheartening and unacceptable. They confirm a systemic invisibility of Latinx actors across the industry.

Since the inception of Latinx Theatre Commons (LTC) in 2013, we have joined the LTC's efforts to champion the visibility of Latinx artists. We laud the work and scholarship of the LTC, which has advanced the craft of Latinx creatives through its convenings. With *Latinx Actor Training*, we contribute to their efforts to transform the narrative by intentionally centering the Latinx actor, along with Latinx practitioners and pedagogues who guide them in training.

In assembling this book, we have brought together scholars and practitioners of theatre to offer historical, pedagogical, and theoretical approaches to the practice of acting. We seek to redefine the scope of our community and positively recast the perception of our work. The book includes 25 chapters to examine our intersectional and multidimensional identities and practices, and although it is not all-encompassing, we strive to bring the scholarship forward and invite further investigations. The range of expertise our community possesses is not always represented in traditional academic publishing; thus, in this collection, you will find academic scholars, practitioners, and theatre makers authoring chapters.

This book uses the synonyms Latinx, Latine, and Latino/a to be inclusive. We welcome unidimensional terminology. The variety of economic, social, and political ideologies of Latinidad demands self-identification. Our 2019 collection, *Scenes for Latinx Actors*, describes Latinx identities as "hyphenated, multiple, constructed, reclaimed, colonized, vilified, commercialized, internalized and inevitably evolving with the intersectionality of race, class, gender, sexuality, and politics."[7] We stand by the usage of Latinx because it offers an inclusive attitude toward gender and sexual identities, celebrates the vast expression and experiences of our community, and embraces intersectionality. We acknowledge that there are arguments for and against its use, but we believe "Latinx" provides the possibility of expansion within the bipartite of cultural heritage and American identity.

Dr. Jorge Huerta, professor emeritus at the University of California, San Diego, draws on his expertise in Chicano and Latinx theatre to offer a foreword to the chapters in this book. We begin with historical and theoretical perspectives in Latinx actor training that may not be widely known. Finally, the most extensive section offers a myriad of lenses into the practice of acting through the Latinx experience. The contributors of this book display a variety of writing styles from pedagogical examinations to narrative formats in order to mirror the diverse expression of our community. Spanish and Spanglish—sounds that are often omitted in classrooms of training—are interlaced in these chapters to make language visible.

In this collection we offer new perspectives, curricular innovations, and reconfigurations of traditional approaches to empower a new generation of Latinx actors, and to assist educators who are entrusted with their training. We hope Latinx actors and communities find themselves represented in this book, which can foster a sense of belonging that comes from understanding one's history. We anticipate that Latinx actors will read these pages to find culturally competent mentors, coaches, and champions to help them navigate training toward a clearer pathway of academic and professional success. Finally, we are optimistic that this book will bring visibility to Latinx creatives and champion positive narratives to combat pervasive and damaging stereotypes. Ultimately this book is for all who are dedicated to creating culturally responsive pedagogy. We strongly believe that if we change the training, we change the industry.

## Notes

1. Micha Espinosa and Antonio Ocampo-Guzman, "Identity Politics and Training of Latino Actors," in *The Politics of American Actor Training*, eds. Ellen Margolis and Lissa Tyler Renaud (New York: Routledge, 2010).
2. BIPOC stands for Black, Indigenous, and People of Color.
3. An average of 6 percent according to the UCLA Hollywood Diversity Report 2022 (2021 television and film 7 roles) and the 2021 USC Annenberg report (5% of film roles between 2007 and 2019). Darnell Hunt and Ana-Christina Ramón, "Hollywood Diversity Report 2022," *socialsciences.ucla.edu*, March 24, 2022, https://socialsciences.ucla.edu/wp-content/uploads/2022/03/UCLA-Hollywood-Diversity-Report-2022-Film-3-24-2022.pdf.
4. Ariana Case, Zoily Mercado, and Karla Hernandez, "Hispanic and Latino Representation in Film," *uscannenberg.org*, September 13, 2021, https://assets.uscannenberg.org/docs/aii-hispanic-latino-rep-2021-09-13.pdf.
5. According to the Actors Equity Diversity and Inclusion report of 2020, and the AAPAC Visibility Report of 2018–19 reported, Latinx actors worked 3.46 and 3.9 percent, respectively, of all the jobs reported. "Total—Actors' Equity Association," *Actors Equity Association Diversity and Inclusion Report 2020*, November 18, 2020, https://actorsequity.org/news/PR/DandIReport2020/diversity-and-inclusion-report-2020.
6. Pew Research Center reported a projected change in the US Hispanic (Latinx) population by 2050 from 133 million to 106 million, still reflecting an increase of double the population of the reported 2020 US Census. Jens Manuel Krogstad, "Census Bureau Lowers Forecasts for Hispanic Population Growth," *Pew Research Center*, September 4, 2020, www.pewresearch.org/fact-tank/2014/12/16/with-fewer-new-arrivals-census-lowers-hispanic-population-projections.
7. Micha Espinosa and Cynthia DeCure, *Scenes for Latinx Actors: Voices of the New American Theatre* (Hanover, NH: Smith and Kraus, 2018), 23.

# PART 1
# History and Theory

# 1

# ANCESTRAL ECHOES

## Excavating Latinx Histories in Actor Training

*Chantal Rodriguez*

In the fall of 2020, amidst an online year at the David Geffen School of Drama at Yale, I attended a meeting of El Colectivo, the School's student Latinx affinity group.[1] As Associate Dean of the School I support student life including affinity groups, and as Associate Professor Adjunct of Dramaturgy and Dramatic Criticism, I teach a variety of courses, including Latinx Theatre. During the meeting, I was chatting with an international student from Mexico who is enrolled in the Technical Design and Production program, and they asked if I knew about Nancy Cardenás, a famous alum from the school. I was not familiar with her, and the student recounted how friends and family in Mexico, upon hearing that they were coming to Yale to study Drama, immediately mentioned Nancy and that they were going to "her school." The student explained that Cardenás was a famous artist from Mexico, who studied directing at Yale in 1961, and was well known for her work as an actress, playwright, poet, and director. She catapulted to queer icon status when she became the first woman to publicly declare that she was a lesbian on Mexican television in 1973. I felt a sense of pride knowing that this trailblazer trained at Yale, and then immediately wondered why I had never heard that she was an alum. Later that year, Sebastián Eddowes Vargas, a then first-year M.F.A. candidate in Dramaturgy and Dramatic Criticism, profiled Cardenás in the School's annual alumni magazine. Reflecting on her art, he states, "Nancy's words are urgent. We keep invoking her voice, as ancestor and queer mother. Creating genealogies to feel less alone, to open a space for us, for those who are on their way."[2]

The process of uncovering Latinx ancestors in theatre training, particularly in predominantly white institutions, is challenging. Archives are incomplete and unstable. As we try to discover those who have come before, we scan surnames of alumni in an imperfect search for their traces. We know that Latinx representation

DOI: 10.4324/9781003021520-3

is complex and must be understood in terms of cultural, linguistic, geographic, ethnic, and racial categories. We also know that it might be impossible to uncover lineages that may have been obscured as a means of survival. Archives and oral histories become key tools for Latinx students, faculty, and staff seeking confirmation that they walk in the steps of their collective ancestors as they work to also leave imprints "for those who are on their way."

I'm writing this essay from my personal perspective as a Latina who originally began my education in the theatre with the goal of being an actress. My path toward studying the history of Latinx theatre was sparked by a course on August Wilson's Century Cycle taught by Professor Aldo Billingslea at Santa Clara University. As the best academic courses do, it served as a catalyst for me to learn more about the many theatre histories that I had not yet been exposed to as I marveled at Wilson's brilliance. I felt compelled to seek out Chicano/Latinx theatre histories and play a part in documenting and teaching them.[3] While I consider my acting training fundamental to my work as a dramaturg, educator, and administrator, I have often wondered how my training might have progressed had I been exposed to the works of Dolores Prida, María Irene Fornés, Luis Valdez, René Marqués, and so many others earlier in my studies. I coupled my formal academic training in the doctoral program of Theater and Performance Studies at UCLA, with post-graduate professional work with the Latino Theater Company in Los Angeles, which served as a training ground for me and so many other artists. I offer this exploration as a contribution to spark further scholarship documenting the influence and impacts of Latinx actor training histories. There is no singular history so as an entry point, I engage two key threads: highlighting some of the historic and contemporary training opportunities offered by Chicano/Latinx theatre companies, and exhuming key institutional Latinx theatre initiatives and programs, which have led to experiments with new models in training for Latinx actors.

## Chicano/Latinx Theatre Companies as Fertile Training Grounds

In tracing influences of Latinx actor training, it is vital to honor the legacy of companies who have preserved and developed performance traditions, and created laboratories on their stages for actors to train. Revered scholar Nicolás Kanellos has expertly documented the early history of Spanish-language troupes and resident companies throughout the late 19th century across the United States. These companies engaged in diverse theatrical forms from Latin America including the *pastorela*, *juguete*, *zarzuela*, *circo*, *revista*, *carpa*, and religious and historical dramas.[4] Contemporary Chicano/Latinx theatre is most often understood as emerging in the 1960s and 1970s with activist theatre companies on both the East and West coasts, using theatre as an artistic tool for social justice. As a Chicano/Latinx theatre movement emerged, companies grew in their aesthetic and political approaches to the work which has led to a wide spectrum of theatre-making practices. Through Chicano/Latinx and Latin American ensemble-based practices in these companies, many Latinx actors have gained experience in approaches to performance including but not limited to the development of *rasquache* aesthetics, devised work, naturalism, magical realism, documentary theatre, heightened language, bilingual theatre, agit-prop and political theatre, avant-garde theatre, ritual drama, and so much more within embodied artistic and cultural practices. What follows serves as a roll call of key companies across the United States that have served as training grounds for Latinx actors seeking culturally rooted storytelling models that expand beyond traditional European models. This list is by no means exhaustive, but in its scope I hope it will inspire an understanding of the immense breadth of this essential work.

The history of El Teatro Campesino (ETC) and its role in the development of the Chicano Theatre Movement on the West Coast have been well traversed by scholars like Jorge Huerta and Yolanda Broyles-González, who chart its seismic impact on the field. Originally created as a theatre by, for, and about farmworkers, the life of the *teatro* itself became a formative training ground for people who may have otherwise never considered themselves actors. Focusing on three branches—professional arts, community arts, and arts education—ETC continues to center access to the theatre for artists at all stages of their development. Most recently, the publication of Luis Valdez's *Theatre of the Sphere: The Vibrant Being* has given theatre practitioners unprecedented access to a model of actor training developed by Valdez, that reflects a syncretic practice blending Aztec and Mayan philosophy, along with Mexican and European performance traditions.[5] ETC inspired the creation of teatros across the country, many of which began as student groups in colleges and universities. Two other foundational companies rooted in the teatro tradition are Su Teatro in Denver Colorado and Borderlands Theater in Tucson Arizona. Su Teatro is the third oldest Chicano theater in the county, founded as a student theatre group at the University of Colorado at Denver in 1972. Led by Executive Artistic Director Tony Garcia, the company's mission is "the preservation of the cultural arts, heritage, and traditions of the Chicano/Latino community."[6] In providing theatre training in acting, singing, technical elements, playwriting, directing, music, and movement, their Cultural Arts Education Institute aims "to teach the next generation of teatro students the skills necessary for success."[7] Borderlands Theater also traces its roots to the teatro movement with many of its original members having been part of the Chicano group Teatro Libertad in the 1970s. Borderlands Theater was officially founded in 1986, by Barclay Goldsmith and has been committed "to the development and production of theatre and education programs that reflect the diverse voices of the U.S./Mexico border region."[8]

On the East Coast, the history of the Puerto Rican Traveling Theatre (PRTT), founded by Míriam Colón in 1967, and Pregones Theater, founded by Rosalba Rolón and a group of artists in 1979, is also well documented as being rooted in the power of the artistic collective, honoring the richness of Puerto Rican culture and a commitment to Latinx-centered artist training.[9] Central to the foundation of both companies, which merged in 2014, has always been an educational branch dedicated to training Latinx actors. The famed Raúl Julia Training Unit, founded in 1969 as the Training Unit, was originally the leading place for Latinx actors to train in New York. The program continues through innovative partnerships with groups like R. Evolución Latina and the SITI Company, and approaches to interdisciplinary actor training.[10] International Arts Relations, better known as INTAR, is another pillar of Latinx theatre on the East Coast. Founded in 1966 by Max Ferrá, INTAR is committed to nurturing the professional development of Latinx artists. INTAR's programs include a New Works Lab and Unit 52. Created in response to the lack of Latinx actors in Actor's Equity Association, Unit 52 is a key program for actors of color to hone their skills with legendary artists at INTAR for free through a year-long training program.[11] One notable collaboration inspired by connections made at INTAR is the birth of the LAByrinth Theater Company, originally known as Latino Actors Base, which was founded at INTAR in 1992 by a group of actors who wanted to expand their artistic limits and engage in more inclusive forms of storytelling to challenge the boundaries of mainstream theatre.[12]

The desire to work in an ensemble method is also central to the history of the Latino Theater Company in Los Angeles which also has roots in the Chicano Theatre Movement. Originally created as The Latino Lab in 1985, Artistic Director José Luis Valenzuela initially brought together 22 Latinx actors to rehearse and read Latinx plays.[13] While the core ensemble has changed in size over time, the company continues to provide access to training opportunities for artists at all stages of their careers.[14] The Latino Theater Company also operates the Los Angeles Theatre Center (LATC), a multi-theater complex in downtown Los Angeles. Through their stewardship of the LATC, the company works to give Latinx actors a home for the development of new work. The company's educational programming includes rigorous training for high school students through a Youth Summer Conservatory and the Play at Work after school program. Most recently the company announced an innovative partnership with Los Angeles Mission College for a directed study course with founding artistic director and UCLA Emeritus Distinguished Professor José Luis Valenzuela, including attending productions at the LATC.[15]

Another key company in Los Angeles is Casa 0101 in Boyle Heights, which was founded by Josefina López in 2000 and has become a leading organization in Los Angeles dedicated to "providing inspiring theatre performances, arts exhibits and educational programs in Boyle Heights, thereby nurturing the future storytellers of Los Angeles who will someday transform the world." Since its inception, Casa 0101 has offered year-round adult and youth classes in acting and writing. In reflecting on his time at Casa, television and film actor Johnny Ortiz has said "*Casa is what made me. Casa is what brought me to this place in my career. When I come here I feel safe. I feel I can let everything out.*"[16]

Chicano/Latinx theatre companies have also flourished throughout Northern California and the Pacific Northwest. Teatro Milagro in Oregon was founded in 1985 by José Eduardo González and Dañel Malán. In addition to a full season of programming, its touring and arts education programs "embrace a cradle to career approach in arts education" and feature original bilingual plays and educational residencies.[17] In San Francisco, California, Brava! For Women in the Arts was founded in 1986 by Ellen Gavin along with a group of women artists dedicated to "cultivating the artistic expression of women, LGBTQIA, people of color, youth, and other underrepresented voices."[18] Brava's Artist-in-Residence program provides professional development for actors and other artists and in return, they mentor youths in the company's education programs. Brava's youth programming provides artists with professional training through the Mission Academy of Performing Arts at Brava. One arm of that program includes the Young Thespians Theatre Lab, which integrates instruction in acting, dance, music, and stagecraft. Another anchor of Chicano/Latinx theatre is Teatro Visión located in San Jose, California. Founded by Elisa Marina Alvarado in 1984, the company is committed to amplifying Latinx voices and through its mainstage and formal youth training programs seeks to ensure the future of Chicanx theatre by "training the next generation of teatristas—skilled actors who are committed to culture-based, bilingual theatre."[19]

In Texas, there is another thriving landscape of Chicano/Latinx theaters. Two of the largest Chicano/Latinx companies are both in Dallas, Cara Mía Theatre and Teatro Dallas. Founded in 1985, by Cora Cardona and Jeff Hurst, Teatro Dallas supports emerging local artists through mainstage productions, festivals, and educational workshops centering on performance techniques.[20] Founded in 1996 by Eliberto Gonzalez and Adelina Anthony, Cara Mía supports a resident artistic ensemble, community programs, and robust educational initiatives including bilingual touring shows, youth theatre classes, and student matinees.[21]

Chicago has also become an important hub for Chicano/Latinx theatre and actor training. Two companies of note include Teatro Vista and Teatro Luna. Teatro Vista, founded in 1990 by Edward Torres and Henry Godinez, was also created to address a lack of opportunities for Latinx artists and other artists of color and to explore new work by Latinx writers that challenge the actor, director, and audience.[22] Teatro Luna was founded in 2000 by Coya Paz and Tanya Saracho as an all-Latina ensemble. This company is now made up to two regional ensembles in Chicago and Los Angeles, both with a rich history of developing devised work centering the lived experiences of women of color.[23] Chicago's oldest Latinx theater, Aguijón Theater, was founded in 1989 by actress/director Rosario Vargas and is an important company committed to Spanish-language theatre. In its first ten years of existence, Aguijón was headquartered at Truman College and operated as a traveling theater bringing shows to schools and community centers across the city. This company now operates out of the northwest side of Chicago and continues to produce both Latin American and U.S., Latinx work in Spanish, in addition to providing acting classes and workshops for adults and youths.[24] Aguijón's work serves as an example of another vital thread in the history of Chicano/Latinx work, Spanish-language theatre.

One of the most significant companies dedicated to Spanish language theatre in the United States is Repertorio Español, founded by René Buch and Gilberto

Zaldívar in New York City in 1968. Since its inception, Repertorio Español has been dedicated to producing Spanish classics, renowned playwrights from Latin America and US Latinx writers. Repertorio primarily produces Spanish-language plays with English captions. Education and training are also fundamental to Repertorio's mission. Their educational arm consists of a matinee and in-school residency program, which are grounded in the concept of *dignidad*. Inspired by both of its meanings—dignity and self-esteem—Repertorio's educational programming aims to "share the excitement of the theater with students, introduce them to their theatrical cultural heritage, challenge the lack of knowledge that exists about Latinx culture, and create a generation of future dramatists, theater artists, administrators & theater-goers."[25] Another historic company in this regard is GALA Hispanic Theatre in Washington, D.C. GALA stands for Grupo de Artistas Latino Americanos and was founded in 1976 by Hugo Medrano, Rebecca Read, and a consortium of visual artists, writers, dancers, singers, musicians, and actors. Initially GALA produced fully bilingually, with plays presented in both Spanish and English but working in this way had its challenges. Eventually GALA abandoned the alternating language approach and has produced almost exclusively in Spanish. Their educational programming is also vital to their mission. Through their Paso Nuevo program, GALA offers free, year-round, bilingual theatre education incorporating acting training, playwriting, and mentorship with opportunities for public performances.[26] In Los Angeles, California two pivotal companies provide training opportunities for Spanish speaking Latinx actors, The Bilingual Foundation of the Arts (BFA) and Grupo de Teatro SINERGIA, otherwise known as Teatro Frida Kahlo Theater. Founded in 1973 by Carmen Zapata and Margarita Galban, BFA produces professional mainstage plays in English and Spanish and offers in-school educational programs.[27] Founded by Rubén Amavizca-Murúa in 1987, Teatro Frida Kahlo Theater stages professional bilingual productions and offers classes in advanced acting, Meisner method in Spanish, and Voice and Diction workshop in Spanish, among others.[28] In giving Latinx actors dedicated access to Spanish-language production work, these theaters, and so many others like them, make a vital contribution to the training grounds available for actors seeking multilingual modes of expression.

Latinx actor training has also been profoundly influenced by Latinx playwriting initiatives and artist laboratories that have developed throughout the United States. Some of the largest Latinx theatre initiatives were developed as a result of funding programs in the 1980s and 1990s dedicated to supporting the development of Latinx work and to diversify audiences at major regional theaters. Three of the most influential programs include the Latino Theatre Initiative at the Mark Taper Forum (1992–2005), the Hispanic Playwrights Project at South Coast Repertory (1986–2004), and the Hispanic Playwrights-in-Residence Laboratory at INTAR (1981–1992).[29] These programs served as fertile ground for playwrights as well as Latinx actors and directors to deepen their craft in new play development, and to nurture important networks with Latinx artists across the country. Contemporary theatre initiatives like the Latinx Theatre Commons, the Dominican Artists Collective, Latinx Playwrights Circle NYC, Arizona Theatre

Company's National Latinx Playwriting Award, and the Nuestras Voces National Playwriting Competition, to name only a few, continue this important work.

Another source of connection, training, and networking has occurred in the long history of the festival tradition in Chicano/Latinx theatre. As scholars have documented, the theatre festivals of El Teatro Nacional de Aztlán (TENAZ), the national organization made up of individual Chicano theatre companies in the 1960s and 1970s, were important sites for artistic exchange and the advancement of Chicano theatre as an artform. In addition to performances of plays, the festivals included workshops in many forms of theatre practice and often a sharing of aesthetic approaches from artists and companies across the United States and Latin America. The festival tradition has been sustained by companies like Teatro Avante in Miami, Florida, who under the leadership of Mario Ernesto Sánchez has produced the annual International Hispanic Theatre Festival of Miami since 1986. The Goodman Theatre's Latino Festival curated by Henry Godinez, Two River Theater's Crossing Borders (Cruzando Fronteras) Festival curated by José Zayas, Teatro Vivo's Austin Latinx New Play Festival, and San Diego Repertory Theatre's Annual Latinx New Play Festival are other important examples.[30] Most recently the Latino Theater Company's series of Encuentro Festivals and accompanying Latinx Theatre Commons convenings have sought to revitalize a national network of Latinx artists, producers, and scholars in communication and collaboration.[31] Central to each Encuentro festival has been the sharing of artistic practice between festival artists in the spirit of the workshops of the early TENAZ festivals. These sites of embodied learning and collective practice are a vital part of the history of Latinx theatre training.

As is already evident in this brief review, many important connections have also existed between the lineage of Chicano/Latinx companies and colleges and universities. These connections created an important path for Latinx actors seeking formal training. Two historic programs include Teatro Bilingüe of Texas A&I University (now Texas A&M) in Kingsville, founded by Joseph Rosenberg and Teatro Bilingüe at California State University Sacramento directed by Romulus Zamora, both programs were active in the 1970s and 1980s and produced original bilingual work as well adaptations and translations of Latin American and Spanish plays.[32] Additional examples of these partnerships include Teatro Prometeo in Miami and Teatro Espejo in Sacramento. Housed at Miami Dade College, Teatro Prometeo was a professional Spanish-language conservatory for actor training. Founded in 1985 by Teresa María Rojas, its mission was "to preserve the Spanish-language and Hispanic culture through theater." For over 12 years, Prometeo offered classes at the College in Acting, Voice and Speech, Movement, Singing, Playwriting and Camera-acting Technique as well as specialized workshops.[33] On the West Coast, Teatro Espejo was founded as a community theatre company in 1975 initially supported by the Washington Barrio Education Project, an educational center sponsored by Sacramento City College. Five years later Teatro Espejo became an official part of the Theatre Department at Sacramento State University, producing over 30 shows on campus under the leadership of Artistic Director and Professor Manuel José Picket until he retired in 2012. Teatro Espejo is now a non-profit organization which continues to thrive in its mission "to advance the craft of teatro while honoring our traditions."[34]

While I have only highlighted a few of the many Chicano/Latinx theatre companies that make up the landscape, it is abundantly clear that Chicano/Latinx companies, initiatives, festivals, and programs have long provided a hub for Latinx actor training. Through the preservation of cultural performance traditions, interdisciplinary training, and opportunities for networking, many Latinx actors have found a home in these companies and others for the development of their craft. It is also important to note that given the diversity of Latinx identities many Latinx actors have found significant opportunities for training and belonging in Native/Indigenous, Black, Asian, and LGBTQ companies as well as companies dedicated to artists with disabilities, while not being explicitly Chicano/Latinx in focus.

## Institutional Training Programs

In *Acting in the Academy*, Peter Zazzali traces the history of professional actor training in the United States, highlighting the influence of professional theatre companies, acting studios, and university training programs. Noting an increase in university programs in the 1960s, Zazzali sees the rise of these programs as interconnected with the success of the regional theatre movement and the need for resident acting ensembles. This led to the establishment of the League of Professional Theatre Training Programs—a group of 11 schools formed at universities that adhered to a set of unifying principles in training actors for the stage.[35] Zazzali's fascinating study explores how rapid shifts in the economics of regional theatre making and the commercial pathways for acting graduates have influenced the method and efficacy of actor training over time. Absent from Zazzali's study however is an engagement with changing demographics within M.F.A. programs, barriers to entry, and the impacts of acting training on students from marginalized backgrounds.

In Chicano/Latinx theatre, there has also been a connection between the growth of theatre companies, the interest of regional theaters in Latinx work, collaboration between companies and universities, and the impact of academic training programs on Latinx actors and their success. The 1980s and 1990s saw a rise in the professionalization of Chicano/Latinx Theatre. Throughout these decades there was an increase in Latinx students formally training in university theatre programs, a robust network of Latinx theatre companies around the country, and the emergence, though not proliferation, of Latinx plays on regional stages. At this time of unprecedented opportunity, Professor Jorge Huerta, then a faculty member at the University of California San Diego (USCD) Department of Theatre, understood the need for Latinx actors and directors to train in an environment where they could honor the fullness of their being.[36] Professor Huerta was the first person to earn a Ph.D. in the study of Chicano Theatre. His extensive experience in leading and working with teatros, regional theaters, and teaching in universities gave him a keen understanding of the gaps in the landscape of

Chicano/Latinx actor training. Noting that no graduate programs in theatre at the time offered a specialization in Hispanic-American Theatre, Huerta proposed a new Master of Fine Arts (M.F.A.) program that would do just that.[37] From 1989 to 1992, Huerta created and ran UCSD's first, and only, M.F.A. in Hispanic-American Theatre for actors and directors, designed "to meet the specific needs of a growing network of professional Hispanic-American theaters."[38] Additionally, the program would prepare actors for the growing amount of work available to them in Latinx theatre companies across the United States. Most important to Huerta's vision was that "the proposed program would offer the actor and director an opportunity to express a cultural reality closer to his/her experience."[39] Huerta argued that artistic directors seemed to agree on the importance of training, but that too few theatre departments had addressed, or even considered, the needs of their Hispanic students. Moreover, he lamented that "from coast-to-coast, it seems that Hispanic theatre students must put aside their cultural identity and blend into the mainstream."[40]

In a memo to the Dean of the Office of Graduate Studies and Research, Adele Shank, Chair of UCSD's Theatre Department, and Huerta as Head of the Hispanic Theatre Program outlined early recruitment efforts for the new program which would "complement and affirm our existing affirmative action efforts."[41] Their recruitment plans included campus visits as well as a brochure campaign to undergraduate theatre departments across the country with a specific focus on Hispanic-serving institutions, as well as to Hispanic theaters and cultural centers. The memo also identifies the need to reach out to other institutions with large Hispanic populations or ongoing Hispanic/Chicano programs at the undergraduate level. These programs included Teatro Espejo at California State University, Sacramento, UCLA School of Theater, University of Texas, El Paso and Texas A and I University.

The Hispanic-American Theatre Program admitted ten students in its first and only cohort, though the goal was to admit a new cohort every two years. Students followed a three-year curriculum, with the first two years being studio-oriented with production opportunities on campus, and a tour with the Department's Teatro Ensemble, and the third year consisted of a professional residency on campus, in a local venue or on tour, a thesis production, and a professional showcase. Academically, the Hispanic-American Theatre students were meant to follow the same curriculum as the traditional M.F.A. students, but with a concentration in Hispanic-American Theatre production opportunities in both Spanish and English. Additional elements of the program included an "externship" with a professional theater across the country for one semester. The externship would be curated so that the student would participate as an actor or as a director "in a play that is either Latino, multicultural, or an example of a theater's non-traditional casting philosophy."[42]

The curriculum included traditional acting classes like Movement/Combat, Voice, Scene Study, New Plays workshop, Acting Process, and Scripts to

**FIGURE 1.1** Copy of brochure from the Hispanic-American M.F.A. program (1989–1992), headed by Dr. Jorge Huerta (see Chapters 9 and 10 for additional reference).

*Credit Line:* Jorge Huerta papers. MSS 142. Special Collections & Archives, UC San Diego Library.

Performance. It also included specific courses in the concentration including Hispanic-American Dialects, Hispanic-American Theatre History, Chicano Dramatic Literature, and a Teatro Seminar Course exploring the artistic, political, and financial realities of a life in the teatro. The Hispanic-specific courses were taught by Huerta and Tony Curiel, an acclaimed Chicano theatre director who was hired to the faculty for this program. Curiel was also serving as the Associate Artistic Director of ETC during the time of the program which gave the program a direct link to one of the most well-known teatro companies in the world.

After the summer of the first year of the program, the students went on tour to Europe and dubbed their company "Teatro Nuevo Siglo" (Theater of the New Century). Some of the productions they produced in their second year included María Irene Fornés' *The Conduct of Life*, Milcha Sanchez-Scott's *Roosters*, and

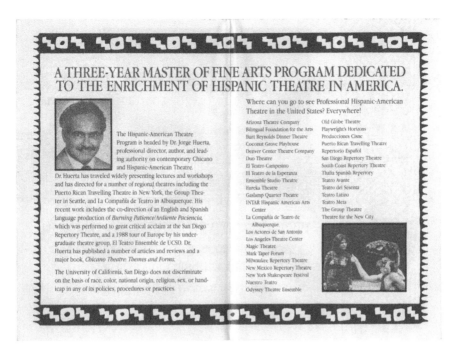

**FIGURE 1.2** Copy of brochure from the Hispanic-American M.F.A. program (1989–1992), headed by Dr. Jorge Huerta (see Chapters 9 and 10 for additional reference).

*Credit Line:* Jorge Huerta papers. MSS 142. Special Collections & Archives, UC San Diego Library.

both a bilingual and fully Spanish production of *La Maestra* by famed Colombian teatrista Enrique Buenaventura. Some of the externship placements included San Diego Repertory Theatre, Mixed Blood Theatre, Latino Chicago Theatre, Bilingual Foundation of the Arts, Magic Theatre, Eureka Theater, and San Francisco Shakespeare Festival. Students also secured internships at significant Chicano/Latinx companies including ETC, El Teatro de la Esperanza, and Repertorio Español.

A variety of challenges impacted the program's success which led to not recruiting a second class, though the entire cohort of ten students did graduate from the program. Issues ranging from funding, sharing of space, and challenges with meeting the needs of all students in both M.F.A. programs led Huerta and the Department's leadership to determine that the program was simply not feasible without more resources. When Huerta originally proposed this program to the university, he noted that he was the only Chicano professor in the theatre department. With the appointment of Curiel he received important support, but it was still not enough to sustain the intense demands required to run the program

**FIGURE 1.3** Copy of brochure from the Hispanic-American M.F.A. program (1989–1992), headed by Dr. Jorge Huerta (see Chapters 9 and 10 for additional reference).

*Credit Line:* Jorge Huerta papers. MSS 142. Special Collections & Archives, UC San Diego Library.

effectively. His proposal also explicitly stated that the new program would share the department's facilities and equipment equally with the other M.F.A. disciplines to avoid having a "Hispanic corner" of the department. After two years of the program, it was clear that without additional space, staff, and increased enrollment in design disciplines for example, it was impossible to provide the program production support in an equitable manner.

Feedback from students in the Hispanic-American Theatre program expressed frustration with aspects of the curriculum and a lack of clarity about issues ranging from casting to course schedules. In an open letter posted on a department call board, a design student who was not a member of the Hispanic-American Theatre program addressed the Chair of the Department and cited issues of concern with the program. These concerns included Hispanic students being denied opportunities in the larger theatre department; the status of the two M.F.A. programs as "inherently unequal"; a desire to have an integrated student body while preserving the integrity of both programs; a call for instituting an African-American and an Asian-American program which would benefit all students; and a need for the school to provide "training in the skills necessary to understand differences across boundaries."[43]

Student and faculty concerns led to a review of the program in the spring of 1991 to determine the best path forward. Ultimately, the department shuttered the Hispanic-American Theatre M.F.A. but vowed a commitment to continue to support the recruitment and training of Hispanic students. Moreover, Shank expressed the need for the Department of Theatre to embrace a multicultural approach to recruitment and curriculum offerings and committed to supporting courses in Hispanic-American, African-American, and Asian-American dramatic literature along with a commitment to producing a season of plays that would enrich the education of a diverse student body. Though the Hispanic-American Theatre M.F.A. program was short-lived, it remains an important moment in the history of Latinx actor training as it attempted to address historic inequities with radical structural change, and also illuminated many in the process. In looking at contemporary models of Latinx actor training within academic institutions, I believe Huerta's M.F.A. program is an ancestor to many contemporary programs that are providing the distinct production opportunities that he was envisioning. One such program is Duende CalArts.

Established in 2009 by Marissa Chibás, Acting faculty member in the School of Theater at California Institute of the Arts (CalArts), Duende CalArts is "an initiative of the CalArts Center for New Performance dedicated to developing and producing innovative work emerging from Latinx and Latin American communities and sources."[44] Inspired by Federico García Lorca's articulation of *duende*, the program invites students to work with established and emerging artists from Latin America and the United States to develop new projects at the Center for New Performance. While Latinx actors at CalArts follow the same curriculum as their cohort, Duende CalArts gives them a space to engage in a form of theatre making that at once honors ancestral roots while also inviting students into collaboration to wildly experiment.

## Latinx Theatre Training Today

In his landmark 1982 study *Chicano Theater: Themes and Forms*, Jorge Huerta discusses a key challenge for Chicanos seeking theatre training. He writes "when they go to the drama department for help, they find that there are no Chicanos on the faculty and few Chicano students, if any." Furthermore, he notes that the Chicano theatre student "lives a sort of double life, engaged in traditional theater as a student and in Chicano theater as an activist."[45] While much has changed since 1982, these quotes still resonate today. Many Latinx students in training programs today feel as though they need to earn two degrees, one in "traditional/European" theatre and the other in Chicano/Latinx theatre. Moreover, there is also a direct relationship to the state of the theatre industry and training methods. If Latinx students don't see themselves in the faces of faculty, other students, or on professional stages, it is difficult to envision a sustainable career.

According to the Asian American Performers Action Coalition (AAPAC) 2018–2019 Visibility Report on racial representation on New York City stages, 58.6 percent of all roles went to White actors during the 2018–2019 season, compared to 4.8 percent of roles that went to Latinx actors. This represented a drop for Latinx actors who in the 2017–2018 report held 6.1 percent of roles.[46] Another important turning point and moment of reckoning came in the summer of 2020, when in response to civil unrest after the murder of George Floyd, a collective of Black, Indigenous, and People of Color (BIPOC) theatre makers formed a collective "to address the scope and pervasiveness of anti-Blackness and racism in the American Theater." The collective issued a testimonial letter, *Dear White American Theater,* and a subsequent list of demands with a specific section addressing academic and professional training programs.[47] One of the demands explicitly states, "we demand the prioritization of recruitment and retention of BIPOC theater faculty in full time and tenure track positions."[48]

As theatre training programs have begun to diversify their student body, and their faculty albeit more slowly, the question of how curriculums can provide actors with the tools needed for an ever-changing industry, but also not divorce them from their cultural identities or attempt to find a so-called neutral self, remains. The calls for radical accountability in the American Theatre have led to explicit and renewed work toward the development of anti-racist theatre practice and pedagogy at institutions around the country. This work is crucial for both traditional training institutions and Latinx companies and collectives. Interrogating a history of Eurocentric training methods, anti-Blackness, and anti-indigeneity in all of our work is a critical imperative. While many educators and artists have acknowledged their need to develop or expand their cultural competency, there is still much work to be done.

While we acknowledge the work ahead, it is also important to celebrate the leaders in the classroom who not only pass down ancestral knowledge but also foster a space of belonging and possibility, while they themselves may navigate hostile academic terrains as Latinx faculty. To trace all Latinx faculty members in all theatre training programs in the United States is beyond the scope of this chapter. Instead, I offer a humble excavation of a portion of the current Latinx actor trainer landscape. I offer a call of ¡presente! for appointed Latinx faculty in a variety of Master of Fine Arts (M.F.A.) and Bachelor of Fine Arts (B.F.A.) Acting programs in the United States at the time of this writing. An important dynamic to name is that there are many Latinx actor trainers who are contingent faculty or who teach in other theatrical disciplines and absolutely play a significant role in supporting Latinx actors in their training across all levels of training programs. This roll call, much like this essay, is not exhaustive and invites others to continually uplift all those supporting Latinx actors within and outside of formal training grounds.

When I think of acting trailblazers, Dr. Alma Martinez, Associate Professor of Theatre at the University of La Verne, is one of the first to come to mind. She is renowned for her work as an actress on stage and screen and holds an M.F.A. in Acting and a Ph.D. in Directing and Dramatic Criticism. At UCLA's School of Theater, Film and Television, J.Ed Araiza serves as the Chair of the Department of Theater and is a professor in the Acting program. He is a principal actor and original member of the SITI company and offers students Suzuki and Viewpoints training. As mentioned earlier, Marissa Chibás is on the Theater School faculty at CalArts where she teaches Acting. Her recently published book *Mythic Imagination and the Actor* is another profound contribution to the field as it offers an approach to actor training that embraces the mythic and the poetic. At the University of Southern California's School of Dramatic Arts, award-winning actor Coleman Domingo was recently appointed Professor of Acting.

At the University of California, San Diego, Robert Castro is on faculty in both the Acting and Directing programs. At the University of San Diego (USD), Jesse Perez is the Director of the Graduate Theatre program at USD and The Old Globe. Perez is an actor, director, and choreographer/movement director who taught at Juilliard for 12 years before coming to USD. In the spring of 2022, Robert Ramirez was appointed the Head of the School of Drama at Carnegie Mellon University. He previously served as the Chair of the Department of Theatre and Dance and Head of the Acting Program at the University of Texas at Austin. Ramirez is a renowned vocal coach, actor, and director, and he also currently serves as the Vice President of the University Resident Theatre Association.

Two key faculty members at Northwestern University's Department of Theatre make clear the vital relationships between Latinx companies and institutional training. Henry Godinez, Resident Artistic Associate at the Goodman Theatre and director of its Latino Festival is the Chair of the Department where he teaches Acting and offers a specific Acting course on Latino Theatre. Sandra Marquez, an ensemble member at Steppenwolf Theatre and Teatro Vista where she previously served as Associate Artistic Director, is Assistant Professor of Theatre at Northwestern where she teaches a variety of courses in Acting. At the Theatre School at DePaul University, Michelle Lopez-Rios is Associate Professor of Voice and Speech and the Artistic Director of the School's Chicago Playworks for Families and Young Audiences. She was previously the Head of the B.F.A. Acting Program at the University of Wisconsin-Milwaukee.

At Elon University's College of the Arts and Sciences, Julio Matos Jr. is Associate Professor of Performing Arts and the Music Theatre Director in the B.F.A. Acting Program, where he teaches courses in Acting and Musical Theatre. At the University of South Florida School of Theatre and Dance, Dora Arreola is Associate Professor of Theatre teaching courses in Acting ranging from Grotowski to Suzuki and Movement. At Kean University Theatre Conservatory, actor, and voice and dialect specialist Joshua Feliciano-Sánchez Moser is Assistant Professor of Voice and Movement. From 2019 to 2022, they were the Interim Head of Voice and Speech at Brown University/Trinity Repertory.

At Boston University College of Fine Arts, Melisa Pereyra is Assistant Professor of Theatre, where she teaches Acting courses in Shakespeare and in Voice. At Northeastern University College of Arts Media and Design, Antonio Ocampo-Guzman serves as the Chair of the Department of Theatre where he teaches courses in all levels of Acting, Voice and Speech, and Improvisation. At Emerson College, Nathaniel Justiniano is Assistant Professor specializing in courses on Performing Arts and Comedic Arts. At Dyson College of Arts and Sciences at Pace University, renowned acting teacher Jorge Luis Cacheiro is the Chair of the Performing Arts Department. At the University of Puerto Rico (Rio Piedras) Department of Drama, Jacqueline Duprey is Associate Professor who teaches courses in multiple styles of Acting. She is joined by Edgar M. García, Associate Professor of Acting and Voice and Speech.

Lastly, I recognize the editors of this volume themselves. At Arizona State University's School of Music, Dance and Theatre, Micha Espinosa is a Professor of Voice and Acting. She is an actor; teacher; voice, speech, and dialect coach; the editor of *Monologues for Latino Actors: A Resource Guide to Contemporary Latino/a Playwrights for Actors and Teachers*; and co-editor of *Scenes for Latinx Actors: Voice of the New American Theatre* with Cynthia Santos DeCure. A bilingual actor, playwright, teacher, and dialect coach, Cynthia is an Associate Professor Adjunct of Acting at the David Geffen School of Drama at Yale.

Latinx actor trainers—¡PRESENTE!

Reflecting on the political possibilities of the phrase *¡presente!* scholar Diana Taylor has offered that it is

> as much an act, a word, and an attitude, *¡presente!* can be understood as a war cry in the face of nullification; an act of solidarity as in responding, showing up, and standing with; a commitment to witnessing; a joyous

accompaniment; present among, with, and to, walking and talking with others; an ontological and epistemic reflection on presence and subjectivity as process; an ongoing *becoming* as opposed to a static *being*, as participatory and relational, founded on mutual recognition; a showing or display before others; a militant attitude, gesture, or declaration of presence.[49]

This multiplicitous definition encapsulates the many ways that Latinx actor trainers show up to support the next generation and how the presence of Latinx actors can bring to them closer to their own practice. Each person and company mentioned in the lists earlier and throughout this chapter represent a continuum of artists and educators who showed up to make the work possible, to create a stage where there was none, to create a program where there was none, and to excavate the echoes of artists that have always been there.

## Concluding Thoughts

In the spring of 2020, I learned that a titan of Latinx theatre had passed away. At the age of 94, René Buch, co-founder of New York City's Repertorio Español, left an artistic legacy marked by his impact on an entire generation of artists and audiences.[50] Upon reading about Buch's life I gasped when I learned that he had graduated from the Playwriting program at Yale School of Drama in 1952. A mix of immense pride and frustration filled my heart yet again. I wondered why I had not heard of Buch's legacy at the school, and also vowed to remember and honor it through my teaching.

I recognize his spirit in the bilingual work happening at the school in recent years. During the spring 2021 term at Yale, a course titled "Shakespeare in Spanish" was offered for the first time, taught by Cynthia Santos DeCure and Daniela Varon. The course illuminated the power of working in a bilingual space with heightened text. In the fall of 2021, a bilingual production of Lorca's *Blood Wedding/Bodas de Sangre* was produced as the Acting Program's Fall Project, adapted by Cynthia Santos DeCure and Tatiana Pandiani, who also directed. One of the project's central goals was to allow students to engage in reclamation of language. At the same time, the production supported non-Spanish speakers to strengthen their language skills and engender empathy for the experience of living in translation. While bilingual and Spanish language productions have been an important thread in the history of Chicano/Latinx theatre, there has also been a renewed interest in this work across training programs and regional theaters. A few recent productions include Dallas Theater Center's 2022 production of *Our Town/Nuestro Pueblo* by Thornton Wilder; Oregon Shakespeare Festival's 2019 Play On! bilingual adaptation of *La Comedia of Errors* and the Arizona State University School of Music, Dance and Theatre production of the piece in 2022; a Spanish production of Lope de Vega's *Fuenteovejuna* at the Lewis Center for the Arts at Princeton in 2022; and Teatro en el Verano's bilingual production of *La Mancha*, an adaptation of Don Quixote, produced by Rhode Island Latino Arts in association with Trinity Rep, to name only a few.

I return again to the legacy of René Buch as I close this chapter. I am reminded of Repertorio Español's centering of *dignidad* as part of its education program. In the spirit of the tenacious Chicano/Latinx companies, artists, and educators that have been nurturing Latinx actors for decades, we must nurture training models that support pride and self-esteem in Latinx actors so that the next generation of theatre artists will not only have a love and respect for their art but also be able to hear their ancestors' echoes within it.

## Notes

1 In July 2021, Yale School of Drama's name was formally changed to David Geffen School of Drama at Yale University in recognition of a $150 million gift from the David Geffen Foundation which will ensure that the school will be tuition-free for all degree-seeking students in perpetuity.
2 Sebastián Eddowes, "To Remember Nancy, We Dream of Her: A Portrait of an Overlooked Pioneer," *Yale School of Drama Annual Magazine*. (2020–2021) David Geffen School of Drama at Yale, August 12, 2021, www.drama.yale.edu/alumni/annual-magazine/ (24–25).
3 A note on terminology: I use "Chicano/Latinx" here to acknowledge a history of evolving terminology that is used to refer to people of Latin American cultural descent or ethnic identity. The terms Chicano, Latino, and Hispanic are also used throughout the essay when referencing the formal names of companies or initiatives. Otherwise, I use the term Latinx on its own as a gender-inclusive term.
4 Nicolás Kanellos, *History of Hispanic Theatre in the United States: Origins to 1940* (Houston: University of Texas Press, 1990).
5 Luis Valdez, *Theatre of the Sphere: The Vibrant Being* (London: Routledge, 2022).
6 "Mission & Values," *Su Teatro Cultural and Performing Arts Center*, March 25, 2021, http://suteatro.org/about-us/mission-and-values/.
7 "Cultural Arts Education Institute," *Su Teatro Cultural and Performing Arts Center*, April 10, 2021, http://suteatro.org/education/.
8 "About Borderlands Theater," *Borderlands Theater*, May 13, 2021, www.borderlandstheater.org/about/.
9 For a detailed history of Pregones, see Eva Vasquez, *Pregones Theatre: A Theatre for Social Change in the South Bronx* (London: Routledge, 2003).
10 "Category Archives: Education," *Pregones/PRTT*, July 18, 2022. https://pregonesprtt.org/category/education/.
11 "Programs," *INTAR Theatre*, July 18, 2022, www.intartheatre.org/programs/.
12 "About Labyrinth Theater Company," *LAByrinth Theater Company*, accessed March 2, 2022, https://labtheater.org/history.
13 José Luis Valenzuela, "*Latino Theater* Company: How We Grew, and Why," *American Theatre*, February 2, 2017, www.americantheatre.org/2016/11/21/latino-theater-company-how-we-grew-and-why/.
14 The core ensemble has changed over time; in 1990, there were nine active members and for the last several decades, the core ensemble has been five members, which include José Luis Valenzuela, Evelina Fernández, Sal Lopez, Geoffrey Rivas, and Lucy Rodriguez.
15 To learn more about the Latino Theater Company visit https://www.latinotheaterco.org/
16 "Our Mission Statement," *CASA 0101 Theater*, March 13, 2022, https://casa0101.org/about.

17  "About Teatro Milagro," *Teatro Milagro*, July 18, 2022, https://milagro.org/about/.
18  "History of Brava," Brava for Women in the Arts, March 4, 2022, www.brava.org/history.
19  "About Teatro Vision," *Teatro Vision*, July 18, 2022, www.teatrovision.org/about_teatro.
20  "Who We Are," *Teatro Dallas*, July 18, 2022, https://teatrodallas.org/about/.
21  "About Cara Mía," July 18, 2022, www.caramiatheatre.org/about.
22  "History and Mission," *Teatro Vista—Theater with a View*, March 1, 2022, www.teatrovista.org/history-mission.
23  "Home," *Teatro Luna*, July 18, 2022, https://teatroluna.org/.
24  "History of Aguijón Theater," *Aguijón Theater*, July 18, 2022, https://aguijontheater.org/history/.
25  "Repertorio Español Education Programs," *Repertorio Español*, February 6, 2022, https://repertorio.nyc/#/education.
26  "About GALA Hispanic Theatre" *Gala Hispanic Theatre*, March 1, 2022, www.gala-theatre.org/about.
27  "About," *Bilingual Foundation of the Arts*, July 24, 2022. https://www.bfatheatre.org/about.
28  "Classes," *Frida Kahlo Theater*, July 24, 2022. https://www.fridakahlotheater.org/classes.
29  For a history of the Latino Theater Initiative see Rodriguez, Chantal. *The Latino Theatre Initiative/Center Theatre Group papers, 1980–2005* (Los Angeles: UCLA Chicano Studies Research Center Press, 2011).
30  As of June 19, 2022, San Diego Repertory Theatre has suspended all operations.
31  From 2014 to 2021, the Latino Theater Company produced a series of three Latinx theater festivals—Encuentro 2014 A National Latinx Theater Festival, Encuentro de las Américas 2017, a festival between Latinx and Latin American artists, and Re: Encuentro 2021 a national, virtual, Latinx theater festival.
32  Jorge Huerta, *Chicano Theater: Themes and Forms* (Arizona: Bilingual Review Press, 1982), 223.
33  "Teatro Prometeo," *Miami Art Guide*, July 24, 2022. https://www.miamiartguide.com/teatro-prometeo/.
34  "Our History," *Teatro Espejo Sacramento's Latinx Theatre Company*, January 25, 2022, https://teatroespejo.com/history.
35  Peter Zazzali, *Acting in the Academy: The History of Professional Actor Training in US Higher Education* (London: Routledge, 2016).
36  Dr. Jorge Huerta is a Chancellor's Associates Professor of Theatre, Emeritus at UC San Diego. He remains a leading authority on all things Chicano/Latinx theater.
37  In his 2020 dissertation, From *La Carpa to the Classroom: The Chicano Theatre Movement and Actor Training in the United States*. Dennis Sloan, Ph.D. chronicles a full history of this program through detailed research of Huerta's archives, and I am indebted to his research.
38  Jorge Huerta Papers. MSS 142, Box 30, Folder 9. Special Collections & Archives, UC San Diego Library.
39  Ibid.
40  Ibid.
41  Ibid.
42  Ibid.
43  Ibid.
44  "Duende CalArts," *Center for New Performance*, February 18, 2022, https://centerfornewperformance.org/duende/.
45  Jorge Huerta, *Chicano Theater: Themes and Forms* (Arizona: Bilingual Review Press, 1982).
46  The Asian American Performers Action Coalition. 2018–2019 Visibility Report, February 25, 2022, www.aapacnyc.org/2018-2019.html.

47 We See you White American Theater, December 15, 2021, www.weseeyouwat.com/.
48 To see the full list of demands, visit https://www.weseeyouwat.com/demands.
49 Diana Taylor, ¡Presente! *The Politics of Presence* (Durham: Duke University Press, 2020).
50 To read stirring testimonials about Buch's impact read Caridad Svich's, "Rene Buch: Tough Love in Two Languages," *American Theatre Magazine*. Theatre Communications Group, April 28, 2020, www.americantheatre.org/2020/04/28/rene-buch-tough-love-in-two-languages/.

## Bibliography

"About," *Bilingual Foundation of the Arts*, July 24, 2022. https://www.bfatheatre.org/about.
"About Borderlands Theater." *Borderlands Theater*, May 13, 2021. www.borderlandstheater.org/about/.
"About Cara Mía." *Cara Mía Theatre*. Accessed July 18, 2022. www.caramiatheatre.org/about.
"About GALA Hispanic Theatre." Accessed March 1, 2022. www.galatheatre.org/about.
"About Labyrinth Theater Company." *LAByrinth Theater Company*. Accessed March 2, 2022. https://labtheater.org/history.
"About Teatro Milagro." *Teatro Milagro*. Accessed July 18, 2022. https://milagro.org/about/.
"About Teatro Vision." *Teatro Vision*. Accessed July 18, 2022. www.teatrovision.org/about_teatro.
"The Asian American Performers Action Coalition. 2018–2019 Visibility Report." February 25, 2022. www.aapacnyc.org/2018-2019.html.
Broyles-González, Yolanda. *El Teatro Campesino: Theater in the Chicano Movement*. Austin: University of Texas Press, 1994.
"Category Archives: Education," *Pregones/PRTT*, July 18, 2022. https://pregonesprtt.org/category/education/.
"Cultural Arts Education Institute." *Su Teatro Cultural and Performing Arts Center*, April 10, 2021. http://suteatro.org/education/.
"Classes," *Frida Kahlo Theater*, July 24, 2022. https://www.fridakahlotheater.org/classes.
"Duende CalArts." *CalArts Center for New Performance*. Accessed March 2, 2022. https://centerfornewperformance.org/duende/.
Duprey, Jacqueline. *Faculty Bio. University of Puerto Rico, Rio Piedras. Department of Drama*, February 28, 2022. http://humanidades.uprrp.edu/drama/?page_id=261.
Eddowes, Sebastián. "To Remember Nancy, We Dream of Her: A Portrait of an Overlooked Pioneer." *Yale School of Drama Annual Magazine*. (2020–2021). David Geffen School of Drama at Yale, August 12, 2021. www.drama.yale.edu/alumni/annual-magazine/.
"History and Mission." *Teatro Vista-Theater with a View*, March 1, 2022. https://www.teatrovista.org/history-mission.
"History of Aguijón Theater." *Aguijón Theater*. Accessed July 18, 2022. https://aguijontheater.org/history/.
"History of Brava." *Brava for Women* in the Arts, March 4, 2022. https://www.brava.org/history.
"Home." *Teatro Luna*. Accessed July 18, 2022. https://teatroluna.org/.
Huerta, Jorge. *Chicano Theater: Themes and Forms*. Ypsilanti, MI: Bilingual Press, 1982.
———. "Moving Forward, Never Forgetting the Past." *HowlRound Theatre Commons*, November 2, 2014. https://howlround.com/encuentro-2014.
Jorge Huerta Papers. MSS 142. Special Collections & Archives, UC San Diego Library.

Kanellos, Nicolás. *History of Hispanic Theatre in the United States: Origins to 1940*. Houston: University of Texas Press 1990.
"LAMC Presents Latino Theater Company Experience Class." *Los Angeles Mission College*. Accessed March 2, 2022. www.lamission.edu/news/newsitem.aspx?id=580.
"Mission & Values." *Su Teatro Cultural and Performing Arts Center*, March 25, 2021. http://suteatro.org/about-us/mission-and-values/.
"Our History." *Teatro Espejo Sacramento's Latinx Theatre Company*, January 25, 2022. https://teatroespejo.com/history.
"Our Mission Statement." *CASA 0101 Theater*, March 13, 2020. https://casa0101.org/about.
"Programs." *INTAR Theatre*. Accessed July 18, 2022. www.intartheatre.org/programs/.
"2022 Raúl Julía Training Unit." *Pregones/PRTT*, February 6, 2022. https://pregonesprtt.org/2022-raul-julia-training-unit/.
"Repertorio Español Education Programs." *Repertorio Español*, February 6, 2022. https://repertorio.nyc/#/education.
Rodriguez, Chantal. *The Latino Theatre Initiative/Center Theatre Group papers, 1980–2005*. Los Angeles: UCLA Chicano Studies Research Center Press, 2011.
Schillinger, Liesl. "The Playwright Rewriting Latino Theater." *New York Times*, December 12, 2004.
Sloan, Dennis. "From La Carpa to the Classroom: The Chicano Theatre Movement and Actor Training in the United States." Diss., Graduate College of Bowling Green State University, 2020.
Svich, Caridad. "René Buch: Tough Love in Two Languages." *American Theatre Magazine*. Theatre Communications Group, April 28, 2020. www.americantheatre.org/2020/04/28/rene-buch-tough-love-in-two-languages/.
Taylor, Diana. *¡Presente!: The Politics of Presence*. Durham: Duke University Press, 2020.
"Teatro Prometeo," *Miami Art Guide*, July 24, 2022. https://www.miamiartguide.com/teatro-prometeo/
"We See you White American Theater." December 15, 2021. www.weseeyouwat.com/.
"The Asian American Performers Action Coalition. 2018–2019 Visibility Report." February 25, 2022. http://www.aapacnyc.org/2018-2019.html
"Who We Are." *Teatro Dallas*. Accessed July 18, 2022. https://teatrodallas.org/about/.
"Who We Are." *GALA Hispanic Theatre*, February 19, 2022. www.galatheatre.org/about.
Valdez, Luis. *Theatre of the Sphere: The Vibrant Being*. London: Routledge, 2022.
Valenzuela, José Luis. "Latino Theater Company: How We Grew, and Why." *American Theatre*, February 2, 2017. www.americantheatre.org/2016/11/21/latino-theater-company-how-we-grew-and-why/.
Zazzali, Peter. *Acting in the Academy: The History of Professional Actor Training in US Higher Education*. London: Routledge, 2016.

# 2
# DIANE RODRÍGUEZ'S ACTING ACTIVISM

*Marci R. McMahon*

> *Actors brought her great joy; she loved actors, performers, actors especially. She knew how to work with actors because she was an actress. . . . She knew how to draw performances out of actors.*[1]

In her keynote speech at the first Latinx Theatre Alliance/Los Angeles (LTA/LA) convening in 2013, the late Diane Rodríguez—Obie award-winning actor, director, nationally recognized artistic producer, and iconic member of El Teatro Campesino (the Chicano/a theatre company co-established by Luis Valdez and Agustín Lira)—remarked on fellow troupe member Socorro Valdez's vocal power:

> When I was in the teatro, I had to act next to Socorro Valdez. To this day, one of the two best actresses I have ever worked with. She was an inspiration. *She was excellent.* She could act like a man better than a man. Do a back flip. And then let out a sorrowful wail that would chill your backbone. Brilliant. . . . And me, the one with the tiny voice to balance the not so tiny body who wasn't very deep. Who mugged and over acted.[2]

Rodríguez's praise of S. Valdez as "one of the two best actresses" she worked with was one she made numerous times throughout her career, and provides a glimpse into Rodríguez's emphasis on excellence.[3] According to Rodríguez, the excellence of an actor emerged, not in a "tiny" voice that "mugged and over acted," but with a big voice and presence on stage. In contrast to Rodríguez who felt she had to limit her voice in her body, she was in awe of S. Valdez who could "act like a man better than a man." Rodríguez's statement underscores the gendered

DOI: 10.4324/9781003021520-4

politics that inform the theatre and film industry's assessment of actors, where Latina actors often have to work harder than their male counterparts to be heard.

This chapter focuses on Rodríguez's emphasis on excellence as central to her "acting activism" in her last directing opus before her passing in April 2020: Janine Salinas Schoenberg's *Las Mujeres Del Mar* at Atwater Village Theatre (September–October 2019). "Acting activism," according to Rodríguez, is where "good acting, social consciousness, and activism [are] all intrinsically connected."[4] In Rodríguez's last directed production, her acting activism required both excellence and the physical embodiment of storytelling through ensemble work to amplify Latinas' voices and stories. Salinas Schoenberg reflects on Rodríguez's requirement of excellence with the actors in the production:

> What she demanded of all those around her, was excellence, and how we, particularly, as artists of color, had to be virtuosos. It wasn't enough to be good or even great, you had to be a virtuoso, and she demanded that rigor of herself, first and foremost, as well as everybody around her.[5]

Here, the playwright remarks that Rodríguez's emphasis on excellence with Latina actors responds to the racial/gender inequalities in US theatre, film, and television, in which Latinas and other women of color are expected to exceed expectations in their craft; such requirements are not placed on their white male peers with neither the same intensity nor the same impact.[6]

Drawing on my interview with playwright Salinas Schoenberg and actor Adriana Sevan (formerly Adriana Sevahn Nichols), a cast member of *Las Mujeres Del Mar*, this chapter shares specific acting techniques Rodríguez used with the actors to broadcast Latina excellence both on and off stage.[7] While Rodríguez developed her acting activism during her time with El Teatro Campesino (ETC), this chapter asserts (as were the late Rodríguez's wishes) that her approach to working with actors was informed not only by her experiences with the iconic company but also by her experiences working in US theatre as an actor, director, and artistic producer. While Rodríguez's work with actors pays homage to ETC, Rodríguez was able to leverage her numerous artistic producing roles to uplift marginalized storytellers and to advocate for Latinx stories. As Salinas Schoenberg notes, Rodríguez utilized her large orbit toward social change:

> One of the extraordinary things about Diane is that wherever Diane was, she somehow brought everybody with her into that space. Whatever doors she helped to open, whatever opportunities she made happen, she shared with others. Everybody that was in Diane's orbit was welcomed, supported and encouraged. Her ambition was never personal, it was instead a mission to continuously cultivate other artists and to help build up and inspire her community.[8]

As a scholar of Rodríguez's acting and directorial work, I was asked by the editors of this volume to contribute this chapter.[9] I first met Diane in 2005 when I was a Ph.D. student at the University of Southern California; at that time, I was working on a dissertation on Chicana feminist performances, writing about Rodríguez's navigation of gender roles in her work with ETC, as an actor in Hollywood, and as a theatre director and actor. I interviewed Rodríguez several times, and this work became a chapter in my book *Domestic Negotiations*.[10] I was in awe when Rodríguez cited my chapter about her theatre career in my book so publicly in her online biographies, public lectures, and podcast interviews. I was also honored when Rodríguez requested that I write about her play, *The Sweetheart Deal*, at the Mark Taper in 2017.[11] Such exchanges between us signal that the late theatre artist not only trusted my writings about her work but also appreciated my Chicana feminist analyses of her work.

## Rodríguez's Acting Philosophies From El Teatro Campesino to the White House

Rodríguez's performances with ETC—a theatre troupe initially founded during the Delano Grape Strike in 1965 and under the cultural arm of the United Farm Workers (UFW) Movement—shaped her acting philosophies and rigorous approach to acting. ETC's early performances were defined by their actos, or short skits intended to incite social action. Grounded in Mexican working-class popular culture aesthetics from the *carpas*, and European performance aesthetics from *commedia dell'arte*,[12] ETC first performed their actos on flatbed trucks in the fields for farm workers and in union halls, to dramatize the struggles and activist causes of the farmworkers. When ETC separated from the UFW in 1967, they wielded performance to address broader social issues of the Chicanx Movement—a political and artistic renaissance of the era that focused on labor, educational, and political rights for Mexican Americans. During this period, ETC emerged as a theatre troupe, gaining national and international attention with their innovative agit-prop performances.[13] At the same time, the troupe ignited Chicanx students across California and the United States to establish Chicanx theatre companies of their own.[14] In 1971, the troupe established a theatre company in Juan Bautista, a small rural town an hour drive from San Jose, California.[15] Rodríguez, whose family was from San Jose, California, and had a history with migrant farm work (like co-founder Valdez's family), volunteered and interned for ETC at the company's theater for several summers while she was pursuing a bachelor of arts degree in theatre arts from the University of California, Santa Barbara. When Rodríguez graduated in 1973, she joined ETC as a performer at the height of the troupe's recognition and prestigious invites to perform across the United States, Europe, and Mexico. These performances occurred during a global and Latin American theatre movement that both drew from and rejected Euro-centric thinking and philosophies. During this time, ETC, with Valdez's vision, developed several acting methods, including the troupe's "Theatre of the Sphere"—derived from Mayan mathematics and metaphysics, and which included the "veinte pasos," or 20-element exercise sequence that comprised the troupe's core principals of strengthening the mind and body in service of community.[16]

Rodríguez's experiences acting under the direction of the late theatre and film director, Peter Brooke, shaped her disciplined approach to acting. Rodríguez reflected on her experience working with Brooke in the production of *Conference of the Birds* with other ETC performers and members of Brooke's Centre of International Theatre Research at ETC's theatre company in San Juan Bautista in 1973. Rodríguez stated: "That is where I put my ten thousand hours, as a theatre maker, starting off very broadly and then refining the craft until we left. It took that kind of dedication, from morning until night, to completely submerge."[17] During the intensive performance workshops leading up to the *Conference of the Birds* production and in the production itself, Rodríguez acted alongside English and Hollywood actor Helen Mirren. Rodríguez's time spent acting, sharing a room, and "cruising" with Mirren through San Juan Bautista in a red convertible during the production was a pivotal experience for her. In Mirren, Rodríguez found another model of "acting excellence." Rodríguez frequently put Socorro Valdez and Mirren alongside each other as acting inspirations:

> Never had two mujeres moved me so profoundly. Socorro was a comic, short, dark, Indian featured, and from San Jose, my hometown. Helen was sultry, blond, voluptuous, and English. . . . both were razor sharp, willful, strong. . . . *In a male-dominated field, their strong presence was a political act*" (my italics).[18]

Even as Rodríguez's terms evoke the popular stereotypes society places on "Latinas" and "white" woman, the late theatre artist's description of these two women demonstrates that she desired a diverse spectrum of female actors as role models.

With numerous performances and acting excellence under her belt after touring with ETC for ten seasons, Rodríguez began to pursue work as an *actriz*[19] in Hollywood in the 1980s; here, she experienced the stereotypes ascribed to Latinas in Hollywood (as the Latina domestic, servant, the devoted wife, and suffering mother in numerous high-profile Hollywood performances).[20] Her immediate response to playing these roles was not to leave Hollywood behind but to use her acting craft and rigor to provide complexity to these roles.[21] After frequent typecasting, however, Rodríguez soon left Hollywood acting to focus on theatre. In 1988, Rodríguez co-founded the comedy troupe Latins Anonymous as a response to the Hollywood stereotypes she and the other performers in the group confronted.[22] After years of performing in the troupe, Rodríguez turned to direction. She directed the collective's collaboratively created performance, *Latins Anonymous*, at the Borderlands Theater in Tucson, Arizona, in 1991. A few years later, when Rodríguez acted in the world premiere production of Tony Kushner's adaptation of Bertolt Brecht's *The Good Person of Setzuan* at La Jolla Playhouse in 1994 under Obie award-winning director, Lisa Peterson, she met a director who made a significant impact on her. Through Peterson, Rodríguez saw the potential to enact social change in the director's role. A year later, both Peterson and Rodríguez began a ten-year stint at the Mark Taper (1995–2005), with Peterson as Resident Director and Rodríguez as co-director/director of the Latino Theatre Initiative (LTI).

While Rodríguez was a recognized and Obie award-winning actor in her own right, appearing in notable and award-winning theatre productions throughout her career,[23] her most significant impact in the field of acting was through her direction of numerous play readings and many full productions, playing a role in artistic development of many new works. Through artistic producing and directorial roles, Rodríguez staged complex images of Latinx communities in response to the Hollywood stereotypes she experienced. In the last play Rodríguez wrote and had produced, *The Sweetheart Deal*, in 2017, she used her voice as a playwright and director to challenge the gendered stereotypes that she not only experienced in Hollywood but also confronted in those early years with ETC.[24] Remarking on her play, Rodríguez stated: "Now I have the opportunity of telling the story of our people, through a woman's perspective and that is what I am doing now."[25]

Called to social action throughout her career, Rodríguez was a fierce advocate of Latinx stories in her role as an artistic producer in several national roles and platforms. As the co-director of the LTI with playwright Luis Alfaro at the Mark Taper Forum in Los Angeles from 1995 to 2003, Rodríguez and Alfaro worked together to diversify the stage's play productions, which included ushering in new Latinx playwrights, producing Latinx stories, and providing community-engaged programming.[26] In this role, Rodríguez and Alfaro oversaw the production of over a dozen Latinx plays and developed new plays by Latinas specifically during the course of the initiative on the Taper's main stage.[27] Rodríguez then carried forward these initiatives as a sole director of the LTI until 2005.[28] During this time, Rodríguez worked with several national theatre artists to diversify the Taper, including Lisa Peterson, Chay Yew, Rachel Hauck, Timothy Douglas, Annie Weisman Macomber, Brian Freeman, Vicky Lewis, the late John Belluso, and Pier Carlo Talenti, among many others.

Commenting on Rodríguez's contributions to amplifying Latinx voices specifically as co-director of LTI, Adriana Sevan recalls how the initiative was

> one of the incredible contributions that Diane made to augmenting Latinx voices through the Center Theatre Group, especially her leadership of the LTI Latina Women's Writers Retreat; in this space, I wrote my first play, *Taking Flight*, produced by Center Theatre Group; the work's birth, world premiere and subsequent successes would not have happened without Diane.[29]

Salinas Schoenberg remarks that, in these roles, Rodríguez

> became a fierce advocate for artists who would have never been given the resources or the opportunity to be in those spaces. Starting from when she and Luis ran the Latino Theater Initiative. . . . She used any and all platforms she had to empower and support artists and introduce them to American theatre audiences. She was always out there pounding the pavement, searching for authentic and inspiring new storytellers.[30]

As a result of her work with the LTI at the Mark Taper, theater companies reached out to Rodríguez for collaborations, and she utilized those networks to advocate for Latinx actors and playwrights through spearheading theater partnerships and artist residencies. In her role as Associate Producer, Director of new play production, and Associate Artistic Director at the Center Theatre Group in Los Angeles (CTGLA) from 1995 to 2019, she developed the work of more than 75 theater artists to the CTGLA stages, working to create a more inclusive US theatre; in this capacity she also advocated for Latinx actors.[31] For her extensive career advocating for theatre arts, Rodríguez was appointed by President Obama to the NEA's National Council on the Arts and inducted into The College of Fellows for the American Theatre in 2018.[32] As a member of the NEA's National Council on the Arts, Rodríguez pressed the NEA to use its funding to support ensemble work (the least funded form of US theater) and to elevate the cutting edge work of international theater companies, using her voice once again to amplify marginalized storytellers.

## The "Personal Is Political" in *Las Mujeres Del Mar*

As with the other Latinx plays that Rodríguez directed throughout her career, *Las Mujeres Del Mar* amplifies a third world feminist of color tenet that the "personal is political," where larger structural systems of race, gender, and socio-economic inequality weigh on women's personal and intimate family relationships. Set in both Mexico and Los Angeles, California, *Las Mujeres Del Mar* narrates the structural factors impacting three generations of Chicanas coping with generational and historical cycles of trauma, a familiar trope in Chicanx/Latinx literature (i.e. Lorna Dee Cervantes's poem "Beneath the Shadow of the Freeway," Sandra Cisneros's *House on Mango Street*, among numerous other cultural texts). In Salinas Schoenberg's play, we see these mother-daughter relationships traverse across various structural systems, including family, community, migration, and the U.S. prison system. The play follows Virginia (Dyana Ortelli), Marina (Sevan), and Lupe (Gabriela Ortega) as they reconcile and learn to love one another across these traumas. As with her many other directorial projects, Rodríguez's direction of the world premiere of *Las Mujeres Del Mar* amplifies the Chicanx women's voices at the center of the story, and, gives depth and nuance to the personal, intimate, lives of these women. While much of the play is set in the prison system following Marina's confinement, the play is not about these structural systems, but about the characters' intimate relationships to them, which Rodríguez skillfully approaches in her direction of the ensemble.

## Cultivating the Physical Embodiment of the Storytelling

> *Diane was one of the most sensorial people I have ever met, as evidenced by how she not only worked and lived, but how she adorned herself through the artistic expression of her clothes, the sounds of her bangles, her chancletas, her sassy red lips, and her laughter. She was an explosion of life. More than any director I've ever worked with, Diane brought every art form into the process—visuals, music, movement, which helped us deepen our physical and emotional response to the text, each other and the space between the words. Diane knew how to build a world in which the soul of each actor and character could thrive.*[33]

In her direction of *Las Mujeres Del Mar*, Rodríguez prioritized the physical embodiment of the storytelling through ensemble work. Drawing on acting techniques culled from her time with ETC, her direction focused on getting actors to find their inner strength and to stand in their power. Rodríguez's focus on the body and power in her direction of a play rooted in a female-centered story performed by a female-centered ensemble is significant. For *Las Mujeres Del Mar*, Rodríguez first worked with the actors separately from the script, foregoing the traditional table read where the playwright is present, an unconventional approach for a world premiere of a play. As Sevan recalls,

> Diane decided to start rehearsals two days before Janine could physically be with us. Those two days were filled with improvisation and extraordinary exercises of exploration, where we moved together with music and attention to our breath, listening and responding to each other's innate rhythms. When we sat down on the third day with Janine and had our first read-through, the molecules of a family, of a company, of breathing life into a world together, had already begun.[34]

By foregoing the awkward table read where the cast and production team typically do not know each other in prior, Rodríguez valued and emphasized the female connections and community central to Salinas Schoenberg's storytelling. Salinas Schoenberg recalls Rodríguez's reasons for prioritizing ensemble work: "I just want to get them in their bodies, and then on Friday we'll all sit down."[35] The impact of getting the actors "in their bodies" led the cast, according to Salinas Schoenberg, to be "so comfortable with each other, it was extraordinary. I felt like everyone was so dialed in from the very beginning."[36] Salinas Schoenberg further describes that Rodríguez's power as a director was her ability to amplify the "essence of these women."[37] As a result of Rodríguez's emphasis on ensemble work, both Sevan and Salinas Schoenberg noted the strong sense of family and community created among the actors, which worked to uplift *Las Mujeres Del Mar*'s narrative of women coping with gendered and racialized trauma.

During the two days prior to the official table read with Salinas Schoenberg, Rodríguez implemented several acting exercises focused on somatic knowledge and awareness of the body, which were intended to create deep connections among the cast members. One technique included guiding the actors in a sensorial activity that involved blindfolds. While blindfolded, each actor moved through the rehearsal space to find and feel each other's presence. As Sevan recalls,

> Diane put on music and had us begin to move around the space. Then we put on our blindfolds. She asked us to notice how the air shifted when we took away our sight. What did that feel like on our skin? Was there any change in temperature or any shifts in our breath? Could you tell when you were coming close to somebody? Then she led us until we were all coupled with someone else. And then with music by the composer for the play, Adam Schoenberg, Diane had us explore the hands of someone in front of us, guiding us in noticing every nuance about them.[38]

This somatic activity was especially important for Sevan because the approach helped the actor to deepen her character Marina's relationship with her daughter Lupe, played by Gabriela Ortega. In a hallmark scene where Marina is trying to throw Lupe a perfect party for her tenth birthday to redress her neglect of her daughter due to drug addiction, Marina asks Lupe: "Can I promise you something? That this won't ever change again. (Beat) You believe me?"[39] As Sevan recalls,

> I took my daughter Lupe's hand in mine and instead of an actor doing this from a heady intention, a visceral wave moved through my heart as I held her warm soft hands feeling them like Braille . . . those hands I knew and loved and could find in the dark. And that was a connection that had been created during the blindfold exercise that first day, which left a cellular imprint every time I held my daughter's hands.[40]

Additionally, Rodríguez would begin each rehearsal with a two-minute meditation, which led the actors to approach the rehearsal space as, Sevan describes, a "living ritual."[41] As Sevan explains, "it was a way of working cellularly, spiritually, soulfully, intellectually, but all in some kind of harmony, and an alchemy that was unlike anything I had ever experienced before."[42] Sevan also notes the significance of the set designer Tanya Orellana's choice to have the entire floor of the stage covered in sand:

> As trauma survivors, immigrants, and women carrying our own ancestral wounds, the sand had a moment to moment impact on my nervous

system. . . . [i]t made it impossible to ever be grounded and balanced. The sand became the perfect obstacle . . . to have to keep fighting to stay on my feet.[43]

With the above techniques, Rodriguez helped the actors find their bodies in relationship to the women's generational traumas expressed in the play.

## Acting Technique: Listening to the Body of an Actor & Collaboration

*Diane had a tremendous capacity to listen deeply. She was never hasty or automatic in her response. She would consider everything . . . really taking you in . . . being with you, and I think that that's what made her such an incredible director, collaborator, and friend.*[44]

Rodríguez's work with the cast cultivated a circular leadership rooted in collaboration. One specific technique used in this production was the use of an assistant director, Sonia Sofia Rivera, who had just recently graduated from high school. Rodríguez strategically chose Rivera as the assistant director to mentor and usher in a new generation of Latina directors. Sevan explains Rodríguez's choice of assistant director:

I loved that Diane saw that as an opportunity to not only educate, but to bring this young gifted Latinx artist to the table to contribute, yes, but also for us to grow from her wisdom. Diane did not have her sit in the background as a silent witness to the process. Instead, she invited Sonia Sofia to actively contribute as a collaborator, signaling that you not only belong here but that you are needed here.[45]

Sevan continues: "Diane was like, 'I'm on a mission to change this girl's perspective.' To show her that Latinx Theatre can be something special and different from what she maybe has seen or not seen."[46] Furthermore, as Sevan explains, "her voice in the room was as fertile and contributing to the process as anyone else's."[47] By choosing Rivera as an assistant director, Rodríguez used her hard-earned privilege to usher in a new generation of Latina directors that would carry the work of Latina inclusivity forward.

Rodríguez's non-hierarchical leadership as a director enabled her to listen deeply to her actors. One prime example of her listening approach included the re-staging of a scene where Sevan's character confronts her mother Virginia when she visits her in prison. In rehearsals, Marina initially faced Virginia in that scene, so the audience only saw the back of Marina's body. When Sevan communicated to Rodríguez she wanted to re-shift the arrangement so she would face the audience, Rodríguez was open and re-staged the scene. Sevan recalls as a result of the change, "suddenly it just opened everything up for me and gave me my voice because I was now facing the world, no longer facing a wall and the past."[48] Going back to the role of voice that opened this chapter, Rodríguez's re-staging honored and amplified Sevan's voice. Sevan explains: "she trusted that in my body something didn't feel right," and that this scene was "built from Diane's listening and being willing to even in a moment where she's conducting an orchestra say, 'Let's see what else we can do with these notes.'"[49] In these moments, Rodríguez listened to the actors she worked with, instead of deciding, choosing, or choreographing scenes.

Furthermore, Rodríguez's collaborative approach goes against convention where the director is typically the lead voice in the room, and the playwright does not have much input in the process. As a result of this mutual exchange, Sevan and the other actors felt they had input into the script. This "sculpting" of the script was exciting for the actors.[50] As she recalls,

> One of the things that was so exciting about working on this play with her was she wanted different drafts of the scene in terms of the acting every time. It's not like, "Okay, do it again and now add some things." Instead, it's "Throw it away and let's see it from a whole new light". . . . It was constant sculpting.[51]

This collaborative process of working with actors also honored Salinas Schoenberg's vision and the story that she wanted to tell. Salinas Schoenberg remarks that Rodríguez's collaborative approach is one of the main reasons she worked with Rodríguez on her play: "Diane was the only person who could direct this play the way that I had envisioned it, because she understood on a visceral level who these women were and where they came from."[52]

## "Be the Bridge": The Legacy and Impact of Rodríguez's Acting Activism

Rodríguez's acting techniques with the Latina cast of *Las Mujeres Del Mar* cannot be underestimated in the continued hierarchical spaces of US theatre. Through collaboration, advocacy, and a fierce generosity of mentorship, Rodríguez navigated these exclusionary spaces to uplift marginalized voices throughout her career. Salinas Schoenberg comments on Rodríguez's perspective of the inequities that Latinas continue to confront as they navigate US theatre:

> She would tell me, 'As a woman and as a woman of color, you need to make yourself indispensable because otherwise they will always find a way to push you out the minute you start to question them or say things they don't want to hear. You have to speak up for what you believe in and continuously pursue your passions while always making sure that you are

creating a space for yourself to thrive and succeed. A space where they know they need you.' And that's exactly what she did.[53]

The strategic work and collaborations Rodríguez implemented in her direction of *Las Mujeres Del Mar* were intentional. As Sevan explains,

> The depth of connections that were made by creating this work feel very deliberate and lasting. Seeds were planted. This wasn't just Diane's last directing opus but, through her care in bringing us together, we continue to create brave work in honor of all that Diane has given to us.[54]

Rodríguez's acting activism continues to live on in the numerous actors and artistic teams she worked with, ensuring they are bridges for each other, not waiting for the structural systems to change, but changing them from within with clarity of purpose and vocal power.

## Notes

1 Jose Delgado, "Celebrating the Legacy Lessons of Theatre Artist Diane Rodríguez," *Filmed*, Friday July 17, 2020. *HowlRound Theatre Commons*. Posted Friday July 18 2020, www.youtube.com/watch?v=WKdPrCBNH2g.
2 Diane Rodríguez, "Keynote Speech: The First Latinx Theater Alliance/Los Angeles (LTA/LA) Encuentro/Convening," *Filmed*, July 13, 2013. Vincent Price Art Museum. East Los Angeles College. *HowlRound Theatre Commons*. Posted July 13, 2013, https://howlround.com/happenings/latino-theater-allianceencuentro-2013-los-angeles.
3 Diane Rodríguez, "Searching for Sanctuaries: Cruising Through Town in a Red Convertible," in *Puro Teatro: A Latina Anthology*, eds. Alberto Sandoval-Sánchez and Nancy Saporta Sternbach (Tucson: University of Arizona Press, 2000).
4 Ibid., 316.
5 Marci R. McMahon, Interview with Janine Salinas Schoenberg and Adriana Sevan (September 23, 2020).
6 Salinas Schoenberg notes the structural factors underlying Rodríguez's demand of excellence from the actors she worked with:

> She understood that as artists of color, we have to try 10 times as hard and we have to be 10 times as good in order to get that foot in the door. And every single time she opened a door, she invited everyone through her orbit.
> 
> *(Marci R. McMahon, Interview with Janine Salinas Schoenberg and Adriana Sevan. September 23, 2020)*

7 McMahon, Interview with Salinas Schoenberg and Sevan.
8 Ibid.
9 Before Rodríguez's passing in April 2020, she planned to contribute a chapter to this volume. Rodríguez was adamant about establishing her work with actors as unique from her experiences as an ensemble member of El Teatro Campesino. And Rodríguez indicated to the editors of this collection that she wanted the title of the piece to be "Acting Activism." With the help of Patricia Garza (Producer and Director of Los Angeles Programs at Los Angeles Performance Practice), both a mentee of Rodríguez and one of the members of "Team Diane," and with guidance from the editors, we

decided that the best approach to Rodríguez's intended contribution was to focus on her last directing opus before her passing.
10 Marci R. McMahon, *Domestic Negotiations: Gender, Nation, and Self-Fashioning in US Mexicana and Chicana Literature and Art* (New Brunswick, NJ: Rutgers University Press, 2013).
11 Marci R. McMahon, "A Chicana Heroine Redirects El Movimiento: Diane Rodríguez's *the Sweetheart Deal*," *Ignited Series for Café Onda: Journal of the Latinx Theatre Commons* (October 12, 2017).
12 The *carpas*, or vaudeville-style traveling tent shows, toured the US Southwest from the 1850s to the 1940s. The *carpas* are rooted in Mexican working-class popular performance aesthetics of "una burla colectiva," or collective mockery, sounding bawdy irreverence through humor, singing, and mime. See Yolanda Broyles-González, *El Teatro Campesino: Theatre in the Chicano Movement* (Austin: University of Texas Press, 1994). Luis Valdez's use of clowning and mime from *commedia dell'arte*, or Italian Renaissance marketplace comedy, derived from Valdez's training and acting with the San Francisco Mime Troupe prior to his co-founding of El Teatro Campesino.
13 For a further understanding of El Teatro Campesino's extensive history and acting methods, see El Teatro Campesino, *El Teatro Campesino: The Evolution of America's First Chicano Theatre Company 1965–1985* (San Juan Bautista: El Teatro Campesino Inc., 1985); Jorge Huerta, *Chicano Theater: Themes and Forms* (Ypsilanti, MI: Bilingual Press, 1982); Broyles-González, *El Teatro Campesino: Theater in the Chicano Movement*; Luis Valdez and Michael Chemers, *Theatre of the Sphere: The Vibrant Being* (New York: Routledge Press, 2021).
14 In 1971, inspired by the Second Annual Chicano Theater Festival, and Luis Valdez's idea of a national Chicanx theatre company, the leaders of some of the Chicano theatre companies create a national network of teatros called, TENAZ, standing for El Teatro Nacional de Aztlán. Some of the Chicanx theatre companies that were formed during this period include Teatro Chicano (Los Angeles, CA, 1968); Teatro Mestizo (San Diego, CA, 1969); Teatro de la Esperanza (Santa Barbara, CA, 1969); El Teatro de la Tierra (Fresno, CA, 1970); El Teatro de los Barrios (Phoenix, AZ, 1971); El Teatro de los Pobres (El Paso, TX1971); Su Teatro (Denver, CO, 1971); El Teatro Chicana (San Diego, CA, 1971); El Teatro Espiritú de Aztlán (Fullerton, CA, 1972); and El Teatro de La Gente (San Jose, CA, 1972).
15 Ten years later, ETC acquired a warehouse in the town in 1981, converting it to ETC's first playhouse, a 200-seat theater, which allowed the troupe to experiment and offer acting workshops with a focus on music and dance and theatre, which resulted in national and international attention to the group.
16 For an in-depth discussion and analysis of ETC's "theatre of the sphere" acting method, see Valdez and Chemers, *Theatre of the Sphere*.
17 Samantha Gregg and Daniela Lieja Quintanar, "An Homage to Diane Rodríguez," *Los Angeles Contemporary Exhibitions (LACE)*, https://welcometolace.org/lace/an-homage-to-diane-rodriguez/?utm_source=rss&utm_medium=rss&utm_campaign=an-homage-to-diane-rodriguez.
18 Rodríguez, "Searching for Sanctuaries," 316.
19 See Diane Rodríguez, "About," accessed January 3, 2021. www.diane-rodriguez.com/about.
20 For a further discussion of the stereotypical roles Rodríguez played in Hollywood, see McMahon, *Domestic Negotiations*, 161–162.
21 For a further discussion and analysis of Rodríguez's acting and subversion of the Hollywood stereotypes ascribed to Latinas, see McMahon, *Domestic Negotiations*, 164–72.
22 In the late-1980s, Rodríguez co-founded Latins Anonymous, an L.A.-based comedy troupe that incorporated satire to critique the typecasting of Latinas and Latinos in

Hollywood; the project was a response to the limited roles Rodríguez persistently encountered while pursuing an acting career in Los Angeles.
23 In 2007, Rodríguez received an Obie Award for Best Ensemble Performance in Heather Woodbury's *Tale of 2 Cities*. She also performed in leading roles in two world premiere productions at the Mark Taper: Luis Alfaro's *Breakfast, Lunch and Dinner* (2003) and Lisa Loomer's *Living Out* (2003).
24 Rodríguez explains how, because of the limited roles for women in the troupe, she often chose to play more "androgynous" characters in El Teatro Campesino:

> It is true, the Teatro repertoire of women's roles, the wives, the girlfriends, the loose women, the Virgins, was tiresome and limiting. I was never very good at playing any of them. Looking back, I realize it was my way of resisting those roles. I was most comfortable playing androgynous characters: La Muerte in *La Carpa de los Rasquachis* or Satanas in *La Pastorela*, a shepherd's play. These roles offered more versatility and power. We women complained but, in the end, we accepted the roles.
> *(Qtd. in Broyles-González, El Teatro Campesino: Theater in the Chicano Movement, 317)*

25 Gregg and Lieja Quintanar, "An Homage to Diane Rodríguez."
26 Chantal Rodríguez, *The Latino Theatre Initiative/Center Theatre Group Papers, 1980–2005*. (Los Angeles: UCLA Chicano Studies Research Center, 2011).
27 Ibid.
28 Rodríguez and Alfaro supported new works by playwrights seeking to represent diverse images of Latinx in US theatre, producing scripts by now well-known Latinx dramatists such as Nilo Cruz, Octavio Solis, Oliver Mayer, Ricardo Bracho, Ann Garcia Romero, Marga Gomez, Evelina Fernandez, and Cherríe Moraga, among many others. The LTI also supported the development of work by Caridad Svich, Monica Palacios, and Carmelita Tropicana, among numerous other Latina artists (Rodríguez, *The Latino Theatre Initiative/Center Theatre Group Papers*).
29 McMahon, Interview with Salinas Schoenberg and Sevan.
30 Ibid.
31 During this time, Rodríguez helped develop numerous works, including Young Jean Lee's *Straight White Men* (the first play by an Asian American female playwright on Broadway in 2018), and Jessica Blank and Erik Jensen's *How to Be a Rock Critic*. Both productions were both part of a major initiative she directed at Center Theatre Group from 2009 to 2018 with the support and partnership of the Andrew W. Mellon Foundation. Rodríguez utilized this funding to collaborate with over 80 artists from around the world.
32 Rodríguez also served as President of the board of Theatre Communications Group from 2013 to 2016.
33 Adriana Sevan, from McMahon, Interview with Salinas Schoenberg and Sevan.
34 McMahon, Interview with Salinas Schoenberg and Sevan.
35 Ibid.
36 Ibid.
37 Ibid.
38 Ibid.
39 Salinas Schoenberg, Janine, *Las Mujeres Del Mar*. Unpublished Script (2019: 18).
40 McMahon, Interview with Salinas Schoenberg and Sevan.
41 Ibid.
42 Ibid.
43 Ibid.
44 Adriana Sevan, from McMahon, Interview with Salinas Schoenberg and Sevan.
45 McMahon, Interview with Salinas Schoenberg and Sevan.
46 Ibid.

47 Ibid.
48 Ibid.
49 Ibid.
50 Adriana Sevan, from McMahon, Interview with Salinas Schoenberg and Sevan.
51 McMahon, Interview with Salinas Schoenberg and Sevan.
52 Ibid.
53 Ibid.
54 Ibid.

## Bibliography

Broyles-González, Yolanda. *El Teatro Campesino: Theatre in the Chicano Movement*. Austin: University of Texas Press, 1994.

El Teatro Campesino. *El Teatro Campesino: The Evolution of America's First Chicano Theatre Company 1965–1985*. San Juan Bautista: El Teatro Campesino Inc., 1985.

Huerta, Jorge. *Chicano Theater: Themes and Forms*. Ypsilanti, MI: Bilingual Press, 1982.

McMahon, Marci R. *Domestic Negotiations: Gender, Nation, and Self-Fashioning in US Mexicana and Chicana Literature and Art*. New Brunswick, NJ: Rutgers University Press, 2013.

———. "A Chicana Heroine Redirects El Movimiento: Diane Rodríguez's *The Sweetheart Deal*." *Ignited Series for Café Onda: Journal of the Latinx Theatre Commons*. Accessed October 12, 2017. https:/howlround.com/chican-heroine-redirects-el-movimiento.

Rodríguez, Chantal. *The Latino Theatre Initiative/Center Theatre Group Papers, 1980–2005*. Los Angeles: UCLA Chicano Studies Research Center, 2011.

Rodríguez, Diane. "Searching for Sanctuaries: Cruising Through Town in a Red Convertible." In *Puro Teatro: A Latina Anthology*, edited by Alberto Sandoval-Sánchez and Nancy Saporta Sternbach. Tucson: University of Arizona Press, 2000.

Salinas Schoenberg, Janine. *Las Mujeres Del Mar*. Script, 2019.

Valdez, Luis, and Michael Chemers. *Theatre of the Sphere: The Vibrant Being*. London: Routledge Press, 2021.

# 3

# "LET ME DEFINE MYSELF"

## An Interview With Puerto Rican *teatrera* Rosa Luisa Márquez

*Priscilla Meléndez and Aníbal González*

As Professor of Language and Culture Studies at Trinity College (Priscilla Meléndez), and Professor of Modern Latin American Literature at Yale, (Aníbal González), we share a common interest in the rich history of Puerto Rican theatre. This rich history is tied to Rosa Luisa Márquez, who is a Puerto Rican theatre director and Professor *emerita* of the Drama Department of the University of Puerto Rico (UPR). We have known Rosa Luisa Márquez since 1990 for an article on contemporary Puerto Rican theatre. We first met her in person, along with her long-time collaborator, Puerto Rican visual artist Toño Martorell, in 1992, when we invited both to lecture, perform, and teach a miniseminar on techniques of popular theater at Michigan State University. Since then, we have become friends with Rosa Luisa and with her husband, photographer and documentarian Miguel Villafañe, and have followed her career closely. In a sense, we have been "interviewing" Rosa Luisa for the last 32 years, since she is an inexhaustible source of information about the Puerto Rican cultural community of which she is a key figure.

Rosa Luisa's four decades of teaching and working with theatre groups in Puerto Rico and the United States, such as Teatreros Ambulantes de Cayey, Puerto Rican Traveling Theatre (PRTT), and Pregones Theater, have had a decisive influence in the careers of numerous Latin American and Latinx actors.[1] For this chapter, we interviewed Rosa Luisa via Zoom, in Spanish, for about an hour and a half. What follows is a translated, condensed, and reworked version (with Rosa Luisa's collaboration) of that interview, shaped like a brief monologue. It begins with her reply to our main question:

> How do you explain to an audience that is not familiar with the Puerto Rican theatrical experience the way you deal with the island's complex

DOI: 10.4324/9781003021520-5

artistic and political reality, and how you have established bridges with the tradition of Latino or Latinx theatre in the US. When and how do those connections begin?

RLM: Today is January 14, 2022, the second year of COVID-19 and some months into the Omicron variant. In order to answer your question, I'd have to go back in time to my college years in the 1960s. I joined the UPR in 1965 and graduated in 1969. During those years, I studied theatre history and performed plays from Europe and the Americas (North, South, and the Caribbean). I was particularly impressed by Spanish playwright Valle Inclán's theatre of the grotesque and by the existentialist movement and its connections to the "theatre of the absurd." I was also active in the popular theatre movement in Puerto Rico. From 1969 to 1970, I studied for my master's degree in NYU in the midst of the Vietnam War era. Those years were very important in the development of my political and aesthetic awareness. Puerto Ricans from the island died in Vietnam without being able to vote for the President that sent them there.

The war and its effects in Puerto Rico, along with the worldwide liberation movements in both politics and theatre, led me to consider a "people's theater" (*teatro popular*) as a professional option. Theatre departments at the time emphasized the study of the classics, yet the whole world was experiencing a moment where traditional hierarchies were being questioned—from May 1968 in Paris to the protests against the Vietnam War in the United States, to the development of collective theatre projects in Latin America. Those conflictive events echoed with Puerto Rico's political instability. Furthermore, the influence of the Cuban Revolution was of particular significance in generating a sense that Puerto Rico existed as an independent cultural entity strongly connected to the rest of the Latin American nations.

My first contacts with the theater experience in the US and the Latino presence in it emerged in response to the aforementioned international political events (as it often happens in Puerto Rico), which led to start the creation of a theatre that dealt not just with the Vietnam War but also with political events in Latin America (México, Argentina, Chile). Of particular influence to my understanding of politics and theatre was the visit to Puerto Rico of Argentine playwright Osvaldo Dragún in 1979, in which I greatly benefitted from reading, watching, and directing his plays and attending his playwriting seminars. Dragún then traveled to New York to work with Miriam Colón—head of the PRTT—who produced his plays in the streets for Latino audiences. Colón's PRTT was inspired by Federico García Lorca's 1930s *Teatro La Barraca* in Spain and by the UPR's Traveling Theatre project which began touring in 1947 and continues to this day.

It was a time for theatrical experiments and explorations. At the Brooklyn Academy of Music, I was able see in 1968 *Paradise Now* by the Living Theatre and had the opportunity to experience Richard Schechner's "environmental theater," which is performed in exterior spaces and in which action envelops the audience.

I followed the work of Luis Valdéz's *Teatro Campesino* in California, as well as the Latino theater criticism and history of Nicholas Kanellos, who is of Puerto Rican descent. Both coincide in their creative and critical works with Dragún's aesthetics and ethics, which is based on the encounter between audience and actors—what Argentine theater historian Jorge Dubatti calls the *convivio*, or a fundamental sense of conviviality. Valdéz's theater draws from the tradition of circuses and traveling shows common to Argentina, Mexico, and Puerto Rico, and Kanellos' groundbreaking anthology (with Jorge Huerta), *Nuevos Pasos: Chicano and Puerto Rican Drama* (1979), was a key reference for my Ph.D. thesis.

These theatrical movements in the United States were closely related to what was being developed in Puerto Rico with directors and teachers such as Victoria Espinosa and Pablo Cabrera, who encouraged us to perform everywhere—streets, squares, churches, even in traditional theaters. We were also influenced by the work of Pedrito Santaliz, who had performed in the UPR's traveling unit and founded his own group, the "Teatro Pobre de América," in New York based on a grassroots version of Grotowski's "Poor Theatre." Later Santaliz brought back his project to the island.

The notion of being regarded as a US Latino theatre person is new to me, because as a Puerto Rican from "the island" I don't think I can legitimately identify myself as a US Latino. However, I can't ignore the great presence in my career of US traditional as well as alternative theatrical influences, such as Bread & Puppet Theater in New York and Vermont, and the San Francisco Mime Troupe in California, with whom I share a common vocabulary that rejects strict distinctions between playwrights, producers, directors, set designers, and actors. We defined ourselves as "teatreros" (theatre people), who play many roles. Like Bread and Puppet, we used in Puerto Rico a horizontal organizational structure that turned all kinds of spaces into performance spaces. This would later become Augusto Boal's mantra when I chose him as a mentor during the 1980s, as he constantly reminded us that everyone, not just actors, can do theatre, and that theatre can be played anywhere, even in theaters.

Soon after I arrived at NYU, the university was closed down due to student protests and threats to destroy the computer center. Streets were taken over by policemen on horseback, and theater, inspired by some of our teachers, occupied those same streets. We held sit-ins, happenings, and other massive events with lighted candles, songs, and slogans. I realized that there was an affinity with what we had been doing in our own performances with Anamú, a popular theatre group founded in the late 1960s in Puerto Rico. Anamú performed what was then called "guerrilla theatre," and the group sought to give communities a voice in the midst of Puerto Rico's colonial status, persecution of independence activists, and growing inequality.[2]

Back in Puerto Rico in the 1970s, I met Colombian theatre director Enrique Buenaventura, who developed a method of collective theater creation in which all members participated in the writing and directing of their pieces. I was almost tempted to follow his company instead of continuing graduate studies, but ultimately, I decided that academic life offered me room for reflection as well as for action. I opted for a teaching career that allowed me to direct as well, joining the UPR's theatre department in 1978 and retiring in 2011.

In 1973, I returned to the United States to enroll in Ph.D. studies at Michigan State University, which offered a theatre program that was adaptable to my interests and had an Asian culture component. At MSU, I became a member of the Acting Company, but because I spoke with an accent, I was only given roles that would justify using that accent: Bernarda in *La casa de Bernarda Alba*, a lizard in Edward Albee's *Seascape*—because lizards of course speak with accents— Katherine in *Henry V* because she was a French princess who spoke English.

As part of my graduate degree, I taught creative drama at the public school system in East Lansing, and also performed for the students. Spanish language became a source of cultural resistance. I played the little engine in *The Little Engine that Could*. The character spoke in Spanish so that when she said "Yo creo que puedo" instead of "I think I can," all Spanish-speaking children understood the message and translated it to their peers, becoming an empowering experience for them.

My stay at MSU also opened the doors for other compatriots, such as Puerto Rican director Vicente Castro, who staged Luis Rafael Sánchez's classic *La pasión según Antígona Pérez* as well as an experimental theatre version of *La casa de Bernarda Alba*. Other Puerto Ricans followed, and slowly but surely, our work had a multiplying effect.

Yet, at the same time, I experienced prejudice due to our professors' lack of information about Latin American culture and theatre and their unwillingness to explore this field. There was a classic moment of monumental cultural ignorance. I remember a production of the musical *Guys and Dolls,* which had scenes set in Havana before 1959. The costume designer, without doing any historical research on the Cuban scene during the 1950s, designed costumes in which women would wear grass skirts and men would be wearing loincloths!

And of course, there was an impasse when I had to choose a dissertation topic. I had originally proposed writing on a Puerto Rican playwright, Gerard Paul Marín, but the subject was rejected because there was no one connected to a cultural experience in the Spanish language who could become my adviser. A compromise was reached, and the department allowed me to write about Miriam Colón's PRTT, which had already a ten-year history. I conducted my research in Puerto Rico on the first chapters that centered on the history of modern theatre in the island, and finally approached the PRTT's New York experience with its profound connections to Puerto Rican theatre.

My thesis became another important connection with Latino theatre in the United States. Miriam Colón anchored her work in the tradition of the Puerto Rican Theater Festivals sponsored in the island by the Institute for Puerto Rican Culture since 1958. She produced classic plays such as René Marqués' *La carreta* and *La muerte no entrará en palacio*, the latter well before it was premiered in Puerto Rico. She also produced other Latin American plays—for example *O pagador de promessas* by Brazilian playwright Alfredo de Freitas Dias Gomes—in Spanish as well as in their English translations. The PRTT's work was bilingual, and actors would perform each play in Spanish one night and in English the next. It was truly challenging for performers, since actors were a mixed group from the Puerto Rican diaspora in New York as well as Latin American actors from other origins.

Miriam had also created an experimental theatre branch and a training program. Plays were staged in a small room turned into a theater space. Jaime Carrero, a Puerto Rican artist raised in the United States who later returned to Puerto Rico, wrote *Pipo Subway no sabe reír*, a highly successful play about a kid who desperately wants a bicycle and his mother who wants to have more babies. It's a grotesquely funny play written deliciously in Spanglish.

Miriam was clearly committed to presenting Latin American and Spanish plays to New York audiences. She also staged many of García Lorca's comedies such as *La zapatera prodigiosa* and other pieces from his *teatro de guiñol* (puppet theater). In studying how Miriam worked, I could see the coherence in her trajectory from her student days in the Teatro Rodante Puertorriqueño at the UPR to the creation of her own PRTT in the United States. Her choices of playwrights, texts, and directors were often the ones I later chose to direct and teach in my professional life.

By the time I was doing my research at the PRTT in New York, I had been influenced by the works of Bertolt Brecht. This connected me again with Osvaldo Dragún's plays, filled with "epic theater" conventions, even though he claimed that when he wrote some of his best-known plays he still had not come in contact with Brecht!

Speaking of Brecht, a key moment of my experience in New York was attending the 1976 revival of his *Threepenny Opera*, in which the lead role was played by Puerto Rican actor Raúl Juliá. I was fascinated by the conjunction of Brecht's bizarre universe of epic, narrative theatre, placards, and songs, with Juliá's placing the *boricua* (Puerto Rican) accent in English in the center of the protagonist's discourse. And he did it naturally and freely without asking anyone's permission. All these experiences have left an indelible mark in the irreverent ways I approach theatre directing.

Dragún became in 1989 the director of the Escuela Internacional de Teatro de América Latina y el Caribe. The itinerant and non-government-sponsored school of theatre invited my artistic collaborator Antonio Martorell and me to become teachers in the school seminars. For 15 years and throughout Latin America, the United States and Europe, the school held more than 30 workshops to train and connect performers with teachers and theatre groups from all of the Americas. This experience marked my teaching methods for the years that followed. Exchanges were established by students and professionals with groups such as

Yuyachkani in Perú, Malayerba in Ecuador, Boal in Brazil, Bread and Puppet in the United States, La Candelaria in Colombia, and the Odin Teatret in Denmark.

One of the most important influences on my work is that of the Bread and Puppet Theater. I met them in 1979, around the same time I started teaching at the UPR's Drama Department. Their ethics and aesthetics have strongly impacted the work I have co-created with visual artist Antonio Martorell over the course of three and a half decades. Their influence is also present on other contemporary Puerto Rican theater groups such as Y No Había Luz and Agua, Sol y Sereno who work with masks, stilts, music, speaking about peace, the environment, and freedom.

Academia has certainly been a part of my life that has allowed me to develop a wide range of ties with US theater. In 1981, I participated in a heavily intellectual post-doctoral seminar at NYU with Herbert Blau, a theatre director and theorist famous for staging *Waiting for Godot* in St. Quentin Prison. He was a practitioner of the avant-garde, and a philosopher as well. The seminar day was packed with activities—eight hours of reports, readings, etc.—but sadly the participants in that group did not know about Augusto Boal's life and works. I had gotten to know Boal several years before in a conference at the O'Neill Center in Connecticut, had read his book *Theatre of the Oppressed*, and later, in the 1980s, became his apprentice in his research center in Paris. I introduced Boal's theory and practice to our colleagues, and the seminar allowed me to network with people who later had important academic positions in the field of theater in the United States. One of them was Alan Brody, who became director of MIT's Theater & Music Department. Because MIT students seemed to lack communication skills, the university had taken up the mission of offering its engineers a humanistic background, including a theater and music program.

When I became MIT's artist in residence in 1993, the students found some of the workshops threatening since their daily work was mostly passive, isolated, and competitive. They had difficulties expressing their feelings and learning to work collectively. I was also constantly expected to focus my work on so-called minorities, and had to teach courses about the African American or Asian-American experience without knowing what it was really like, as if as a Puerto Rican—a member of another "minority"—I would instantly understand these students' needs.

We once had a complex discussion among colleagues about how to deal with "minorities" in my field. I told them:

> I didn't choose to be born in Puerto Rico, and I was, nor did I choose to be born a woman, and I was. I accept those "given circumstances" with pride. However, I did choose to study, teach, and create theatre, and you are forcing me to teach exclusively theatre for minorities, which I do with rigor, but I feel uncomfortable about this imposition from the outside: let me decide, let me define myself! In Puerto Rico I'm not a minority, so don't define me as such.

When Diana Taylor established the Hemispheric Institute of Performance and Politics at NYU, one of my former students at UPR helped organize a database of Latin American theatre artists and groups that include many from Puerto Rico. The archive includes some of my work, as well as that of Antonio Martorell, Viveca Vázquez, Teresa Hernández, Javier Cardona, and many other island performers.

My relationship with Pregones Theater group based at the Bronx—who have become heirs to the PRTT's legacy—has been a source of great satisfaction. It's amazing how things sometimes fall into place: Alvan Colón, the co-director of Pregones, was a former member of the Anamú theater group in Puerto Rico in the 1980s, who shares with me the same background in people's theatre, street theatre, and collective theatre. Before moving to the United States and joining Rosalba Rolón in Pregones, Alvan had played the character of Mr. Terence in *Pipo Subway no sabe reír*, and I played the character of Lina, the girl who's in love with Pipo. Over the years I have traveled from Puerto Rico with Antonio Martorell to hold workshops produced by Pregones with New York's Latino community. Our strong collaboration is a testament to the reality that three and a half million Puerto Ricans live in the island and five and a half live in the mainland and we share a very strong, coherent culture and the same colonial past.

My latest directing dance/theatre project in 2017 was *Hij@s de la Bernarda*. It was presented at Pregones just after Hurricane María devastated Puerto Rico, and is based on *La casa de Bernarda Alba*, but staged in experimental dance and flamenco fashion. Dealing with five daughters who struggle under their mother's yoke, the play's atmosphere is oppressive. Some of the local references relate to the wave of femicides happening in the island and to resistance from imposed authority. It touched universal fibers, and was a success in San Juan during the Casals Festival and in New York at Pregones, as well as in other cities to which it traveled: Cádiz, Miami, and Havana, where it received the important cultural recognition of *El Gallo de La Habana*. Ultimately, I credit the staging of *Hij@s de la Bernarda* for the lifetime achievement award I received at the 33rd International Hispanic Theatre Festival of Miami in 2018.

Today, I'm a retired professor from the University of Puerto Rico. I direct plays and documentaries and have recently published my memoirs with the collaboration of a Peruvian theatre director: *Rosa Luisa Márquez, memorias de una teatrera del Caribe: Conversaciones con Miguel Rubio*. I am focused on what makes Puerto Rican theatre unique: Its rhythms, sounds, movements, and meanings, and with what still makes theatre such a fascinating communal experience. I go often to New York to nurture my insatiable hunger for good theatre wherever it is staged, and there I reconnect with colleagues and friends and members of the diaspora, who together with us continue imagining and recreating Puerto Rican theatre in the island and abroad.

## Notes

1. Rosa Luisa Márquez is the author of *Brincos y saltos. El juego como disciplina teatral: ensayos y manual de teatreros ambulantes* (Ediciones Cuicaloca and Colegio Universitario de Cayey, 1992). The 95-minute documentary based on her book, produced in 2010 in association with Miguel Villafañe, is available in the media archive of the NYU's Hemispheric Institute (Permanent URL: http://hdl.handle.net/2333.1/gtht78w4). Her most recent book is *Rosa Luisa Márquez, memorias de una teatrera del Caribe: conversaciones con Miguel Rubio Zapata* (Ediciones Cuicaloca, 2020), www.teatropublicopr.org/libro-rosaluisamarquez.
2. See *Performing Arts Legacy Project: Alván Colón Lespier*, https://performingartslegacy.org/colonlespier/art-for-all-the-anamu-collective/.

# 4

# ACTOR TRAINING WITH GLOBAL PERSPECTIVES

## A Historical Narrative of the Only Spanish-Language Theatre Conservatory in the United States

*Joann Yarrow*

Teatro Prometeo's Professional Theatre Conservatory holds a platinum place in my heart and career. I served as artistic director for 12 years of its nearly half-century existence as a hallmark of Spanish-language actor training in the United States. Prometeo's story as the only Spanish-language theatre conservatory in the nation is revealed in its historic influence on actors and directors and designers. By weaving my story with the story of building the Professional Acting Conservatory, my hope is that I can inspire new cultural possibilities for theatre programs in the United States and establish this last iteration of Teatro Prometeo in theatre history.

This Spanish-language theatre conservatory thrived in Miami. Miami is the largest metropolitan area in the state and the most ethnically diverse city in the United States. The Latin American community, especially, maintains a robust and diverse presence there attracting Cubans from Baracoa to Matanzas, Colombians from Bogota to Barranquilla, Chileans from Santiago, and Argentinians from Bahia Blanca, plus immigrants from all across the South American continent and Central American region.

Miami presents an opportunity for immigrants to create a new way of life that encompasses not only their new US identities but also their proud Latin American heritage. Some are established professionals, and some are students from academies or universities; others follow a passion they could not express in their home countries due to war, politics, or a lack of resources. Miami offers a haven where artists can speak Spanish anywhere. In this unique *sancocho* of Hispanic flavors, Teatro Prometeo flourished as a theatrical oasis.

In 2006, I was offered the position as Artistic Director of Teatro Prometeo. My desire was to continue the theatre's mission of preserving Hispanic culture through theatre, which it had promoted for more than three decades. I also wanted to develop it into a unique and powerful Spanish-language theatre conservatory.

DOI: 10.4324/9781003021520-6

Founded in 1973 by Teresa Maria Rojas, Teatro Prometeo found a home at Miami Dade College. With the vision and support of its then President, Eduardo Padrón, what began as the first bilingual theatre courses in the Department of Arts and Philosophy grew into a community theatre program with annual productions and non-credit courses offered through the college's continuing education department. Teatro Prometeo became the cultural center for many artist/immigrants and Latinx actors who wished to train and perform in Spanish. The program, ripe for evolution, served as a unique niche for a large community of artists and performers. To support this new chapter, Teatro Prometeo partnered with the Florida Center for the Literary Arts, led by its executive director, and former Prometeo actress, Alina Interián, who also spearheaded Miami Book Fair International.

Partnership with the Center meant that its staff supported Prometeo with publicity, programming, budget management, and grant development. Together, we created a structured professional acting program and repertory in Spanish. As a result, Teatro Prometeo was swiftly recognized in the nation as the primary Spanish-language professional theatre conservatory housed and supported by an academic institution. This recognition gave Prometeo the ability to attract and recruit faculty, students, guest artists, and designers.

My life journey, academic experiences, and professional opportunities provided the path toward taking the reins of this budding conservatory. I grew up in a series of disparate and, thus, culturally distinct places. I was born in Barranquilla, Colombia. My mother is Colombian and my father is British. When I was a month old, my mother and I joined my father in Korea, the first leg of a journey that took our family all across the world. I have lived in more than a dozen countries. However, I always maintained a deep connection to my Colombian heritage. As a child, I visited my *abuelos* in Barranquilla every summer. My grandfather, who loved poetry and literature, would recite Rubén Darío in the garden until all of us knew these passages by memory. It was a house full of music, magical realism, history, and love.

Theatre became the place I most connected with. I attended prominent institutions for undergraduate and graduate study in theatre. Though I received excellent training, I struggled to find a cultural space as an artist. What countered this was a directing internship with Double Edge Theatre, who introduced me to Odin Teatret, an international theatre group based in Denmark headed by Eugenio Barba. At Odin, I worked with core company member Roberta Carreri on how to use performance as a global language connecting distinct cultures and disciplines to create powerful theatre.

I needed a place to sift through my cultural and lived experiences and to experiment with global aesthetics and philosophies. With Vernice Miller, I founded A Laboratory for Actor Training (ALAT). We continued the work across performance disciplines and later, during my tenure at Union College, I explored my deep desire to integrate and diversify the American theatre experience. The Chair of the Department, Bill Finlay, and I were both excited about offering a unique, non-cookie cutter experience inside a small but mighty theatre program. We offered theatre history, play analysis, and performance opportunities from various cultural and global points of view. When the opportunity arose to help nurture and develop Teatro Prometeo, a long-standing Spanish-language theatre school, I was excited to make a difference and to fulfill this vision of global theatre training.

The first action I took as artistic director was to assess the program. I realized immediately that nothing like it existed in the United States. Teatro Prometeo existed in Cuba before Castro's revolution. Francisco Morín founded Prometeo in Havana in 1948. His star actress, Teresa Maria Rojas, brought the name from Cuba as a tribute to Morín and fearlessly led a Spanish-language theatre school at Miami Dade College for 32 years.[1] It offered community classes in acting, voice, and children's theatre, and it produced one show a year that focused on community engagement. I saw this community theatre as fertile ground to build the first US professional acting conservatory in Spanish. I believed it important that the conservatory be a non-credit, professional program. I wasn't interested in grading artists. I was interested in getting artists to work.

One of the unique features of Teatro Prometeo's Professional Actor Training Program was the curriculum. Each season comprised a first-year presentation, a second-year performance, and a production at the International Hispanic Theatre Festival of Miami founded by another Prometeo company member, Mario Ernesto Sanchez, and director of Teatro Avante. Since its inception in 1986, Teatro Prometeo participated at and co-presented this international theatre festival that continues to feature professional theatre companies from Latin America and Spain. Prometeo also provided opportunities for students to participate in MicroTeatro Miami, the Miami Book Fair International, and the Miami Hispanic Showcase. At the showcase, students auditioned for local and national casting directors, agents, and industry professionals. In addition, actors in the program also toured with Prometeo productions nationally and internationally every year. Teatro Prometeo was invited to present in Colombia, Ecuador, Peru, Dominican Republic, New York, Los Angeles, and Boston.

More than a "Latinx" theatre, Prometeo was an international center for theatre training where actors, directors, and playwrights from Chile, Cuba, Venezuela, and New York City could create productions that did not strip away their cultural identities but, instead, acknowledged and honored them. Spanish, like English, has different accents, regionalisms, socio-economic slang, and colonial influence. It was important to dive into classical, contemporary, and commissioned plays that came from countries across South America, Central America, North America, and Europe.

To build the conservatory, it was essential to me that the faculty consists of a diverse group of seasoned theatre professionals who worked successfully within the core classes or offered master classes and workshops. The curriculum consisted of acting, voice, movement, Latin American and Global theatre history, camera-acting technique, and specialized workshops in stage combat, *Commedia dell'arte*, contact improvisation, rasaboxes, and acrobatic stilt performance. Prometeo drew in world-renowned theatre directors, designers, choreographers, and historians, award-winning playwrights, actors, and singers, as well as film and television professionals from all parts of the globe to share their unique style and cultural flavor, their discipline and expertise with our students. Prometeo's core faculty and staff comprised Vivian Ruiz, Cristina Rebull, Zaida Castellanos, Humberto Gonzalez, Jorge Hernandez, Maria Garcia, Pedro Balmaseda, Jorge Noa, Liliam Vega, Susy Lechuga (Cuba), Beatriz Rizk, Orlando Arias, Maria Christina Mustellier (Colombia), Yarani del Valle Piñero (Puerto Rico), Sonia de Martin Iriarte, Carlota Pradera, Olga de Martin Eugenio (Spain), Neher Jacqueline Briceño, Fernando Calzadilla, Melissa Messulam, Julio Bouly (Venezuela), Ana Maria de Lima, Sara McCranie (the United States), and Carlos Cedano (Dominican Republic). We worked together to create a structured and professional acting program and repertory in Spanish that rivaled American programs.

Beatriz Rizk was Prometeo's resident artist/scholar. She specializes in Latin American Theatre and Global History. To this day, her curricula are some of the most sought-after globally. She had a gift for choosing and directing staged readings of culturally relevant plays. These plays connected our actors to their cultural heritages, which empowered them to see themselves beyond North American stereotypes.

Vivian Ruiz, a graduate of Prometeo, was affectionately known as "the heart" of Prometeo. She has a highly successful film, television, stage, and voice-over career. She was a professional role model for our students; as a working bilingual actor, she navigated fluidly in English and Spanish markets. At Prometeo, Vivian taught both levels of voice and diction and the camera-acting class. Her presence and talent were nothing short of incredible. With many ties to the industry, she networked to ensure that Prometeo actors found work.

Prometeo professors also served as resident playwrights. Cristina Rebull and Neher Jacqueline Briceño are award-winning, published writers from Cuba and Venezuela. They are also professional actors who taught the second- and third-level professional acting courses. It is an odd practice in US Conservatories to silo artistic disciplines as opposed to cultivating the artist holistically. Our goal was to train the *artist* to professionally navigate through all parts of the industry. With the company of actors in mind, Cristina Rebull developed and adapted several plays at Prometeo including *Cena para seis, Cyrano mío,* and *Cacerâ (The Crucible)*. Neher Jacqueline Briceño's *Chejov vs Chekov* and *Mujeres de Shakespeare* toured nationally. Yaraní del Valle Piñero came to Miami from Pregones Theatre, NY, and taught a full second year intensive, directing *Pequeños absurdos, grandes abrazos,* and *A puerta cerrada (No Exit)*.

What is also important to note was the classes themselves came from different cultural and global perspectives. Humberto Gonzalez, a first-year movement teacher, came from the National Ballet of Cuba. Orlando Arias had trained in Colombia in Commedia and clowning. Sonia de Martin Iriarte brought her training from RESAD (Royal Academy of Performing Arts) in Spain. Fernando

Calzadilla from Venezuela is only one of six master teachers of rasaboxes who could teach in Spanish. Although everyone lived in Miami, the training and experience were global.

In addition to the classroom curriculum, Prometeo's support staff were involved in the programming and culture of the conservatory. María Cristina Mustelier, my administrative coordinator, brought an understanding and appreciation of the different cultural nuances each person brought to the theatre. Beyond correcting my Spanish guffaws, she was instrumental in recognizing and empathizing with the journeys each student took in order to be in this country, many supporting their families, let alone showing up for class and rehearsals. Students' ages ranged from 18 to 65. Average age was 30. This created a mature company atmosphere. They would propose projects, such as creating short films, doing children's theatre, and going out into the streets and communities performing on stilts and bringing classical theatre and music to the elderly. María Garcia was our director of photography for the Camera classes and included them in various film projects. After completing the program, one of our graduates created a TYA company, and our production coordinator Melissa Messulam proposed Prometeo produce "Play Time! An International Theatre Festival for Children." She invited companies from Colombia, Ecuador, Brazil, and Italy to Prometeo and showcased them at various theatres in Miami during the Miami Book Fair International, an advantage of our collaboration with that organization.

The faculty created a protective space for students to do theatre in their native language while at the same time raising the bar of artistic excellence. This was not limited to acting. Prometeo wouldn't have been able to bring to life its magical productions without the nimbleness of our technical director, Carlos "Carlitos" Cedano. Carlitos was a genius at translating and transforming the visions of designers. Whether we were performing in the United States or at a theatre school in Peru, he made the creative team feel respected, could adapt to any system, and could build whatever was needed. Carlitos, like Vivian, worked fluidly between US institutions and Latin American companies. Prometeo did not have a "scene shop" or a "costume shop." Everything was done off-site by carpenters and seamstresses with whom we had relationships. If sets were built on stage, the whole company was involved. What this engendered was that several graduates went on to direct, produce, and form their own theatre companies.

From the first production through to our final show together, designers Pedro Balmaseda and Jorge Noa were cultural mentors for each show and my linchpins to creating a Prometeo community. We translated the collaborative process that defines devised theater into our production meetings. That meant that we didn't have to have it all figured out before the actors started rehearsal. Many times, they would watch a rehearsal and then add or subtract scenic elements during run-throughs.

Each show had its own cultural identity. The designers, director, mentors, and actors in that rehearsal room were all committed to preserving and expressing the cultural heritage of each specific production in every detail. The designers would easily flow from experimenting with the lighting to helping an actor walk in new shoes.

Passion was defined as egalitarian. Each culture expresses it differently—one is not more or less than the other. Although Spanish was the designers' primary language, they worked with English-language American productions as well. They didn't adapt their Cuban identity to be more "American"; they entered the process with a spirit to amplify both their experience and the rest of the production team. This was the key. "We don't have to change ourselves," they believed. "There is enough room in theatre training, production, and design for everyone."

I directed many productions at Prometeo. An example of adapting an American Latinx production from English to Spanish was *Filo al Fuego*, a new translation of Oliver Mayer's *Blade to the Heat* that was presented at the International Hispanic Theatre Festival of Miami. In 2009, I approached Oliver and asked if he would be open to collaborating on a new translation/adaptation of his play. By changing the language and the specificity of the details, we found the Caribbean-ness, the Miami-ness, and the very special and individual connections to the acting company and the audience. The play, which examines the way Latino men define themselves by country, sexuality, and violence, took on an explosive significance in the hands of Prometeo's actors with its fiery and poetic translation of the original dialogue.

To prepare for this play, Oliver and I discussed the possibility of shifting some of the characters' ethnic identity so that the fact that the characters were speaking Spanish would be organic to the company and public. For example, some African American characters morphed into Afro-Cuban or Afro-Dominican. The Jackie Wilson impersonator became the Benny Moré impersonator. I wanted to preserve Oliver's story and make it culturally accessible to the actors and audience. The television announcer, who spoke English in the production, was played by an African American actor. This cultural distinctiveness was important in a society that would lump them together because of race.

In addition to the script revisions, the actors needed to know how to box. I needed to set up a promotional photo shoot at a boxing gym in downtown Miami. The owner, Mickey Demos, quickly stepped in and offered to train these Spanish-speaking actors at his gym. "With a healthy dollop of good luck" as Oliver would later say, Mickey introduced me to Dwayne Simpson, who had been the Olympic trainer for the US boxing team. Then retired, Dwayne had a storage unit full of boxing memorabilia and equipment, which he generously lent to our production. Bill Finlay came down from Union College to set the fight choreography. Ferdie Pacheco, Muhammed Ali's fight doctor, consulted dramaturgically, with a treasure trove of stories of the history and time period. A colleague from Disney Studios in Orlando helped build the ring and the designers scoured Goodwill for costumes. Gonzalo Rodriguez, with his expertise at lighting rock concerts, lit our production magnificently.

The process was seasoned with all the right human ingredients: Mexican American playwright; actors from Colombia, Cuba, Chile, Puerto Rico, Honduras, Venezuela, Mexico, Nicaragua, as well as African American actors from Miami; Greek, Irish, and Italian trainers and choreographers; Cuban designers; and a Colombian-British director. This impressive mix of people from varied cultures and professions worked passionately on a production that questioned identity in America.

Another example was the production of *Papeles*, one of our most traveled shows. It opened for MicroTeatro in Miami and went on to Los Angeles, New York, Peru, and Colombia. Co-written by Hector Pino and Brad Beckman, this 15-minute piece placed the audience inside an immigration room at Miami International Airport. That's the room where officials take travelers when passport control is an issue. *Papeles* manifested an immersive theatrical experience because it placed actors in the audience whispering to each other, questioning, judging, and subtly discriminating against each other—and the audience. We performed this play in English, Spanish, and Spanglish, a sample of which can be seen below:

MARIA: ¡Todos somos Mexicanos para ellos! ¡No saben la diferencia de un país latinoamericano al otro!
JUAN: ¡Cálmate! If you want to live in this country, stop complaining so much! Aquí todos vivimos al borde del pánico. Por eso nos tienen encerrados aquí. El miedo hace que la gente se sienta culpable sin haber hecho nada.

*Papeles* allowed international audiences to understand, empathize, and recognize— the immigrant experience of being "othered." The productions were certainly a highlight of the program.

The other highlight of our program was the students themselves. For the purposes of this essay, I interviewed actors Esther Banegas Gatica and Claudia Quesada, both graduates of Prometeo and working professionals who went on to study in US graduate programs. Esther Banegas Gatica spoke honestly about her experience:

> After leaving Prometeo, I was most aware that the professors at Prometeo would give us context as to why our productions mattered to us, to our audience. They explained how we were connected to the material and its historical context. It didn't matter if we were doing an absurdist play like *Pierrot Pierrot* or naturalistic productions like *Emily Dickinson*; everything we did was connected to the community. In other programs, I have felt like the theatre season did not connect to what was happening in the community, the city, or the student body.

Esther's reflection questions how theatre institutions choose their seasons. Is it for training experience, work with texts, character development, or the need to make a difference in their community? At Prometeo, we had the unique opportunity to select productions because we had a resident playwright, access to a huge library of plays from all over Latin America, and the capability to translate and adapt plays from English to Spanish. Esther further offered:

> Prometeo didn't pit the students against each other for a role. Prometeo productions were tailored to the company of actors. Our training stretched us, challenged our limitations, and included us. We trusted the process, no matter how long it took. Whether it was the lead actor or a person in a supporting role, we understood that we all had to be present. We all had to care. Part of our process was that all the actors were called to rehearsal, whether their scene was being worked on or not. It was never considered wasted time. In each rehearsal, we dove deeper into why we were doing this play, what it meant to us. Where it rang true or where it felt inauthentic. We managed ourselves, ensured we got where we needed to be, and supported each other through breakdowns and triumphs. It was a family dynamic. You may not always like every member, but you always have each other's back. We had a bond of trust.

Claudia Quesada also reflected on how trust played a crucial role at Prometeo:

> Yes, trust is everything. During a trust exercise at my graduate school, the class let me fall and hit the ground. They didn't catch me. I had to go to the hospital for a concussion. That was literal, but it also mirrored what I was going through in an emotional and creative sense—I could not trust. At Prometeo, I could have a tough night and still count on the respect and support of my classmates the next night.

In contrast to the training at Prometeo, Claudia offered an example of what she encountered at her graduate program:

> I remember my accent in English being a problem in my actor training. I was excited to present a monologue in class because the character hates roaches, and I hate roaches, and it was funny. I didn't know that the character was from the South, and I was told it needed to be done with a Southern accent. But I felt that my accent was sufficient; I wanted to embody the character because the character spoke to me. Then the same happened with a Shakespeare scene. I explained to the professor that at Prometeo, we did Shakespeare in Spanish with an Argentinian accent, a Cuban accent—the dialect didn't matter. I informed the faculty in the program on how to deal with me, how to teach me and how to approach my way of speaking. I still wanted them to guide me to be better, speak clearer and be better understood. For the most part I was typecast and pigeonholed into playing Latina

characters and wished I had the opportunity to explore other roles within this education setting, roles that I probably wouldn't have in the professional world. I wanted to be cast for who I am, not what I am.

Claudia's experience in "English-only" training programs is, unfortunately, not unique. Standardized arts education models dampen the student's artistic values, especially when those values do not culturally reflect the creative spirit. At Teatro Prometeo, we emphasized cultural distinctions with clarity and compassion. According to Esther:

> Prometeo actor training was very culturally different at its core. Prometeo had professors with different experiences and cultural backgrounds. Their expectations were always high, and you could feel the pressure from our professors to do good work because we would be competing in a national market that would discount us before we even stepped on stage. Students learned by example—seeing them navigate their lifework and artistry.

Esther's comments reinforce the concept that Teatro Prometeo was not a building or a place or even a curriculum. Prometeo was comprised of people who had the utmost respect for its craft. At the end of every production, we engaged in the methodological tool of cultural mapping to strengthen and empower our student's unique cultural identities and memories.

Until Esther unpacked the technique in our conversation, I had not realized its importance. Esther explained:

> During our talkbacks, we always had the chance to say our full name and the country we came from. That is such a powerful thing to do. Because we're not just Latinx. We're not these brown people in a conservatory. We got to say, 'My name is Esther Banegas Gatica de Honduras,' and then we recognized those in the audience who were also Honduran. And this was true for the Cubans, Nicaraguans, Chileans, everyone. We represented our backgrounds with pride. That is not a thing that happens regularly in any other space.

Esther's comments strike at the heart of what made Prometeo's cultural understanding different from Eurocentric/English-language actor training. In my personal experience and opinion, the Eurocentric/US conservatory offers theatre students strong technique, but in one-size-fits-all model that fails to consider individuals' cultures and accents, and, most importantly, the reasons they are called to be artists.

The Professional Actor Conservatory at Teatro Prometeo had an amazing 12-year run completing a span of 44 years of Spanish-language theatre at Miami Dade College. In 2018, after significant cuts in state arts funding, we finished our season and our tenure with sold-out performances of Lorca's *Doña Rosita la*

*Soltera*. Directed by Gonzalo Rodriguez, designed by Pedro Balmaseda and Jorge Noa, with outstanding performances by Cristina Rebull, Vivian Ruiz, and the graduates and students of Teatro Prometeo, the production beautifully saluted an incredible legacy.

Looking back on my time as artistic director of Teatro Prometeo as well as looking at the global perspective for Latinx actor training makes me hope this essay continues the conversation for educators developing curriculum in drama programs, for Latin American and Latinx artists seeking formal training, for theatre directors choosing their seasons, and for playwrights developing their voices. How can our institutions awaken to include global perspectives while nurturing and empowering young creators? Within our art programs, we have performers and activists, mentors, world leaders, and dreamers. An army of creators with the right tools and inspiration can offset apathy, anxiety, destruction, and divisions. Stories bridge cultures. Arts institutions can be culturally distinct and still empower stories of identity through differing cultural lenses. Prometeo was a mish mosh that didn't homogenize its population but emphasized its heterogeneity.

The living organism that was Teatro Prometeo is best encapsulated in a moment from our tour to the New England Russian Theatre Festival in Boston in 2007. Teatro Prometeo had presented Neher Jacqueline Briceño's *Chejov vs. Chejov*, a Spanish adaptation of Anton Chekhov's short stories. The audience of academics enthusiastically received the play. At the end of our performance, someone asked "How do you teach passion?" I simply responded "We never snuffed it out."

Teatro Prometeo showed the world just how powerful developing a strong identity and holding fast to the tenets of inclusivity and diversity could be. Directors, actors, playwrights, designers, and more were trained to nurture and honor their cultures, to value them, and to meet new cultures with curiosity, empathy, and expansion. If "all the world is a stage," then it is important that we expand what the artists and audience can experience.

## Note

1. For the complete history of Teatro Prometeo and its productions under the direction Teresa Maria Rojas, see the digital collection, which is curated by Lilian Manzor and Dr. Beatriz J. Rizk at the University of Miami: Knight Foundation, "Cuban theatre in Miami: 1960–1980," *University of Miami Library*, accessed January 21, 2022, http://scholar.library.miami.edu/miamitheater/.

## Bibliography

Knight Foundation. "Cuban theatre in Miami: 1960–1980." University of Miami Library. Accessed January 21, 2022. http://scholar.library.miami.edu/miamitheater/.

# 5

# DR. ALMA MARTINEZ

## A Narrative Toward Becoming a Chicanx Actor

*Alma Martinez*

*The following is a historical narrative of how I came to find my acting technique and identity as a Chicana only when I stepped outside white-dominant American theatre training.*

### 1953–1971 Birth Through High School

I am Mexican-born and immigrated to the United States in 1954 with my family at four months. Dad had a primary school education, and my mom completed high school. Spanish was my first language. Migrating was a gamble my parents were willing to take, given the limited opportunities in Mexico. I am the first in my family to graduate from college. I hold a Ph.D. in Directing and Dramatic Criticism from Stanford University, an M.F.A. in Acting from the University of Southern California (USC), and a B.A. in Drama from Whittier College. I am a Fulbright Scholar, a Dartmouth College Cesar Chavez Dissertation Fellow, and a Smithsonian Research Fellow. My decades of acting work in theatre, television, and film were recognized by the Academy of Motion Picture Arts and Sciences when I was inducted in 2013 and by the Academy of Television Arts and Sciences in 2005. I have acted on Broadway and Off-Broadway, and in regional theaters, intimate theaters, public arenas, and improvised spaces across the United States, Mexico, and Europe. I am a proud member of the actors' unions: SAG-AFTRA, Actors' Equity Association (AEA), Stage Directors and Choreographers Society (SDC), and Asociación Nacional de Actores (ANDA), the Mexican actors' union.

From 1954 to 1961, from the ages of one to seven, I did not go to pre-school or kindergarten. Television programs and the commercialization of consumers' most mundane items, with their catchy jingles, were my first English lessons: "Brylcreem—a little dab will do you"; "Oh, I'd love to be an Oscar Meyer Wiener"; "Snap, what a happy sound."

DOI: 10.4324/9781003021520-7

Looking back over a 50-plus-year career as an actor and a scholar, I understand that I gravitated and excelled in high school, educational institutions, generally, and acting, specifically, because of my early indoctrination to English and American culture through television.

Stepping onto pristine campuses and performing in plays about the white American experience reminded me of the idyllic, utopian television shows where I saw myself as the leading lady in each fictitious scenario. Immersed completely into popular American culture but raised in a culturally Mexican home, I easily grew into the role of the "perfect" middle school and high school student as a master "code-switcher," the label applied to those of us who alternate among languages and cultures. Brainwashed and internally colonized? You bet. Did I think I was white? Absolutely. Did the dystopian illusion eventually crumble? Undeniably so.

I first set foot on an actual stage when I was 15 years old in high school productions of *Spoon River Anthology*, *America Hurrah*, and *How to Succeed in Business Without Really Trying*. Performing in these plays not only spurred me forward to continue acting but also confused me to no end after I left high school and delved deeper into the study of acting as a university freshperson. You see, up until I first entered the USC with a full scholarship in 1971, I continued to think I was just like everyone else: White.

Point of information: I'm a brown-skinned, dark-haired, brown-eyed, Indigenous Latina. In 1968, the US educational system did its best to inculcate in us an education that espoused "our" American history, our literature, our science, biology, etc. I must give the system credit. It succeeded—so much so that in 1970, I went to a large cattle call at Disneyland for the role of Snow White. I was not cast (no surprise), so I returned to my high school regimen. I learned, absorbed, and emulated all that I was taught vis-à-vis performing whiteness. I was rewarded time and time again as an outstanding actor and student. By the time I graduated in 1971 at the top of my class, I had learned that the more I emulated whiteness, the more I was rewarded.

## 1971–1972 USC, Department of Drama: Whose Psychological Realism Exactly, Mr. Stanislavski?

I was excited to go to USC because they had a good football team—the extent of my knowledge of the campus. My family lived only 28 miles from there but had never ventured beyond the Million Dollar Theater on Broadway and 3rd Street in downtown Los Angeles. USC resembled the idyllic college campuses I had grown up seeing on television. Beautiful and green with imposing architecture and staffed by primarily white, male professors strolling across campus with briefcases or with books piled high, plus hundreds of white college students, who, I thought, looked just like me. I remember the unsolicited stares when I walked across the mall; I assumed students were admiring my sharp "college" look.

When I registered, the class that most excited me was theatre, taught by Professor Bill White. I was, after all, one of the best actors in my high school, so, surely, I assumed, I would continue my success at USC.

However, the first sign things would go array occurred when I was told that my full scholarship did not cover books. Given my family's tight finances, asking them for money was not an option. So, I found classes that required the least and cheapest books possible. Bye-bye, French, Russian history, music, and fencing classes.

Once in classes, I realized that those looks I was scoring were not assurances of my inclusion. They were quizzical stares. For the first time in my educational life, I was often the only brown-skinned Latinx student in the room. My pattern became to sit alone in class and just observe. Be invisible. The confidence I had, having excelled in high school, crumbled when I was in a room with students who not only had excelled as I had but also were actually white.

However, in my theatre class, I had been surprised and relieved to see two Mexican-Americans. Professor White introduced the class from an elevated stage, informing us what we would cover in the semester: acting, psychological realism, plus someone named Stanislavski.[1] He prompted us to be natural, be ourselves.

The next thing I knew—and I do not recall how this happened or even that I volunteered—I was on stage with Professor White, who had asked me to improvise a phone conversation with my father. My memory of the moment: I am on stage, standing, alone. My mind races, assessing. The class is mostly white, and the professor is white. The two Latinx may only speak English, so, I figured, no improvising in Spanish. English it is. I had to figure out what "would" I say to my dad "if" he spoke English? I thumb through my mental file of television father/daughter scenarios and decide to riff off a scene from "Gidget." Be cute, adorable, and spunky.

Only seconds had transpired—a lifetime for an actor on stage. I held my hand up to my ear as if I were holding a phone. "But, Dad, why do I have to come home by 9 pm?" As I was fully inhabiting my imaginary white world, the professor commanded, "Stop!" I froze, eyes wide and expectant as he told the class that what they had just seen was a cliché, not real and not acting.

What happened that afternoon was not *de rigueur* critique by an acting teacher of his student. Rather, this was a critique of a young Latina, a critique that led to the public realization—and humiliation—that she was not white, not an actor, and weeks later when her grades fell to B's and C's—a failure unto itself, not cut out to be an American college student. My American dream shattered.

What happened next was a steady, deep decline into isolation and depression. When I auditioned and was cast in the chorus for "Gypsy," I was thrilled but then had to drop out because rehearsals were in the evenings, and I had to work evenings to pay for books. I marked the finality and failure of my life as a college student by piling all my papers, files, and class notes into a laundry basket, carrying it outside, tossing all of it into a cement pit, lighting it all on fire, and watching it burn. This ritual burning was a dramatic ending befitting a young Chicana diva in the making. I left USC mid-semester and lost my scholarship.

I went home and spent days lying in bed, tears rolling down my face. My parents were so concerned that they even took me to a psychologist—unheard of in a blue-color Mexican-American family. I remember being asked question after question as the tears flooded my eyes. As the psychologist, a white female, spoke, I could not help but harken back to my acting class with Professor White and think, "You won't understand me if I speak because you don't speak Spanish, and I no longer have the energy or will to make myself understood." I never said a word about what happened at USC to the psychologist or my parents. Those months at home healed me enough to start thinking of the next step. I was Mexican so perhaps I belonged in a Mexican university. Looking for acting training and, more specifically, acting training that would guide me to my actual identity and place in the world, I saw Mexico as my only option and hope.

## 1972–1973 Universidad de Guadalajara: Finally, Jerzy Grotowski[2]

My parents allowed me to stay in Mexico and to study on the condition that I enroll in the Instituto Pan Americano, a private, bilingual, executive secretarial school. The school's director was a US Latina, and many of my classmates, all women, were Latinas and spoke English at various proficiency levels. I attended classes Monday through Friday mornings, dutifully dressed in my navy blue polyester top, pleated skirt, knee socks, and penny loafers. This secretarial school was not where I wanted to be, so as soon as possible, I enrolled in theatre performance classes at the Universidad de Guadalajara (UDG) in the afternoons. On the weekends, we toured our theatre productions to Sinaloa, Zacatecas, and other states within driving distance of Guadalajara. I remember the afternoons fondly when I tossed off my secretarial uniform, put on my boho theatre persona, and headed to the UDG Escuela de Artes Plásticas. The building was an old, majestic colonial mansion with doors wide enough for horse-drawn carriages and a central courtyard that opened up to two stories of painting, sculpture, music, and theatre classes.

I had found a "home" in the theatre department but was still the "American" who could not roll her r's. My colleagues called me "la pochita," a derogatory word made an endearment by the infantilizing suffix "ita." The theatre course was intense because it was my introduction to the methodology of Jerzy Grotowski's "Poor Theatre."[3] Our instructor/director, Rafael Sandoval, took us through the highly physical and emotive exercises five days a week. Grotowski's methodology was not contingent on verbal communication or the nuances of the psychological underpinnings of quotidian social behavior. Instead, the work was visceral. Actors did not portray an emotion; their body and entire being "were" the emotion. Although I was still the *pochita*, I had found an acting style that, for the first time, allowed me to reach a level of emotive and physical expression that freed me from the necessity of code-switching in either Spanish or English. Grotowski's methodology made me confront and come to terms with the psychological and socially conditioned roadblocks that I held as a Latinx actor. In retrospect, at its most profound, this acting work was the first time I truly confronted my life-long, conditioned-white identity with my subsumed ancestral identity as an Amerindian woman.

The actor training in Guadalajara not only taught me to open channels of deep expression, but it also introduced me to theatre that served restorative Mexican justice. Our theatre troupe performed polemical plays like *Esperando al Zurdo* (*Waiting for Lefty*) by Clifford Odets in trade union halls across the state. *El Testamento del Perro* (*The Dog's Will*) by Adriano Suasunna addressed the colonial, Afro-Latinx economic caste system in northeast Brazil that resonated with Mexico's colonial past and Indigenous and Afro-Latinx caste systems. We toured this latter play to small towns and villages in Jalisco, Michoacan, and Zacatecas. *Yo También Hablo de las Rosas* (*I Also Speak of Roses*) by Emilio Carballido was based on the poor and ostracized "trash scavengers" endemic to major urban cities across Mexico. We performed the play in the poorest, marginalized rural communities, urban barrios, and in central markets and plazas across the country. When not touring, our acting troupe conducted workshops in women's prisons.

Although the training was Grotowski-based, our plays were text-based, so table work and rehearsals were primarily conducted in the style of Stanislavski: a deep read of the play, that is, breaking down the play, characters, scenes, beats, objectives, actions, etc. As a Latinx actor whose primary language was now English, this meant that, as I delved into the script, I had to code-switch in reverse, from English to Spanish. As any Latinx actor who has performed a play in rotation knows— English one night, Spanish the next—a literal translation of the text is impossible, for English cannot be translated directly into Spanish and vice versa. I would begin working on the text to understand the Spanish slang, idioms, allegories, metaphors, and historical–cultural references and hear where the beats landed and dramatic arcs rose and fell. Then I translated these discoveries into English to hit the right emotional tone, pace, rhythm, and emphases. Again, this was not a direct literal translation of the text but a cultural translation that superseded the literal.

At the age of 19 years, I had no idea how connecting so profoundly with Grotowski's work and touring plays that addressed Mexico's deep social issues would begin to expand my heart and mind to the theatre. I attribute this period as the impetus to seek alliances with other Latinx performer-activists (*teatristas*) across the Americas and, years later in 1977, with Chicano theatre.

## 1974–1976 Whittier College: No Longer White but Not Mexican

In 1973, I returned to the United States when my parents found out I was studying theatre. With no connections in the wider professional theatre/acting community,

Dr. Alma Martinez **65**

I continued to forge my path in the only way I knew how: re-enrolling in college. Regrettably, I had to wait for a year to renew my scholarship, so I took a job at Whittier High School's New Horizon's Office, a national program focused on retaining students of color. Over that year, my eyes slowly continued to open as I learned how the United States' K-12 educational institutions had historically and systemically denied Chicanx-Latinx students the right to maintain their culture, history, and language and how this denial had further subsumed their identities to privilege a white paradigm. My experience in Mexico had politicized me by showing me that people of my ethnic, racial, class, gender, and skin color were as disenfranchised in the United States as they were in Mexico. I now understood that, as a Latinx woman, I had not failed at USC. Rather, USC had failed me.

Whittier College is a small liberal arts institution with a small drama department. Dr. Robert Treser, my professor and director for many productions, supported me greatly, always pushing me to complete my B.A. With renewed confidence in my talent and in smaller classes, I felt emboldened to follow my goal to become a better actor. I was an itinerant acting student with little money. I had no car or checkbook. I rented a room in a large house. My only savings came from what I amassed in my year at the New Horizons Office. My scholarship had been restored, but I now knew I had to get a job to pay for books and my personal expenses. I was unaware that on-campus jobs were available for me to apply my skills as a bilingual executive secretary, so I sought jobs only at places where I saw other students of color: bussing tables in the cafeteria and campus cleaning crews. (Colleges and universities were still decades away from realizing that first-generation, low-income students of color needed an "orientation" uniquely suited to their lived experience.)

For two years, I took theatre and general education classes and performed in productions such as of *Harvey*, *Days and Nights of Bebe Fenstermaker*, *A . . . My Name is Alice*, and *Picnic*. Yet, I kept thinking back to the Jerzy Grotowski's work and the impact socially conscious plays had made on Mexican audiences. I was two years away from my B.A., but earning a degree was never my goal. My goal had always been to become a better actor.

I figured out that I could spend a semester of foreign exchange in Mexico City and then remain in Mexico and apply to the Centro Universitario de Teatro (CUT)[4] at the Universidad Autónoma de Mexico (National Autonomous University of Mexico) under renowned Mexican director, playwright, and theorist, Héctor Mendoza.[5] CUT, at Universidad Autónoma de Mexico, was the premier acting conservatory in Latin America. This three-year program with a 7:1 student–teacher ratio offered ballet classes, tap, tumbling, voice, music, music theory, art history, and acting. An average of 200 students from across the country applied for 14 slots. Students who were admitted spent their first year focused on Grotowski's style, their second year concentrating on Konstantin Stanislavski's methods, and the third year dedicated to synthesizing and applying these styles into fully staged productions. Only Mexican nationals could apply, and tuition was free. I had a green card and had not yet become a US citizen, so as a Mexican citizen, I would pay no tuition. But months before I was to leave for Mexico City in 1974, a moment in my actor's trajectory transpired that pivoted my acting training, work, and life in an entirely new direction.

A theatre company called El Teatro Campesino (ETC), founded by Luis Valdez, was touring Southern California. I was intrigued by the name "The Farm Workers Theatre." I did not immediately relate to the "farmworker" experience as my grandparents and extended family on both sides in Mexico were railroad workers or miners, truck drivers, mechanics, and store keepers (*abarrotes*). Seeing ETC perform *La Gran Carpa de los Rasquachis* in 1974[6] changed my life.

I had found the theatrical home/troupe I had been seeking without even knowing it, yet I was set to leave for Mexico City in a few weeks. The ETC company was scheduled to give a workshop, organized by Dr. David Flaten, at the Claremont Colleges. I rode a bus for four hours from Whittier to Claremont to participate. The workshop introduced me to Valdez's acting methodology, Theatre of the Sphere.[7] The keystone of the praxis, based on Aztec/Mayan ritual and mysticism, is highly physical theatre. It relates more to *Commedia dell'arte* in its performative relationship, that is, incorporating audiences as active participants. My previous Grotowski training (1971–1973) had been more subjective and actor-based, an emotive/physical/mystic practice that looked at audiences as "witnesses." Yet, having studied the latter, I could easily transfer the emotive physicality of this training to Theatre of the Sphere and *Commedia dell'arte*. I longed to work with this company, but I had to wait—for now.

I was one of only 14 students invited into the CUT program. Many years later, a Chicana theatre friend, working with Grupo Los Mascarones, the renowned Mexican political theatre company in 1974, told me that word had come down to them that the ultra-conservative CUT had "accepted their first Chicana." This achievement was the "first" of my many as I continued to chart a path in American theatre and academia as a Chicanx theatre, film, and television actor and as a professor.

## 1976–1977 The Centro Universitario de Teatro (CUT): Mexico City and Grotowski

I started at the CUT in the spring of 1976. This intense period of Grotowski-based training, led by Luis de Tavira,[8] instilled in the actors the freedom and the "irrational" and non-realistic power of physical expression. We did not perform an emotion: We were the emotion. At each class, we strived for the highest level of personal expression, which, in communion with other actors, superseded the individual in service to a deeper level of truth and authenticity in a performance not dissimilar to a ritual.

Grotowski training did not ask that I identify as a Mexican or American. Yet, once I left the safety of the studio, in Mexico, just as in the United States, I was tagged different, a "*pocha*." This label was not the endearing name *pochita* that my Guadalajara friends had called me but the pejorative that looked down on me as a brown-skinned American not belonging to either country. This dissonance between the studio and day-to-day life kept me yearning for that theatrical home, so my mind frequently harkened to ETC.

While still at the CUT, I knew that, one day, I would bring ETC and my professor and colleagues at the CUT together to produce a show in Mexico City. In retrospect, I am surprised that even at the age of only 23 years, I was envisioning a trans-national theatre production to bring not only two countries together but also my two identities. Thirty-two years later, I accomplished just that by bringing Valdez's play, *Zoot Suit*, with Valdez directing, to the National Theatre Company of Mexico, where de Tavira was the artistic director. The production won Best Mexican Musical—the first for a non-Mexican play. (*Zoot Suit* remains one of the most requested productions in the company's extensive touring repertoire.)

In 1977, the 1976 election of a Mexican president shifted the leadership of all national colleges and universities: Hector Mendoza, the director who had brought me to the CUT, was out. Soon after, I left Mexico City, and, for the first time in my life, I had no plan other than to follow my boyfriend to San Francisco, California.

## 1977–1978 El Teatro Campesino's Theatre of the Sphere and Grotowski's Poor Theatre

I arrived at my new digs in the Haight in San Francisco in March 1977. Thanks to my parents' sage advice that a woman can always find a job if she has secretarial skills, I secured a job as an executive secretary at a Comprehensive Employment Training Act (CETA) office in San Mateo. In addition to my full-time job, I wanted to stay creative, so I signed up for a tap-dancing class. At the studio, a flyer on the bulletin board announced auditions for a master workshop with Grotowski and the Para Theatre Lab actors. I was beside myself! Finally, a chance to work with Grotowski himself. At the audition in Berkeley, we were to be led through exercises by Grotowski and the key actors from his company. I signed up and spent a full day in highly physical exercises. At day's end, my name was among the 20 actors selected.

At Mills College, the workshop participants met in a 19th-century clapboard structure with wooden plank floors. The large room had an open floor and large glass-paned windows that let natural sunlight fill the room. Each day, Grotowski watched his core company members—Rena Mirecka, Ryśzard Cieslak, and Zygmunt Molik—lead us in a variety of exercises. The training was not broken down into smaller contained units as I had learned from my training in Mexico; instead, the physical work, breath, and vocalizations were integrated into a whole. Sometimes, body led; other times, breath or vocalizations. No words or text. There were no predetermined expectations or "final" objectives, and corrections for the actor centered on understanding the process. Each of us was on a unique journey of exploration and liberation.

All the while, Grotowski paced, circling the room, watching, spine hunched, arms crossed, one hand tugging at his beard. He interjected periodically in Polish, but, primarily, he keenly observed. My most vividly remembered moments of the workshop occurred in the late afternoons when the setting sun cast long beams of light through the paned windows facing west. That sun filled space was my space in the sun at the end of each day. I breathed and spoke in rich, supported sounds as if my whole body were a heart, taking in and expelling oxygen, light, breath, and sound in the rhythmic cadences of life itself.

Soon after the workshop, a friend, and a new ETC company member, called to tell me that ETC was holding auditions for a ten-month tour of Europe and the United States. ETC had its home base in San Juan Bautista, California, about two hours south of San Francisco. I went south in a heartbeat. I drove to San Juan in my boyfriend's 1960s orange VW bus a day early to follow my pattern of visualizing myself where I wanted to be. I auditioned, was cast with five others, quit my CETA job, and moved to San Juan Bautista within weeks for the term of my contract.

The six of us were contracted as "guest artists" and we received a small weekly salary. ETC provided housing around the corner from the main rehearsal/office space. Each day we gathered, trained with acting exercises, practiced music for the shows, rehearsed, built sets, sewed costumes, and maintained the workspace. Our first four months of the tour were to be in Europe performing *La Gran Carpa de Los Rasquachis*. When we returned from touring in Europe, we would tour *El Fin del Mundo* for six months in the Pacific Northwest, California, and the Southwest. Besides touring, we also produced and performed in the yearly San Juan Bautista "Día de Los Muertos Parade." I had never been more exhilarated and happier to be an actor. This acting community was what I had longed for; here, I truly understood what it meant to be a Chicana.

Luis Valdez, who had founded ETC, was not around much as he was commuting from his home in San Juan Bautista to Los Angeles in preparation for the premiere of his play, *Zoot Suit*, at the Mark Taper Forum. His sister, Socorro Valdez, the iconic actor of the early Chicano Theatre Movement, served as the director for my whole contract period. Several ETC core members assisted Luis Valdez, so we had been hired to fulfill touring contracts. When in town, Luis Valdez looked into rehearsals. He would give notes, edit scripts, and direct and conduct workshops. With ETC, Valdez developed his lifelong journey to know, understand, and bring his indigeneity and "genetic memory" to the stage.

Valdez's training did not feel unfamiliar to me because I found many similarities to Grotowski's "Poor Theatre" theory and praxis. Both relied on actors' reaching the full potential of a physically based, emotive expression, grounded in a spiritual connection with ancestral roots. An almost semi-hypnotic state induced by

Dr. Alma Martinez  **69**

**FIGURE 5.1**   Alma Martinez at El Teatro Campesino (spring 1978).

the highly physical and singular search of a mind-body-heart-spirit link. Neither used text nor leaned on psychological realism to access the actor's emotional core. Instead, Valdez's work focused on ancient, Indigenous understandings of humans' place in the universe. As a result, actors reached for the full potential of their expressive "vibrant being" that connected them to the larger cosmic whole. As such, Valdez's exercises had a deep spiritual aspect that strived to keep us continually connected viscerally to the other actors while never forgetting connection to the universe. Like Grotowski, Valdez's work focused on the full expression of the actors' body, breath, and sound but always in the context of Aztec/Mayan cosmology. Similarly, Grotowski's exercises slowly guided us to find that same profound physical awareness within the spiritual depth of our notions of self.

The similarities of their acting theories and practice extend even more profoundly if one delves into how their time and place in history propelled them to seek new theatrical languages.

When Grotowski privileged a poor theatre over a rich theatre, his was not a choice but rather an acceptance of historical circumstance. After World War II, Poland was parceled out to Russia, and the country became a nation of the Eastern Bloc. The economy devastated and unemployment rampant, Poles emigrated across Western Europe in the hundreds of thousands. Grotowski's "Poor Theatre" emerged as a visceral response to its people's social devastation and genocide. To embrace "rich" theatre would have meant accepting the exclusion and disenfranchisement that had been experienced by Poles at the hands of Russia, Europe and its allies. His theatre was stripped of costumes, lights, and sets. Theatre was deconstructed to its essence: the actor, the stage, and the actor/audience relationship. The bare actor on stage was all that was needed. Audiences would cease to be spectators and, instead, become witnesses and active participants. Rather than seek to replicate Western theatre, Grotowski turned the search inward. As a result, his theatre was defined as marginal, visceral, intense, and "not beautiful."

By comparison, Valdez, a dark-skinned Indigenous Chicano of Yaqui descent, was born and raised by farmworker parents. As a child, he and his siblings worked with their parents following the seasonal harvests across the country. Farmworkers represent one of the lowest paid and unprotected labor classes in the United States. In 1965, Valdez created ETC (The Farm Workers Theatre) when he joined the United Farm Workers' (UFW) Union. First, Valdez, a block captain on the picket lines, soon gathered farm laborers to produce skits (actos) that urged audiences, comprising other farmworkers, to join the UFW. Like Grotowski's, Valdez's theatre was born out of poverty, discrimination, and socio-political disenfranchisement. The theatre was as "poor" as its audiences, mostly Mexican immigrants, that is, monolingual Spanish speakers with minimal formal education and mostly from rural towns and villages. Similar to Grotowski's Poor Theatre, ETC invited audiences to be witnesses, not spectators. Audiences saw their lives and experiences, the depth of the abuse, and discrimination laid out before them, asking "Is Life Art or is Art Life?" The audiences (farmworkers) were moved to awareness and action.

## 1979–1980 Zoot Suit and Chicanx Identity

My ten-month tour in Europe and the United States ended when we double-billed with the San Francisco Mime Troupe and performed at the Fox Theater in Venice, California. That next day, the company members saw *Zoot Suit* at the Mark Taper Forum; afterward, our company was invited to a company party in South Pasadena. The entire cast and production team were there, as was Valdez. A core member of ETC approached me during the party and said "Luis would like to invite you to audition for *Zoot Suit*." The Mark Taper Forum production was headed to Broadway, and tickets were in high demand. Rather than close the play, the producers had decided to cast a second company to continue the run at the Aquarius Theatre. I auditioned and was cast in the role of Della, the romantic lead. I had no idea what it meant to be in a professional production, earn my union card, follow AEA rules, rehearse in "nice" halls, be fitted for costumes, and have hair and make-up tests, publicity pictures, interviews, VIP dinners, and after parties. The whole of this experience was the antithesis to the "poor" theatre, yet, for all its fancy professional trappings, *Zoot Suit* was still a Chicanx play and *rasquache*[9] theatre at its best.

## A Chicana Academic

Both Grotowski and Valdez created a new theatrical language out of their historical circumstances of colonization/occupation, the genocide of Polish and Amerindians, discrimination, disenfranchisement, and poverty. At the USC, as an American of Mexican descent, a brown-skinned Indian woman, bilingual and bicultural, and a young actor, I had been unaware of my "difference" because of my white education. Still, back then, I could not find an explanation as to why I did not fit into USC's actors' training. Grotowski and Valdez's "poor" theatre was created by and for marginalized, disenfranchised, and materially impoverished actors and audiences. Their theatre and acting aesthetic sought a connection with the human race, the cosmic whole since geopolitics had splintered and broken any semblance of "home" or "native land." This theoretical position extended into the acting theory. Grotowski's and Valdez's acting methodology/praxis led actors to psychological realism/truth, but this was not based on quotidian social interactions but a higher truth devoid of abstractions based on Western notions of cultural-racial-ethnic-sex orientation as defining characteristics. These restless, brilliant theatre makers for whom the theatre was their lives—and maybe their salvation—sought a new paradigm of theatre making that was personal, spiritual, and committed to connection with the audience.

Their acting methodologies were fundamental and vital to my continued growth as an actor. The Grotowski technique freed me physically and psychologically at a time in my life when I felt lost in the paradigm of US-based Stanislavski training. But Theatre of the Sphere, ETC, and Valdez opened my heart and mind to my being Chicana. This awareness completely altered my proprioception and forever changed my life and acting trajectory. Theatre of the Sphere showed me how my Mexican indigeneity could become the foundation of my acting practice. It helped me understand and embrace the origin of my brown skin, my language, the food I favor, the colors I am drawn to, and my yearning as an American to be fully Mexican.

As a Chicanx actor and scholar, I seek to balance the demands of my creative research and community service with my academic practice. To that end, I strive daily to impart the lessons I learned throughout this narrative in my pedagogy with its focus on decolonizing hearts and minds, preparing critical thinkers for a hopeful future. Embracing an inclusive perspective of culture and identity was essential to my evolution and success. However, above all else I look back now and regard these acknowledgments as the direct result of the countless, international, accidental and courageous acts of a young Chicana actor striving for basic self-preservation and survival.

## Notes

1. Konstantin Stanislavski, *An Actor Prepares* (London: Read Books Ltd., 2013).
2. Domingo Adame and Prieto Antonio Stambaugh, *Jerzi Grotowski: Miradas Desde Latinoamérica*, ed. Antonio Prieto Stambaugh (Veracruz: Universidad Veracruzana, 2011).

3. Jerzy Grotowski, *Towards a Poor Theatre* (New York: Simon & Schuster, 1968).
4. C.U.T. Centro Universitario de Teatro (University Theatre Center) is an acting conservatory offshoot of the Department of Dramatic Literature at the National Autonomous University of Mexico (Universidad Autónoma de Mexico). It was founded in 1962 by Héctor Azar to further the avant-garde theater movements in Mexico. CUT continues to be one of the premiere training conservatories for actors, playwrights, set designers, and stage directors in Mexico and Latin America.
5. Héctor Mendoza (1932–2010), renowned Mexican director, professor, playwright, and translator, introduced Modernism to Mexican theater and renewed the vocabulary of directing and actor training. He worked in depth on Stanislavsky's techniques and later investigated the mysteries of Grotowski's ritual theater. He taught and directed theater at the UNAM for over 40 years.
6. Three years later, I performed *La Gran Carpa de los Rasquachis* and *El Fin Del Mundo* on tour with ETC across Europe and the US Southwest.
7. Theatre of the Sphere is a theory and methodology developed by Luis Valdez, "inspired by ancient Mayan/Aztec concepts of motion, form and kinetic energy." See Luis Valdez, *Theatre of the Sphere: The Vibrant Being* (London: Routledge, 2022).
8. Luis De Tavira taught all the first-year actors in the program and later became the artistic director of the National Theatre Company of Mexico. A director, professor, playwright, essayist, translator, and creator of a method of tonal analysis that unravels the elements of the scenic language and is currently practiced in Colombia, Costa Rica, Mexico City, and Spain.
9. *Rasquache* is theory developed by Chicano scholar Thomás Ybarra-Frausto—aesthetically it can be defined as "making the most from the least."

## Bibliography

Adame, Domingo, and Prieto Antonio Stambaugh. *Jerzi Grotowski: Miradas Desde Latinoamérica*. Edited by Antonio Prieto Stambaugh. Veracruz: Universidad Veracruzana, 2011.

Grotowski, Jerzy. *Towards a Poor Theatre*. New York: Simon & Schuster, 1968.

Stanislavski, Konstantin. *An Actor Prepares*. London: Read Books Ltd., 2013.

Valdez, Luis. *Theatre of the Sphere: The Vibrant Being*. London: Routledge, 2021.

# 6
# PERFORMANCE FOR INNOCENTS

Live Art Pedagogy for Rebel Artists With Guillermo Gómez-Peña and Luz Oropeza

*Paloma Martínez-Cruz*

> This text is a response to two challenges. The first is to demystify the art of performance, in particular the work of Gómez-Peña, for a new generation of rebel artists. . . . The other challenge is to tackle the doubts that a non-specialized public may have about why so many artists from all the world's cultures choose this strange and difficult path of live art: a path that leads them to question every form of moral, aesthetic, and political authority.
> 
> —*Performance for Innocents*[1]

The following exchange of conceptual ballistics between Luz Oropeza, a poet and performer based in Mexico City, and performance artist Guillermo Gómez-Peña comes from a series of unpublished conversations that took place in Mexico City and Oaxaca between 2012 and 2017. The larger conversation addresses the themes of performance and its relationship to the body, identity, language, politics, and the development of performance personas in the shifting cultural climate of the US–Mexico border. In the excerpt included below, their exchange centers on the distinction between the genres of dramatic arts and conceptual performance—a thin line that is vividly assembled and dismantled repeatedly by the interlocutors.

Guillermo Gómez-Peña (born in Mexico in 1955; based in Mexico City and San Francisco, California) has contributed to cultural debates on borderlands identity for over 30 years, with seminal performance pieces including, but not limited to, *Border Brujo* (1988–1989), *Couple in the Cage: Two Undiscovered Amerindians Visit the West* (with Coco Fusco, 1992–93), *The Cruci-fiction Project* (with Roberto Sifuentes, 1994), *Temple of Confessions* (1995), *The Mexterminator Project* (1997–99), *The Living Museum of Fetishized Identities* (1999–2002), and multiple

DOI: 10.4324/9781003021520-8

award-winning solo performances that combine racy and rebellious aesthetics, anti-capitalist politics, and hybrid, borderlands' humor to create immersive experiences that blur the boundary between the audience and the performer. A MacArthur Fellow, USA Artists Fellow, and a Bessie, Guggenheim, and American Book Award winner, he directs La Pocha Nostra (LPN), a trans-disciplinary arts organization he founded with Roberto Sifuentes and Nola Mariano in 1993.

A loose network of rebel artists from various disciplines and cultural identities, the common denominator across Pocha Nostra collaborators and productions, is the desire to interrogate borders between art and politics, practice and theory, and artist and spectator. Every year, LPN conducts summer and winter performance art schools in which the troupe's radical pedagogy (a body-based methodology developed over the last 20 years) is shared internationally with groups and individuals seeking to cultivate a live art practice that decries the experience of national exclusion at the behest of capitalist, colonial, patriarchal, and homonormative social orderings. Current Pocha Nostra active core members include Guillermo Gómez-Peña, Balitrónica Gómez, Emma Tramposch, Saúl García-López, Micha Espinosa, and myself.

As expressed by Gómez-Peña and company members on web platforms, print publications, public-facing keynotes, and intimate Q&As, the workshops have constituted a key aspect of the company's offerings for the last 20 years. Sought by actors, directors, activists, conceptual performance artists, educators, dancers, visual artists, musicians, scholars, curators, and more, the pedagogical sessions can be offered as one-day introductory experiences all the way up to 12-day intensives culminating in site-specific immersive performances. LPN's creative partners demonstrate the breadth of its reach and the diversity of its methods: Pocha's Co-Artistic Director Saúl García-López is a professor at the Norwegian Theatre Academy; performances and workshops have been featured in each of the Hemispheric Institute of Performance & Politics annual conferences; and core member (and this volume's co-editor) Micha Espinosa is a professor at Arizona State University School of Music, Dance and Theatre. Alumni include practitioners from all reaches of the world of theatre and film production, from scenic design professionals, photographers, curators, costume designers, filmmakers, directors, and devisers to the hard-to-label, multi-hyphenate actor-activists who apply all the aforementioned ingredients to generate new forms of cultural expression. New networks of LPN alumni invariably emerge from the workshops and go on to forge socially engaged arts interventions using the techniques of performance.

With this overview in mind, let's hone in on the prospects of Pocha work that are particularly relevant to Latinx actor training. The Latinx actor's body exists at the interstice of cultural/racial/linguistic inheritances and the combined inevitability, strange messianism, and ancestral accountability that is the privilege and burden of artists of color who wear the imprint of the border in their vocabularies of creative expression. In the following verbal dance between Gómez-Peña and Oropeza, he points to the concept of time as one of the major distinctions between performance art and scripted theatre. Gómez-Peña states: "The time zone of performance is ritual, not theatrical . . . it unfolds somewhere between real time and shamanic temporality. Performance time is not linear but quantic." I propose that the "quantic" time, or the nonlinear, ritual aspect of time engaged in Pocha Nostra performance art is a specifically Americas-based, Mesoamerican/non-Western contribution. By understanding it is a heritage practice, we can reach beyond the logic of Western ego and individualism to access a decolonial performance register.

In the vein of political rebellion against institutions of dominance and oppression in the hemispheric Americas, the recurring Pocha Nostra injection of shamanism appears in two significant ways in the Pochaverse. First, it emerges in order to point to its commercialization and fetishization in the Western consumer world order as a live art motif. However, it also figures prominently as a decolonial path toward healing in Pocha performance training that is rooted in Chicanx, Latinx, and/or Mesoamerican informed ways of knowing. Both implications need to be understood more plainly here to provide the necessary context for the conversation between Gómez-Peña and Oropeza that follows.

Mircea Eliade, a seminal thinker in the Western study of religious experience, defines a shaman as a healer who relies on the ecstatic journey—or altered states of consciousness—to interact with the divine in order to perform healing.[2] Involuntary or self-induced trances, prophetic raptures, visions and dreams, and the interpretation of these states on behalf of their patients are all attributes of the shamanic vocation. In Mesoamerica (and places influenced by Mesoamerican cultures), these guides provided messages from the gods, wielding specific medical, spiritual, and political authority in their communities. The shaman designation has become heavily beleaguered by new age and Western consumer fads that seek to extract supernatural mind trips and quick fixes from the magical Other, which is certainly one of the reasons why Gómez-Peña has featured the communicative power of this persona in his live art.

In Richard Schechner's seminal *Performance Theory*, he proposes a distinction between the goals of live performance and the goals of ritual that he describes as a continuum with "entertainment" and "efficacy" as its end points.[3] Ritual practices represent the efficacious end of the spectrum, with a repertoire of actions that conduct the receiver of the performance to a different state of being, as with coming-of-age ceremonies, healings, nuptials, funerals, and other rites that establish a connection to the divine. Conventional theatre practices, on the other hand, would constitute entertainment, wherein laic, aesthetic, and recreational outcomes distinguish these performances from those with the spiritual purpose of bridging the gap between the profane and the sacred.

Several of GGP's works have embodied the shamanic, magical real, and/or Mexican notions of the supernatural at the center of the performance zone. In *Border Brujo* ("Border Warlock") (1988–1989), he appeared at an altar decorated with a kitsch collection of cultural fetish items in a border patrolman's jacket decorated with buttons, bananas, beads, and shells to deliver an acerbic indictment of US colonial attitudes toward Mexican culture and history. As a "brujo," Gómez-Peña exorcised the psychic disease load of Western imperialism, articulating fear, trauma, and desire with layered combinations of English and Spanish, and humor and anger. Shamanism as a fetish appeared again in his early 1990's collaboration with conceptual artist James Luna. The team generated an ongoing project titled "The Shame-man meets El Mexican't," in which the two artists challenged stock stereotypes about ethnicity and the magical Other. We find another example of brujerismo (witchcraft) in the *Temple of Confessions* performance (1995–1996) in which two "end-of-the-century saints" from an "unknown border religion" seek sanctuary while inviting confessions on cultural fears, dreams, and desires. On the "Chapel of Desires" platform, Roberto Sifuentes performed the persona of "El Pre-Columbian Vato" (styled as a beatific gang member), while Gómez-Peña presided over the "Chapel of Fears," dais as "San Pocho Aztlaneca," an exaggerated version of a Mexican tribal elder, wizened and stoic, for the benefit of spiritual tourists: a fun house mirror distortion that shows us how the extractive logic of the Western gaze disfigures Mexican/mestizx/Chicanx vocabularies of self-representation.

These aforementioned instances would perhaps fit what Schechner intimated with the "entertainment" end of the continuum. In an act of disidentification, which was performance theorist José Esteban Muñoz's way of describing when BIPOC and/or queer performers seize and reappropriate stereotypes and ethnic clichés to expose their absurdity, Gómez-Peña, as the Border Brujo, lays claim to Mexican shamanism with a wink: He is not casting a hex or summoning the supernatural but embodying a Western desire for the exotic, mystical Mexican.[4] Rather than actual brujería, the Western viewer is gazing at their own fantasy of Mexicanness, which Gómez-Peña incarnates in order to subvert.

The world of Pocha Nostra training, on the other hand, is infused with abundant references to shamanic practices, but this time without the wink. Examples abound in the recent *La Pocha Nostra: A Handbook for the Rebel Artist in a Post-Democratic Society* (Routledge, 2021). From the very first description the company extends to its workshop participants, the notion of shamanism is evoked as a path to achieving a heightened state of awareness that allows the body to communicate new meanings. In *La Pocha Nostra* (2021), the description of their intensive workshop states:

> Participants are exposed to La Pocha Nostra's most recent performance methodologies, an eclectic combination of exercises borrowed from multiple traditions including performance art, experimental theatre and dance, the Suzuki method, ritual shamanism, performance games, and live jam sessions.[5]

Among exercises that contain explicit reference to the shamanic state of consciousness, the Gaze, the Skeleton Dance, the Prop Archeology Bank, Staging

Conceptual Funeral, and the Closing Rituals figure prominently. Lacking the space here to analyze all of these exercises, I'll only go into detail about the Gaze and Conceptual Funeral below.

The "Gaze" is a foundational exercise that should be familiar to all Latinx actors and performance artists, but it is employed in the Pochaverse consistently throughout the workshop so that, over a short period of time, each participant has engaged in the act of gazing with everyone else in the workshop. The exercise requires a room with dim light large enough to allow participants to move freely. LPN recommends a soothing soundscape or simply to practice in silence.

To implement the exercise, the group begins by walking randomly around the workshop space in silence, mindfully changing direction to avoid any collisions. Participants briefly make eye contact with each other as they pass one another and they continue to walk until the facilitator directs them to stop. Depending on the goals of the workshop, the facilitator might instruct them to stop in front of someone they don't know very well, or someone who is as "different" as possible in obvious ways (race, gender, age, body type, subcultural affiliation, etc.). Once the entire group has split into pairs, the partners stand two feet apart facing each other. The objective is to maintain eye contact, maintaining a neutral but open and relaxed gaze and overcoming those initial nervous impulses—giggling, coughing, or blinking excessively. The goal is simply to be present and express nothing more than a mutual acknowledgment of a shared moment in life and art: that is enough. The facilitator may choose a duration of anywhere from three to five minutes.

The Pocha facilitator will often offer verbal cues and instructions during the implementation of this exercise that help the participant dive deeper into its potential to overcome the barriers of self-consciousness and ego, hence moving the participant away from Western individualism and toward a more collective and ancestral way of seeing themselves in relation to their gathered peers. The objectives state:

> This exercise is one of the oldest shamanic exercises we know. It is very likely that you may have tried it out informally without realizing its implications. Kids, lovers, witches, brujos, and madmen do it all the time, and in certain cultures it is used to diagnose diseases. Pocha contextualizes this action as a way to re-enact the primary form in which humans recognize each other, just like the first time that Neanderthals traveled north and met other tribes, or when Cristóbal Colón met the Arawak in the so-called first encounter between Europeans and Amerindians: gazing as a tool to fully recognize our physical similarities and differences and enter into a deeper state of awareness.[6]

While no initiation into acting or performance training is complete without incorporating gazing exercises, the Pocha context here, and its decolonial intention, matters: the Pocha ethos is based on dangerous border crossings as well as the attendant creation of spaces of radical tenderness and safety for all bodies, origin stories, gender identities, and languages. As such, the gaze is not just an exercise in emotional dexterity for the purpose of becoming more capable entertainers, but rather a ritual to transcend the individual ego in favor of extending, and receiving, tenderness from the community.

Another Pocha exercise that draws on non-Western, ancestral ways of knowing is the Conceptual Funeral. As explained in this exercise's introductory remarks in *La Pocha Nostra*, the world of psychomagic actions has been part of contemporary performance art since the 1960s, and Pocha's work is particularly influenced by Alejandro Jodorowsky's *Psychomagic: The Transformative Power of Shamanic Psychotherapy* healing path using the power of dreams, theatre, poetry, and shamanism.[7] The exercise begins by asking participants how they would like to be remembered, and are given the opportunity to stage their own funeral. In teams of two, the body of one person becomes the "raw material" and the other partner is the "artist." The artist stages or creates an installation representing their own funeral, which may incorporate local architecture, relics, costumes, props, and inventive lighting. After constructing the scenic installation, the artist styles their "raw material," and the human sculpture is then introduced into the installation. The exercise is then repeated by inverting the roles of artist and raw material. An exercise of identity reinvention, the shamanic principles, and Indigenous altar rituals from around the world are at the center of this exploration.[8]

So far, I've provided details about how Gómez-Peña has infused his performances with exaggerated Western desires as these relate to the "magical Mexican" in Border Brujo and Temple of Confessions. Another kind of recourse to the shamanic register takes place in the intimate space of the Pocha Nostra pedagogical workshops, where we enlist shamanic practices anchored in Mesoamerican, Indigenous ways of knowing in order to bring new aesthetic acceptance, ancestral alignment, and political purpose to our modes of training in which the efficacy of ritual takes precedence over the aims of entertainment. What follows is my translated and adapted version of the conversation between Gómez-Peña and Oropeza, provided here accompanied by a sincere invitation for you to jump into Pocha's performance zone as a fully enfranchised, quantic participant in our ever-evolving playscape that celebrates you: Latinx artist devising new identities from a place of innocence and impurity, ritual and profanity.

## Performance for Innocents

The legendary "performancero" and writer Guillermo Gómez-Peña and his sparring partner and accomplice Luz Oropeza, "The Geisha of Coyoacán," undertake a series of conversations and provocations in an attempt to delineate and poetically chart what is a highly misunderstood art form of Latin America.

In the present dialogue that spans the course of five years, Oropeza compels Gómez-Peña to encounter, explain, and elaborate on several themes that, while they had not been new to him, resulted in important re-visitings that serve to shine new light, particularly in this time in which the convergence of conceptual arts, political discourses, and contestatory aesthetics is at a moment of profound tension at the global level. Included among these themes are performance and its relationship to the body, identity, language, activism, borders, and, here and there, a detail or two from the life of the controversial persona: "the Neo-Mexica Jode-rowsky of Performance."

As for the language, the "chilango" regionalisms (native to Mexico City) and the Spanglish and Chicano slang that appear throughout the conversation will not be translated or clarified, with a few notable exceptions. This decision was made by Gómez-Peña in order to remain consistent with his body of work and to demonstrate to the reader and listener the experience of fractional exclusion that is part and parcel of the global migrant experience.

Gómez-Peña and Oropeza have something in common: an obsession for resolving conflict between hard theory and the playfulness of performance as well as a love of discovering points of convergence between the two. The following text achieves this without resorting to "teoría lite." The objective is to think about and articulate the living and agonizing project of performance art in an accessible register for a broad public, and to address some of the most common doubts about the discipline of performance that invariably surface in non-specialized interviews. As Gómez-Peña once said, "One day I'd like to write a book about experimental art and performance that doesn't fall into my aunt's hands before you get to page twenty."

## Track 04. The Quarrel Between Performance and Theatre

### The Opera Bar, Mexico City, October, 2012

LO: Today I'd like to talk about a typical theoretical problem having to do with performance art. What is the main difference between conceptual performance art and the rest of the performing arts?

GP: We're starting with theory just like that? First lets order an appetizer and something to drink, no? That's better. Let's head straight into this byzantine dialogue that worries you so much. Salud!

LO: Salud!

GP: Look, the difference between theatre and dance that take place in a designated space, is that performance takes place in the body itself.

LO: But Guillermo, dance and theatre also take place in the body. Without the body there is no theatre or dance. Don't you think that you're being unfair to these poor art forms?

GP: You're more cruel than I am. In truth, I don't look down on them, I just qualify some of the differences. Isn't that what you wanted? Across traditional performing arts, bodies are in space; bodies move across a neutral space. In

LO: the case of dance, bodies articulate meaning and ambulate in the fictional world of theatre. On the other hand, with performance.

LO: But in performance art there can also be bodies in space, bodies in movement, that are there to communicate a message. I'm skeptical about how you envision the fictional world of theatre. Is this fiction the thing that marks the difference between the two?

GP: In performance, body and language are prosthetic extensions of the artist's own identity, and the space is real, not fictive. The blood is also real.

LO: Calm yourself, García Lorca.

GP: So drive a knife through my hand, see if I don't bleed.

LO: Just stop. Look, since we've already spoken about fiction, explain to me the difference between performance and more experimental schools of theatre, device theatre, for instance, in and what the difference is between your performance identities (personas) and the characters in the theatrical sense.

GP: In scripted theatre, the actor *represents* someone they are not. In performance, the performer *presents*; they exhibit *their own* alternate identities and inner demons. In theatre, time and space, I repeat, are fictive, even though they may seem "real." With performance, on the other hand, it takes place in the here and now. Obviously, the paratheatrical "desmontaje" ("deconstructed") movement in Latin America and the aforementioned British device theatre, are exceptions. They have been directly influenced by performance.

LO: Mmm. I disagree. Time is highly complex in theatre. It contains both the represented dimension (or the fictive) as well as the actual—the time frame that coincides with the spectator. Could you expand on your answer a bit more?

GP: You've got some attitude, loca. Performance takes place in an amplified present, but is never fictive (unless the goal of the work is an investigation into the difference between real and fictive time). The time zone of performance is ritual, not theatrical . . . it unfolds somewhere between real time and shamanic temporality. Performance time is not linear but quantic. ¡Carajo! Now you have me talking like a German philosopher. Seriously, we need to change the subject. Aren't you bored with this? We haven't even order the second round.

LO: No. And don't go off on a tangent! Tell me what other differences separate theatre and performance.

GP: ¡Qué la @$#%^! Fine. Here is another: performance has open, modular structures, sensu stricto, there is no beginning and no end. What we think of as a "performance" is a segment of a continual process for the artist but invisible to the public. When the public enters the space where a performance takes place it's only to be the temporary witness (or participant) in part of a process that is unrepeatable.

LO: I really like what you're saying, but honestly, I think that a theatre performance's public is also only seeing a fragment of a process that at times takes months of rehearsal, and is never the final product because each production is unique.

GP: "Unique" but very similar to the one from the night before. But since you keep fucking with this topic, I'll answer with a text I wrote about exactly this issue. *(GP looks for a file on his computer and then reads the following):*

*I dreamed I was a good actor, not a performance artist but an actor, a really good one. I could realistically represent others in a film or staged play, and I was so convincing as an actor that I could transform into that other person, forgetting completely who I really was. The theatrical "persona" I represented in my dream was a performance art essentialist, someone who hated naturalism in theatre as well as psychological and social realism; someone who looked down on artifice, makeup, costumes, memorized lines. In my dream, the performance artist began to rebel against the actor, that is to say, against myself. He did strange things like not speaking for an entire week, moving in slow motion for an entire day or applying tribal makeup and going out in the street to disrupt the sense of the familiar among the unsuspecting neighbors of the barrio . . . He was clearly playing with my mind, and me, the "good actor," I confused myself so much that I ended up having a total identity collapse. I didn't know how to act. I went into a classic fetal position and I was frozen in a huge exhibit window for a whole week. Fortunately, it was only a dream. When I finally woke up, I kept being the same old performance artist, and I felt grateful that I didn't know how to act.*[9]

## Notes

1. Guillermo Gómez-Peña and Luz Oropeza, "El arte del performance para inocentes" (unpublished manuscript, 2017).
2. Mircea Eliade, *Shamanism: Archaic Techniques of Ecstasy* (Princeton, NJ: Princeton University Press, 2020).
3. First published under the title *Essays on Performance Theory, 1970–1976* (New York: Drama Book Specialists, 1977), Schechner's essays continue to be the gold standard for understanding performance as a spectrum of behaviors that includes the performativity of everyday life and rituals as well as theatre. Richard Schechner, *Performance Theory* (New York: Routledge, 2003).
4. José Esteban Muñoz, *Disidentifications: Queers of Color and the Performance of Politics* (Minneapolis: University of Minnesota Press, 1999).
5. Guillermo Gómez-Peña and Saul Garcia-Lopez, *La Pocha Nostra: A Handbook for the Rebel Artist in a Post-Democratic Society*, ed. Paloma Martinez-Cruz (New York: Routledge, 2021), 41.
6. Ibid., 89.
7. Alejandro Jodorowsky, *Psychomagic: The Transformative Power of Shamanic Psychotherapy* (Rochester, VT: Inner Traditions, 2010).
8. Gómez-Peña and Garcia-Lopez, *La Pocha Nostra*, 115.
9. Guillermo Gómez-Peña, "En Defensa del Performance," *Horizontes Antropológicos*, Porto Alegre 11, no. 24 (2005): 199–226.

# 7

## CONFESSIONS OF A RACIAL NOMAD

### Indigenous-Mestizx Ethnicity in the World of Eurocentric Performance Practices

*Saúl García-López aka La Saula*

### Early Stages: A Mexico City Puto-Prieto-Chacal From the Ghetto

When I was 11 years old in Mexico City, my family and I watched telenovelas almost every night on television. Like many people, I decided to become an actor not because of working in the theatre but because of soap operas and popular television. I looked at myself in the mirror and compared myself to the Caucasian cast and was swarmed by the insults my country has coined to put down someone inhabiting my multiple identities: *puto* (faggot), *prieto* (dark-skinned), *chacal* (jackal). These offensive words describe queer, working-class people with brown skin and Indigenous looks. I often heard these slurs in Mexico. This was my only frame of reference for my body and identity at the time. Gender, class, and racial markers were imprinted on me by elementary and high school peers, who bullied and sexually abused me for my hazy gender. These slurs represent and reflect the problematic racial and class tensions in Mexico. I can still hear my classmates' voices: "Hey, you puto-prieto-chacal, wake up!"

Despite feeling uneasy, knowing that my gender complexity and ethnicity contradicted the images I saw in popular media, I still pursued an acting career. When I started to train formally as an actor in my late teens, my difference was even starker. So were the feelings inside me—not just because I perceived my body to be at odds with the traditional representations in casting but also due to the limiting views of performing gender. When I was training as an actor, the only gender role I could assume was a constricted version of masculinity. My queerness was made invisible.

DOI: 10.4324/9781003021520-9

My rigorous education as an artist required a lot of sacrifices for my working-class family. I grew up in the ghettos of Mexico City, every day witnessing the traumas of violence and drugs around me. Meanwhile, in my training as a traditional actor, I learned Eurocentric acting techniques rooted in the fundamentals of Stanislavsky, popularly known in Mexico as *el método*.[1] During my studies, teachers and directors refused to cast me—and others like me—in any of the studio and professional productions because we, "the jackals" (the urban, Indigenous mestizo actor students), did not look like the cast Western dramaturgs required for the play. Thus, I was deemed unsuitable to be cast in plays written by Miller, Strindberg, Chekhov, Calderon, and Shakespeare—or even in classic Mexican plays. At the time, I had a deep, unspoken, and hard-to-articulate realization regarding a lack of awareness of the oppressive colonial implications of my ethnicity and gender complexity.

I quickly learned that in order to enter the training and rehearsal room, I had to leave behind my intersecting ethnic and gender complexities. I always felt uncomfortable, however, when teachers and guest artists asked us to *leave ourselves* outside of the rehearsal or training room so that we could "become the character." It was like performing a gender and whitewashing ritual. Consequently, I felt deeply at odds when interpreting roles that did not suit my ethnicity or had a stereotypical masculinity. It baffled me that my teachers (both those with more Caucasian looks and those who looked like me) were unable to address ethnicity and gender while teaching and creating. Indeed, they did not know how; they understood only that Eurocentric performance methods, plays, and forms of production required them to be color blind and queer blind. As a result, by the end of my training, I possessed no skills with which to pursue authenticity. Moreover, I felt oppressed, voiceless, and invisible. I was also left knowing that I would have fewer job opportunities, less social mobility, and more stress.

After graduating and upon entering the acting profession, I encountered the reproduction of oppressive identity forces from "color-blind/queer-blind" casting agents and producers. I entered my short-lived professional career in soap operas, independent and commercial theatre with no ability to name or question the oppressive forces that subjugated me, embodying and internalizing a self-colonizing attitude that naively translated to: Mestizos and Indigenous actors, like me, can make a living only playing the stereotypical roles of ugly, uneducated criminals.

From the 18th to the 20th century, dark-skinned, Indigenous-looking actors in Mexico have always faced discrimination. The entertainment industry in Mexico is just beginning to discuss the deep racism embedded in the Mexican culture. The recent social justice/anti-racist movements for fair casting in Mexico through the collective movement using the hashtag Poder Prieto (Proud to be Brown) have brought me some hope. Nowadays, Mexican actors are finally declaring that this racism will be acknowledged and that new and equitable casting is a matter of political urgency.

## The Radical Nomad

The political urgency I sensed started my shift into performance art, where I felt fewer restrictions regarding my identity. I also practiced Eurocentric dance forms, but I soon noticed that the field was dominated primarily by the same inherent patterns of discrimination.

I decided to focus, therefore, on studying directing in Australia and television in South Africa, ultimately ending up in the United Kingdom, where I did most of my artistic practice. Abroad, I experienced the same color-blind/queer-blind casting. Audiences commented that I did not look Mexican or queer on stage. Then, I moved to Canada to study for my Ph.D. in theatre and performance. As part of my nomadic journey and informed by my ethnicity, I experienced the mechanisms of discrimination and colonialism in both Spanish and British colonies.

Throughout this radical, nomadic adventure, I have experienced several times, in multi-layered ways, versions of Fanon's third consciousness[2] and Munoz's disidentification of gender and ethnicity,[3] as my identity extended from a Puto-Prieto-Jackal, marginalized and excluded in Mexico and the United States, to a Queer Common Wealth and a Polite Mexican, subordinated and regulated in Canada and the United Kingdom. Independent of my location, from North America to Europe, I dealt with outright discrimination to subordinated inclusion.

## La Saulas Meets La Pocha Nostra

In 2010, I encountered the life-changing work of La Pocha Nostra. La Pocha Nostra is a transdisciplinary arts organization founded in 1993 that provides a support network and multi-media platforms for artists of various disciplines, generations, gender complexities, and ethnic backgrounds. For over 25 years, LPN has brought a particular focus to the notion of border crossings, and foregrounding the markers of race, gender, and generation as borders to be explored and disrupted in politically and aesthetically meaningful ways.

A clear example of their work can be found in our most recent book: *La Pocha Nostra: A Handbook for the Rebel Artist in a Post-democratic Society*. This book marks a pedagogical matrix suited for use as a performance handbook and conceptual tool for artists, activists, theorists, pedagogues, and trans-disciplinary border crossers of all stripes.[4]

Through the troupe, I got to know Guillermo Gomez-Peña and the radical performance pedagogy of La Pocha Nostra, which has had a radical impact on my creative work. In contrast to the color-blind/queer-blind practices of my earlier Eurocentric performance training, the Pocha work invited a heightened awareness of the signifiers of my body, my ethnicity, and my gender. I started to learn how to bring my whole queer-mestizo self into my creative work.

In 2013, I became a core member of the troupe so was invited to give a series of workshops for the prestigious Erasmus Mundus Program, included in the

Master of Arts in International Performance Research (MAIPR), where I served as one of the Pocha pedagogues. Thirty-one students from diverse cultural and ethnic backgrounds studied for 16 months in four locations: the University of Warwick, the University of Amsterdam, the University of Helsinki, and, for the culmination of the academic program, the University of Arts in Belgrade.

For the last chapter of this pedagogical adventure in Serbia, I teamed up with former Pocha member, Erika Mott, teaching an advanced Pocha Nostra workshop on border-crossing, gender, cross-cultural and generational creative exchanges, nationality, ethnicity, and body identity and politics. We held several discussions with academics and students and, at the end of the project, hosted a presentation on embodied practices in performing arts.

For the final presentation, we employed La Pocha Nostra border aesthetics.[5] We intended to present a performance to test the boundaries of theatre and performance. We decided to adapt and re-enact one of the most evocative actions in the imagery of La Pocha Nostra: The Illustrated Body.[6] The Illustrated Body is a performance that offers the opportunity to explore body politics, gender, and race representations by using the body as a living canvas. On a "racialized" nude body, the audience is invited to inscribe phrases, words, poetry, political slogans, personal statements, and drawings. Different languages and writing styles are encouraged.

Aware of my ethnicity and gender-queer complexity, I enacted this performance for the students and professors, testing the intersections of embodied practice, ethnicity, and gender in theatre and performance. We used soft lights and a ritual sound to create the performative atmosphere. I lay nude on a work table in the middle of the room. My Pocha colleague explained the exercise and presented the impulse phrases: *Theatre is . . . is not, Performance is . . . is not*, and *My body is . . . is not*. The group started writing with markers on my body.

Once my body was covered with words and drawings, the group was invited to read the lines. Afterward, I stood up to read the words and lines myself; once finished reading, I covered myself and returned to my chair.

The music stopped. Tension filled the room. I was simultaneously aware of the "provocation" around the constructs of a racialized, Indigenous, queer, and nude body on stage, the power of this ritual, and the poetic image that exposed the groups' resistances and historical assumptions. This powerful ritual, which invites questioning, is one of the best exercises to teach embodied theory. When the performative action ended, the discussion started.

Two different conversations ensued: one led by the students and the other by the professors in the room. The students from classical theatrical training and traditional religious backgrounds and beliefs criticized the presence of a nude body by arguing that we were trying to be provocative. They viewed the action as a distasteful stage tactic from the 1970s; these students claimed that theatre had evolved from presenting nude bodies. In contrast, the liberal and multidisciplinary students focused on the function, purpose, and aesthetics of the body on stage and asked whether the action presented was theatre or not.

One of the most intriguing aspects of this conversation with the students was the resistance (or unawareness) to how to address my queer body, gender, and ethnicity. During the conversation, I became invisible; for them, I was a "generic" body on stage, and I was, by default, rendered as a "man" bearing the attached connotations of patriarchal politics. The effects of this event resonated with my experiences during my early actor training in Mexico City, again, in their inability to address my gender and ethnicity on stage.

The professors' discussion focused solely on my ethnicity. Professors from a Caucasian background—with much urgency—took the microphone to point out that I was totally unaware of the consequences of my performance because I was putting myself in a denigrating position in relation to my Indigenous ethnic origins. The critics continued focusing on my "unawareness" of the ethnic politics embedded in the performance action. According to them, the color of my skin and my nude body highlighted a self-subjugating role in association with the forces of colonialism and racism.

The event turned into a lecture led by a theorist showing the students the issues that emerged when displaying "stereotypical" representations of ethnicity on stage. I was shocked to know that, by merely presenting my body as it was, I was automatically seen as a "typical," colonized body. My race and body became a case study for "experts" to elaborate on their post-colonial arguments. The few professors of color remained silent. Strange.

During this experience, I became "re-otherized." I went back to being the primitive, the ignorant, the ugly, the exotic, the genderless, as well as the one without body agency and who needed to be rescued ("Poor Indian knows no any better"). I was stripped of self-determination.

I was thrown back to the start of my story, to those early years of actor training in Mexico City. Hey, Puto-Prieto-Chacal, wake up!

During the event, the post-colonial theory shifted dangerously to transform into a weapon against my ethnicity and body. The theory successfully became an embodied experience for everyone in the room—including me. However, the theory of the living paradox, instead of liberating me, oppressed me. I realized that the theoretical view co-opted by hegemonic, academic whiteness barred me from all forms of involvement that would allow me to exercise self-determination.

My experience in Serbia propelled my search for the meaning of my body in different contexts. I not only resonated with Fanon and Muñoz's theories, but also started to question pedagogical environments. What assumptions and structures are in place that propelled my experiences? What happens in performance-pedagogical practices that render ethnicity and bodies like mine invisible?

I keep reflecting on how my Indigenous/queer/brown body created a "shock wave" in which theory, propelled by the view of hegemonic whiteness,[7] encountered difficulties to address the living interpretations of my identity. I served as a generic, colonized body, having to bear the re-encryption of historical racial objectification to validate the aims and purposes of post-colonial theory and Eurocentric performance methods.

## Latin Embodiment and Eurocentric Performance Techniques

After these experiences, I emphasize that Eurocentric performing methods in post-colonial territories can reinforce oppressive colonial structures that hinder creative attempts to eradicate the constrictions of subordination and unfair representations of the "Other." If "Othering" is not pedagogically exposed and managed while teaching Eurocentric performing arts methods, the Latinx's body remains invisible and oppressed.

The colonial structures of subjugation are reinforced when Eurocentric performance techniques do not consider the colonial effect that the methodology carries for the Latinx.[8] The inherent problem for Latinxs being seen as the "Other" is the danger of their being encapsulated in fixed representations, thus minimizing the disruption of established forms of productions and allocating Caucasian bodies as the center of performance art education.[9]

Despite the focus on multi-cultural pedagogies in actor training, a system prevails in which Eurocentric performance methods remain privileged. Eurocentric performance is an education system embedded in pedagogical practices dominated by the privileges of hegemonic whiteness.[10] Consequently, this process undermines and denies the Latinx body the possibility of challenging oppressive representation structures.[11]

Addressing the impact of Eurocentric performance methods on the "Other's" identities during the training process is uncommon. Most researchers still focus on the impact of the training in relation to the representation on the stage and the phenomenological aspect of the representational experience.[12] Some performance techniques such as those of Stanislavski, Artaud, Grotowski, Meyerhold, and Brecht have been examined from distinct theoretical views such as deconstructivism,[13] feminism,[14] semiotics,[15] culturalism and multi-culturalism,[16] and post-colonialism.[17] In Latin America, creative strategies fundamentally understand the politics of body identity, such as those coming from the company Grupo Yuyachkani in Peru and Augusto Boal's Theatre of the Oppressed (Brazil-Europe).

If Eurocentric performance instructors are serious about deconstructing the subjugating structures in actor training, the field should address the body in all its ethnic and gender identity complexities during performance training itself. To decolonize a methodology, it is necessary to employ strategies that facilitate re-interpretation and adaptation of the method to the local culture.[18] It is imperative to help performers and performance instructors gain awareness of how Eurocentric performance training intersects with local body politics and how this performance-training influences identity representation.

Implementing techniques of the Eurocentric performing arts, without pedagogically addressing the cultural and ethnic specificities of the local student, continues as an unchecked pedagogical issue in many post-colonial countries.[19] By not addressing this, the training becomes a tool for the re-colonization of the "Other," specifically the Latinx body. In order to reverse this, the implementation of post-colonial and de-colonial theory, together with culturally relevant pedagogy[20] methods and performance exercises, could enable a re-interpretation and de-colonization of Eurocentric performance training.

If "Othering" is not addressed, methods of Eurocentric performing arts will keep rendering Latinxs invisible, unaware of how to use their inherent ethnic signifiers as a tool to open creative ways to stir the terms of unfair and oppressive identity representations in art and society in general. This is even more conspicuous for the queer Latinx body and other queer peoples of color, burdened with that double layer of oppression.

## Arriving at an Experiential, Philosophical, and Epistemological Shift

The above reflection does not just mine the colonial chronicle embedded in performance training. This stance also opposes hegemonic whiteness and colonial and imperialist thinking in performing arts education. By calling for a new pedagogical perspective, culturally relevant pedagogies assessed by queer educators, students, and artists have the potential to minimize the impact of oppressive colonial comprehensions on Latinx performers.

A de-colonizing pedagogy, furnished with practices of re-interpretation, as well as an adaptation to local culture and ethnicity, is necessary to allow opportunities for open conversations of self-representation with the purpose of recontextualizing the colonized body.[21] That is why emancipatory performance methodologies that address "Otherness" are necessary.

## As an Indigenous Queer, Brown, and *Puto-Prieto-Chacal* Artist and Pedagogue, I Declare That

> **From an anti-imperialist, Indigenous, and de-colonial perspective,** Eurocentric training practices need to be purposefully questioned and contested when taught to Indigenous and "colonized" bodies.
>
> **This meditative rant** is not just mining the colonial chronicle embedded in performance training; it also hopes to offer a solid ground to defy and question hegemonic whiteness in the performing arts methodology.
>
> **This meditative rant** aims to say that we—"brown," "red," and "colonized" bodies—have not raised our voices or been loud enough. We need to expose the tension and mechanisms of re-colonization embedded in Eurocentric performing arts techniques.

**This thoughtful tirade** invites readers to imagine emancipatory performance educational tools that address body identity and color-blind environments for teaching acting.

**I dream of** performance methods and teaching environments that facilitate awareness of what our bodies "represent" by making students aware of the identities of their bodies and the creative ways to challenge oppressive learning processes concealed in Eurocentric performance methodologies.

## Notes

1 Method acting is an acting technique in which an actor focuses on creating sincere and emotionally representations of a character. For history of the Method look to, Steve Vineberg, *Method Actors: Three Generations of an American Acting Style* (New York: Schirmer Books, 1994).
2 Frantz Fanon, *Black Skin, White Masks*, trans. Charles L. Markmann (London: Pluto Press, 1986).
3 Jose E. Muñoz, *Disidentifications: Queers of Color and the Performance of Politics* (Minneapolis: University of Minnesota Press, 1999).
4 Guillermo Gómez-Peña and Saul Garcia-Lopez, *La Pocha Nostra: A Handbook for the Rebel Artist in a Post-Democratic Society* (London: Routledge, 2020).
5 Pocha Nostra Border aesthetics can be found in the *Pocha Nostra Manifesto*, Guillermo Gómez-Peña, "La Pocha Nostra," *Guillermo Gómez-Peña*, accessed July 25, 2022, www.guillermogomezpena.com/la-pocha-nostra/.
6 The Illustrated Body in Gómez-Peña and Garcia-Lopez, *La Pocha Nostra*, 139.
7 Hegemonic whiteness is a theoretical perspective that points to the ways white supremacy is reproduced by systemic social and cultural structures (Michael Omi and Howard Winant, *Racial Formation in the United States* (New York: Routledge, 2014)). Its main purpose is to naturalize the inequality produced by social interactions alongside the color line of race. In our society the results of this inequality manifest as white privilege, racial inequality, and anti-minority effect. "Each one of these three levels is mutually reinforcing as the cultural sphere normalizes inequality and racist practices that, in turn, serves to leave systemic white supremacy uninterrogated and unchallenged" (Nolan L. Cabrera, "Where Is the Racial Theory in Critical Race Theory? A Constructive Criticism of the Crits," *The Review of Higher Education* 42, no. 1 (2018): 223, https://doi.org/10.1353/rhe.2018.0038).
8 Christopher B. Balme, *Decolonizing the Stage: Theatrical Syncretism and Post-Colonial Drama* (Oxford: Oxford University Press, 1999); Rustom Bharucha, *Theatre and the World: Performance and the Politics of Culture* (London: Routledge, 2003); Zeynep G. Çapan, "Enacting the International/Reproducing Eurocentrism," *Contexto Internacional* 39, no. 3 (2017): 655–72, https://doi.org/10.1590/S0102-8529.2017390300010; Savo Heleta, "Decolonization of Higher Education: Dismantling Epistemic Violence and Eurocentrism in South Africa," *Transformation in Higher Education* 1, no. 1 (2016): 1–8.
9 A. J. Aldama et al., eds., *Performing the US Latina and Latino Borderlands* (Bloomington: Indiana University Press, 2012); Janet O'Shea, "Decolonizing the Curriculum? Unsettling Possibilities for Performance Training," *Brazilian Journal on Presence Studies* 8, no. 4 (2018): 750–762, https://doi.org/10.1590/2237-266078871.
10 Marie Battiste and James (Sa'ke'j) Youngblood, "Naturalizing Indigenous Knowledge in Eurocentric Education," *Canadian Journal of Native Education* 32, no. 1 (2009): 5–17; Joe L. Kincheloe and Shirley R. Steinberg, "Addressing the Crisis of Whiteness: Reconfiguring White Identity in a Pedagogy of Whiteness," in *White Reign: Deploying*

*Whiteness in America*, eds. Joe L. Kincheloe, Shirley R. Steinberg, Nelson M. Rodriguez, and Ronald E. Chennault (New York: St. Martin's Press, 1998), 3–29.

11 Gloria Anzaldúa, *Borderlands/La Frontera: The New Mestiza* (San Francisco: Aunt Lute Books, 1987); Frederick Luciani, "Spanish American Theatre of the Colonial Period," in *The Cambridge History of Latin American Literature*, eds. Roberto G. Echevarría and Enrique Pupo-Walker (Cambridge: Cambridge University Press, 1996), 260–85, https://doi.org/10.1017/CHOL9780521340694.010; Araceli Rivas, "Postcolonial Analysis of Educational Research Discourse: Creating (Mexican) American Children as the 'Other'" (PhD diss., Texas A&M University, 2006).

12 Balme, *Decolonizing the Stage*; Erincin, 2020; Serap Erincin, "Decolonizing Identity in Performance: Claiming My Mother Tongue in Suppression of Absence," *Frontiers: A Journal of Women Studies* 41, no. 1 (2020): 179–95, https://doi.org/10.5250/fronjwomenstud.41.1.0179; Esiaba Irobi, "A Theatre for Cannibals: Images of Europe in Indigenous African Theatre of the Colonial Period," *New Theatre Quarterly* 22, no. 3 (2006): 268–82, https://doi.org/10.1017/S0266464X06000479; Mariel Marshall and Lisa C. Ravensbergen, "The Doing That Can Undo: Decolonizing the Performer-Audience Relationship in Lisa Cooke Ravensbergen's Citation," *Canadian Theatre Review* 179, no. 17 (2019): 80–82, https://doi.org/10.3138/ctr.179.017.

13 Philip Auslander, "Toward a Concept of the Political in Postmodern Theatre," *Theatre Journal* 39, no. 1 (1987): 20–34, https://doi.org/10.2307/3207618; Philip Auslander, "Postmodern Theatric (k) s: Monologue in Contemporary American Drama," *Theatre Journal* 47, no. 1 (1995): 157–59; Kurt Lancaster, "Theatrical Deconstructionists: The Social 'Gests' of Peter Sellars's Ajax and Robert Wilson's Einstein on the Beach," *Modern Drama* 43, no. 3 (2000): 461–68, https://doi.org/10.1353/mdr.2000.0059; Hans-Thies Lehmann, *Postdramatic Theatre* (London: Routledge, 2006).

14 Tracy C. Davis, "Questions for a Feminist Methodology in Theatre History," in *Interpreting the Theatrical Past: Essays in the Historiography of Performance*, eds. Thomas Postlewait and Bruce A. McConachie (Iowa City: University of Iowa Press, 1989); Elin Diamond, "Brechtian Theory/Feminist Theory: Toward a Gestic Feminist Criticism," *TDR* 32, no. 1 (1988): 82–94, https://doi.org/10.2307/1145871; Elin Diamond, *Unmaking Mimesis: Essays on Feminism and Theatre* (London: Routledge, 2003); Lynda Hart and Stephanie Arnold, eds., *Making a Spectacle: Feminist Essays on Contemporary Women's Theatre* (Ann Arbor: University of Michigan Press, 1989); Linda W. Jenkins and Susan Ogden-Malouf, "The (Female) Actor Prepares," *Theater* 17, no. 1 (1985): 66–69.

15 Elaine Aston and George Savona, *Theatre as Sign System: A Semiotics of Text and Performance* (London: Routledge, 2013); Marco De Marinis, *The Semiotics of Performance* (Bloomington: Indiana University Press, 1993); Umberto Eco, "Semiotics of Theatrical Performance," *The Drama Review* 21, no. 1 (1977): 107–17, https://doi.org/10.2307/1145112; Keir Elam, *The Semiotics of Theatre and Drama* (London: Routledge, 2003).

16 Bharucha, *Theatre and the World*; Richard P. Knowles, *Theatre and Interculturalism* (London: Red Globe Press, 2010); Jacqueline Lo and Helen Gilbert, "Toward a Topography of Cross-Cultural Theatre Praxis," *The Drama Review* 46, no. 3 (2002): 31–53; Phillip B. Zarrilli, *Psychophysical Acting: An Intercultural Approach After Stanislavski* (London: Routledge, 2009).

17 Balme, *Decolonizing the Stage*; Brian Crow and Chris Banfield, *An Introduction to Post-Colonial Theatre* (New York: Cambridge University Press, 1996); Gilbert and Tompkins, eds, *Post-Colonial Drama: Theory, Practice, Politics* (London: Routledge, 1996).

18 Sam Halvorsen, "Decolonizing Territory: Dialogues With Latin American Knowledges and Grassroots Strategies," *Progress in Human Geography* 43, no. 5 (2019): 790–814, https://doi.org/10.1177/0309132518777623; Jonathan Murphy and Jingqi Zhu, "Neo-Colonialism in the Academy? Anglo-American Domination in Management Journals," *Organization* 19, no. 6 (2012): 915–27.

19  Halvorsen, "Decolonizing Territory: Dialogues with Latin American Knowledges and Grassroots Strategies"; Gavin Jack and Robert Westwood, *International and Cross-Cultural Management Studies: A Postcolonial Reading* (New York: Palgrave Macmillan, 2009).
20  Culturally Relevant Pedagogy can be described as teaching strategies that outline "theoretical and practical considerations for critical reflection asserting that the development of culturally relevant teaching strategies is contingent upon critical reflection about the race and culture of teachers and their students." See Tyrone C. Howard, "Culturally Relevant Pedagogy: Ingredients for Critical Teacher Reflection," *Theory into Practice* 42, no. 3 (2003): 195–202, https://doi.org/10.1207/s15430421tip4203_5.
21  Ali A. Abdi, "Decolonizing Philosophies of Education: An Introduction," in *Decolonizing Philosophies of Education*, ed. Ali A. Abdi, 1–13 (Rotterdam: Sense Publishers, 2012); S. Fryberg et al., "The Ongoing Psychological Colonization of North American Indigenous People: Using Social Psychological Theories to Promote Social Justice," in *The Oxford Handbook of Social Psychology and Social Justice*, ed. Phillip L. Hammack (New York: Oxford University Press, 2018), 113–28.

## Bibliography

Abdi, Ali A. "Decolonizing Philosophies of Education: An Introduction." In *Decolonizing Philosophies of Education*, edited by Ali A. Abdi, 1–13. Rotterdam: Sense Publishers, 2012.
Aldama, Arturo J., Chela Sandoval, and Peter J. García, eds. *Performing the US Latina and Latino Borderlands*. Bloomington: Indiana University Press, 2012.
Anzaldúa, Gloria. *Borderlands/La Frontera: The New Mestiza*. San Francisco: Aunt Lute Books, 1987.
Arrizón, Alicia. *Queering Mestizaje: Transculturation and Performance*. Ann Arbor: University of Michigan Press, 2006.
Aston, Elaine, and George Savona. *Theatre as Sign System: A Semiotics of Text and Performance*. London: Routledge, 2013.
Auslander, Philip. "Toward a Concept of the Political in Postmodern Theatre." *Theatre Journal* 39, no. 1 (1987): 20–34. https://doi.org/10.2307/3207618.
———. "Postmodern Theatric (k) s: Monologue in Contemporary American Drama." *Theatre Journal* 47, no. 1 (1995): 157–59.
Balme, Christopher B. *Decolonizing the Stage: Theatrical Syncretism and Post-Colonial Drama*. Oxford: Oxford University Press, 1999.
Battiste, Marie, and James (Sa'ke'j) Youngblood. "Naturalizing Indigenous Knowledge in Eurocentric Education." *Canadian Journal of Native Education* 32, no. 1 (2009): 5–17.
Bharucha, Rustom. *Theatre and the World: Performance and the Politics of Culture*. London: Routledge, 2003.
Cabrera, Nolan L. "Where Is the Racial Theory in Critical Race Theory? A Constructive Criticism of the Crits." *The Review of Higher Education* 42, no. 1 (2018): 209–33.
Çapan, Zeynep G. "Enacting the International/Reproducing Eurocentrism." *Contexto Internacional* 39, no. 3 (2017): 655–72. https://doi.org/10.1590/S0102-8529.2017390300010.
Chuang, Angie, and Robin C. Roemer. "Beyond the Positive—Negative Paradigm of Latino/Latina News-Media Representations: DREAM Act Exemplars, Stereotypical Selection, and American Otherness." *Journalism* 16, no. 8 (2015): 1045–61. https://doi.org/10.1177/1464884914550974.
Crow, Brian, and Chris Banfield. *An Introduction to Post-Colonial Theatre*. New York: Cambridge University Press, 1996.

Dabashi, Hamid. *Brown Skin, White Masks*. London: Pluto Press, 2011.
Davis, Tracy C. "Questions for a Feminist Methodology in Theatre History." In *Interpreting the Theatrical Past: Essays in the Historiography of Performance*, edited by Thomas Postlewait and Bruce A. McConachie. Iowa City: University of Iowa Press, 1989.
De Marinis, Marco. *The Semiotics of Performance*. Bloomington: Indiana University Press, 1993.
Diamond, Elin. "Brechtian Theory/Feminist Theory: Toward a Gestic Feminist Criticism." *TDR* 32, no. 1 (1988): 82–94. https://doi.org/10.2307/1145871.
———. *Unmaking Mimesis: Essays on Feminism and Theatre*. London: Routledge, 2003.
Eco, Umberto. "Semiotics of Theatrical Performance." *The Drama Review* 21, no. 1 (1977): 107–17. https://doi.org/10.2307/1145112.
Elam, Keir. *The Semiotics of Theatre and Drama*. London: Routledge, 2003.
Erincin, Serap. "Decolonizing Identity in Performance: Claiming My Mother Tongue in *Suppression of Absence*." *Frontiers: A Journal of Women Studies* 41, no. 1 (2020): 179–95. https://doi.org/10.5250/fronjwomestud.41.1.0179.
Fanon, Frantz. *Black Skin, White Masks*. Translated by Charles L. Markmann. London: Pluto Press, 1986.
Fiddian, Robin, ed. *Postcolonial Perspectives on the Cultures of Latin America and Lusophone Africa*. Liverpool: Liverpool University Press, 2000.
Fryberg, Stephanie, Rebecca Covarrubias, and Jacob A. Burack. "The Ongoing Psychological Colonization of North American Indigenous People: Using Social Psychological Theories to Promote Social Justice." In *The Oxford Handbook of Social Psychology and Social Justice*, edited by Phillip L. Hammack, 113–28. New York: Oxford University Press, 2018.
Gilbert, Helen, and Joanne Tompkins, eds. *Post-colonial Drama: Theory, Practice, Politics*. London: Routledge, 1996.
———, eds. *Post-colonial Drama: Theory, Practice, Politics*. London: Routledge, 2002.
Gómez-Peña, Guillermo. "La Pocha Nostra Manifesto." *Guillermo Gómez-Peña*. Accessed July 25, 2022. www.guillermogomezpena.com/la-pocha-nostra/.
Gómez-Peña, Guillermo, and Saul Garcia-Lopez. *La Pocha Nostra: A Handbook for the Rebel Artist in a Post-Democratic Society*. London: Routledge, 2020.
Halvorsen, Sam. "Decolonizing Territory: Dialogues With Latin American Knowledges and Grassroots Strategies." *Progress in Human Geography* 43, no. 5 (2019): 790–814. https://doi.org/10.1177/0309132518777623.
Hart, Lynda, and Stephanie Arnold, eds. *Making a Spectacle: Feminist Essays on Contemporary Women's Theatre*. Ann Arbor: University of Michigan Press, 1989.
Heleta, Savo. "Decolonization of Higher Education: Dismantling Epistemic Violence and Eurocentrism in South Africa." *Transformation in Higher Education* 1, no. 1 (2016): 1–8.
Howard, Tyrone C. "Culturally Relevant Pedagogy: Ingredients for Critical Teacher Reflection." *Theory into Practice* 42, no. 3 (2003): 195–202. https://doi.org/10.1207/s15430421tip4203_5.
Irobi, Esiaba. "A Theatre for Cannibals: Images of Europe in Indigenous African Theatre of the Colonial Period." *New Theatre Quarterly* 22, no. 3 (2006): 268–82. https://doi.org/10.1017/S0266464X06000479.
Jack, Gavin, and Robert Westwood. *International and Cross-Cultural Management Studies: A Postcolonial Reading*. New York: Palgrave Macmillan, 2009.
Jenkins, Linda W., and Susan Ogden-Malouf. "The (Female) Actor Prepares." *Theater* 17, no. 1 (1985): 66–69.

Kincheloe, Joe L., and Shirley R. Steinberg. "Addressing the Crisis of Whiteness: Reconfiguring White Identity in a Pedagogy of Whiteness." In *White Reign: Deploying Whiteness in America*, edited by Joe L. Kincheloe, Shirley R. Steinberg, Nelson M. Rodriguez, and Ronald E. Chennault, 3–30. New York: St. Martin's Press, 1998.

Knowles, Richard P. *Theatre and Interculturalism*. London: Red Globe Press, 2010.

Lancaster, Kurt. "Theatrical Deconstructionists: The Social 'Gests' of Peter Sellars's *Ajax* and Robert Wilson's *Einstein on the Beach*." *Modern Drama* 43, no. 3 (2000): 461–68. https://doi.org/10.1353/mdr.2000.0059.

Lehmann, Hans-Thies. *Postdramatic Theatre*. London: Routledge, 2006.

Lo, Jacqueline, and Helen Gilbert. "Toward a Topography of Cross-Cultural Theatre Praxis." *The Drama Review* 46, no. 3 (2002): 31–53.

Luciani, Frederick. "Spanish American Theatre of the Colonial Period." In *The Cambridge History of Latin American Literature*, edited by Roberto G. Echevarría and Enrique Pupo-Walker, 260–85. Cambridge: Cambridge University Press, 1996. https://doi.org/10.1017/CHOL9780521340694.010.

Marshall, Mariel, and Lisa C. Ravensbergen. "The Doing That Can Undo: Decolonizing the Performer-Audience Relationship in Lisa Cooke Ravensbergen's *Citation*." *Canadian Theatre Review* 179, no. 17 (2019): 80–82. https://doi.org/10.3138/ctr.179.017.

Muñoz, Jose E. *Disidentifications: Queers of Color and the Performance of Politics*. Minneapolis: University of Minnesota Press, 1999.

Murphy, Jonathan, and Jingqi Zhu. "Neo-colonialism in the Academy? Anglo-American Domination in Management Journals." *Organization* 19, no. 6 (2012): 915–27.

O'Shea, Janet. "Decolonizing the Curriculum? Unsettling Possibilities for Performance Training." *Brazilian Journal on Presence Studies* 8, no. 4 (2018): 750–62. https://doi.org/10.1590/2237-266078871.

Omi, Michael, and Howard Winant. *Racial Formation in the United States*. New York: Routledge, 2014.

Ray, Aveling. "La Pocha Nostra." *Guillermo Gomez-Pena*. Accessed September 21, 2021. www.guillermogomezpena.com/la-pocha-nostra.

Rivas, Araceli. "Postcolonial Analysis of Educational Research Discourse: Creating (Mexican) American Children as the 'Other.'" PhD diss., Texas A&M University, 2006.

Rivera-Servera, Ramón. *Performing Queer Latinidad: Dance, Sexuality, Politics*. Ann Arbor: University of Michigan Press, 2012.

Said, Edward W. *Orientalism*. London: Pantheon Book, 1978.

Taylor, Diana. "Scenes of Cognition: Performance and Conquest." *Theatre Journal* 56, no. 3 (2004): 353–72.

Vineberg, Steve. *Method Actors: Three Generations of an American Acting Style*. New York: Schirmer Books, 1994.

Zarrilli, Phillip B. *Psychophysical Acting: An Intercultural Approach after Stanislavski*. London: Routledge, 2009.

# PART 2
# Acting

# 8
# THE COMPLEXITY AND POETRY OF LATINX IDENTITY AND ACTOR TRAINING, A NARRATIVE

*Micha Espinosa*

> *Not barrio enough Chicana*
> *Only an academic Chicana*
> *I'll find a coupon for anything Chicana*
> *Muggle Chicana*
> *El Rey loving Chicana*
> *Right to choose Chicana*
> *Take care of my mama for life Chicana*
> *Spoil my prince Chicana*
> *Non makeup wearing Chicana*
> *No spanks Chicana*
> *Embarrassed by my Spanish Chicana*
> *Empowered by my Spanglish Chicana*
> *Latines, Latinx, Latin@ Chicana*
> *Google Translate Chicana*
> *Won't handle your Machismo Chicana*
> *Can't handle my tequila Chicana*
> *I hear mescal is better for me Chicana*
> *Joder Marianismo Chicana*
> *Take a Knee Chicana*
> *Cholas Matter Chicana*
> *Forgot my hot sauce again, Chicana!*

Not Barrio Enough is an identity poem that was published in 2020 for Glossolalia,[1] a multilingual poetry experiment produced with La Pocha Nostra. I begin with poetry because throughout the essay I merge my creative and scholarly voices. I am a spoken-word performance artist, actor, coach, and a Professor in

DOI: 10.4324/9781003021520-11

the School of Music, Dance, and Theatre at Arizona State University in Tempe, Arizona. I teach a variety of voice and acting classes at the university in a multicultural environment. For purposes of this chapter, I will focus on the teaching of Latinx students. I offer insights and best practices, coupled with quotes from Latinx students from the recent past and present, and from Latinx luminaries in the field. These quotes allow us to hear "the voice of the student," signal changes in thought, and affirm that Latinx students in actor training need to be met with cultural knowledge and understanding.

This work builds on my creative research in and dedication to Latinx actor training, which began in the early 2000s. I use narrative memory as a springboard to examine the complexities of discovering one's *voz cultural* (cultural voice). I put myself at the fore to incorporate history into meaningful learning that I can share with my fellow actor-trainers. I teach and write from my wounds (a concept and now a practice given to me by my mentor, Catherine Fitzmaurice).[2]

My upbringing, training, and education in the late 1980s assumed meritocracy, exceptionalism, and assimilation. Like many Mexican-Americans of my generation, assimilation into US society meant English-only at school. Throughout my childhood, I was directed to become American, and that identity was singularly defined for me by every internal and external force in my life.

In fact, I did not see myself represented until I went to graduate school at University of California, San Diego (U.C.S.D.). At U.C.S.D., I met the renowned historian of Chicano theatre, Professor Jorge Huerta, my very first Latino professor ever. Just meeting him and knowing he existed changed my life. Not until graduate school did I learn that Latinos created theatre for Latinos. Not that I wasn't curious or not looking for this history of my field, but my education had directed me toward only Anglo-American theatre. Moreover, Huerta ran a program devoted to training the Hispanic actor! I was in the "traditional" actor training program, but the Latinx *cultura* on campus—with students, playwrights, guest artists, designers, directors at U.C.S.D. during those years (1990–1994)—was exciting.[3] Learning parallel to the students in Huerta's Hispanic Acting program, I saw how I fit into the traditional program yet how I did not. I deeply felt the invisibility of my bi-culturalism and the shame of speaking Spanglish and having an Arizona accent. I remember feeling that I was both not Latina enough and, at times, too Latina—*Ni de aqui/ni de alla.*

At U.C.S.D., I also learned about Chicanos, a chosen identity for American people of Mexican descent. Nowhere in my upbringing in Arizona had I been exposed to Chicano culture—Mexicano, *claro que si*, but not Chicano. In that Chicano culture, I discovered a politically oriented identity. The Chicano identity rejected stereotypes, embraced Spanglish, aligned with the global majority, celebrated bi-nationalism, and spoke to the greater Southwest, the region that my family was from.

While I began to study and learn about the complexities of the Chicano movement, one of many social justice movements that have become important to me, I went to my first MEChA (*Movimiento Estudiantil Chicano de Aztlan*) meeting during my time at U.C.S.D. I was also introduced to the work of Luis Valdez's Teatro Campesino and, subsequently, to the heroes of the farm workers' movement, César Chávez and Delores Huerta. I had the honor of working in the same spaces and having conversations with Chicano artists, like Culture Clash (Richard Montoya, Ric Salinas, and Herbert Sigüenza). Learning Chicano history and joining with a Chicanx-identifying community gave me a path towards finding my own authentic voice—a voice that could integrate my past and my culture.

Understanding and exploring my cultural identity helped me navigate my identity as an actor. That didn't mean it wasn't confusing and full of challenges, but it gave me a place to begin to value my hyphenated, mixed-blood, border-crossing ways.

Early on as a teacher in the academy, I found that the institutions wanted me to replicate those same practices that had made me feel unseen and unheard as a student.[4] Usually, I was the only Latinx faculty member, and although it was hard to be a sole voice, I began to stake boundaries and push back. I realized that I did not want my students to have the same experiences I had had. I wanted to equip them for the field and, more importantly, for life.

I dived into Latinx Literature and theatre studies, Chicano psychology, Chicano anthropology, critical race theory, Latino critical theory, border theory, liberation theory, feminist and gender studies, and trauma-informed voice and acting practices. In addition, I immersed myself in the national and local social justice movements and theatre in service of staying actively connected to the current and emerging voices in the Latinx socio-political sphere and also to be able to provide a fabric of network opportunities with Latinx theaters across the United States. Lastly, I discovered the work of Guillermo Gomez Peña and La Pocha Nostra, which gave me a container to subvert stereotypes and to perform and write from my truth using my Chicana identity, politics, and aesthetics. My immersion in these subjects and pedagogies allowed me to self-define and position myself as a bicultural feminist with a voice.

I wanted to prepare my Latinx actors so they could understand the perils of the industry, value their unique offerings, and speak truth to power. As my mentor, Catherine Fitzmaurice, taught me, "*one should teach what is in front of them.*" To that end I had to be *conscious* of the overt and underlying realities, beliefs, and values of being part of the Latinx diaspora. In Paulo Freire's essay "Cultural Action and Conscientization," Freire defines "conscientization" as "the effort to enlighten men about the obstacles preventing them from a clear perception of reality. In this role, conscientization effects the ejection of cultural myths that confuse people's awareness and makes then ambiguous beings."[5] Luis Valdez's acting philosophy resonates with conscientization: "As actors in life, we must all seek truth to the root, reaching for a wholistic consciousness that will liberate us from our own irrationality."[6]

I invite this heightened state of knowing that Freire describes, and, like Valdez, I find it fundamental to actor training. This critical consciousness is imperative to developing authenticity. To that end, in preparation for this article, I used critical consciousness that Valdez and Freire invoke to write a journal of narrative memory of my early actor training. This painful remembering might be retraumatizing to others if shared.

In summary, I was subjected to damaging eroticized stereotypes. I experienced sexual harassment from producers, directors, photographers, and other players in my training and in the industry. I also faced the challenges of balancing a career with the traditional expectations of familia, and I struggled to break free of toxic, old-world belief systems that were part of my Mexicana upbringing. My Mexicana values of *simpatía* and *marianismo*[7] did not empower me and, therefore, left me vulnerable to the brutality of a misogynistic and patriarchal profession. I wrestled with my reclamation of Spanish and the reimagining of my Chicana-activist identity. I remembered not only mentors and education opportunities that had provided moments of impact that empowered my cultural voice but also others that silenced me. I remember moments of belonging and moments of isolation and othering.

Author Penelope Harnett in *Exploring Learning, Identity, and Power Through Life History and Narrative Research* confirms my process of reflection: "Narrative is valued across a range of subject domains. From the beginning of time, it has been a feature of humankind to explain the present through recourse to the past."[8] She further states: "Stories of individual lives are also important as acts of remembrance ensuring that certain events and episodes of the past do not fade into obscurity."[9] By remembering and examining my journey, I am able to question and exploit my identity to better understand myself, my agency, and my relations with others. Betty Franklin Smith, a scholar of the Theatre of the Oppressed, offers insight into how inner exploration leads to understanding.

> Placing ourselves at the struggle of transformation means knowing our own stand points, our specific ways of being in the world. Sometimes we get to know ourselves (our visions and blindness's) through our cataclysmic introduction to others. Here in these interactions the contrast becomes stark. We explore the meanings of our own shock and awe and come closer to knowing the boundaries of what we have been doing, of who we are. We come to consider who we are and what we might do in the world.[10]

Smith's words confirm that, through the act of remembering and engaging in the scope of the process, I am more equipped as an actor, coach, and teacher to be able to see world orders (old and new), embedded generational values, and shared belief systems. I am also better able to discern the commonalities and differences with my Latinx students in order to improve and disrupt teaching norms.

> If the fastest growing population in this country is Latino, that means we are the future of this country. And, we have proven we have talent. Now we need the tools to succeed.[11]

> *Shakira*

Shakira's statement captures the spirit and emotional tone of my findings as I look to the current state of Latinx students in the classroom. Recruiting Latinx students into our programs without understanding their needs, or not providing them with essential knowledge, then, further, expecting them to assimilate into Anglo-centric ways of being may be reasons we fail to see enough Latinx creatives in the field. Therefore, what follows are reflections, insights, and practices to improve the future of Latinx actors' training.

Unlike my assimilationist upbringing, many of my Latinx students view their multiculturalism and their multilingualism as an asset. For that reason, I have worked with a handful of Latinx students who do not want to be pigeon-holed into playing only Latino/a/x parts. I honor their request. They are comfortable with their Latinx identity, have explored it or rejected it, and are eager to work on their skills of transformation without having to think about their cultural identity.

However, it has been my experience that the majority of Latinx students are eager to explore the canon of Latinx playwrights and dive with critical consciousness into their Latinidad because it was not part of their K-12 performance training or experience. My Latinx students, keenly aware of the deficit in their Latinx knowledge, are eager to exploit their cultural backgrounds and biographies to engage in meaningful connection with texts that reflect their cultural knowledge and sense of self.

> Can you help me find a monologue? My acting teacher said I need one that shows I can speak Spanish. I was afraid to tell him that I don't, but I bet I can fake it.
>
> *Unidentified Mexican-American, male student*

Well-meaning voice and acting teachers fail their Latinx acting students by assuming language ability and by simply substituting Latinx classics for Anglo classic plays. These teachers think this is enough. The assumption is that the Latinx student can easily access a character because it mirrors their world experience and, possibly, their phenotype (physical appearance). This assumption burdens the student tremendously.

> I'm sorry I'm crying. It's just that, I been acting since middle school—I've never played someone who looked like me, and I have no idea how to access this character."
>
> *Unidentified Mexican-American, female student*[12]

Becoming Latinx or Chicano relies not solely on heritage but on a complicated choice full of dilemmas going toward identity. Further complicating this process is that these students may be reclaiming or rejecting their identities. And, most likely, they have never seen their culture reflected in performance. Nuanced discussions about identity are the only way to face these challenges. The students of today have a lot of cultural intelligence and are identity-conscious, but we must ask.

> It so frustrating everyone thinks I'm Mexican! I've never even been to Mexico. I don't sound Mexican. My accent is totally different. (sigh) Can you give me some resources so I can hear what a Fresa from Mexico City sounds like?"
>
> *Unidentified Chilean, female student*

Creating a consent-based culture, using self-identifying practices when diving into identity, is always best. Don't be afraid to ask students how they identify and whether they would like to work on a piece that might speak to their cultures. If we don't have enough cultural knowledge to coach the material, we should seek out a qualified coach with expertise, or, at the minimum, reveal to the student that we are not familiar with their particular cultural context. Prior to working on any monologues or scenes in a course, I discuss identity early on—usually the first day of classes—through a variety of exercises and discussions.[13] This way, the student can incrementally delve into their experience of identity.

Another dangerous trap, aforementioned in the quote from the Chilean student, is clumping Latinos together. Latinx culture, values, and belief systems are not all alike. During a recent adjudication of a bilingual show, a production pursued an all-inclusive vision of Latinidad, mixing many cultural markers—Peruvian, Mexican, Puerto Rican, and even Spanish cultural elements—into one show under a giant umbrella of Latinidad. From my perspective, the play was confusing and bordered on an insult. Due diligence when it comes to entering Latinx worlds is rarely done. Take time to appraise the project, that is, to understand the customs and beliefs of the myriad of cultures within the Latinx community. Without doing the research, teachers and producers run the danger of falling into stereotypes.

> I was so thankful my professor gave me Josefina Lopez' Real Women Have Curves, I thought in order to be actress I had to be skinny.
>
> *Unidentified Mexican-American, female student*

> At that film shoot they asked me to bring wardrobe. I brought a bunch of clothes from home but they said I needed to bring clothes that looked dirtier "like a Mexican."
>
> *Unidentified Mexican-American, male student*

> My career is getting better. When, I first moved to L.A., I was always playing pool boys, vegetable sellers, and farm workers. I try to humanize my characters. Those are my ancestors and I'm going to play them with dignity. Representation is really important me. I believe I'm now being

looked at for other roles because I brought charm, a warmth to my roles. I didn't give into the stereotype.

*Unidentified Mexican-American, male actor*

Each one of these quotes shows actors in different stages of their careers and in different stages of consciousness toward identity. All three felt the cultural bumping of limiting stereotypes, which sadly still exist. I have found that if actors have not been exposed to their Latinx cultures, they may easily fall prey to the stereotype without being able to subvert it. I have also seen many actors impose a world of their own understanding onto the play. But Latinx plays do not have the supportive resources readily at hand for actors to find. If I'm an actor and want to enter an Elizabethan world, resources and books stand ready for me to enter that world. Looking to Shakespeare, an actor would need to understand heaven, hell, purgatory, the church, and witches and fairies—the cosmic order of the macro- and microcosms. To enter a Latinx world as an actor, I will need to understand the history, the manners, my feeling about beauty, the images I might see, and the ways in which I would succeed or fail in this world. Learning the customs, rituals, and ways of these worlds with a special eye toward the understanding of old-world and new-world belief systems offers the student actor confidence in which to play. The rules of a world inform the style of a play, help the actor understand the stakes, and aid in embodiment.

Without resources, actors, vulnerable to stereotypes, are left to look inward; that can lead to a deep sense of not being Latino enough. I spend many hours looking for resources to empower Latinx students; these resources include books, films, and podcasts. Historical novels and memoirs like *Caballero*, *House on Mango Street*, and *Native Country of the Heart* are excellent examples of resources to understand class, patriarchy, and gender embedded in 19th-century Mexican-American life.[14]

> I thought I had to move to LA or NY. I had no idea Chicago had so many Latinx theatre companies!
> 
> *Unidentified Mexican-American, male student*

It always breaks my heart when I meet Latinx students who are not made aware of the large Latinx theatre community because I remember that deep sense of not belonging. There is an abundance of professional Latinx theaters across the United States and a tremendous canon of material.[15] Theatre departments need to include the rich history of Latinx theaters, playwrights, and creatives as a regular part of the curriculum. I believe that not sharing the history and the resources is a great disservice. This ignorance of Latinx theatre, creatives, and playwrights is not history. It continues. At the 2018 Association of Theatre in Higher Education conference, I was handing out a flyer for my book, Monologues for Latino/a Actors, and a fellow Anglo acting teacher said to me, in all seriousness, "*They would share the flyer with their colleagues in Latin American studies.*" I smiled and kindly informed them that these playwrights and their texts were part of the New American Theatre.[16]

I am also cognizant of a new layer of pressure that millennials face: a dark anti-immigration/anti-Latino/a/x/e sentiment so prevalent in some far-right media and in the highest offices of our country. Arizona is a hostile place for Latinos.

> May I perform my poem for you during office hours. My poem is about my immigration status and I'm not ready to share that in front of the class.
> *Unidentified Dreamer, male student*

Arizona passed some of the worst anti-immigration laws in the country: The now-defanged, 2010 Arizona S.B 1070 law was one of the broadest and strictest anti-immigration laws in the United States. The law, criticized for legalizing racial profiling, ushered in a decade of racial politics creating fear of racial self-identification.[17] Arizona is also the last remaining state to have English-only laws.[18] These laws have a ripple effect. They do not lead to Latinx success. They are ineffective and offensive. In the politically hostile environment of Arizona, my students who were English-language learners studying performance often struggled with linguistic confidence and, during the height of the racial profiling, feared for the solo drives home after evening rehearsals.

It is imperative that teachers understand the social and political stressors their Latinx students may be facing in their communities. We must stand ready with resources. We must remove the stigma of the old-world Hispanic belief that "we do not ask for help." I experienced sexual harassment and the humiliating performance of stereotypes while training and working as an actor, but because of my cultural upbringing, I did not feel I had a right to speak up; therefore, I feel that community agreements that support safety and promote ethical performance practices are essential. We are fundamentally purveyors of voice; the highest levels of actor training address not only the sound of the voice but also its constitution.

To that end, over the last two years, after numerous conversations with our departmental community groups at Arizona State, the faculty and staff created new policies and procedures for safe-set protocols, ensuring multiple options for reporting concerns, including anonymity. I have been especially proud of the commitments to cultural context and safe-set protocols and designation of assigned faculty representatives to be intimacy coordinators and cultural-context representatives on every production.

My last insight centers on the role of family in my Latinx student's lives. Even as new-world values and belief systems move away from patriarchy and strict gender constructs, I believe that family culture, norms, and expectations (*familismo*) continue to rule the life of my Latinx students.

> I turned down the scholarship, I'm not going to graduate school, my mom got really upset when I told her it was out of state. She needs me.
> *Unidentified Mexican-American, female student*

> I'm not interested in doing the showcase. I'm staying in Arizona to work. I help with our family business.
>
> *Unidentified Mexican-American, nonbinary student*

In my 14 years at ASU, I have had only one Mexican-American undergraduate student pursue a higher degree away from Arizona. The majority have all chosen to stay close to home. I also see that my students are often working to support family even while going to school, so the traditional evening rehearsals often prove to be a problem. At ASU, we continue to experiment with flexible rehearsal times and encourage devised projects in new media, video, or Zoom, to ensure that our students with family obligations can honor them yet pursue their craft.

An extension of *familismo* is community. Just like when I discovered the radical performance pedagogy of La Pocha Nostra, I have found that my Mexican and Mexican-American students experience a high level of engagement and satisfaction when they are offered the opportunity to look beyond self to community. For Latinos who face many pressures as they define themselves in a society that disparages their identities and imposes definitions, finding their identities as artist-citizens can be extremely empowering.

As my Mexican and Mexican-American students navigate their education within the hostile political climate, myths are exposed, and students need an anchor, as well as a vessel, for their creativity, an anchor and vessel that allow them to create for and against the causes in which they believe. The struggle for inclusion requires consistent awareness, getting involved with local student chapters and creating projects that include community causes help Latinx students participate in the socio-political so they are heard and seen. They are offered an alternative identity. They become advocates, activists, and leaders.

In Valdez's Theatre of the Sphere, he offers a way of being in communion with *gente* by using the Mayan concept of InLak'ech (I am you and you are me).

> In other words, you should love your brother or sister as yourself because they are yourself. The requires acknowledgment of our collective genetic and psychosocial identity as a human species; an idea that flies in the face of diametrically opposed beliefs in rugged individualism, particularly in the West. Yet the concept was not alien to the great ancient civilizations in Asia, and no less fundamental to the moral and spiritual ethos of ancient America. Ultimately, as one of the highest expressions of collective art, world theatre itself thrives on the very vibrations and love expressed in the root idea of *IN LAK'ECH*.[19]

I resonate within Valdez's vision and model the practice of InLak'ech by supporting Latino initiatives, programs, and media. But, ultimately, I practice InLak'ech by accepting and loving myself.

If I could speak to my younger self entering actor training, I would tell her this:

*Having a satisfying and enriching life as a performer can take many shapes. There is not one way. You can choose, challenge, and transform your identity. You have a myriad of choices. Embrace your hybrid identities, create new identities. Mine the social, political, creative, and linguistic power in your body. With pride and confidence, keep the best values from your biculturalism/multiculturalism and disregard what no longer works for you. Heal the mind-body split. Slow down. Listen deeply. Value your body as the site of understanding and creation. You hold ancestral memory in your bones. Notice where you are: the land speaks, too. You have to quiet the noise of your mind to listen. Your wounds need healing, but they are also sites of knowledge and growth and creativity. Lean in to the discomfort. You don't have to do it all today—take the time you need to breathe. If you need help, reach out to others, see a therapist, find a mentor, form community, ask questions, be curious, record your family's histories. The more you engage with your cultural identity(ies) or your heritage(s) on your journey toward identity, the stronger your voice will be. Write your own story. Embrace your complexity. Don't wait. No one has ever expressed your story as well as you can. Use your voice. The world needs your story.*

## Conclusion

> By creating a new mythos—that is, a change in the way we perceive reality, the way we see ourselves and the way we behave—la mestiza creates a new consciousness—Making Face.[20]
>
> Gloria Anzaldúa

The purpose of this chapter is to explore cultural identity and Latinx actor training. I offer new ways of being that can only come from introspection, understanding of structural relations, and grace that emerges from examination of beliefs and values.

Influenced by work with radical performance pedagogy and the liberation practices of theorists—Freire, Boal, Gomez-Peña, and Fitzmaurice—and the real-world reality of my Latinx student experiences, I offer my teaching philosophy for working with Latinx students.

I acknowledge complex identities, current events, and the history of class, race, and gender inherent in ethnic and language identity and its complexities with national identity as the point of entry into teaching. As teacher and artist, I seek to challenge identity politics, transform social dynamics, and embrace Latinx narratives and ways of knowing. I believe we must foster development of authenticity and empowerment of the cultural voice. I believe that we must reject stereotypes and any reductionist views of Latinx culture. Lastly, I reject the toxic patriarchy of the industry and the dominant lens of Anglo-centric pedagogy and narratives in the field of actor training.

My story continues; my identity is ever-changing as a single mother, a sister, and a senior teacher in my communities. I see the evidence of my new role as an elder in my thinking but also by the thinness of my skin. I hope that this remembering and the insights that followed contribute to understanding of Latino/a/x/e actors' journeys. That my remembering will offer a conduit through which others may see themselves reflected and, thus, continue to develop the muscle of empathy. This muscle of empathy can be used in service of world-making for performance, creating theory and pedagogy, y *por su puesto*, poetry.

## Notes

1. Border Poetics Against the Wall, *Posnacional 2: Glossolalia* (San Francisco: La Pocha Nostra, 2020), http://book.flipbuilder.com/saulgarcialopez/.
2. I have been practicing Fitzmaurice Voicework since 1998. Catherine Fitzmaurice's Voicework and physical practices are based on bioenergetics and are trauma-informed. The idea of teaching and writing from one's wounds invites the practitioner to use and transform their most challenging life experiences into relevant learning. The practitioner models vulnerability and authenticity in creative practice and teaching.
3. For a full account of the history of the program, see Dennis Sloan, "From La Carpa to the Classroom: The Chicano Theatre Movement and Actor Training in the United States" (PhD diss., ProQuest Dissertations Publishing, 2020), www.proquest.com/openview/bd22df4ec1002b4daca44f8f0e21ab51/1?pq-origsite=gscholar&cbl=18750&diss=y.
4. The majority of actor training programs in the mid-1990s insisted that actors be trained in theatre standard or general American, so plays by Latinx authors were rarely produced or used in the classroom.
5. Paulo Freire, "Cultural Action and Conscientization," *Harvard Educational Review* 68, no. 4 (1998): 517, https://doi.org/10.17763/haer.40.3.h76250x720j43175.
6. L. Valdez, *Theatre of the Sphere: The Vibrant Being* (Milton: Routledge, 2021), 137.
7. *Marianismo* (prescribing the Roman Catholic Virgin Mary as a role model) is a belief system given to females within the Latino culture. The term was coined by political scientist Evelyn P. Stevens as a counter-point to machismo and is widely used in the field of psychology. For studies that examine the concept and its application, see Linda G. Castillo, Flor V. Perez, Rosalinda Castillo, and Mona R. Ghosheh, "Construction and Initial Validation of the Marianismo Beliefs Scale," *Counselling Psychology Quarterly* 23, no. 2 (2010): 163–75; Miguel De La Torre, "Marianismo," *Hispanic American Religious Cultures*, 2009. *Simpatía* can be strictly translated into English as being sympathetic, sweet, and agreeable. The term helps define the sexist paradigms that can lead to abuse because of the avoidance of conflict, see Amanda M. Acevedo, Clara Herrera, Sharon Shenhav, Ilona S. Yim, and Belinda Campos, "Measurement of a Latino Cultural Value: The Simpatía Scale," *Cultural Diversity & Ethnic Minority Psychology* 26, no. 4 (2020): 419–25.
8. Penelope Harnett, *Exploring Learning, Identity, and Power Through Life History and Narrative Research* (London: Routledge, 2010), 160.
9. Ibid., 162.
10. Betty Smith Franklin, "Freire, Boal, You and Me," *Transformations: The Journal of Inclusive Scholarship and Pedagogy* 10, no. 2 (1999): 1, www.jstor.org/stable/43587652.
11. Silvana Paternostro, "Shakira's Colombian War: The Latin Pop Star on Why She's Spending Millions on Schools in Her Home Country and Beyond," *Wall Street*

*Journal*, accessed April 3, 2010, www.wsj.com/articles/SB10001424052702304252704575156063289919070.

12. Used with permission from Tiffany Ann Lopez. Vice Provost Lopez used this quote from her student at UC Riverside to discuss Latinx dramaturgy during an interview in April 2016.
13. A variety of "I am" poem templates are accessible on freeology website and provide a great way for students to play with language and explore identity. See Freeology, accessed September 16, 2021, https://freeology.com/.
14. To springboard conversations about cultural and aesthetic complexity in Latinx worlds, I recommend, Patricia Ybarra, "How to Read a Latinx Play in the Twenty-First Century: Learning from Quiara Hudes," *Theatre Topics* 27, no. 1 (2017): 49–59, https://doi.org/10.1353/tt.2017.0001.
15. Latinx Theatre Commons defines itself as a movement that advances the state of Latinx Artists in the United States. Latinx students can network with Latinx creatives throughout the United States. For more information on the organization, see Teresa Marrero, "The Latinx Theatre Commons: A Commons-Based Approach Movement," *Theatre Topics* 27, no. 1 (2017), https://jhuptheatre.org/theatre-topics/online-content/issue/volume-27-number-1-march-2017/latinx-theatre-commons-commons.
16. The new American Theatre is a term coined by Luis Valdez to describe the multicultural future of the American theatre and its audiences. I first heard him reference the new American Theatre at the Boston Latinx Theatre Commons in 2013.
17. Christina M. Getrich, "'Too Bad I'm Not an Obvious Citizen': The Effects of Racialized US Immigration Enforcement Practices on Second-Generation Mexican Youth," *Latino Studies* 11, no. 4 (2013): 462–82, https://doi.org/10.1057/lst.2013.28.
18. Corey Mitchell, "'English-Only' Laws in Education on Verge of Extinction," *Education Week*, accessed October 23, 2019, www.edweek.org/teaching-learning/english-only-laws-in-education-on-verge-of-extinction/2019/10.
19. Valdez, *Theatre of the Sphere: The Vibrant Being*, 126.
20. Gloria Anzaldúa, *Making Face, Making Soul/Haciendo Caras: Creative and Critical Perspectives by Women of Color*, 1st ed. (San Francisco: Aunt Lute Books, 1990), 379.

## Bibliography

Anzaldúa, Gloria. *Making Face, Making Soul/Haciendo Caras: Creative and Critical Perspectives by Women of Color*. 1st ed. San Francisco: Aunt Lute Books, 1990.

Border Poetics Against the Wall. *Posnacional 2: Glossolalia*. San Francisco: La Pocha Nostra, 2020. http://book.flipbuilder.com/saulgarcialopez/.

Franklin, Betty Smith. "Freire, Boal, You and Me." *Transformations: The Journal of Inclusive Scholarship and Pedagogy* 10, no. 2 (1999): 1–10. www.jstor.org/stable/43587652.

Freeology. Accessed September 16, 2021. https://freeology.com/.

Getrich, Christina M. "'Too Bad I'm Not an Obvious Citizen': The Effects of Racialized US Immigration Enforcement Practices on Second-Generation Mexican Youth." *Latino Studies* 11, no. 4 (2013): 462–82. https://doi.org/10.1057/lst.2013.28.

Harnett, Penelope. *Exploring Learning, Identity, and Power Through Life History and Narrative Research*. London: Routledge, 2010.

Marrero, Teresa. "The Latinx Theatre Commons: A Commons-Based Approach Movement." *Theatre Topics* 27, no.1 (2017). https://jhuptheatre.org/theatre-topics/online-content/issue/volume-27-number-1-march-2017/latinx-theatre-commons-commons.

Mitchell, Corey. "'English-Only' Laws in Education on Verge of Extinction." *Education Week*. Accessed October 23, 2019. www.edweek.org/teaching-learning/english-only-laws-in-education-on-verge-of-extinction/2019/10.

Paternostro, Silvana. "Shakira's Colombian War: The Latin Pop Star on Why She's Spending Millions on Schools in Her Home Country and Beyond." *Wall Street Journal*. Accessed April 3, 2010. www.wsj.com/articles/SB10001424052702304252704575156063289919070.

Paulo Freire, "Cultural Action and Conscientization." *Harvard Educational Review* 68, no. 4 (1998): 452–77. https://doi.org/10.17763/haer.40.3.h76250x720j43175.

Sloan, Dennis. "From La Carpa to the Classroom: The Chicano Theatre Movement and Actor Training in the United States." PhD diss. ProQuest Dissertations Publishing, 2020. www.proquest.com/openview/bd22df4ec1002b4daca44f8f0e21ab51/1?pq-origsite=gscholar&cbl=18750&diss=y.

Valdez, Luis. *Theatre of the Sphere: The Vibrant Being*. London: Routledge, 2021.

Ybarra, Patricia. "How to Read a Latinx Play in the Twenty-First Century: Learning From Quiara Hudes." *Theatre Topics* 27, no. 1 (2017): 49–59. https://doi.org/10.1353/tt.2017.0001.

# 9
# FROM METHOD TO MYTHIC

Why Latinx? Why Mythic? How Mythic? Why Now?

*Marissa Chibás*

**Why Latinx?**

Let's start with a story. It's 1994. I walk into the workshop rehearsal room for *The Floating Island Plays* written by Eduardo Machado and directed by Oscar Eustis at the Mark Taper Forum in Los Angeles. I am brimming with excitement to be in my first all Latinx cast and to work on these delicious roles I have been assigned. Up until now I have played parts outside of my ethnic background. This is my opportunity to share a story that is close to me, to the culture in which I belong. As I walk in, salsa music is playing and Willie Marquez is filling small cups of *cafecito* for everyone around the large group of tables pushed together to make a sort of squarish circle. This is so unlike the usual way we in the theater set up to rehearse on those first days. This rehearsal room is like no other I have entered before.

I look around the room and see Latinx folks from many different geographical backgrounds: Cubans, Mexicans, Spaniards, Puerto Ricans, etc. There is an exuberance in this space, a feeling of joy and celebration fills us. Willie gets the dancing started and soon we are all up on our feet, letting loose, warming up in order to enter the epic world of these plays. We laugh and shake our hips, releasing to the dynamic moves many of us grew up learning. Ancestors seem to present themselves energetically, and we smile with a recognition that something in this space is very special and sorely needed.

Eduardo looks like the *gato* who ate the canary, a contained joy spills over his entire being. Oscar has his mouth and eyes wide open with warm appreciation and wonder at what is happening. Soon we gather around the table and start to unpack the text and put our hearts and souls in to these beautifully crafted plays. That was my introduction to working with a group of Latinx actors. Our unplanned ritual

DOI: 10.4324/9781003021520-12

cracked us open to be fully ourselves, unapologetically, and to meet each other through this material with the understanding that we were all Latinx.

But what is that? Honestly, I don't know. We are not a monolith. We are not a race. We are different cultures within a culture. Regardless, I know that we exist and that there is great strength and community despite our differences.

Iberia was occupied for 800 years by North African Muslims and those of Berber descent.[1] Therefore, to be of Spanish lineage means to have within you North African blood and/or culture. African culture is a central part of Hispanic identity and needs to be honored and celebrated, as Federico García Lorca beautifully wrote in his lectures published as *In Search of Duende*.[2] Of equal importance to what makes the Latinx community is the integration of Africans who were enslaved and brought to the New World and whose culture, religion, and customs have become interwoven within all of Latin America. This is true of the Indigenous cultures and lands those of us living in the Americas stand on and occupy. This mixing of peoples and places has created some of the most dynamic arts and culture our world has known under the banner of Latinx and Latin American. We are Black, Asian, White, Indigenous, and every combination thereof. We eat different foods, sometimes speak different languages, but we have landed together in the United States and have become a powerful demographic. In my circle of Latinx friends, we have understandings and ways of being and expressing that come from what our different cultures within a culture share. Some of this coming together evolved out of necessity and needing to find a way to unite in a country that was hostile to us. Often, we Latinx folks splinter out and see each other as enemies, inventing cruel falsehoods about one another. But that is not what I choose to focus on. I choose to focus on what we share, what our potential is when we come together, and how Latinx *sabor* infuses the work we make.

I am included in this book because I am a Latina performance practitioner, and teacher of acting. Everything I do, all the work I create, comes from that particular cultural lens. That lens began specifically as Cuban, then Nuyorkina, then was hugely influenced by Mexico and Central America from living in Los Angeles for the past 20 years. The approaches I share as a teacher with my students were developed out of necessity. I found training in acting classes to either be too invasive in the personal lives of the students, and sometimes very inappropriate, or terribly soul draining, pedantic, and overly technical. I needed the abandon, joy, and serious fun I experienced in the Floating Islands rehearsal room. I needed something that spoke to my soul. I needed the mythic.

## Why Mythic?

In my book, *Mythic Imagination and the Actor*,[3] I define the mythic as tied to the collective human story, that which inspires and grounds us as individuals while connecting us to what is age old. Myths speak to our deepest dreams, fears, and wisdoms. Although the mythic is with us every day, it is often ignored in our busy and sometimes soul crushing modern lives. When we access the mythic, we are aligned with our true nature and that which stirs deeply in us and to our soul's purpose. Myths are great stories that serve as guides for us to better understand our experience of humanity. They are stories that stand the test of time because they speak profoundly through metaphor. Just as the great teachers throughout history have used parables and kōans to lead people to a deeper understanding of human experience, so too do myths through metaphor and symbols. In my work with actors, I seek to mine the mythic that is stirring within them in order to connect their work to that deeper purpose. Metaphor is key to connecting to the mythic.

The mythic approach acknowledges that we as artists have a poetic purpose and that we are all on a hero's journey. My process as a teacher includes teaching skills for the art of acting as well as helping actors connect to that purpose. Too many of us actors go along for years without ever asking essential questions: What am I passionate about? What stories do I need to tell? Who is doing the work I am drawn to and how do I connect with that work? We are propelled by the machine of an industry that rarely bothers to notice their audience except on the crudest level of product information gathering. We run along our busy lives, out of breath, barely able to consider who we really are. What we need as artists, as people, are those ways to connect with those powerful life-sustaining stories and places of meaning and belonging.

For a long while now I have contemplated that meaning and belonging are the most intrinsically necessary elements for a human being to thrive. Without meaning, we are lost in an empty soulless void. There has to be meaning to find our purpose, to know that our little life matters and that we are here to share our gifts. Once I am connected to that purpose, to that deep meaning, I need to bring the fruits of those discoveries to community. It is community that feeds meaning and gives us the sense that we belong. This search is very circular, for as soon as we find that purpose and bring that to community, a new purpose arises. The acting life, and later writing and filmmaking have enabled me to find meaning and places where I felt I belonged, such as in that Floating Islands' rehearsal room. As one who trains those in the art of acting, I need to open pathways for that meaning and belonging to come forward. Myth and story are the perfect portals for that.

During my actor training at SUNY Purchase, I found myself often diminishing who I was in order to fit in to the idea of human behavior that was prevalent. The focus in that training was method acting. "The Method," as it has come to be known, asks an actor to use personal memory as the core of their work. Founded on some of Stanislavski's training ideas, the Method evolved as an American variant focusing on drawing from intimate private experiences to find authenticity. Popularized by Lee Strasberg[4] at the Actors' Studio in New York City, it became important in the post-World War II period and is particularly associated with actors such as Marlon Brando and Dustin Hoffman. The alienation I felt was not created consciously by any of my teachers; it was just that a certain Anglo way of being was seen as "believable" and anything outside of that "unreal" or "fake." I was taught to explore my own experiences in order to overlap my emotional life to the characters. In my view, that overlap is inevitable whenever we read, see, or listen to a piece of theatre or film work. Where we need attention and energy is outside of what Method acting gives us, it is an opening to what we do not know or have not experienced. Since we all have the memory of human history in our bones, it is in our bones, beyond our singular life, that we can look to for that deep knowledge. I am not saying there is no place for method acting and I am not putting forward an alternate to the method. What I propose with this mythic acting invitation is an approach that works alongside the method and allows for a wider view of what it means to authentically represent a role.

With mythic acting, we are asked to push beyond the limits of our singular life experience and move to a realm where dreams and imaginations thrive. It is a way to invite poetry, mystery, and metaphor into the actors training and everyday practice. In mythic acting, we release into the deep wisdom of the archetypal, rather than incorporate work that has moored itself solely to the rational.

## How Mythic?

Now that I have laid out my perspective on Latinx and introduced the mythic approach, let us talk about ways to invite the mythic into our practice. One of the first exercises I like to do with the actors I work with is to center and listen. Here is an exercise to get to there—

- Sit with your eyes closed, if you can, or look straight on to the horizon. Notice your breath as it travels in and out of your body. Feel your feet making contact with the floor. Imagine that you have roots that extend from the bottoms of your feet deep down into the earth. Connect with the energy line moving through the center of your body, through the center of your head, and roots that extend upward toward the sky. Feel the point between your belly button and your pubic bone, your center, and how that point connects to the core of the earth. Feel the place your shoulder blades connect with your back, where your wings are, and imagine those wings spreading wide. Now, with this full body, earth, sky, core of earth connection, just breathe, nice and easy. Take a moment to acknowledge the great gift of simply and fully being in the here and now.
- Imagine that behind you are your parents, whether by blood, spirit, or kindred, and they've got your back. Behind them your grandparents, of blood, spirit, or kindred. Behind them your great grand-parents and so on extending as far back millennia. These are the folks who made it possible for you to be right here, right now and in the beauty of your breath and the present moment.

- Now imagine those who will come after you, your children, whether of blood, spirit, or kindred. They are in front of you. Then imagine their children and so on. Imagine the myriad of people whose lives you can and will affect, just by being you, stretching out before you.
- Now come back to the here and now. Be in the space that you are in, in between those who came before you and those to come. Feel those who have your back and those whose lives you will affect. Breathe that in.

That is a centering exercise to open your channel and to aid in feeling your mytho-poetic place in the cosmos. Below is an exercise that can follow. It is the Duende exercise and is meant for an actor to connect deeply with the material they are working on. The writings of Lorca on Duende made such an impact on me that I named the initiative that I run, Duende CalArts, after this idea. Although, it is more of a life force than an idea. With this exercise you can participate using any text. The main thing is to be open to whatever may emerge and allow for as much physical and vocal expression and liberation as possible. Below is an explanation of Duende by the master, Federico García Lorca, himself—

- Center yourself as in the exercise above. Read aloud the following words from Lorca's lectures that are published in the book *In Search of Duende*:

  *The duende is a momentary burst of inspiration, the blush of all that is truly alive, all that the performer is creating at a certain moment. . . . It is truly deep, deeper than all the wells and seas in the world, much deeper than the present heart that creates it or the voice that sings it, because it is almost infinite. . . . The figure of the cantaor[5] is found within two great lines, the arc of the sky on the outside, and on the inside the zigzag that wanders like a snake through his heart. . . . When the cantaor sings he is celebrating a solemn rite. He rouses ancient essences from their sleep, wraps them in his voice, and flings them in to the wind. He has a deeply religious sense of song. . . . Through these chanters the race releases its pain and its true history. They are simple mediums, the lyrical crest feathers of our people. . . . They are strange but simple folk who sing hallucinated by a brilliant point of light trembling on the horizon. The duende, then, is a power, not a work. It is a struggle, not a thought. I have heard an old maestro of the guitar say, 'The duende is not in the throat; the duende climbs up inside you, from the souls of the feet.' Meaning this: it is not a question of ability, but of true, living style, of blood, of the most ancient culture, of spontaneous creation. This 'mysterious power which everyone senses and no philosopher explains' is, in sum, the spirit of the earth.*[6]

- Gather in a circle. Take a few moments as a group to feel the energy between you and allow Lorca's words to resonant and fill you. Feel that spirit of the earth as it travels from the souls of your feet up through your entire body. When one actor feels ready, they will come in to the center of the circle. The others will close the circle to fill in the gap of the person stepping in. The actor in the center will now act as a conductor of sorts, and silently lead those in the circle in some kind of sound to support their exploration of their text. It may be a soft clap, or wind type sound through the teeth, or stomping of feet. The person in the center will signal to those in the circle to bring the sound up or down, like a conductor, as the outer circle acts as musicians supporting the person in the center's exploration. Those in the outer circle must pay close attention, be in complete active listening to the one in the center and their "conducting" of the sounds to support their text. The person in the center then will give in to the Duende and begin to speak with this support of sounds all around them. They can stop the sound, adjust, and change it at any time. The goal is to release into the Duende and find new power, abandon, breaking of patterns with the text. It may come out completely different from what was practiced, that's just fine. The main thing is to crack open the heart, the channel and submit to the Duende. When that person has done several lines of their text, they can return to the circle and the next person can go.

This exercise can be very invigorating, as well as emotionally and physically exhausting. Please be aware of that before you do the exercise. Usually, a group of about 12 or so can do this exercise in an hour and a half. It is a great way to open that mythic portal and invite something other than the left brain work in to your process. Actors I have worked with through the years have communicated to me that this exercise has become a central part of their practice.

## Why Now?

We are in the midst of a tectonic human shift, and we need great art to meet the changing landscape. We need great stories that speak to our conditions and great interpreters of those works, actors, who can meet those much-needed stories and lift us up to help us imagine a better future with dignity for all. Our practice needs to be inclusive, needs to raise us out of our limited experiences and move us toward the expansive. We need to move away from our industrial assembly line approach to actor training and toward those grand circles that remind us of our lineage, a storytelling history and practice that has existed for over 40,000 years.

As a Latinx actor, I know the importance of bringing this practice that invites the imagination full force forward. Without this the work is hollow and lacks inspiration. We need that *sabor*, that serious fun, that the mythic invites to make our practice come alive, because it is connected to the ancestral.

For actors and practitioners alike, allow into your process the mytho-poetic, that which makes your soul sing. Remember that no one has the market cornered on great stories. Wherever you come from, whoever you are, you come from great stories, great performance traditions. Do not be afraid to bring forward from whatever particular cultural, racial, gender, ability, and ethnic lens you come from that which stirs deeply within. That is your mythic at work. It is connected to both your personal history AND that which is anchored in the cosmos and your imagination. Rely on those soul stirrings that don't entirely make "sense" but call you to follow. Our art form cannot lead with the rational; it must lead with the intuitive, that is the mythic. You do no one any favors leaving yourself out of the process, or trying to fit a frame, a mold, that cannot contain your enormity. When you enter the work, the environment you are brought to, and share your mythic self, everyone benefits. I invite you to center in your acting practice, your full, soulful, mythic self.

## Notes

1. To further explore this rich history, I recommend reading *Ornament of the World* by María Rosa Menocal and *Aristotle's Children* by Richard E. Rubenstein.
2. Federico García Lorca, Christopher Maurer, and Giovanni N. T. Di, *In Search of Duende* (New York: New Directions, 1998). Print.
3. The book offers ideas and practices that will help actors to build a sustainable and nourishing life. It explores awareness work, solo performance creation, the power of archetypes, character building exercises, creating a body/text connection, and how to be the detective of your own process. Marissa Chibás, *Mythic Imagination and the Actor* (London: Routledge, 2021).
4. Lee Strasberg, *The Lee Strasberg Notes* (Routledge, 2010).
5. Cantaor is a singer, in this case, of the Spanish tradition called Flamenco. One can easily substitute actor for cantaor as the sentiment can apply for both art forms.
6. García Lorca, *In Search of Duende*, viii.

## Bibliography

Chibas, Marissa. *Mythic Imagination and the Actor*. London: Routledge, 2021.
García, Lorca F., Christopher Maurer, and Giovanni N. T. Di. *In Search of Duende*. New York: New Directions, 1998. Print.
Strasberg, Lee, and Lola Cohen. *The Lee Strasberg Notes*. London: Routledge, 2010.

# 10
# THE LATINX ACTOR'S LINGUISTIC IDENTITY

## Preserving Our Culture in Speech Training

*Cynthia Santos DeCure*

The act of recognizing and honoring the truth of our linguistic identity can ground and fuel our impulses as Latinx/e actors. However, when speech training stifles cultural linguistic identity, the actor may find bringing their full self to the work challenging. In this essay, I contextualize how standard speech training, as a component of actor training, has led to sound erasure and gatekeeping for the Latinx actor. Although many of the examples in this essay may apply to actors of the Global Majority, I purposely narrow the scope to the Latinx/e experience in an effort to center our community. I briefly chronicle the historical lineage of speech training, and how teaching toward a prescriptive sound can erase identity. I further connect how oppressive practices in American actor speech training can result in linguistic insecurity for some Latinx actors, and how the media contributes to a vicious cycle in training that perpetuates the ongoing stigmatization of non-standard speakers. Finally, I share some of my teaching strategies and culture-sustaining practices for honoring and preserving linguistic identity in Latinx actor training.

As an actor, I have spent over 30 years working in theatre, television, and film in both Spanish and English. My work as a voice, speech, and dialects professor has led me to teach at several Hispanic Serving Institutions (HSIs), in Bachelor of Arts (B.A.), conservatory Bachelor of Fine Arts (B.F.A.), and Master of Fine Arts (M.F.A.) acting programs. I have discovered that regardless of the institution, many Latinx actors in training encounter stumbling blocks due to biased attitudes about how they should sound. This gate-keeping mentality is pervasive, has prevented countless Latinx/e actors from experiencing actor training as a playground for expanding themselves as artists, and has even kept some from entering training programs altogether. These biases exist in many facets of academia and can be linked to attitudes and policies about language competencies in education.[1] Linguistic and language scholars refer to this situation as a "state of emergency"

DOI: 10.4324/9781003021520-13

for Latinos in education and argue that labeling languages as "foreign" has fueled the practice of "continued inequalities."[2]

Education scholars have found that although our classrooms are now more culturally and linguistically diverse, teaching approaches have not fully embraced diversity as a strength, yet Latinx diversity continues to grow.[3] "By 2024, 29 percent of all students will identify as Latinx, 6 percent as Asian/Pacific Islander, and 15 percent as African American. Today, 9.2 percent are classified as English learners."[4] Research reveals that "rather than building on students' linguistic and cultural backgrounds, schools often 'subtract' these rich resources from students' learning experiences."[5] By acknowledging the many biases about language embedded in the education system, we can interrupt their manifestation in actor training.

The practice of voice and speech training for actors in the United States has evolved in the last century and is a foundational part of actor training programs. While our classrooms are diverse with multilingual and multi-dialectical performers whose idiolects, or individual accents, span the globe, the curriculum of most training programs across the United States still focuses on teaching to a prescriptive "Standard American" sound. This mode of teaching has been in use for nearly a century and, hence, restructuring and replacing it is a challenge. Historically, teaching speech in actor training has focused on shifting the actor's accent[6] or dialect[7] toward the "standard" sound accepted by the dominant culture or the individual program. American actor training has adopted the notion that in order for an actor to be well trained, they must align their speech patterns to a "neutral," "unmarked American" sound; the rationale is that this equips the actor with more possibilities beyond merely playing characters within their own accent. This pedagogical practice has been particularly evident in the approach to training Latinx actors; as Espinosa and Ocampo-Guzman noted, "Latino students are typically required to standardize their speech sounds. With this standardization practice, programs may inadvertently shut down an inherent part of the individual's identity and diminish their students."[8]

## Standard Accent and the Legacy of "Good American Speech"

In order to examine the current practices of teaching speech, I will offer a brief summary of its historical context. Sociolinguist Rosina Lippi-Green describes in her research the common notion of standard U.S. English as ". . . the language spoken and written by persons

- with no regional accent;
- who reside in the Midwest, far west or perhaps some parts of the north east (but never in the south);
- with more than an average or superior education;
- who are themselves educators or broadcasters;

- who pay attention to speech, and are not sloppy in terms of pronunciation or grammar;
- who are easily understood by all;
- who enter into a consensus of other individuals like themselves about what is proper in language."[9]

Lippi-Green charges "standard language" and "non-accent" speech both as "abstractions and as myths,"[10] pointing out that we all have accents, and further noting that "the myth of standard language"[11] has served to empower certain social groups and disempower others. In essence, this constructed formula of what is "standard" can be regarded as both an ideology and a myth.

This standard language or pronunciation myth in American actor training derives from a similar ideology in the use and teaching of British Received Pronunciation,[12] also known as the Queen's English. The US standard training modality harkens back to the early days of elocution classes. The late actor and speech teacher Dudley Knight extensively documented the lineage in his article *Standard Speech: The Ongoing Debate*."[13] Knight traced it back to Australian-born elocution teacher William Tilly, who taught in Germany, England, and at Columbia University as a phonetics instructor. Tilly developed a "distinctive ideology of speech standards and a distinctive pedagogy."[14] Two of Tilly's prominent students, Margaret McLean and Edith Skinner, further expanded the standard speech idea in the United States. Together, they cultivated a regimented system of speech training that singled out speakers outside their prescribed pedagogy, deeming "the influences of masses of uneducated foreigners who speak English with many non-English sounds, foreign stress . . . and intonation" as a primary cause for America's supposedly "poor" speech.[15] McLean and Skinner described their approach as teaching "Good American Speech." In the introduction of her influential book *Speak with Distinction*, first published in 1942 and revised in 1966, Skinner detailed that "Good Speech is a dialect of North American English that is free from regional characteristics; recognizably North American, yet suitable for classical texts; effortlessly articulated and easily understood in the last rows of a theater."[16] With this book, Skinner—and many of her students who became teachers themselves—disseminated a system of selected phonetic "sounds of spoken English" that offered two dialectical variations, General American and Good Speech. The system employs the use of selected sounds of spoken English, a specific cursive style of phonetic transcription, a reduction of R-colored vowels, and an alternative pronunciation of words utilizing the intermedial [a] vowel for an "Ask-List" of words among various other features. The "Ask List" offers a pseudo-British sound as recommended pronunciation for classical texts. Knight recognized this "prescriptive" methodology as mired in "a model of class, ethnic, and racial hierarchy that is irrelevant to the acting of classical texts," and oppressive to "one's cultural essence."[17] Many teachers of Skinner's method disagreed with Knight and have defended the intent and the benefit of her work.[18] Some have abandoned the "value-loaded terms" of "good" or "standard" and have shifted to teaching it as a "model, a point of reference, a map."[19] At any rate, Skinner's contribution to American actor training is recognized and respected by many teachers and students alike. Yet, regardless of the intent of her work, which may well have been to open possibilities for the actor, the work's prescriptive nature—coupled with the rigid manner in which some teachers teach it—has been injurious to the cultural voice of the Latinx actor. As more actors of the Global Majority continue to participate in actor training, many have found standard speech training processes to be "othering" toward them.

Although Knight developed a more inclusive, descriptive approach to speech training in his Knight-Thompson Speechwork[20] (KTS), Skinner's "Good Speech," or a variation of her method, is still taught in several programs across the country today and continues to influence the manner in which many Latinx actors encounter training. My intent is not to vilify one methodology over another, but simply to contextualize how the legacy—and mainly the interpretation, or misinterpretation—of Skinner's work has influenced and maintained assumptions that speech training for the actor, and specifically the Latinx actor, must focus on standardizing their sound. In examining this issue, I acknowledge that I base my opinions about Skinner's method on my own experience as a student of her work as part of my initial speech training, and having had to teach the work years ago in an acting program. I also acknowledge that I am trained and certified in KTS, which approaches speech training from different perspectives. However, my experience as a student and teacher of multiple methods of voice and speech allows me to examine the subject matter through a broader lens. Latinx actors in training may not question the pedagogies offered, but may rather accept them as a part of their training. Yet, oppressive methodologies—those that repeatedly single out one community as "non-standard" versus another "standard" group—are doing damage. Voice and speech and Linklater Designated teacher Louis Colaianni agrees and notes that since publishing his book, *The Joy of Phonetics and Accents*, in 1994, he has been "changing the central column of authority" and does not teach to a "standard."[21]

Today, a growing number of voice and speech teachers, including many members of the Voice and Speech Trainers Association (VASTA), are raising awareness of oppressive practices in our pedagogies and seeking strategies to eliminate them.[22] In fall 2020, as a part of my role as VASTA's director of Equity Diversity and Inclusion, I curated and moderated an anti-oppression panel. Our panelists, Nicole Brewer (Anti-Racist Theatre Training), Kaja Dunn (Theatrical Intimacy), and Leslie Ishii (artEquity) had a robust discussion urging voice and speech practitioners to center the most vulnerable students in training, value the actors' culture, and continuously interrogate the inherent biases embedded in speech, accent, and dialect training. VASTA members Melissa Tonning-Kollwitz and Joseph Hetterly, in their research of standard dialect use in teaching speech pedagogy, concluded that "there is a shift [in the use] away from SSD [Standard Stage Dialect]" and toward "GenAm [General American]" and a "desire for better contextualization of the inherent racial . . . implications of standard dialects."[23] In their research into the use of a standard stage dialect in selected regional theaters and Broadway, they concluded that the growing practice is that of coaching for the demands of the project rather than requiring the actor to possess a unified standard sound.[24]

But voice, speech, and dialects are not exclusively taught by members of VASTA. In fact, many general theatre practitioners and scholars are often assigned to teach these courses without the necessary training, nor an understanding of the inherent bias contained in "standard speech" and how this prescriptive sound can oppress students of the Global Majority. Additionally, private acting studios may employ an actor or a director with only the experience in voice and speech they know from their own training, but no culturally inclusive knowledge or voice and speech expertise. Hence, many continue to teach this prescriptive work. I believe that, ultimately, university programs, acting studios, professors, and coaches share equal responsibility for the proliferation of teaching and training that has led so many actors, directors, and theatre and film makers to believe that one codified sound is superior and should be the standard for all speakers.

## Speech Training or Linguistic Bias?

> *So, if you really want to hurt me, talk badly about my language. Ethnic identity is twin skin to linguistic identity—I am my language.*[25]
>
> Gloria Anzaldúa

The late scholar Anzaldúa connected identity directly with language in a way with which I, as a bilingual Latina, can also identify. I understand the oppressive harm that some Latinx actors experience in terms of their cultural linguistic identity. When I moved from Puerto Rico to California in the ninth grade, a teacher immediately told me my English was not good enough to enter a "regular" English classroom and instead enrolled me in English as a Second Language (ESL) classes. Although I had learned English as a part of my elementary to middle school instruction in Puerto Rico, at the time I was primarily a Spanish-language speaker. I spent the semester in ESL with students from Mexico, Guatemala, and El Salvador. We used our class time reciting greetings, listening to recordings, and practicing pronunciation drills. One thing was consistent: Our teacher spoke to us as if we lacked intelligence, rather than recognizing that we simply did not possess the English language fluency to express ourselves. The teacher also displayed a biased assumption that our lack of English language comprehension and pronunciation impaired our capacity to succeed academically.

Years later, in my actor training speech classes, I experienced what Anzaldúa describes as an attempt to "tame the wild tongue."[26] That meant doing countless pronunciation exercises and taking ample criticism for my non-standard Puerto

Rican accent. Teachers told me my "R's" were "too strong," and my pronunciation of the /ɪ/ vowel KIT,[27] in Standard American English, was wrong, as I was using the "Spanish" long /iː/ FLEECE instead. They told me that to truly learn Standard American English pronunciation, I had to stop speaking Spanish altogether. No other choice was offered. I wondered: Is there a way in my training to embrace my bilingualism and natural sound? Through these challenging experiences, I began to imagine ways to train actors that would not strip them of their cultural linguistic identity, which I also equate with our natural impulses in acting.

In my training and career, I have been increasingly aware that our voices reveal the essence of who we are. Every time we speak, we are sharing aural clues to the listener about our identity. Our individual voices and dialects are a reflection of our own existence. Although we may be adept at code-switching, or being multidialectical, Latinx actors are oppressed when we are criticized for our sound. Hence, much of the challenge in training is tied to listening, and the perspective with which we listen. Professor and sound researcher Jennifer Stoever posits, "the sonic color line connects sound with race in American culture, showing how listening operates as an organ of racial discernment."[28] This concept of "color listening" creates an expectation that the Latinx actor should perform their Latinx identity via their sound, perpetuating a racialized representation of sound, such as expecting a Mexican actor to sound as if they have an accent, even if they do not own that accent. All the while, the actor is urged to strip all traces of their accent and perform to the established standard. Essentially, the actor feels as if they must simultaneously conform to the expected stereotyped sound and the prescribed standard. These demands have tangible consequences, as teachers and program directors may not consider the actor for casting in the mainstage plays, classics, and other contemporary works where they are expected to have a "neutral" sound, and may underestimate the actor's ability and talent to embody the character. Instead, they may only cast these actors in parts that call for a "Latinx sound," or small roles with little dialogue. In academic program speech classes, the student may even receive a low course grade for not achieving the learning objectives—that is, the expected transformation of their sound—in the given time of a semester, regardless of the actor's efforts.

These harmful practices pressure the Latinx actor to acquiesce to the standard training, often perpetuating a sense of "linguistic insecurity,"[29] or causing anxiety and shame about their sound, as the actor submits to countless classes of accent reduction or modification. These experiences may eventually lead to a denial or erasure of personal identity. Anti-racist theatre facilitator, Nicole Brewer contends that the process of erasure "privileges the experience of the white students" because the training favors those in the dominant culture.[30] To this point, anthro-political linguist Ana Celia Zentella argues that education is geared toward the dominant narrative language and supports the power structure.[31] She adds that linguistic insecurity "is exacerbated by continued critiques . . . contributing to the 'Chiquita-fication,' i.e., the diminishment and disparagement of Latina/o languages and identities."[32] Some students may experience speech training as if they are constantly under added corrective scrutiny from both their teachers and peers. The consequences of the Latinx actor choosing not to conform to the expected speech standard, especially in a conservatory program, may result in their being deemed "difficult" to train or excluded from training altogether.

Why, then, do programs continue to rely on these practices when many educators today recognize that such methods disproportionately "otherize" the cultural voice? For many programs, the answer is: Tradition—and the perception that if these methods are altered or replaced with culturally inclusive processes, the rigor and status of a program will somehow be diminished. Another rationale is that some programs are training for the demands of the "industry," which continues to prize a neutral sound. I believe these justifications are seriously misguided.

As actor trainers we need to continuously reflect on "who" and "why" we are training. Is it for the actor? Or are we serving the expectation of audiences already conditioned by what they routinely see and hear on stage, television, and film? We also need to examine how media feeds the training. The media promotes and reinforces stereotypical attitudes about non-dominant sounds and displays a constant preference for the "standard language ideology" of the correct speech.[33] Many years ago, the established "standard accent"—a construct of a Midwest American sound—became a model for broadcasters. Thus, the media has inculcated the ears of generations of listeners with the perceived "correct" sound. Historically, once this model became embedded in our media and education systems, it replicated and took hold as the "accent perceived to be standard."[34]

The media creates a cycle of sound preferences as they reinforce stereotypes,[35] because we as audiences have been accustomed to expecting a certain accent or dialect to represent education or authority.[36] As Zentella notes, "Latinas/os are usually portrayed as speakers of disparaged dialects."[37] Hence, actor trainers must interrogate how the hierarchy of power and voice affects our conscious and unconscious biases as listeners, and how speech is taught in a performance studio. Is the training creating a vicious cycle? Actors are often trained to emulate the perceived correct sound in the industry, but that sound is already filtered, or curated, based on the perceptions of those who teach, create, and produce the work in those industries and bring their own distinct aesthetics and attitudes to decide how the actor ought to sound.

The popular belief within programs that we are training for the industry is misinformed because today's audiences are growing more discerning, and demand stories that reflect our communities with linguistic authenticity. Therefore, bringing this authenticity to storytelling requires expanding the linguistic palette and restructuring the way actors are trained in speech and dialects, not diminishing their linguistic value. I propose a conscious shift in speech training, which includes training the actor in a way that preserves the cultural voice, implementing inclusive approaches and hiring expert faculty who can teach with cultural specificity. In my pedagogy as a voice, speech, and dialects teacher, I work to empower actors to recognize the beauty and uniqueness of their idiolects. I believe we can train actors via a skills-based approach that is comprehensive, rigorous, and culturally inclusive.

## Reclaiming and Reaffirming *Nuestras Voces*. Building a Culturally and Language Inclusive Pedagogy

In my classroom, I celebrate the linguistic diversity and identity of each actor and champion their visibility and audibility. I place a high value on cultural specificity of identities in voice, speech, accents, and dialects. My approach embraces a competency perspective rather than a deficit perspective. I recognize the complexities and nuances of our Latinx identity and communities. My bilingualism serves as a model for students to take pride in their own multi-lingual and multi-dialectical selves, reminding them that they are the experts of their own sounds.

For more than a decade, I have been building a "culturally relevant"[38] and "culturally sustaining"[39] pedagogy in my acting, speech, accents, and dialects teaching practice. Education scholar Gloria Ladson-Billings describes this approach as work aimed at helping students succeed by maintaining a connection to their culture and their native language as part of their schooling.[40] This pedagogy also "acknowledges the legitimacy of cultural heritages of different ethnic groups, both as legacies that affect students' dispositions, attitudes and approaches to learning and as worthy content to be taught in the formal curriculum."[41] I view this practice of including culture in academic and studio actor training as one that can empower and counteract the type of erasure in which "we are taught to suppress our voices and accents, and with them, our identities."[42] This inclusive practice recognizes the importance of "engaging the full cultural context of the actor"[43] as a part of their artistic development. "[T]hrough embracing difference in theatre arts training, all students can be empowered to perform to their full potential, regardless of their heritage and identity—and indeed because of the power of each student's unique cultural context."[44] I recognize the value of this approach from both the student's and teacher's perspective. Hence, I embrace a clear shift in the training to a mode that is more inclusive and celebrates our cultural and linguistic identities, while widely expanding the actor's skills.

This culturally sustaining approach does not diminish the complexity and rigor of teaching speech, accents, and dialects. It means that by first centering the linguistic identity of the actor, all other sound learning that follows is offered as accents or dialect options, not as a prescriptive standard. The actor's linguistic identity is the center point from which all other sounds are learned. I describe this in my teaching practice as *transforming from self*.

Another way to describe this process is to think of the actor's sound as being the central location, and the movement toward a new sound—based on the demands of the character—as the vocal transformation journey. The actor's vocal journey returns home upon the completion of the performance or sound exploration. Most importantly, the process does not demand or suggest that the actor eliminate their home sound as a part of their speech training.

This approach differs from other processes, as it calls on actors to use their idiolect as the *center point* of learning. In order to do so, actors must first have the opportunity to discover their home sound without judgment and celebrate its uniqueness. One way I approach this is to prepare for this exploration by researching and validating the actor's idiolect, which adds to my cultural competency to teach the actor in front of me. I work with the actor to discover the physical actions of their articulation. For the Latinx actor with a Spanish-influenced idiolect, this work may entail helping them discover where, in their vocal tract, they realize certain sounds. For example, where do they articulate the /t/ and /d/ phonemes, at the dental ridge or the alveolar ridge? As we learn how they articulate sounds, I help them discover other possibilities, but avoid making corrections. Instead, I demonstrate and help them feel in their vocal tracts how they can shape those phonemes in a myriad of accents. I refer to this as "learning the choreography of sounds." This process helps the actor expand their awareness of transformation. They develop body memory and flexibility in their vocal tract. Most significantly, the Latinx actor has agency to choose if, how, and when they want to shift their sound for the demands of a particular role. No prescriptive standard is imposed.

The actor exploration may be in the form of a heritage, personal accent, or idiolect project by which the actor investigates their idiolectical sound production. It often includes listening to recordings of their speech as well as the sound of close relatives or others in their hometown and taking a phonetic inventory of their pronunciation and prosodic[45] features to create a vocal guide of their idiolectical sound. This personal vocal guide serves as a reference point for all other accent and dialect learning. This exploration of one's sound is not solely for the Latinx actor, but is for all actors in the classroom. It is a way for the actor to discover their own cultural context or personal given circumstances. Actors learn how they articulate each sound in order to take ownership of their own linguistic identity, and sometimes even reclaim an accent that may have been lost or repressed. Although different versions of the home project exist, my approach includes modeling with my own linguistic journey, experience, and cultural knowledge as a way to inspire actors to bravely explore their idiolectical sounds.

My instruction begins with contextualizing the history of speech training and sharing my anti-racist theatre ethos. The actor learns how sounds have been colonized and historically codified. This process interrogates the power dynamics that have influenced speech training, and allows us to begin to examine the identity of sounds and how they translate into soundscapes around the globe from an inclusive perspective. While learning about our idiolects, I engage some of the foundational precepts of KTS, gently guiding actors to discover their vocal anatomy, the articulatory muscles that shape sounds, and the physical actions of speech utilizing the full International Phonetic Alphabet (IPA) through rigorous play and descriptive exploration. This skills-based approach does not promote one sound as neutral or standard over another, but rather, is inclusive to help train actors from all languages and cultural backgrounds.[46] I introduce all the phonetic sounds from across the globe that make up the IPA rather than merely the sounds of English. In this exploration, students recognize their own linguistic sounds as a part of the larger soundscape of speech. I use my training and understanding of multiple voice methodologies, including Fitzmaurice Voicework®, always searching for which approach works best for the actor in front of me. My cultural knowledge as a Latina and lived experience as a working actor helps me bring nuanced understanding to speech training.

The culmination of this simultaneous exploration of our idiolects and sounds of speech is celebrated with a sharing. Each student performs a sharing for the entire class, which includes the history of each actor's sound as well as a piece of text or song in their idiolect. This offering, or performance of self, is both empowering and educational.* The sharing educates and acculturates the ear of each listener, guiding each classmate toward a more inclusive, culturally competent and empathetic way of working. This learning journey serves to affirm identity. It also allows each actor to learn other accents and dialects from their personal sound perspective with greater investment and freedom to play.

I propose these pathways for supporting Latinx actors in speech training:

- *Cultivate the actor's connection to culture.* Cultural connection and authenticity are essential to, and empower, the actor's development. Encourage actors to use monologue and scene work[47] that allows them to bring their culture into the work.
- *Move away from teaching to a "standard."* Instead, encourage actors to build their skills with all sounds of the IPA, which includes their home sounds. Offer a possible pathway to transform to the demands of the given character, rather than requiring the actor to abandon their home sound.
- *Celebrate the actors' idiolects.* Using either an idiolect project or a personal accent research project, create a way for the actor to center their linguistic identity.
- *Allow the Latinx actor to incorporate Spanish and bilingualism in their work, but do not force it.* The actor needs to have agency to decide when they want to use Spanish. Create a space where the actor can feel like they can use language without judgment, but do not insist that the actor "translate" on the spot. Be aware that forcing translations sometimes creates an injurious impromptu "performance of culture" that "others" and disempowers the actor.
- *Assess each actor's progress from an individual standpoint.* This means approaching speech training from a "capabilities perspective"[48] rather than a deficit perspective. Find new ways to evaluate their expansion. Set the actor up for success by assessing the skills they are acquiring in training, rather than creating an inflexible goal.

- *Re-train educators and employ speech and dialect coaches who have cultural competency and are adept in guiding language.* Actor trainers need to understand the cultural, lexical, and prosodic differences and nuances within Latinx identities. Not all Latinx actors are alike and they should not be treated as such.
- *Continuously re-examine the tools, techniques, and canon of plays employed in your teaching and reframe them through an inclusive cultural lens.* Decolonize the canon and refrain from using resources that reinforce stereotypes. Survey whether the material being offered is out of date or contains attitudes about speech that exclude and even oppress the multicultural voice.

We can empower Latinx actors to acquire highly complex skills of linguistic transformation without stripping them of their identities. Training actors with a culturally sustaining methodology expands their skills in rigorous ways. By interrogating, contextualizing, and replacing historically oppressive systems with inclusive pedagogies, we can welcome actors to bring their entire cultural selves into training and enrich our practice in identity-affirming ways. I believe the future of American theatre is one that is multicultural, multi-dialectical, and multi-lingual. Hence, actor training must foster a path where the actor's individuality is recognized and valued as integral to the learning process. Through these inclusive methods, we can help Latinx actors expand their skills and not merely survive, but thrive in training.

## Notes

1. Glenn A. Martínez and Robert W. Train, *Tension and Contention in Language Education for Latinxs in the United States* (New York: Routledge, 2020), 12.
2. Ibid., 10–11.
3. K. Puzio et al., "Creative Failures in Cultural Sustaining Pedagogy," *Language Arts* 94, no. 4 (2017): 223–33.
4. Between fall 2009 and fall 2018, the percentage of public school students who were Hispanic increased from 22 to 27 percent. The percentage of public school students who were White decreased from 54 to 47 percent, and the percentage of students who were Black decreased from 17 to 15 percent. See National Center for Education Statistics, "Racial/Ethnic Enrollment in Public Schools," accessed May 2021, http://nces.ed.gov/programs/coe/indicator_cge.asp.
5. Puzio et al., "Creative Failures in Cultural Sustaining Pedagogy."
6. An *accent* can be defined as the manner in which language is pronounced and can be associated with region, ethnicity, or socioeconomic status. See Collins and Mees, *Practical Phonetics and Phonology*, 295.
7. A *dialect* is a variety of the language, which includes differences in grammar, vocabulary, and pronunciation within the language. See Collins and Mees, *Practical Phonetics and Phonology*, 297.
8. Micha Espinosa and Antonio Ocampo-Guzman, "Identity Politics and Training of Latino Actors," in *The Politics of American Actor Training*, eds. Ellen Margolis and Lissa Tyler Renaud (New York: Routledge, 2010).
9. Rosina Lippi-Green, *English with an Accent: Language, Ideology and Discrimination in the United States* (London: Routledge, 2012), 60.

10 Ibid., 54.
11 Ibid., 59.
12 Received Pronunciation (RP) is described as the British developed "prestige accent." At one time it was the only accent employed by the British Broadcasting Company, BBC. See Collins and Mees, *Practical Phonetics and Phonology*.
13 Dudley Knight, "Reprint Standard Speech: The Ongoing Debate," *Voice and Speech Review* 1, no. 1 (2000): 31–54.
14 Louis Colaianni, *The Joy of Phonetics and Accents* (Kansas City: Joy Press, 1994), 54.
15 Margaret Prendergast McLean, *Good American Speech* (New York: E.P. Dutton and Company, 1941), 53.
16 Good Speech, as Skinner described it, has been also referred to as "Eastern Standard" or "Theater Standard." See Skinner, *Speak with Distinction*, ix.
17 Dudley Knight, "Reprint Standard Speech: The Ongoing Debate," *Voice and Speech Review* 1, no. 1 (2000): 31–54.
18 David Hammond, "Another Opinion: Reflections on Skinner in the Classroom and in Rehearsal," *Voice and Speech Review* 1 (2000): 131–42.
19 Ralph Zito, "Essay Who I Am, What I Teach, and Why I Teach It," *Voice and Speech Review* 1, no. 1 (2000): 79–88.
20 Knight-Thompson Speechwork, developed by Knight and fellow speech teacher Phil Thompson, is a skills-based approach to speech and accent training for actors that places emphasis on developing the speaker's detailed awareness of the precise physical actions which make up speech. KTS offers a certification program for teachers of speech and dialects.
21 Louis Colaianni, interview by Cynthia Santos DeCure, personal interview, July 24, 2021.
22 Amy Mihyang Ginther, "Dysconscious Racism in Mainstream British Voice Pedagogy and Its Potential Effects of Students from Pluralistic Backgrounds in UK Drama Conservatoires," *Voice and Speech Review* 9, no.1 (2015): 41–60; Daron Oram, "Decentering Listening: Toward an Anti-Discriminatory Approach to Accent and Dialect Training for the Actor," *Voice and Speech Review* 15, no. 1 (2021): 2–26.
23 Melissa Tonning-Kollwittz and Joe Hetterly, "The Current Use of Standard Dialects in Speech Practice and Pedagogy: A Mixed Method Study Examining the VASTA Community in the United States," *Voice and Speech Review* 12, no. 3 (2018): 295–315.
24 Melissa Tonning-Kollwitz, Joe Hetterly, and Ellen Kress, "The Current Use of Standard Dialects in the United States Theatre Industry," *Voice and Speech Review* 15, no. 2 (2021): 1–15.
25 Gloria Anzaldúa, *Borderlands/La Frontera: The New Mestiza*, 4th ed. (San Francisco: Aunt Lute, 2012), 81.
26 Ibid., 75.
27 KIT and FLEECE are part of the 24 lexical sets devised by the phonetician John Wells. Lexical sets serve as a tool for describing the vowel inventory and distribution of different accents. See John C. Wells and John Corson Wells, *Accents of English*, vol. 1 (Cambridge: Cambridge University Press, 1982).
28 Jennifer Lynn Stoever, *The Sonic Color Line: Race and the Cultural Politics of Listening* (New York: New York University Press, 2016).
29 Ana Celia Zentella, "Dime con quién hablas, y te diré quién eres: Linguistic (In)security and Latina/o Unity," in *A Companion to Latina/o Studies*, eds. Juan Flores and Renato Rosaldo (Malden: Blackwell Publishing, 2007), 35.
30 Nicole Brewer, "Training With a Difference," *American Theatre* 35, no. 1 (2018): 54–58.
31 Ana Celia Zentella, "The Power of Words: Keynote" (Presented at South Carolina: The Sustainability Institute, College of Charleston, South Carolina, August 25, 2018), www.youtube.com/watch?v=YIFwIy1IfSg&t=2s.
32 Ana Celia Zentella, "Dime con quién hablas, y te diré quién eres: Linguistic (In)security and Latina/o Unity," in *A Companion to Latina/o Studies*, eds. Juan Flores and Renato Rosaldo (Malden: Blackwell Publishing, 2007), 32.

33 M. Dragojevic et al., "Silencing Nonstandard Speakers: A Content Analysis of Accent Portrayals on American Primetime Television," *Language in Society* 45, no. 1, (2016): 59–85.
34 Thomas Paul Bonfiglio, *Language, Power and Social Process, Vol. 7, Race and the Rise of Standard American* (Berlin and New York: De Gruyter Mouton, 2010).
35 Joe R. Feagin and José A. Cubas. *Latinos Facing Racism: Discrimination, Resistance and Endurance* (Boulder: Paradigm, 2014).
36 Dragojevic et al., "Silencing Nonstandard Speakers: A Content Analysis of Accent Portrayals on American Primetime Television."
37 Ana Celia Zentella, "Dime con quién hablas, y te diré quién eres: Linguistic (In)security and Latina/o Unity," in *A Companion to Latina/o Studies*, eds. Juan Flores and Renato Rosaldo (Malden: Blackwell Publishing, 2007), 26.
38 Gloria Ladson-Billings, "But That's Just Good Teaching! The Case for Culturally Relevant Pedagogy," *Theory into Practice* 34, no. 3 (1995): 159–65.
39 Geneva Gay, *Culturally Responsive Teaching: Theory, Research, and Practice* (New York: Teachers College Press, 2000).
40 Ladson-Billings, "But That's Just Good Teaching! The Case for Culturally Relevant Pedagogy."
41 Gay, *Culturally Responsive Teaching*.
42 Cynthia L. Santos DeCure, "Miss Quince: Writing and Performing Latina Identity" (Thesis., California State University, Los Angeles, 2012).
43 Chris Hay and Kristine Landon-Smith, "The Intracultural Actor: Embracing Difference in Theatre Arts Teaching," in *New Directions in Teaching Theatre Arts*, eds. Anne Fliotsos and Gail S. Medford (Cham: Palgrave Macmillan, 2018), 158.
44 Ibid.
45 Prosody or prosodic features refer to suprasegmentals such as "stress, duration, rhythm, tempo, lexical tone and intonation of an utterance." See Janet Fletcher, "The Prosody of Speech: Timing and Rhythm," in *Handbook of Phonetic Sciences*, eds. William J. Hardcastle, John Laver, and Fiona E. Gibbon (West Sussex: Blackwell Publishing Company Ltd., 2010), 523.
46 Andrea Caban, Julie Foh, and Jeffrey Parker, *Experiencing Speech: A Skills-Based, Panlingual Approach to Actor Training* (New York: Routledge, 2021).
47 *Monologues for Latina/o Actors* by Micha Espinosa *and Scenes for Latinx Actors* by Micha Espinosa and Cynthia DeCure offer a myriad of options for use in classroom. See Micha Espinosa, *Monologues for Latino/a Actors: A Resource Guide to Contemporary Latino/a Playwrights for Actors and Teachers* (Hanover, NH: Smith and Kraus Publishers, 2014); Micha Espinosa and Cynthia DeCure, *Scenes for Latinx Actors: Voices of the New American Theatre* (Hanover, NH: Smith and Kraus, 2018).
48 Martinez and Train define a "capabilities approach" as one that goes beyond language assessments to maintain or revitalize language. See Martínez and Train, *Tension and Contention in Language Education for Latinxs in the United States*, 149.

## Bibliography

Anzaldúa, Gloria. *Borderlands/La Frontera: The New Mestiza*. 4th ed. San Francisco: Aunt Lute, 2012.
Bonfiglio, Thomas Paul. *Language, Power and Social Process. Vol. 7, Race and the Rise of Standard American*. Berlin, NY: De Gruyter Mouton, 2010.
Brewer, Nicole. "Training with a Difference." *American Theatre* 35, no. 1 (2018): 54–58.
Caban, Andrea, Julie Foh, and Jeffrey Parker. *Experiencing Speech: A Skills-Based, Panlingual Approach to Actor Training*. New York: Routledge, 2021.
Colaianni, Louis. *The Joy of Phonetics and Accents*. Kansas City: Joy Press, 2000.
Collins, Beverley, and Inger M. Mees. *Practical Phonetics and Phonology: A Resource Book for Students*. London: Routledge, 2013.

Dragojevic, Marko, Dana E. Maestro, Howard Giles, and Alexander Sinbk. "Silencing Nonstandard Speakers: A Content Analysis of Accent Portrayals on American Primetime Television." *Language in Society* 45, no. 1, (2016): 59–85.

Espinosa, Micha. *Monologues for Latino/a Actors: A Resource Guide to Contemporary Latino/a Playwrights for Actors and Teachers*. Hanover, NH: Smith and Kraus Publishers, 2014.

Espinosa, Micha, and Cynthia DeCure. *Scenes for Latinx Actors: Voices of the New American Theatre*. Hanover, NH: Smith and Kraus, 2018.

Espinosa, Micha, and Antonio Ocampo-Guzman. "Identity Politics and Training of Latino Actors." In *The Politics of American Actor Training*, edited by Ellen Margolis and Lissa Tyler Renaud, 150–61. New York: Routledge, 2010.

Feagin, Joe R., and José A. Cubas. *Latinos Facing Racism: Discrimination, Resistance and Endurance*. Boulder: Paradigm, 2014.

Fletcher, Janet. "The Prosody of Speech: Timing and Rhythm." In *Handbook of Phonetic Sciences*, edited by William J. Hardcastle, John Laver, and Fiona E. Gibbon, 521–602. West Sussex: Blackwell Publishing Company Ltd., 2010.

Garcia, Ofelia, and Wei Li. *Translanguaging: Language, Bilingualism and Education*. New York: Palgrave Macmillan, 2014.

Gay, Geneva. *Culturally Responsive Teaching: Theory, Research, and Practice*. New York: Teachers College Press, 2000.

Ginther, Amy Mihyang. "Dysconscious Racism in Mainstream British Voice Pedagogy and Its Potential Effects of Students from Pluralistic Backgrounds in UK Drama Conservatoires." *Voice and Speech Review* 9, no.1 (2015): 41–60.

Hammond, David. "Another Opinion: Reflections on Skinner in the Classroom and in Rehearsal." *Voice and Speech Review* 1 (2000): 131–42.

Hay, Chris, and Kristine Landon-Smith. "The Intracultural Actor: Embracing Difference in Theatre Arts Teaching." In *New Directions in Teaching Theatre Arts*, edited by Anne Fliotsos and Gail S. Medford, 157–73. Cham: Palgrave Macmillan, 2018.

Knight, Dudley. "Reprint Standard Speech: The Ongoing Debate." *Voice and Speech Review* 1, no. 1 (2000): 31–54.

Ladson-Billings, Gloria. "But That's Just Good Teaching! The Case for Culturally Relevant Pedagogy." *Theory into Practice* 34, no. 3 (1995): 159–65.

———. "I'm Here for the Hard Re-set: Post Pandemic Pedagogy to Preserve Our Culture." *Equity & Excellence in Education* 54, no. 1 (2021): 68–78.

Lippi-Green, Rosina. *English With an Accent: Language, Ideology and Discrimination in the United States*. London: Routledge, 2012.

Martínez, Glenn A., and Robert W. Train. *Tension and Contention in Language Education for Latinxs in the United States*. New York: Routledge, 2020.

McLean, Margaret Prendergast. Papers of Margaret Prendergast McLean, 1878–1961. Archives and Special Collections, Colorado State University.

———. *Good American Speech*. New York: E.P. Dutton and Company, 1941.

National Center for Education Statistics. "Racial/Ethnic Enrollment in Public Schools." Accessed May 2021. http://nces.ed.gov/programs/coe/indicator_cge.asp.

Oram, Daron. "Decentering Listening: Toward an Anti-Discriminatory Approach to Accent and Dialect Training for the Actor." *Voice and Speech Review* 15, no. 1 (2021): 2–26.

Paris, Django. "Culturally Sustaining Pedagogy: A Needed Change in Stance, Terminology, and Practice." *Educational Researcher* 41, no. 3 (2012): 93–97.

Puzio, Kelly, Sarah Newcomer, Kristen Pratt, Kate McNeely, Michelle Jacobs, and Samantha Hooker. "Creative Failures in Cultural Sustaining Pedagogy." *Language Arts* 94, no. 4 (2017): 223–33.

Santos DeCure, Cynthia L. "Miss Quince: Writing and Performing Latina Identity." Thesis., California State University, Los Angeles, 2012.
Skinner, Edith. Edith Warman Skinner Papers, 1902–1981. Curtis Theatre Collection, Archives & Special Collections, University of Pittsburgh Library System.
———. *Speak with Distinction.* New York: Applause, 1990.
Stoever, Jennifer Lynn. *The Sonic Color Line: Race and the Cultural Politics of Listening.* New York: New York University Press, 2016.
Tonning-Kollwitz, Melissa, and Joe Hetterly. "The Current Use of Standard Dialects in Speech Practice and Pedagogy: A Mixed Method Study Examining the VASTA Community in the United States." *Voice and Speech Review* 12, no. 3 (2018): 295–315.
Tonning-Kollwitz, Melissa, Joe Hetterly, and Ellen Kress. "The Current Use of Standard Dialects in the United States Theatre Industry." *Voice and Speech Review* 15, no. 2 (2021): 1–15.
Wells, John C., and John Corson Wells. *Accents of English.* Vol. 1. Cambridge: Cambridge University Press, 1982.
Zentella, Ana Celia. "Dime con quién hablas, y te diré quién eres: Linguistic (In)security and Latina/o Unity." In *A Companion to Latina/o Studies*, edited by Juan Flores and Renato Rosaldo, 25–38. Malden: Blackwell Publishing, 2007.
———. "The Power of Words: Keynote." Presented at South Carolina: The Sustainability Institute, College of Charleston, SC, August 25, 2018.
Zito, Ralph. "Essay Who I am, What I Teach, and Why I Teach it." *Voice and Speech Review* 1, no.1 (2000): 79–88.

# 11

# ACCENT AND DIALECT TRAINING FOR THE LATINX ACTOR

*Cynthia Santos DeCure*

Accents and dialects are an integral part of actor–character construction and offer authenticity to storytelling. Traditionally, institutional or studio-based actor training includes some accent and dialect instruction, but for the most part, it is limited to European accents or regional American accents. Unfortunately, "accents and dialects of Latinx identities"[1] are not routinely taught in US actor training, leaving the Latinx/e actor to either self-study or forgo learning these accents and dialects altogether. The study and performance of Latinx sounds is complex and requires in-depth research, understanding, and cultural specificity. Accents and dialects of Latinx/e identities are specialized and worth studying as a foundational step in Latinx actor training. Without nuanced, skillful learning for actors and directors alike, stereotypes and generalizations of "Latinx accents" are formed, codified, and propagated resulting in erroneous portrayals of our community on stage and screen.

In this chapter, I address the current void of this specialized training for the Latinx actor and its effect on productions that particularly call for accents and dialects of Latinx identities. I share some strategies in approaching the teaching and coaching the work, and offer a sampling of accent-building skills to empower the Latinx actor in their study and the embodiment of the linguistic sounds of our Latinx communities. Lastly, I highlight why I believe authentic linguistic representation can serve as an identity-affirming act for both the performer and the Latinx community.

My foundation of accent and dialect training began as a child in Puerto Rico listening to the syncopated rhythms of Afro-Caribbean music my late father, a saxophone player and arranger–composer, would play. As a native Spanish speaker, I would watch movies and TV programs in Spanish from Mexico, Spain, Venezuela, and Argentina, and practice imitating the accents. I enjoyed performing the different accents to entertain my siblings. Through this playful exploration,

DOI: 10.4324/9781003021520-14

I developed a deep curiosity for the specificity of accents in Spanish. My actor training introduced me to Standard American English, regional American accents, and a few European-based dialects in English. It was only when I began to audition for professional acting jobs in theatre, TV and film in Los Angeles that called for accents of Spanish, that I realized my actor training had not prepared me to work in that capacity. In order to compete for these roles, I returned to my childhood curiosity, which was to listen carefully, examining the rhythm, and to emulate the accent. With each audition, I began to decode another accent and added to my skill set. Soon, other actors were asking me to assist them in their accent preparation. Later, I fortified my education and training with two certifications in voice, speech, accents, and dialects to better understand the work as a player and as a coach. I have presented my continued research at several Association of Theatre in Higher Education (ATHE) and Voice and Speech Trainers Association (VASTA) conferences in hopes of bringing attention to the need for specificity in accents and dialects of the Latinx community. As a part of my practice, I have created numerous accent and dialect breakdowns in both Spanish and English for teaching and coaching, which will be published in a future book. My research is integral to my teaching and coaching, not only in working with Latinx/e actors but also as a contribution to the accurate portrayals of our rich Latinx/e stories in theatre, film, and television.

## The State of Affairs

In American actor training, accent and dialect instruction is framed through the dominant narrative. Traditionally the curriculum ranges from regional American accents, such as American Southern,[2] New York, British Received Pronunciation (RP), Irish, and Scottish to European dialects spoken in English. The accents and dialects commonly taught depend on the program's preferences and, perhaps more often, the personal strengths and comfort zone of the teacher. If an accent of Spanish is introduced at all, it is presented almost entirely in "general"[3] form, without much specificity.

In recent years, more Latinx actors are seeking training in accents and dialects that represent Latinx linguistic identities rather than in traditional European dialects, and some institutions have reached out to me to teach workshops for their Latinx actors. Many professional Latinx actors I have recently worked with bemoan their not having received instruction in accents of Spanish as a part of their actor training. For the most part, these accents are not included in the academic curriculum, even in programs that serve a large number of Latinx actors such as those in Hispanic-serving institutions. As a result, Latinx actors often miss out on the necessary accent and dialect training that can expand their skills to accurately represent our communities in performance.

However, one M.F.A. acting program in the late 1980s and early 1990s offered training for the actor in "Hispanic Accents" in both English and Spanish. The short-lived Hispanic-American Masters of Fine Arts degree in Theatre,[4] a program headed by Dr. Jorge Huerta, a Chicano Theatre scholar and professor emeritus at the University of California, San Diego, offered a variety of courses specifically for the Hispanic/Latinx actor. Huerta recognized the need to prepare our community's actors to be able to tell our stories authentically.

One of the reasons I have found accents, dialects of Latinx identities are not routinely offered is the lack of training and understanding in this area. While we have more trained Latinx acting and voice and dialect coaches working today, not enough are teaching in training programs. If these accents and dialects are taught by other practitioners, the sources used are typically created by non-Latinx, non-native Spanish-speakers and often rely on static, dated materials laden with reductive generalities and lacking culturally inclusive linguistic details. In other instances, popular films with stereotyped representations may be used as models. Moreover, nearly all guides are written for teaching "general Spanish" from the point of view of language used in Spain, and using basic sound changes between the Spanish and English languages, but rarely offer the specificity of a distinct accent and musicality from a particular region or country.

I find one of the greatest challenges to be a lack of cultural competency on the part of the teacher, teaching institution, director, or production company. Often a teacher or director will assume that because an actor is Spanish-speaking or Latinx—even if not Spanish-speaking—they already inherently possess the ability to perform all accents of Spanish. This lack of nuanced understanding of differences in cultural and linguistic identities diminishes the complexity and importance of our sounds. The result is to shift the responsibility to the actor to research and prepare dialect work on their own. For example, the Latinx actor may be tasked to perform an accent of Spanish outside of their own idiolect, cross culturally, such as a Dominican actor playing a character from Mexico City. The burden is placed on the actor to research and learn the new dialect on their own with the mistaken assumption that the linguistic transformation from one Latinx identity to the other is effortless. Sometimes this task is shifted to a Latinx classmate or other Latinx person in the production who does not have any expertise in accents and dialects but simply speaks Spanish.

Latinx actors recognize a double standard in that teachers, directors, and productions are unconcerned about the specificity of the accents of Spanish these actors employ, yet they require the utmost precision when actors use accents representing lionized European identities. This lack of regard for the specificity of accents of Latinx identities results in stereotypical Latinx portrayals on stage and in film.[5]

Accents of Spanish are complex. There is not one "standard Spanish accent,"[6] and hence the study cannot be reduced to one sound. Although many of the accents share a common language, Spanish, they differ distinctly in pronunciation and vocabulary depending on the region. Each accent and dialect bears the nuanced linguistic details of a place of origin, with multiple possible variations within the same country or territory. For example, we cannot simply seek a "Mexican" accent without addressing with specificity a geographic location and the age, gender, and socioeconomic status of the character, among many other detailed "given circumstances." The dialect of a speaker from Mexico City is different from the one from a border town such as Ciudad Juarez, or the Mexican-American sound of a speaker from East Los Angeles. Another significant detail is that not all Spanish speakers have accented English, and for those who do have a "perceived accent," not all features of their first language, Spanish, transfer into an accent sound change in English. Yet, often this lack of knowledge in the classroom or production process can perpetuate bold generalizations and distorted representations of accents of the Latinx community.

## Teaching and Coaching Latinx Accents and Dialects

One of the most perceptible, audible differences between various accents of Latinx identities that I recognize—in Spanish or English—is *prosody*. This feature can be described as the rhythm of the different accents—in essence, the distinct musicality that the native speaker of the language and region uses. This musicality of the accent influences the segmentation of syllables in words and thus the pitch and intonation we hear.[7] This key ingredient in the accent-building recipe is what I most often find missing in an authentic performance, and frequently is the starting point for how I begin to study a sound.[8] In this section I share some of my strategies for building my research to teach accents and dialects of Latinx identities. When I am researching an accent or dialect for class or coaching, I consider the following: cultural context, vocal tract posture (including placement of resonance and energy), phonology, and prosody.

*Cultural context* is an integral part of my process because in order to understand accents and other idiolectical variations, we must understand the people who speak these sounds, which includes history of the region or regions, second language influences—in particular Indigenous languages—how sounds change over time, geography, and more. By researching cultural context of a given accent, I learn vital details to some regional pronunciations and specific phonetic usage and thus contextualize how this cultural sound may inform the storytelling of the character, play, or film.

I listen to multiple native speakers of this sound and examine their *vocal tract posture*, which is the unique way speakers configure their muscles in the vocal tract—their articulators (i.e., the lips, tongue, and soft palate)—and, in other words, what muscles are tense or relaxed or not engaged at all. This posture influences the shaping of the sound. Without a re-acclimation of the vocal tract muscles, some phonetic sounds of a given accent may not form and sound as intended. Accents and dialects in every language have their unique vocal tract postures, and hence this accent-building ingredient allows the actor to create a linguistic transformation that is more authentic and embodied. For example, the phonetic sounds /t/ and /d/ in many American English pronunciations are realized with the tip of the tongue exploding against the alveolar ridge, the bumpy area behind your top front teeth. In many accents of Spanish, the tongue contact of speakers happens against the top front teeth, creating a dental /t̪/ /d̪/ articulation, which indicates that the posture of the tongue may be higher and forward in the vocal tract. The actor working on an accent of Spanish can practice re-orienting their tongue placement for the dentalized sounds to create muscle memory, gain fluency for these sounds, and apply them depending on the character's accent features.

Another key accent recipe ingredient is *phonology*, which involves gathering the phonetic inventory of the sounds the accent or dialect produces. I research the phonology, and then fortify the phonetic information with my perceptive examination of the sound samples. I use the full International Phonetic Alphabet (IPA) as my guide and create a profile. By working with the full IPA palate of sounds, I am able to demonstrate to actors which sounds are new to their linguistic sound usage, and which ones they own or transform in the given accent.

English and Spanish languages have different phonetic inventories. Spanish employs five vowels, whereas American English has 11.[9] When speaking English, some native Spanish speakers will employ their five-vowel inventory to voice words that in English are pronounced with a vowel not used in Spanish. For example, words in English pronounced with the phonetic vowel [ɪ], as in KIT, may be pronounced[10] by a native Spanish speaker when speaking English, with the [i] vowel, as in FLEECE, because [i] is the sound in their Spanish inventory of vowels. Thus, KIT may sound like *keet* [kiːt]. The same can be said for consonant sounds, as some English consonant sounds do not exist in Spanish or are pronounced with a different level of articulatory effort, and hence sound different when speaking English.

However, a few sounds exist in Spanish phonology that are not represented in American English and, to my ear, indicate the geographic placement of the speaker's accent. For example, some Spanish-accent speakers, namely Caribbean, pronounce the initial consonant phonetic sound in the names *Juan* or *Javier* as /h/, a voiceless glottal sound. Other Spanish-accent speakers, such as from certain regions of Mexico and regions of Spain, may routinely utilize the voiceless velar fricative[11] /x/ for [xuan] or [xavieɾ].[12] This vital phonetic information, which many Spanish speakers transfer into their pronunciation in English, allows the actor learning the accents to more accurately differentiate the interpretation of characters from these regions in both Spanish and English.

One of the most challenging misconceptions about accents of our Latinx communities is the representation of the phonetic sound /r/ or the alveolar trill. This is the sound I most frequently hear misused in dialect performances because not all Spanish speakers use a strong treatment of /r/, especially in the initial position of a word. This overemphasis happens when the actor over-articulates the sound or uses it where it should not be substituted. All "r" consonant sounds are not pronounced the same in accents of Spanish and thus do not carry the same degree of rhotic articulation into the speaker's English idiolect.[13] I work with the actor to find the appropriate balance for this sound and avoid stereotyping this feature.

The elements of *prosody*, including the rhythm, intonation, and resonance of the accent, are what I consider the "sauce" in each unique accent recipe. Prosody provides clues that "facilitate human language acquisition" and the perception of accents.[14] This is important to note because English is considered a "stress-timed" language, meaning that stress syllables give an indication of the rhythm, whereas Spanish is considered a "syllable-timed" language and its rhythm is perceived as having a more equal distribution of time between its syllables. Also, there is a closer one-to-one correspondence between the orthographic (the written word), meaning that words spelled in Spanish sound closer to how they are spelled, but words in English frequently sound different from their spelling. A character who is a second-language English speaker and native Spanish speaker may pronounce a word with the syllable segmentation of their native language and the intonation of their accent. The prosody of a speaker, especially in Spanish, offers rhythmic clues as to whether they are, for example, from Bogota, Buenos Aires or Santo Domingo, and so on. Therefore, when approaching an accent of Spanish, we must consider how the rhythm needs to be re-acclimated from the starting point of the actor's idiolect to that of the character's sound. Some accents of Spanish may have a stronger perceived prosody, while others may have a light rhythmic quality. The actor should be cautious not to get stuck in one repetitive intonation. Prosodic phrasing and intonation are not formulaic and do not repeat in an even pattern from sentence to sentence, but rather follow the meaning of what the speaker is communicating. As a strategy, I use multiple sound samples in both Spanish and English to sketch out the movement of the prosody in order to best illustrate it for the actor. I practice with the actor to incorporate the prosody into the sense and meaning of the thought of the given character.

This approach of emphasizing the prosody, vis-à-vis the musicality, was key in coaching the actors in *El Huracán*,[15] Yale Repertory Theatre's premiere of Charise Castro Smith's play. Set in Miami, this story centers on four generations of Cuban and Cuban-American women dealing with forgiveness and the aftermath of hurricanes. The play calls for a Cuban dialect from Havana (both in Spanish and English), Miami Cuban-American accents, and a young Miami (second-generation Cuban) English sound. Honing in on the specific levels of the musicality of each of the sounds helped the actors more fluidly embody the rhythm of the varied Cuban accents.

Because I am an actor, when teaching and coaching I also take into account the process of creating a character. I search for textual clues in the script to ground the accent or dialect choices to the given circumstances of the character. When teaching these accents and dialects in the classroom, I try to offer them in the context of a play. For example, I employ plays by Eduardo Machado or Nilo Cruz for regional Cuban accents, and Luis Alfaro's trilogy of Greek plays to study California Mexican-American or Chicano English (CE).[16] By placing the instruction in the context of a play, we can avoid generalities about all speakers of a given accent and instead concentrate on the character's linguistic actions and how they serve the storytelling.

I create a phonetic blueprint of sounds native speakers of the accent own, and which are appropriate for the given character, to best help the actor transform into the accent. As part of my own culturally inclusive pedagogy, I consider the actor's own idiolect and their phonetic inventory. If working with a native Spanish-speaking actor, I guide them from the perspective of their own specific cultural sound. If working with a non-Spanish-speaking Latinx actor, I start by mapping out the differences between their English stress-timed language and the syllable-timed language that influences accents of Spanish. When working with an Afro-Latinx actor on a Latinx accent, I am mindful to include samples representative of the given Afro-Latinx community. For instance, with a play set in Colombia, I include samples from Afro-Colombian speakers. In essence, because we all come from different cultural and linguistic backgrounds, Spanish-speaking or not, I start my teaching from the particular actor's point of reference toward the target accent. I continue being mindful to avoid biases or generalizations about speakers of any given sound.

One important fact to note is that not all accents and dialects of Latinx identities come from speakers whose first language is Spanish. For example, linguist Carmen Fought describes CE as "influenced by contact with Spanish, and spoken as a native dialect by both bilingual and monolingual speakers."[17] CE is not "Spanglish" although it may employ some code-switching. Unfortunately, actors and teachers not familiar with this variety of English may misinterpret CE as an English learner's or second-language speaker's dialect. For instance, I recently coached two Caribbean (Puerto Rico and Dominican Republic) bilingual actresses on a scene from Luis Alfaro's *Electricidad*. Neither was familiar with the rhythm of Alfaro's language or the sound of the East Los Angeles Mexican-American community. Their first impulse in approaching the dialect was to think of it as second-language speakers of English, and their phonetic sound changes were initially overdone. One of the most salient features of the CE dialect is the prosody, in particular, how speakers employ shifts in intonation and lengthening of syllables.[18] Therefore, in approaching this text we worked with lengthening, pitch, inflection, and tempo, especially in words that were operative in the thought and meaning of what the character was conveying. This approach more accurately reflected the sound of speakers of this dialect and helped the actresses honor and integrate the sound.

Every time I coach a dialect, I enhance my existing research to further expand my cultural knowledge because I understand that accents change over time, and not all speakers from the same area sound alike. For instance, my work on Marissa Chibás' play *Shelter* enriched my cultural insight into Central American dialects. *Shelter* recounts the painful experiences unaccompanied minors from Honduras, Guatemala, and El Salvador encounter when crossing the US border. Several of the play's characters were primarily Spanish-speaking, and spoke Spanish (from their home country) as well as accented English. As part of my research,

I gathered sound samples that were closer to the ages of the characters from youth migrants I interviewed at the Central American Resource Center in Los Angeles. These interviews enhanced my cross-cultural understanding, and served both as a dialect resource for the actors and as an additional dramaturgical reference, which in turn enriched the actors' desire to honor the linguistic identities in the play.

I recognize that not all teachers of accents and dialects have the time or resources to delve into this work with the care and generosity they may want to offer to their students. However, our Latinx actors deserve to learn this work with specificity. Thus, I suggest that academic programs, theaters, and productions hire teachers and dialect coaches who have the linguistic and cultural expertise to teach accents and dialects of Latinx identities. Such intentional action will create opportunities for actors to acquire the skills needed to begin to embody and share these sounds truthfully. I do caution against cultural appropriation, via Latinx accent and dialect work, which is historically problematic in the dominant culture. The aim of this work is to empower the Latinx actor.

## For the Latinx Actor

*Te veo y te escucho. I see you and I hear you.*

In this section I offer suggestions for the Latinx actor to fortify their embodiment of accents and dialects. Learning and integrating an accent or dialect as part of the acting process takes time. It is imperative to work with accents at the start of any rehearsal process—the earlier the better, for any accent. By routinely working on the vocal instrument, you, the actor, are making sure your vocal tract is flexible and can acclimate to the shaping of sounds. Hence, practicing the muscularity of articulation is vital to adjust the vocal tract closer to the needs of the accent. For accents of Spanish the practice of shaping the Spanish vowels is a great way to prime your articulators. I have included a brief offering to warm up into the shaping of Spanish vowels.

### *Spanish Vowel Shaping Warm-Up*[19]

*(This section is part of larger warm-up that I offer when coaching. It is inspired by my childhood Spanish phonetics instruction and incorporating modified exercises from KTS.)*[20].

Begin with a robust body and breath warm-up, such as Fitzmaurice Voicework®[21] or Linklater[22] progression. Breath support is integral to articulatory action.

- **Massage facial muscles**
    - Starting at the forehead hairline, slowly run fingers down the face, releasing the facial muscles, the masseter (that runs along the side of cheecks and jaw).

- Tap your face and scalp to encourage blood flow and awareness.
- Use your fingertips to massage your scalp around your skull and forehead and eye sockets.

- **Move facial muscles**
  - Continuously create extreme shapes or *haciendo muecas*—without sound for 10–15 seconds; then add sound for 10–15 seconds. Breathe.

- **Jaw**
  - *Note: Please work gently on the jaw. The goal is to allow your jaw to release to gravity.*
  - Rub your hands together to warm them. Apply the heel of the hands to your jaw joint and gently massage. Then drag the heel of your hands down the masseter (sides of the face) to your mandible (chin) as you exhale. (Repeat 2–3x.)
  - *Follow with additional jaw release exercises.*

- **The Vowel Shaping [a], [e], [i], [o], [u]**
  - Using a mirror, begin the practice by shaping all five vowels <u>without sound</u>. (It is important to establish shaping body memory without relying on sound.)
  - *Release each shape to an <u>expressionless</u> face in between each vowel so that each shape starts anew.*
  - **[a]** <u>Drop</u> the jaw, opening your mouth, releasing the tongue into a cup or well with the front of the tongue behind the lower front teeth. (This is a lower jaw placement than for words like TRAP.) Pause in the shape for five seconds. *Without sound—feel the breath flow, and energy in the center well of the tongue. Release. Then quickly shape and release three times.*
  - **[e]** <u>Pull straight back</u> your lip corners toward your ears—lateral and flat. Use your index fingers to hold the shape if needed. Pause in the shape for 5 seconds. *Without sound, feel the breath flow, and energy in the middle top of the tongue. Release. Then quickly shape and release three times.*
  - **[i]** <u>Pull up</u> lip corners up to your cheekbones to a high smile. Pause in the shape for 5 seconds. *Without sound, feel the breath flow, and energy toward the top front teeth. Release. Then quickly shape and release three times.*
  - **[o]** <u>Round</u> lip corners into a tight "O" shape. See the shape in the mirror—open the O shape slightly. Use your index fingers to feel how far forward your lip corners have traveled. Check the shape. Pause in the shape for 5 seconds. *Without sound—feel the breath flow, and energy toward the inside of your lips. Release. Then quickly shape and release three times.*
  - **[u]** <u>Purse</u> lips and protrude them forward. Practice the forward motion. Pause the shape of pursed lips forward for 5 seconds. *Without sound—feel*

*the breath flow, and energy toward your lips. Release. Then quickly shape and release three times.*

- Now that you have practiced the shape, *add* the sound. Repeat the shaping sequence again, this time <u>adding the voicing sounds</u> and shapes of the 5 Spanish vowels. *(Remember, you are shaping the sounds of Spanish vowels and they will not sound as you hear them in English.)*
- Repeat the sequence of this exercise 3–5 times. Alternate, not using a mirror, to test your body memory. Practice the flow from one shape to the next. The aim is to work out your vocal tract posture to feel and remember the shape of this new sound and to gain facility to shift from your personal vocal tract posture. You are creating body memory.

Follow with additional warm-up exercises that include the release of the tongue, the movement of the soft palate, and dynamic consonant practice, and conclude with speaking text in the accent.

As you prepare your accent study, be specific to the character. If your script does not provide specific location for the accent, ask your playwright or director and if need be, make a distinct choice so that your accent is rooted in the authenticity of speakers of a specific area. For example, if your character is contemporary, such as, a 22-year-old Mexican-American female from El Paso, Texas, from the 1970s, then your sound model will be that of female Mexican-American speakers from that area, time and preferably the same age range. Interviews and oral histories of the area are often great sources. Remember, a contemporary speaker today may not share the same linguistic features of a speaker from decades ago.

Listen to multiple native speakers of the accent, if possible, in Spanish and in English. Attune your ear to the similarities and differences among the speakers. Collect sound samples from native accent speakers. Interview your *abuela*, or your *tio*, friends, and family who own distinct accents and dialects you are seeking to learn. Watch how they hold and release their articulators as they speak. Practice moving your lips as you watch or listen to your samples. Describe the musicality and, if you can, diagram your impression of the movement. Notate the sound changes you hear in your own words and if possible, using the phonetic symbols of IPA.

This is not a comprehensive guide, but is simply a few accent-acquiring skills to help you get started within the pages of this chapter. Whenever possible, work with an expert.

If you are a Latinx actor who does not own an accent of the Latinx community and are learning this anew, dialect training can serve as linguistic retro-acculturation. You can reclaim the sounds of your cultural history that may have been erased or never been taught to you by learning how to articulate them through accent work. It is never too late to learn to embody the sounds of your ancestors.

## Why Do I Teach This Work? Why Is This Work Important?

There is something so profoundly powerful that happens when we see *and* hear ourselves reflected on stage and screen. Our very existence is validated. I experience what Jill Dolan refers to as "hope in the theatre," an optimistic feeling in which through "utopian" moments in performance we can see a possibility for a better world, recognizing our "human commonality despite the vagaries of difference."[23] For me, the act of being seen and *heard* in our full linguistic identity activates a feeling of belonging. Every act of presenting our Latinx stories authentically is an enunciation of self. I recognize this powerful, affirming effect in Latinx/e actors who embody accents and dialects reflective of our communities. This is one reason I am passionate about this work and take great care in offering it in the classroom and in my professional coaching. It is my hope that through this endeavor, actors and audiences can experience the feeling of belonging and move one step closer to understanding our collective humanity.

## Notes

1. For the purposes of this chapter only, I use the term "accents and dialects of Latinx identities" to refer to accents of Spanish (as represented in Spanish in Latin America), as well as dialects spoken in English by Latin American and/or Latinx speakers in the United States. I acknowledge and value the distinction between each accent and dialect, and by no means reduce the complexity of the myriad of linguistic identities to "one" category, nor do I dismiss the intersectionality of language, culture, and race.
2. American Southern, as termed in many dialect resources, describes a compilation of several variations of accents of the American South.
3. I refer to "general" as broad accent and dialect information.
4. The program existed at University of California, San Diego, from 1989 to 1992 and only graduated ten students. See Jorge Huerta Papers, 1964–2008, MSS 142, Special Collections & Archives, UC San Diego Library, San Diego, California.
5. Cynthia Santos DeCure, "Linguistic Identity and Hollywood: Hoping Spielberg and Sorkin Got the Latinx Accents Right," *Visible Magazine*, accessed December 10, 2021, https://visiblemagazine.com/lingustic-identity-hollywood-hoping-spielberg-and-sorkin-got-the-latinx-accents-right/.
6. The term "Standard" in Spanish, sometimes referred to as *neutro,* is an accent used by broadcasters, announcers or in film dubbing. Several Spanish-speaking countries or regions may have their own *neutro,* but the concept is subjective as there is no one "standard." *Neutro* is problematic because it is laden with attitudes about "standard accents."
7. Adrian Leemann et al., "The Role of Segments and Prosody in the Identification of a Speaker's Dialect," *Journal of Phonetics* 68 (2018): 69–84, https://doi.org/10.1016/j.wocn.2018.02.001.
8. Cynthia Santos DeCure, "The Rhythm of Spanish Accents" (Paper presented at the Voice and Speech Trainers Association International Conference, Central School of Speech and Drama, London, England August 5–9, 2014).
9. Dudley Knight, "American Vowel Phonemes," in *Speaking with Skill: An Introduction to Knight-Thompson Speechwork* (London: Bloomsbury, 2012), 179–84.
10. I say "may be pronounced" because depending on the speaker's level of English language pronunciation fluency, they may be adept at employing the American English phonetic vowels in their speech.

11 The voiceless velar fricative sound /x/ is realized with the middle to rear part of the tongue closing toward the soft palate to create slight friction.
12 Phonetic consonant usage is not consistent throughout all Spanish-speaking countries and regions; thus, the voiceless velar fricative /x/ is employed by some speakers. See Campos-Astorkiza, "Consonants," in *The Cambridge Handbook of Spanish Linguistics*, ed. Kimberly L. Geeslin (Cambridge: Cambridge University Press, 2018), 165–89.
13 In Spanish words with "rr" spelling, the sound is made with the alveolar trill (rolling r), however in other placements 'r'--intial, middle and ending--the manner of articulation may be tapped, slightly trilled, devoiced or even omitted altogether, depending on the particular accent.
14 Philippe Boula de Mareüil, Giovanna Marotta, and Martine Adda-Decker Adda-Decker, "Contribution of Prosody to the Perception of Spanish/Italian Accents," in *Proceedings of Speech Prosody* (Nara: SProSIG, 2004), www.isca-speech.org/archive/speechprosody_2004/boulademareuil04_speechprosody.html.
15 *El Huracán's* premiere in 2018 and was produced in partnership with the Sol Project, a theatre initiative that amplifies the voices of Latinx playwrights in the American Theatre.
16 As referred to by sociolinguist Carmen Fought. She describes it as the English variety spoken by some Mexican American residents in California. See Carmen Fought, *Chicano English in Context* (Basingstoke: Palgrave Macmillan, 2003).
17 Fought, *Chicano English in Context*, 1.
18 Ibid., 70–78.
19 This Spanish vowel section is part of a much larger warm-up. These exercises are particularly helpful for actors in need of strengthening their pronunciation of accents of Spanish, or those acquiring the sounds anew.
20 Knight-Thompson Speechwork is a skills-based approach to speech, accent, and dialect training for actors. Many beginner speech exercises can be found in their new book. See *Experiencing Speech: A Skills-Based, Panlingual Approach to Actor Training* (New York: Routledge, 2021).
21 Fitzmaurice Voicework® is a comprehensive, holistic approach that combines classical voice training with adaptation of several body-based disciplines. It can support speaking for performance, public speaking, singing, voice with movement, and vocal rehabilitation, and aid in developing greater presence.
22 The Linklater Voice progression is a series of exercises that seek to undo habitual tensions that inhibit expression. The progression helps enliven the connection with the voice, body, and imagination.
23 Jill Dolan, *Utopia in Performance: Finding Hope at the Theater* (Ann Arbor: University of Michigan Press, 2008), 171.

## Bibliography

Bassiouney, Reem. *Identity and Dialect Performance: A Study of Communities and Dialects*. London: Routledge, 2017.

Caban, Andrea, Julie Foh, and Jeffrey Parker. *Experiencing Speech: A Skills-Based, Panlingual Approach to Actor Training*. New York: Routledge, 2021.

Campos-Astorkiza, Rebeka. "Consonants." In *The Cambridge Handbook of Spanish Linguistics*, edited by Kimberly L. Geeslin, 165–89. Cambridge: Cambridge University Press, 2018.

Canfield, Delos L. *Spanish Pronunciation in the Americas*. Chicago: University of Chicago Press, 1992.

Chism, Cori, and Norman J. Lass. "Perception and Analysis of Spanish Accents in English Speech." *The Journal of the Acoustical Society of America* 111, no. 5 (2002): 2367. https://doi.org/10.1121/1.4777997.

Collins, Beverley, and Inger M. Mees. *Practical Phonetics and Phonology: A Resource Book for Students*. London: Routledge, 2013.

De Mareüil, Philippe Boula, Giovanna Marotta, and Martine Adda-Decker. "Contribution of Prosody to the Perception of Spanish/Italian Accents." In *Proceedings of Speech Prosody*. Nara: SProSIG, 2004. www.isca-speech.org/archive/speechprosody_2004/boulademareuil04_speechprosody.html.

DeCure, Cynthia Santos. "The Rhythm of Spanish Accents." Conference presentation at the Voice and Speech Trainers Association International Conference, Central School of Speech and Drama, London, August 5–9, 2014.

Dolan, Jill. *Utopia in Performance: Finding Hope at the Theater*. Ann Arbor: The University of Michigan Press, 2008.

Espinosa, Micha, ed. *Monologues for Latino/a Actors: A Resource Guide to Contemporary Latino/a Playwrights for Actors and Teachers*. Hanover: Smith and Kraus Publishers, 2014.

Espinosa, Micha, and Cynthia DeCure, eds. *Scenes for Latinx Actors: Voices of the New American Theatre*. Hanover: Smith and Kraus, 2018.

Fought, Carmen. *Chicano English in Context*. Basingstoke: Palgrave Macmillan, 2003.

Jorge Huerta Papers, 1964–2008, Special Collections & Archives, UC San Diego Library, San Diego, CA.

Knight, Dudley. "American Vowel Phonemes." In *Speaking with Skill: An Introduction to Knight-Thompson Speechwork*, 179–84. London: Bloomsbury, 2012.

Leemann, Adrian, Marie-José Kolly, and Francis Nolan. "Identifying a Speaker's Regional Origin: The Role of Temporal Information." *Speech Prosody* (2016). https://doi.org/10.21437/speechprosody.2016-222.

Leemann, Adrian, Marie-José Kolly, Francis Nolan, and Yang Li. "The Role of Segments and Prosody in the Identification of a Speaker's Dialect." *Journal of Phonetics* 68 (2018): 69–84. https://doi.org/10.1016/j.wocn.2018.02.001.

Lipski, John M. *Varieties of Spanish in the United States*. Washington: Georgetown University Press, 2009.

———. *A History of Afro-Hispanic Language: Five Centuries, Five Continents*. Cambridge: Cambridge University Press, 2010.

Santos DeCure, Cynthia. "Linguistic Identity and Hollywood: Hoping Spielberg and Sorkin Got the Latinx Accents Right." *Visible Magazine*. Accessed December 10, 2021. https://visiblemagazine.com/lingustic-identity-hollywood-hoping-spielberg-and-sorkin-got-the-latinx-accents-right/.

# 12

# FREEING THE BILINGUAL VOICE

## Thoughts on Adapting the Linklater Method Into Spanish

*Antonio Ocampo-Guzman*

Adapting the method of voice training known as "Freeing the Natural Voice" into Spanish has been one of the most fascinating, complex, and empowering experiences of my life: It has shaped my identity as a bilingual theatre artist, creating and teaching in the United States. I currently identify as a white-passing, Colombian immigrant who is the adoptive father of a Black son.

This personal reflection is an attempt to articulate my experience in order to share it with others: There are many nonwhite students, many from the vast Latinx spectrum, encountering Eurocentric voice and speech training methodologies. My hope is that if such students and their teachers read about my experience, they may gain some helpful insights to clarify their own relationship with the training.

## El Viaje Comienza En Bogotá

I first encountered the Linklater method in 1988 through Livia Esther Jiménez, the voice teacher at the Teatro Libre School in my native Bogotá, Colombia, where I trained as an actor. Even though she gave us a basic exposure to the exercises, I found them to be transformational. They helped me achieve an understanding of my voice on a literal level—the physiological mechanism of its functioning—and, more profoundly, of my metaphorical voice—the deep investment of my own self into the characters I was playing. I became even more immersed in Linklater's book as I translated portions of it to share with my peers.

Kristin Linklater was born in the Orkney Islands, off the north coast of Scotland, in 1936. She trained as an actor at the London Academy of Music and Dramatic Art (LAMDA), where she became a pupil of Iris Warren. Staring in the early 1960s, Linklater developed "Freeing the Natural Voice" from the basic

DOI: 10.4324/9781003021520-15

framework of exercises inherited from Warren. She came to the United States in 1963 and developed the method further through her associations with prominent theatre companies, the graduate program in acting at New York University in the 1970s, and with Shakespeare & Company in the 1980s. It quickly became one of the most recognized methods for training actors, encouraging the release of vocal potential through a conscious application of active physical relaxation and deep emotional connection. Drama Books first published the book "Freeing the Natural Voice" in 1976, where Linklater lays out the complete progression of exercises. A second edition, expanded and revised, was published in 2006.

Since the late 1960s, and until her death in 2020, Linklater trained over 200 teachers from around the world to teach her method as Designated Linklater Teachers. It is very rigorous training, including hours of personal work in order to free one's vocal instrument, and hours of observation of master teachers in action in order to deeply understand the profound personal transformation that relaxing the breathing muscles and freeing the voice may generate in a student. The method is currently taught all across the United States and in many other English-speaking countries, including Canada, Australia, and England; a number of DLTs teach in their native languages in Germany, Spain, Italy, Belgium, Russia, Finland, Iceland, Mexico, China, Japan, and Korea.

I came to the United States in 1993, after I graduated from the Teatro Libre School, seeking to further my training with Linklater and other master teachers at Shakespeare & Company. In 1998, I became the first Spanish-speaking Designated Linklater Teacher. Since then, six teachers from Spain and four from Mexico have also completed their training and designation.

## The Return to Spanish

In the early 2000s, the opportunity to teach Linklater in my native tongue appeared at the insistence of several bilingual students at Florida State University, where I taught for two years. In 2006, I began a more intense and frequent practice of teaching the method in Spanish, through two long-term associations: in Mexico, with the Centro de Estudios para el Uso de la Voz (Ceuvoz), a pioneer institution dedicated to the promotion of voice studies, under the direction of renowned Mexican actress Luisa Huertas; and in Spain, with the Estudio Corazza para el Actor, a privately owned acting studio run by Juan Carlos Corazza, where some of Spain's most prominent actors have trained.

After more than 20 years of teaching Linklater in English and more than ten years of teaching it in Spanish, I arrived at the conclusion that for me there are no first and second languages. I learned English at an early age and, since 1993, I have conducted my professional, artistic, and personal lives primarily in English. Of course, Spanish will always be a part of my identity, having been born and raised in Colombia, but it doesn't take second place to English: Both languages co-exist in my accent, in my stammering, in my brain, in my dreams, in my breath, in my voice, and in my sensibility to words. In fact, I had to enrich my own Spanish vocabulary in order to teach the Linklater method effectively. Though I completed a large part of the process of freeing my own voice in English, these experiences have made me realize how free my entire self can be in both of my languages. I now truly and unequivocally call myself bilingual. Some days, this fact arises in me a sense of loss, of detachment, of not belonging anywhere. But most days, it fills me with joy, as I am able to share the training I respect and admire so much with so many different sorts of people and in so many countries. I wonder if these feelings might be true for other bilingual and bicultural artists.

These experiences led to the publication of my book, <u>La Liberación de la Voz Natural: el Método Linklater</u> by the Universidad Nacional Autónoma de México—UNAM (The National Autonomous University of Mexico, the largest university in Latin America) in 2010; it has been reprinted three times. While Linklater's book had been translated into other languages, she gave me permission to put my own name on this book as it isn't a complete, and certainly not, literal translation of her own book. In fact, what I have done, and what is manifested in my book, is an adaptation in action of the entire methodology. When I began to teach the work in Spanish and was translating exercises that I had learned in English, something went amiss. Students were not getting the sort of deep personal connections that I had experienced in my own training. I soon acknowledged that I needed to do more than just merely translate the instructions and expect students to have the same vocal experiences. In Spanish, we don't have effective words for phrases crucial to the Linklater method, such as "release," "let your breath drop in," or "drop down your spine." I had to adjust, and I had to invent. I had to delve deeply into my own sensibility and identity in order to adapt the instructions, communicate the spirit of the method, and assess the results it provokes in the students.

One of the basic premises of the Linklater method is the development of the ability to sense the voice physically. We cannot hear ourselves the same way that others hear us; focusing on the sound of our voice is not useful. It is much more practical to have a physical sensation of our voice: the warm, tingling sensation of its resonance within the body. However, this proves challenging in Spanish. Because the language is mostly written phonetically, when we hear a word, we can immediately know how to spell it; when we spell a word, we can immediately know how to pronounce it. There is a closer intellectual relationship between speaking, reading, and spelling, unlike in English, which has such a spectrum of spellings for similar sounds, allowing for a more physical experience of sound. For example, the sounds of the basic sigh of relief in English can easily be spelled "huh." In Spanish, we do not have a symbol for a neutral vowel. In the book, I chose to spell it using the phonetic symbol "schwa" to keep people focused on the physical sensation of the sigh and not to look for a specific result in the sound of their voice.

## Bilingüe Teacher

One of the most significant experiences in my journey took place in July 2012, when Ceuvoz invited Linklater as the guest of honor for the celebration of their 5th Annual Voice Conference. She gave a splendid speech recounting her career and her interest in the embodied voice. She also taught a series of master classes for over 80 participants from all over the Mexican republic and intensive workshops for the Mexican teacher trainees. For five exhilarating days, I simultaneously translated and adapted her words, teachings, answers to questions, conclusions—even her quotes from various Shakespeare plays. Up until then, my experience of adapting the method had been exclusively solitary: either teaching workshops in Spanish by myself or working on the book at home. Those five days were more of a performance, one that embodied the agile juggling act I have played daily in my head for many years. My understanding of the method and my connection to my two languages achieved a new and surprising level of depth through this "performance act."

In one of the sessions, Linklater laid out an exercise to enliven the soft palate. I could sense her focusing on me like a hawk while I relayed the instruction in Spanish. The exercise uses the phoneme /ng/, which does not appear in written Spanish. We can make the sound, of course, but if we try to spell it, the exercise will not work as efficiently. After I had finished, she barked at me: "I didn't say all those things!" to which I replied: "Leave me alone. English is much more succinct and direct. I have to contextualize the instruction, otherwise it will not work at all!" The 80 participants gasped; being an exquisitely intuitive woman, Linklater backed down and witnessed me translating and adapting on the fly. Afterward, Linklater led everyone in applauding my "performance act" and finally understood the linguistic struggles that are part of my bilingual identity.

That week in Mexico with Linklater certainly helped me refine some of the language I had been using when teaching in Spanish. I will share two major examples here: A basic instruction in English is "feed in a sigh of relief." In Spanish, I was using the verb "*suscitar*," which means "to incite." But, even after so many years of hearing and using that expression, during my "performance act," I heard something quite new and revelatory: We must feed the outgoing sigh with the incoming thought with enough energy to generate an authentic expression. On the fly, I shifted the instruction to "*alimente el suspiro*" (feed the sigh), a more literal yet more visceral image. It proved amazingly useful for the participants. Another basic verb we use is "to let," allowing the involuntary mechanisms to take over the control that we habitually exert with our more clumsy external muscles. In Spanish we have two options for that verb: "*dejar*" and "*permitir*." The first one speaks more to an abandonment of control, which is sometimes useful. However, "to permit" is more of a decision, a commitment that is more empowering. This revelation led me to some deeper considerations about the politics behind my teaching, which I will now attempt to articulate.

## Finding a Better Educational Framework

In adapting and teaching the Linklater method in Spanish, I have had to deeply examine what I believe education is for, as well as the sort of theatre I want to make. In this respect, the works of renowned Brazilian educator and philosopher Paulo Freire have been an incredible inspiration. I now recognize that "Freeing the Natural Voice" is indeed a practice of education toward freedom in the best Freirean spirit. It aims to empower people: to find the means whereby a person may express their most authentic thoughts and feelings using their fullest, most resonant and most articulate voice. When Linklater invites us to feed in a sigh of deep relief, she is encouraging us to reconnect with the involuntary nervous system and with the involuntary breathing musculature, which provokes a more authentic expression of ourselves. However, I must acknowledge that Linklater's work was devised in, and became increasingly popular, in a dominant culture, one in which it is plausible to encourage people to appreciate language and vocal energy while, *at the same time*, encourage them to stake a claim to a free natural voice of their own by asserting their "right to speak." In my opinion, this isn't the same in Spain or in Latin America.

It is my observation that the educational system in Spain, and therefore in much of Latin America, has been influenced dramatically over centuries by its allegiance to the doctrine of the Roman Catholic Church, which makes it an education toward obedience, not toward freedom. As such, society's main educational goals are obedience and the perpetuation of submission. We have almost no sense of "common wealth" and, at best, an awkward sense of community, based on very strict and irrefutable hierarchies. Speaking up freely can be very challenging in our societies, even dangerous, because they have been built on the notion of a few commanding the rest who serve them. Expressions such as *"mande"* (command me), *"estoy para servirle"* (I'm here to serve you), *"con permiso"* (with your permission), *"por favor"* (by your favor) permeate most human interactions. This is why I believe that the main goal of "Freeing the Natural Voice" is harder to achieve for us.

Freire concluded that the educational system in Latin America does not seek to empower people but to oppress them. Throughout my years teaching actors in Mexico and Spain, I have encountered students who only wanted to be taught how to do the exercises well and then to simply be evaluated on the basis of their mechanical execution. These students lacked the curiosity to take the exercises further—that is, to use the exercises for self-empowerment and artistic growth. Furthermore, I have observed that mainstream theatre in Mexico and Spain is mostly dominated by men, many of them educated by Jesuits, who exercise an incredibly tight grip on all aspects of the actors' journey. Most acting is muscular, forceful, and enamored of loud voices and overworked enunciation. Actors are expected to be obedient marionettes: I have witnessed and heard from actors that they are told what to do, where to sit, sometimes even how to deliver lines. This results in actors who are eager to please the director, or their teachers, rather than self-expressed artists who feel free to follow their creative impulses.

Here are a few examples from different classes and workshops: First, the young actor who, after completing a series of exercises designed to re-energize the spine, stated that he felt "violent," even though his peers and myself witnessed him as assertive and tall. He said he wouldn't be able to face his "superiors" with such energy in his spine because it would be disrespectful. He preferred a de-energized spine, even if that meant undermining his breath and his voice. Second, the highly admired actress who shared with us that, when she was 12 years old, she said to her mother that she wanted to be a boy because she had seen how much the mother suffered at the hand of her husband and her sons. The mother slapped her and told her that God would punish her for such thoughts; suffering was women's lot in this life and that she ought to offer such suffering to God for the reward would come in the next life. The actress left home at 13 and built a successful career around a very assertive persona, with a very loud, unhealthy, rough, and manly voice. Lastly, the actress rehearsing Laurencia's well-known speech from *Fuenteovejuna* in which she unleashes her rage and hatred. After some coaching, she performed it with an incredible amount of sheer power coming from deep within and not from the muscles with which she had been pushing her voice to threads, as instructed by her director. Everyone in the workshop knew the speech, but, as many commented, few had truly *heard* it before.

These examples might illuminate why the Linklater method has been a revelation and a revolution in Mexico and Spain. It makes us come to terms with the baggage of our educational system and with our old traditional ways of making theatre. Yet, it also offers a new angle through which to look at theatre pedagogy and, more importantly for me, at the way in which teachers of actors are trained. Training Linklater teachers in Mexico has been the highlight of my entire journey, and my proudest contribution.

## A New Generation of Maestros

When Luisa Huertas first approached me to serve as a consultant to CEUVOZ, she explained that the most pressing need was to train a younger generation of voice teachers. In 2008, with Linklater's blessing, I started the first satellite teacher training program, exclusively conducted in Spanish. Though it had many challenges, through their commitment and determination, four of them received their Linklater designations in 2012 and 2014: Tania González, Indira Pensado, Carmen Mastache, and Llever Aíza. A very significant aspect of the training was our dialogue about the nature of being a teacher: how to guide, encourage, and challenge our students to apply rigor, curiosity, and attention to detail to their training without resorting to old educational models. Particular attention is given to the way that we speak the instructions for the exercises and how we conduct assessments of the students in order to avoid commands and to keep encouraging their empowerment. It makes for a more democratic learning process and in my opinion, to a more freeing experience overall.

These four teachers have begun to disseminate the Linklater method as a revolutionary way of looking at education, not only of actors but also of society at large. Furthermore, they have created a small theatre company whose vision is to bring the method alive on a stage, in front of an audience. One of the main purposes of this enterprise is to investigate the bridge to acting: Voice training needs a direct application to a variety of texts in order to manifest its rewards. Linklater, not surprisingly, tied most of her training to classical verse speaking, namely, Shakespeare. Unfortunately, in my opinion, Shakespeare in translation does not offer the same sort of possibilities that it does in English: The structure of the verse and the rhetorical devises that make it so rich are too distorted by translation. Besides, most Shakespeare translations are done by academics for the purposes of reading the plays; very few are intended for stage productions.

While there is much to be explored in the texts of what is called the Spanish Golden Age—Calderón de la Barca, Lope de Vega and others; during my time working at the Estudio Corazza, I preferred to reconnect with the deeply poetical texts of Federico García Lorca's plays and apply some of the Linklater voice training. The results were delightful: passionate, articulate, and deeply connected to released emotion. In Mexico, at the invitation of the teachers I was training, I discover several amazing Mexican playwrights, such as Víctor Hugo Rascón Banda, Jorge Ibargüengoitia, and Bárbara Colio. These adventures prove that the Linklater method is so adaptable that it serves the training needs of actors in any language.

## Y Entonces . . .

Overall, my journey has been toward empowerment as a bilingual theatre artist. While working to free my natural voice, to find a clear and deep connection to my primary impulse, I have been able to synergize both my languages, and my experience of both cultures. While attempting to balance my thoughts, my breath, and my resonance, I believe I have been able to become an eloquent speaker in both languages. My hope is that others recognize that this is possible, especially in actor training programs, and that multilingual students are encouraged to find such eloquence and not be constrained by old-fashioned educational models.

Kristin Linklater passed away in her home in Orkney in June 2020, just as the world was being convoluted by the COVID-19 pandemic, and as the United States was being gripped by never-ending social and racial violence. This past year, those of us who make and teach theatre have had to face unfathomable challenges that have questioned every single aspect of our art form. I miss Kristin's wisdom and wit. A few days before her death, she wrote to me:

> Nothing I can say can be of any use to you . . . or to those of you who are in the middle of the fear and suffering. All I can do is keep my antennae

alive to the extremities and bear witness to the extremities of suffering and the extremities of viciousness that are the facts of human nature. Howl howl howl. . . . Is that what we need to do now as voice teachers? Build vocal muscle in our students so that they have the strength to rage against the dying of the light?[1]

I must answer yes—we must keep our antennae alive, keep paying attention, and keep sharing our work—especially those of us who are not part of the dominant culture, those of us who tread unusual paths.

It has been an amazing journey from the Teatro Libre to being a true bilingual theatre artist. My debt to Linklater is huge, and the only way I can pay it forward is to continue to grow and to share.

## Note

1. "Email from Kristin Linklater," *Email from Kristin Linklater*, June 3, 2020.

## Bibliography

Guzmán Antonio Ocampo. *La Liberación De La Voz Natural El Método Linklater*. México: Universidad Nacional Autónoma de México, 2015.

# 13

# TOWARD A LATINX-DRIVEN PHYSICAL THEATRE PEDAGOGY

## Acrobatic Theatre for Social Change

*CarlosAlexis Cruz*

I believe we live in a new era of performing arts, where the clear delineations that separated each performing art form (i.e., dance, theatre, circus) are no longer as siloed as they once were. Instead, our audience accepts and desires to experience more collaborative, multi-dimensional projects. Thanks to some visionaries in the latter part of the last century (with whom I had the privilege to work), forgotten eras and genres resurged to make their way to mainstream physical theatre pedagogy. Western European heritages, such as *Commedia dell'Arte* and what we know as vaudeville traditions, magic performance, and circus arts, are being reinvented or, perhaps, re-purposed.

Such disciplines lie at the center of a modern-age circus tent or a large city stage, perhaps ignoring their roots—how these disciplines were shared and what they meant. Contemporary Circus has grown to stand front and center of our modern stages, thanks in part to the work and evolution of companies like Cirque du Soleil. However, I posit we are ignoring the historical context, which is vital in understanding this performance vocabulary. We must look to the performance traditions that come from our Indigenous communities in Latin America.

Being a first-generation immigrant, I ground my career as an actor/creator in my Puerto Rican heritage. My training began in Teatro Siglo de Oro with Professor Dean Zayas as part of Teatro Rodante of the University of Puerto Rico. Simultaneously, I began to work with Rosa Luisa Marquez at the experimental theatre initiative within the university. This led me to work with the companies *Mala Yerba* in Ecuador and *Yuyachkani* in Peru and provided me with direct contact with the Theatre of the Oppressed's pedagogy of Augusto Boal in Brazil. A common denominator among these three practices is the physical approach to performance, which led me to pursue a graduate degree in physical theatre at Dell'Arte with Joan Schirle.

DOI: 10.4324/9781003021520-16

In 2009, after training with Dell'Arte and inspired by the work of Luis Valdez and El Teatro Campesino,[1] I formed the Pelú Theatre project in Portland, Oregon, to address the Latino reality in the Pacific Northwest. My training helped me recognize that physically driven theatre had the power to transcend verbal language and the potential to unify physical languages. I learned that physical gesture keeps the audience engaged and immersed in storytelling. This training led me to further research theatre rooted in gesture, and then eventually to the world of contemporary circus arts and Indigenous acrobatic traditions. This research inspired me to generate theatre in the United States that is rooted in Latino culture and idioms. As a result, I had the privilege to study cultural and artistic heritages of mask and acrobatic practices still staged in Latin America.

In the past decade, I created physical theatre that draws on Indigenous philosophies and practices to build a pedagogy that centers on the Latinx actor and ancestral heritages. In doing so, I have been able to bring to the forefront my passion for telling stories for and about our Latinx communities.

What follows describes cultural heritages that have been imperative to my research: two ritual, high-flying dances, which I encountered in Mexico; the practice of *Acrobacia Indígena;* the practice of the *Voladores de Papantla;* and my creative research with *la Máscara Popular*. In addition, Indigenous popular modern dances of the African diaspora, which have also influenced our Latin American movement traditions.

The mask, acrobatics, and Indigenous dances intrinsic to the people of the Americas form the *base y fundamento* for my physical performance methodology. I believe that as Latinx artists, we should not to rely on Eurocentric physical approaches, given that our history is so rich and varied.

In the Indigenous cultures of Central America and Mexico, many ritualistic traditions of movement traditions resemble modern-day disciplines within the realm of contemporary circus arts. From the use of masks for folkloric dances, which differ from region to region, to full-body percussion, to the *maromeros*[2] walking on a loose wire, to seeing the dancers flying down and around a 50-foot-tall pole, we can see the foundation of modern acrobatic techniques approached from a culturally specific ritual perspective. My research with circus professionals in Mexico led me to discover the Laboratorio de Acrobacia Indígena.

## Laboratorio de Acrobacia Indígena

The Laboratorio de Acrobacia Indígena[3] in Veracruz gathered the acrobatic rituals and expressions from the Totonac and Nahua communities and from the Zapotecas in Veracruz and Oaxaca. This troupe, driven by a collective desire to preserve their rich cultural patrimony, researched these practices and shared the traditions by performing them throughout Mexico. Unfortunately, the Laboratorio de Acrobacia Indígena struggles with financial stability as do most community-based initiatives in Mexico. Yet the troupe, through force of will and passion for its art form, is keeping the effort and research alive as it hopes to move into a better future when this cultural legacy can earn the respect, attention, and support it deserves.

## Voladores de Papantla

As it is currently archived and inscribed at the United Nations Educational, Scientific and Cultural Organization (UNESCO),

> The ritual ceremony of the Voladores[4] ("flying men") is a fertility dance performed by several ethnic groups in Mexico and Central America, especially the Totonac people in the eastern state of Veracruz, to express respect for and harmony with the natural and spiritual worlds. During the ceremony, four young men climb a wooden pole eighteen to forty meters high, freshly cut from the forest with the forgiveness of the mountain god. A fifth man, the Caporal, stands on a platform atop the pole, takes up his flute and small drum and plays songs dedicated to the sun, the four winds and each cardinal direction. After this invocation, the others fling themselves off the platform "into the void." Tied to the platform with long ropes, they hang from it as it spins, twirling to mimic the motions of flight and gradually lowering themselves to the ground. Every variant of the dance brings to life the myth of the birth of the universe, so that ritual ceremony of the Voladores expresses the worldview and values of the community, facilitates communication with the gods and invites prosperity. For the dancers themselves and the many others who participate in the spirituality of the ritual as observers, it encourages pride in and respect for one's cultural heritage and identity.[5]

This cultural heritage often serves as an entry point for most tourists and people unfamiliar with this part of the Mexican heritages, with rituals and performances taking place in oft-visited sites such as the Anthropology Museum in Mexico City.

## La Máscara Popular

Perhaps equally important to these pre-Hispanic ritual dances has been the masked character's presence in traditional dances, *carnavales*, and street performances, including the Danza de Los Viejitos[6] and the Chinelos in Mexico, the rich mask traditions in Central America, to the Vejigantes[7] in Puerto Rico, the Diablos Danzantes[8] in Venezuela, the Huacanada[9] in Perú, and even to the Brazilian Carnival half-masks—each is part of popular culture.[10]

These rich cultural heritages of Latin America, using the larger-than-life masked characters, express communal feelings toward corrupt governments, oppose social injustices, and acknowledge the vast diversity within our regions while never losing the sense of celebration that has been imperative for resiliency in people. Countless examples of these *fiestas de pueblo* exist in all Latin American countries, yet they have been neither valued nor mined for their immense theatrical value.

My creative research with Maestra Mascarera Alicia Mártinez Álvarez[11] of the Laboratorio la Máscara[12] in Mexico City provided insight and inspiration to me. The Laboratory, dedicated to rescuing Mexico's rich mask heritage, undergirds those traditions as foundational in actor training. Maestra Mártinez Álvarez uses traditional masks found in the festivals and celebrations in Mexico to create modern masks to inform contemporary Mexican actor training. Many actor training programs and practitioners in the United States lionize European mask traditions; They deem these pedagogies as of higher artistic value than traditions from the Global South.[13] These European mask traditions include *Commedia dell'Arte*, the theatrical clown, and Lecoq's "Neutral' masks, among others. Instead of looking to European traditions, I suggest that as a community we mine the rich heritage of our ancestors to look back at our Latin American traditions. My work with Laboratorio la Máscara has been instrumental in my recognizing that our ancestral and traditional practices can be employed for American actor training, especially with Latinx actors.

## The Dancing Body—African Diaspora

The extremely physical gestures within our cultures in Latin America reveal the immense impact that the African diaspora has had on our evolution and on how our movement traditions have evolved. Our music, what we know now as popular Latinx music—salsa, bachata, and reggaetón, to name a few genres—would not exist without this convergence of cultures. And with each of those musical worlds, an inherent physical danced expression accompanies the music. A sense of community happens with every step, every spin, every lift. The dances create physical connections and partnerships, performed with the joy of being present with each other.

Within these dance movement practices, I highlight the acrobatic dance heritage of the Capoeira in Brazil. The form of resistance and survival contained in each Capoeira Roda (circular formation of 10) symbolizes a space for the dreams of then-enslaved people; the form now exemplifies physical freedom and readiness for all of us who engage with the practice. Rooted in ancestral traditions brought to the Americas by enslaved Africans and in direct response to the desire for freedom, a new dance was born. Capoeira's complex history ranges from being outlawed and prosecuted, to being practiced at Quilombos—settlements populated by former slaves— to ultimately being adopted and accepted across Brazil as a cultural heritage dance. It is imperative to note that Capoeira has always been a form of resilience and resistance. Within the form, the expression of freedom is communicated through precise martial art-style movements and explosive acrobatic elements.

In my estimation, Capoeira defines the cultural heritage closest to what we have had within our cultures in the Americas as a form of resiliency and rebellion through acrobatic movement, music, and dance. The dance not only became widely accepted within Brazil, but it also became an export and, thus, a point of connection with other countries in the Americas. This Afro-Brazilian tradition practiced across the Americas informs many modern-dance practices.

Other examples of liberation and dance practices include the Puerto Rican *Bomba y Plena*. *Bomba*, as a dance form, represents a form of rebellion and resilience for our Puerto Rican culture. In addition, *Bomba* dances and music have served as an important vehicle and space to preserve Afro-Puerto Rican heritage. Jade Power-Sotomayor and Pablo Luis Rivera brilliantly stated this point in their article, "Puerto Rican Bomba: Syncopating Bodies, Histories, and Geographies":

> Bomba also reveals to us how music and dance enscone silenced stories of survival through the brutal realities of racial-colonial capitalism. Yet it has also helped us imagine a future beyond insurmountable economic and political impasses in which a group of individuals make themselves attentively receptive towards each other as they mutually instantiate a moment of collective energy and liberation, as dancers, drummers and singers do in a batey.[14]

*Bomba* is a similar example of resiliency in Puerto Rican culture. While it is not necessarily a dance driven by acrobatics, the need for joy and freedom, and physical expression in conversation with the music performed live, *Bomba* is a point of commonality between the two. In *Bomba*, the *bailarín* enters and bows to the *tocador*. In call-and-response between the *tocador* and the *bailarín*, they develop a corporeal, rhythmic dialogue with "*piquetes*": sharply articulated movements by female dancers using their skirts or by male dancers with their bodies. The simple dance "vocabulary" communicates emotions and stories without words.

As our cultures have evolved into more modern dances, influenced by, for example, hip-hop, breakdancing, and reggaetón, we can easily see traces of these Afro-Caribbean movement practices as foundational elements within these modern dance forms. These Latinx cultural heritages serve as foundational tools for my practice and pedagogy.

## *De Cero Al Extremo*—A Progression From the Ground to the Air in Actor Training

Within my methodology, I have established a progression of learning circus skills side by side with scene work and physical theatre exercises from ground acrobatics, to borrowing and renaming elements directly from Capoeira, to physically balanced inversions or handstands. I have created this progression to establish a common ground among all students. I often say to my performers that, by balancing only on our two feet, we limit all possibilities within our medium to roughly half of what's possible. The *Maromeros Zapotecos*[15] understood that the performer's presence becomes much richer when encompassing a full 360-degree range. The *Voladores* raised these concepts to great heights.

This progression is gratifying to witness. At the end of the term, student performers have transformed themselves into having fewer inhibitions and a stronger sense of pride in skills they once thought impossible but now are within their reach. Such a concept of a strong presence of the individual performer in breath, balance, and feeling of uniqueness harkens back to the ritual action of Indigenous dance and movement of our pre-Hispanic heritage.

As I continue to evolve this training progression, I follow the basic acrobatics training with aerial acrobatic skills, starting with single-point trapeze and moving to silks, rope, and aerial straps. These skills introduce what is possible physically, which opens a door for the performer to more expressive forms of communication. The training provides students with the foundational elements to select, explore, and expand their artistic vocabulary. Ultimately, what is essential is that students develop an interest in consciously making choices with their bodies. That means taking care of their bodies and training to build on skills that could potentially add

**FIGURE 13.1** Acrobatic exercises with theatre students at University of North Carolina, Charlotte.

*Credit Line:* Photo by CarlosAlexis Cruz.

to the evolving theatrical landscape. Most important, the performer should always keep a sense of active play. To this end, at the conclusion of this essay, I offer an entry into engaged play by offering a sample warm-up and exercise as a way to provide examples of how to develop a common physical vocabulary.

## En Conclusión

The physical heritage of our Latinx cultures exists within us. From our everyday body language to the traditions we are able to preserve in our culture, such as masks and acrobatics, we lay the groundwork for new forms of theatre. If we center our rich heritage as Latinx artists, we will open the door for a visceral theatre that connects to our Latinx audiences here in the United States and, by extension, with our people in our native countries.

I propose a shift in actor training that centers the body and honors but does not overemphasize the text. I value the individual's uniqueness, the inherent physical skills, and the development of the body. Virtuosity inspires imagination. I define my research as an investigation of stories from under-represented communities through the creative lens of physical/circus theatre. I recommend an acrobatic theatre for social change: This means a theatre that promotes justice by starting from a physical common ground.

Finally, I call for the centering of Indigenous philosophies in Latinx actor training. By acknowledging the vast array of histories that live within our ancestral heritages in and around our communities, we are creating opportunities for all members of Latinx communities to potentially find a space within the arts. This philosophy responds to our current needs of equity and justice and also invites Latinx artists to bring their cultural bodies and voices to the stage to tell their stories. This philosophy is a path for **Art to intersect Reality** so as to truly serve all people.

Academic environments often duplicate old systems by employing the same Western European forms, which, in my estimation, have diminished the possibilities of being truthful to the stories of all communities. While I could write in depth about how this systemic inequality contributed to our current lack of diversity on stages, as Latinx actors, theatre makers, and immigrants in this country, I propose that we do not assimilate. Instead, I urge that we dig deep into who we are (our heritage) within the nexus of Latin American cultures to set the fundamental body of our work as Latinx artists.

I believe in creative research that moves beyond the colonial lens. I suggest a blending, a praxis for more points of contact that can help Latinx actors from the diaspora to find more common ground in their work. I am committed to multi-cultural perspectives that include the rich Latinx actor's heritage. I envision actors across the Americas all immersed in research—Puerto Rican, Mexican, and Central American students engaging with their ancestral heritage to bring to life contemporary storytelling. I hope that this Latinx-centered, physical-theatre pedagogy empowers the Latinx actor. These Latin American cultural practices are invaluable to their artistry.

## The Warm-Up

Inspired by some *danzas indígenas* of the Americas, I have adapted the following movement sequence to serve as a point of connection and starting point for the work.

*La Danza del Unísono* (Movement and breath in rhythm)

- Group stands in a circle, with about one meter of space between participants.
- Stand still, shoulder-width apart, eyes forward, open, feeling the body at balance. The perfect equilibrium of the skeletal structure defying gravity and navigating the sudden adjustments needed as the planet, which is our ground, is in constant motion.
- The ensemble, organically, breathes in unison, everyone inhaling and exhaling simultaneously.
- Begin to feel the rhythm of this breath. For example, 1 and 2, 1 and 2, inhale 1, exhale 2. If we were using a 4/4 meter as a reference, we would be inhaling in the 1, exhaling in the three of four counts. Repeat. Note: this inhale-and-exhale sequence happens with a staccato quality, a short and sharp way of breathing.
- When ready, organically, the ensemble begins to move side to side with each inhale and exhale. For example: inhale, step to the left; exhale, step to the right. Given that these breaths/steps happen in the uneven numbers of a four-count, the even numbers in said count become crucial as rhythm markers. Allow the body to trail and feel that internal bounce.
- The breathing pattern does not change in this initial variation.
- Keeping that same rhythm, accentuate the movement a tad more—stronger steps side to side, with the trailing foot touching in the middle. This movement is closer to a step/touch dance, with a sharp and short breathing rhythm. Allow this movement to grow and begin to feel a bounce with each step. At this juncture, allow the middle count, the 2s and 4s, to be an action in the middle for half a count. This move, stepping side to side, should resemble what is commonly known as step, ball change; step, ball change with the ball/change action happening next to the step foot. The movement repeats. Keep the same rhythm in breath and movement.
- Allow the movement to grow. The ensemble begins to get more "airborne" while continuing to step/ball change side to side in the ensemble's circle.
- Incorporate the use of arms in a subsequent step, opening the arms and body with the inhale action and closing the arms and body with the exhale action.
- Break the circle. Move freely through the space, always keeping the breathing rhythm, as well as the movement connection to this constant rhythm.
- Return to the circle.

- Allow the movement to begin to dissipate slowly until we are back standing and breathing together.
- Allow the breathing pattern to slow down until we are able to fall back to each individual's breathing pattern, at ease, standing in the circle re-energized by the connections we just experienced together.

*** *Variations* ***

1. Play with pauses or freezes in the free-moving portion.
2. Accelerate or decelerate the breathing rhythm. Internalize what that means. How does the change signify a different deal to others? How does this change our intention or experience within your body?

## *Pique y Repique*

On the basis of the traditional call-and-response dynamics of African diaspora dances and centered on the ground as the element that sustains all actions and movements, we begin a group dynamic for potential acrobatic gestures and ensemble connections.

- Ground to body connections commonly known as touching the ground with as many parts of your body as you can.
- Identify 15 clear parts of the body: head, two shoulders, two elbows, two hands, chest, mid-front section, two knees, two feet, top back, back mid-section.
- Touch the ground with all 15 parts! Is it impossible? Look for ways. Be creative.
- Now, begin a game with different amounts of parts: 7 . . . 5 . . . 1 . . . 3 . . . The caller vocally signals the action; the individual responds with a body part connection. This action in itself creates a percussive sound as the connection happens. Internalize this. Make this more evident and more audible.
- While doing so, introduce two important circus philosophy concepts:
  - Different performing levels/heights: floor, middle, high
  - Be UNIQUE. Try to rely on what makes you special, something that nobody else can do.
- Share. Look at the structures created.
- Sequence these shapes.

*** *Variations* ***

1. Put three of these shapes in sequence, for example, 3 + 7 + 1. Work on transitions. Constantly think about the floor connection and the role of breathing to ease these unusual shapes. Share the work, perhaps with music. This sequence is your first acrobatic choreography.

2. Same exercise: duos!
    - Follow the same instructions, but in this case, parts are now between the artists, physically intertwined.
3. Ensembles:
    - Same as duos but with more people. Be creative. Take risks!

## Notes

1 El Teatro Campesino, founded by Luis Valdez in 1965, is a Chicano theatre company that advocates for workers' rights and social justice.
2 *Maromeros* are indigenous acrobats. For more information, see Javi Torres, "Danza Tradicional De México: Danza De Los Maromeros," Danza tradicional de México: Danza de los Maromeros (*México Cultural Digital Magazine*, June 23, 2022), www.mexico-cultural.com/2021/12/danza-tradicional-de-mexico.html.
3 Pedro Daniel Godínez Corona, "Clip Corto Laboratorio De Acrobacia Indígena," *YouTube*, accessed May 25, 2018, www.youtube.com/watch?v=I5FNNys00iU.
4 "Ritual Ceremony of the Voladores," *UNESCO*, accessed February 9, 2022, https://ich.unesco.org/en/RL/ritual-ceremony-of-the-voladores-00175.
5 Ibid.
6 El Mictlán, "La Danza De Los Viejitos: Historia y Significado," *YouTube*, accessed July 26, 2021, www.youtube.com/watch?v=T1n-LzYBwXI.
7 Taller Puertorriqueño, "Vejigantes of Loiza, Puerto Rico," *YouTube*, accessed April 15, 2020, www.youtube.com/watch?v=Y_g7s0QWQnA; "Origen De Las Máscaras De Puerto Rico," *EnciclopediaPR*, accessed July 22, 2021, https://enciclopediapr.org/content/origen-de-las-mascaras-de-puerto-rico/.
8 "Diablos Danzantes De Venezuela," *UNESCO*, accessed February 9, 2022, https://ich.unesco.org/es/RL/diablos-danzantes-de-venezuela-00639.
9 "La Huaconada, Danza Ritual De Mito," *UNESCO*, accessed February 9, 2022, https://ich.unesco.org/es/RL/la-huaconada-danza-ritual-de-mito-00390.
10 I refer to popular culture as it defined in Latin America, "*cultura popular*," elements of entertainment, community building that are rooted community traditions and specific to the town and place.
11 "Alicia Martínez Álvarez," *BU College of Fine Arts*, accessed February 9, 2022, https://sites.bu.edu/womenandmasks/alicia-martinez-alvarez/.
12 "Laboratorio De La Máscara," accessed February 9, 2022, www.mexicoescultura.com/actividad/239549/laboratorio-de-la-mascara-alicia-martinez-alvarez.html.
13 I refer to Global South to signify anywhere south of the United States border.
14 Jade Power-Sotomayor and Pablo Luis Rivera, "Puerto Rican Bomba: Syncopating Bodies, Histories, and Geographies," *Centro Journal* 31, no. 2 (2019): 5–39.
15 Miranda Pineda et al., "Patrimonio Cultural Inmaterial: Los Maromeros De Santa Teresa, En Santiago Sochiapan, Veracruz," *Estudios De Antropología Biológica* 18, no. 2 (2017).

## Bibliography

Boal, Augusto. *Games for Actors and Non-Actors*. London: Routledge, 2021.
BU College of Fine Arts. "Alicia Martínez Álvarez." Accessed February 9, 2022. https://sites.bu.edu/womenandmasks/alicia-martinez-alvarez/.
El Mictlán. "La Danza De Los Viejitos: Historia y Significado." *YouTube*. Accessed July 26, 2021. www.youtube.com/watch?v=T1n-LzYBwXI.

Emery, Lynne Fauley, and Lynne Fauley Emery. *Black Dance: From 1619 to Today*. Princeton: Princeton Book Co., 1988.

EnciclopediaPR. "Origen De Las Máscaras De Puerto Rico." Accessed July 22, 2021, https://enciclopediapr.org/content/origen-de-las-mascaras-de-puerto-rico/.

Godínez Corona, Pedro Daniel. "Clip Corto Laboratorio De Acrobacia Indígena." *YouTube*. Accessed May 25, 2018. www.youtube.com/watch?v=I5FNNys00iU.

González, José Emilio. *El Teatro Rodante: Sesenta años después*. San Juan: Seminario Multidisciplinario, 2007. http://smjegupr.net/newsite/wp-content/uploads/2020/05/CATALOGO-RODANTE-1-1.pdf.

López, Armando Josué. "La celebración del carnaval en Morelos, resistencia e identidad: el origen de la danza del chinelo." In *La celebración del carnaval en Morelos, resistencia e identidad: el origen de la danza del chinelo*, edited by Cristina Amescua Chávez and Hilario Topete Lara, 301–27. México: Bonilla Artigas Editores, 2015.

Pineda, Miranda, Joab Emanuelle Isai, Federico Serano Díaz, and Rosalinda Tovar Garcia. "Patrimonio Cultural Inmaterial: Los Maromeros De Santa Teresa, En Santiago Sochiapan, Veracruz." *Estudios de Antropología Biológica* 18, no. 2 (2017).

Power-Sotomayor, Jade, and Pablo Luis Rivera. "Puerto Rican Bomba: Syncopating Bodies, Histories, and Geographies." *Centro Journal* 31, no. 2 (2019): 5–39.

Taller Puertorriqueño. "Vejigantes of Loiza, Puerto Rico." *YouTube*. Accessed April 15, 2020. www.youtube.com/watch?v=Y_g7s0QWQnA.

UNESCO. "Diablos Danzantes De Venezuela." Accessed February 9, 2022. https://ich.unesco.org/es/RL/diablos-danzantes-de-venezuela-00639.

———. "La Huaconada, Danza Ritual De Mito." Accessed February 9, 2022. https://ich.unesco.org/es/RL/la-huaconada-danza-ritual-de-mito-00390.

———. "Ritual Ceremony of the Voladores." Accessed February 9, 2022. https://ich.unesco.org/en/RL/ritual-ceremony-of-the-voladores-00175.

# 14
# EXPERIENCES IN WORKING WITH SHAKESPEARE IN ADAPTATION, SHAKESPEARE IN SPANISH AND BILINGUAL HEIGHTENED TEXT

*Cynthia Santos DeCure and Micha Espinosa*

*Three recent experiences working with Latinx actors and different forms of heightened text at Arizona State University (ASU) and at David Geffen School of Drama at Yale.*

### Tradaptations en La Frontera—With Micha Espinosa

The height of the Trump era in 2017 saw the brutal zero-tolerance policies that created family separations and a humanitarian crisis on the southern border of the United States. Bill Rauch[1] and Lydia Garcia[2] recognized the cultural and societal symmetry of Shakespeare's *The Comedy of Errors* that presaged the crisis. To challenge the national politics, they set their new play, *La Comedia of Errors,* on the *frontera* (the border), allowing Latinx players of Oregon Shakespeare Festival (OSF) and Latinx communities of Ashland, Oregon, to see themselves reflected in Shakespeare's works.

Using culturally specific concepts and rigorous play with languages—Spanglish, Modern and Early Modern English, and Spanish—Garcia and Rauch, thus, reimagined the play as a tradaptation, a category that crosses boundaries of language and genre. Professor of English, Susan Knutson, explains the neologism which sprang from Canadian theatre artist and poet Michael Garneau's work with Shakespeare: "Tradaptations have intentions with respect to the past and the future, but they intervene in the here and now."[3]

The nature of these interventions of the "here and now" appears throughout *La Comedia of Errors,* thus, not only liberating Shakespeare's words but also offering direct and fresh connection for actors and audiences.

Rauch and Garcia began their adaptation with Christina Anderson's translation of *The Comedy of Errors* from the Play On series.[4] The Play On program commissioned modern translations of 39 of Shakespeare's plays. Trevor Boffone's article, "Creating a Canon of Latinx Shakespeare," outlines the Play On process devised between dramaturg and playwright as developed at OSF: "each team had to retain the integrity of the original script. Rather, they were charged with translating the script line by line, adapting the play to Contemporary English as needed." He further offers:

> The playwright had to take into account the meter, metaphor, rhyme, rhythm, rhetoric, themes, and character arcs of the original play, while also maintaining the setting, time period, and any specific references. In this way, OSF has made it very clear that these are translations not adaptations.[5]

During the 2019 production at OSF, I served as voice and text coach. I had immediately recognized that this work would have significant impact on my students and our community in Arizona. As a professor, I have witnessed destabilization of families and its deleterious impact on students' success. Sadly, for those of us who live on the *frontera*, this stress is all too familiar. Many of my students live trans-national lives wherein the anti-immigrant stresses of deportation, racial profiling, and anti-Spanish are present every day.

In February 2022, I saw my wish realized. *La Comedia of Errors*, directed by alumnus, Ricky Ariaza, was performed at ASU.[6] The play was designed and choreographed by students, who envisioned a broad Commedia style with undergraduate actors. The show succeeded with student groups and the bilingual public. For many of the fully bilingual, Spanish-speaking actors in the cast, being in the play was the first time they had been able to use their Spanish within a production. Additionally, students also had the joyful benefit of inviting their Spanish-speaking *familia*, knowing they would fully comprehend the play.

Garcia, using her keen understanding of Mexican imperialism in Latin America, global trade, and linguistic politics and policies effectively intervened the Anderson translation. Talking with ASU students after the production, Garcia said: "*La Comedia* is not a love story of the border."[7]

This short exchange between the Guide and the Antifolo de Mexico shows how she does not romanticize the politics of language usage within the play:

> ANTIFOLO DE MEXICO
>
> (to Dromio)
> *No se permiten Mexicanos, punto.*
> THE GUIDE/EL GUÍA
> Oh, and not a word of Spanish!
> ANTIFOLO DE MEXICO
> (to Dromio)
> *Oye, y ni una palabra de español.*

The actors playing Dromio, Antifolo, and the Guide brilliantly played this curt exchange as each is a bilingual, trans-national actor. They had been victims of English-only education and initiatives, so they appreciated the explicit criticism of those initiatives within the play. Garcia spoke with the actors about the process of tradaptation:

> We respected the original language but followed the prose and verse of the original *Comedy of Errors*. I used contemporary Spanish, but I also looked to Golden Age verse forms to complement the verse in English. Spanish is easy to rhyme. Rhyme is inherent in the language.

She cautioned: "The Spanish heartbeat does not beat in iambic pentameter, and the English heartbeat has a different rhythm than that of the Spanish heartbeat." She cited an excerpt from the wooing speech in the play:

> *Que no soy el esposo de tu hermana triste.*
> *Con su cama conyugal obligación no existe.*
> *No, eres tú, solo tú, quien inspira mi pasión.*
> *Sirena, con tu canto no pidas que me muera,*
> *Ahogado en el llanto de tu afligida hermana.*
> *Canta por ti*, oh mermaid, *y el amor me allana.*

When it is spoken, this example allows the audience to see and feel that Garcia employed a 12-syllable verse and rhyme, and offered a comedic interjection of English for effective tradaptation. The form heightened the moment for the actor and the audience. Another aspect of the play that resonated especially well for our bi-cultural/bilingual audiences was the thematic interjection referencing Mexican telenovelas. As a member of the audience, Ruben Espinosa, Associate Director of the Arizona Center for Medieval and Renaissance Studies and author of *Shakespeare on the Shades of Racism*, said that:

> The quirky comedy reminded me of *Chespirito*,[8] the plaza, with people sitting outside, telenovelas. I enjoyed this sense of people listening and gossiping. There are a lot of Shakespeare plays that deal with perceptions of insiders and outsiders, but what Rauch and Garcia did with this play was brilliant.[9]

Dr. Espinosa's comments tie directly to La Vecina ("the neighbor"), the character who not only translates language but also knits the community together by offering commentary.

La Vecina employs the common trope in the Americas known as "*pueblo chico, infierno grande*" (small town, big hell). Garcia and Rauch understand not just the symbolism of this trope but also its familiarity, so they created a new character. La

Vecina would guide the story, easily flip from English to Spanish, add humor, and offer political commentary. Using La Vecina, the writers carefully created language guardrails so that the listener—regardless of Spanish or English comprehension—would be able to understand the many jokes, the mistaken identities, and the moving plot lines. La Vecina started out to be their tool for comprehension but became, like many clowns in Shakespeare's works, a soothsayer, a truth-teller.

The actor playing La Vecina inherently understood this device and her role. Inspired by Mexican television, she based La Vecina's movements on the character of Carmelita from *Casa de Los Flores*. Her parents, she said, were touched by her final monologue in which La Vecina stops the action of the play to speak truth to power in order to stop the deportation of Egeon, the doting father of the lost twins.

LA VECINA

> You have that chance. And we're going to fight for you like I wish someone had fought for me.
> (to SOLINUS)
> These people are *mis vecinos;* no, they're our neighbors.
> (turning to the audience)
> *Son parte de nuestra comunidad, y los queremos con nosotros.* No, we need them here. *Tenemos que hacer algo.* Yes! We are not powerless. *Aunque somos pocos, somos poderosos. ¡Porque el pueblo unido jamás será vencido!* The people united will never be divided! Say it with me!

The actress added: "My mom teared up when I got to my monologue because my stepdad got deported. I used happy images of him and us together making *sopes* when I spoke my text."[10]

The Arizona audience stopped laughing and fell silent to La Vecina's call to power because the situation within the play reflects the painful history of Arizona, the familiar distribution of sadness within our Latinx community, and the injustices surrounding the incarceration of immigrants in the United States. The actor related about how her role as La Vecina allowed her to find a stronger voice because she was able to explore her identity. She was encouraged to develop her character because the material had cultural and political references that she knew and understood.

Dr. Espinosa agreed:

> "I loved the long stretches of Spanish because, undoubtedly, there are audience members who don't know Spanish. You're relying on the interlocutor [La Vecina] to present what's happening. For my part, I always feel like, if you can make others have that sense of the alienation that one feels with linguistic identity, then you're meeting somewhere where you can begin to understand what it is to have that lived experience."

Border theorist Gloria Anzaldua best describes that alienation, common to those of us who grew up on the border: "Yet the struggle of identities continues; the struggle of borders is our reality still. One day the inner struggle will cease and a true integration take place. In the meantime, *tenemos que hacer la lucha.*"[11] As a voice and text coach, whose profession is imbued with colonizing language, I, too, call for protest. My students struggle with teaching practices that force them to work within the confines of the English-only monolithic Shakespeare.

Garcia and Rauch's tradaptation is imbued with border/bicultural/trans-national themes, modernity, Spanglish, Modern and Early Modern English, and Spanish. Giving Latinx actors material wherein they can reinvent, reclaim, and reimagine is of utmost importance to their education as professional actors and their coming into their physicality and voice as artists—that is, as citizens struggling for social justice in an unjust world.

### ¿Como? Shakespeare en Español at Yale—With Cynthia Santos DeCure

In 2020, due to the COVID-19 pandemic, the Yale School of Drama,[12] like many other schools' programs, shifted its course offerings to online instruction. The faculty was asked to think of other classes we could offer via Zoom in the graduate program. Daniela Varon, a director, long-time member of Shakespeare and Company, and acting faculty colleague, proposed that I co-teach a Shakespeare course in Spanish.

*Shakespeare en Español/Shakespeare in Spanish* is the first-ever Spanish language acting course at the School of Drama. The course was inspired by a cohort of Spanish-speaking Latinx actors at the school, and we set out to engage each actor's imagination and identity with Shakespeare. We asked: How do you bring your own cultural history to his characters and stories so that they may still speak to us today? What happens when your imagination, lived experience, and body encounter Shakespeare in Spanish? Our course invitation acknowledged that, one, such experiences and questions are key to discovering what anti-racist Shakespeare training and performance may be; and two, we could manifest the premise that Shakespeare's themes are universal. The course offered students the opportunity to engage with Shakespeare in Spanish as a means for them to reaffirm their language or reclaim their ancestors' sound through the heightened poetic text of Shakespeare, a new way to embody the text as their own.[13]

Varon describes the impetus for our exploration:

> The actors had everything they needed to play Shakespeare—deep wells of emotion, emotional transparency, and a great willingness to be extravagant with emotion, but perhaps not the immediate visceral connection to the English language the way that their primarily English-language-speaking

classmates did. How can they find the connection that is not in their heads but in their bodies, memories and personal lived experiences?[14]

We recognized how we each connect with language and how we could help the actors access the text. On the syllabus, we emphasized the class as an "exploration" into the challenges, rewards, and discoveries of playing Shakespeare in Spanish. We focused on one play, rehearsed selected scenes, and helped actors find a personalized, embodied connection with their characters. We acknowledged that this exploration would raise political, philosophical, and psychological questions and inquiries into universality, specificity, cultural identity, and access; hence, we embraced wide-ranging discussions as part of the class. Latinx Shakespeare scholar, Carla Della Gatta argues, "the field of Latino Shakespeares demands new tools for theatre making,"[15] and with this class we set out to create novel possibilities.

One challenge in preparing for this exploration was finding a play's Spanish translation that retained the sense and meaning of the text and, yet, still read as "heightened." Ultimately, we settled on merging two translations of *Macbeth*, one by Jorge Plata in El Ancora Editores[16] and the other by Agustin Garcia Calvo, published in Penguin Clásicos.[17]

We opened the class to both native speakers and proficient speakers of Spanish as a second language. We instructed primarily in Spanish, which offered Varon, a non-Latinx Spanish speaker, an opportunity to use the Spanish she acquired in early childhood in the Dominican Republic and Paraguay. Nine students participated: three spoke Spanish primarily, two had grown up with both languages, three were non-Latinx but proficient Spanish speakers, and one was Latinx who had not acquired Spanish growing up.

At the first read-through, some student actors stated they were "*emocionados*," as this was their first experience working this way at Yale. Actors offered these responses:[18]

> "I appreciated working in a way that does not stereotype or infantilize our abilities."
>
> —*Puerto Rican actress*

> "My passion lives in Spanish; in English, Shakespeare doesn't resonate the same way."
>
> —*Venezuelan actor*

> "I am not comfortable speaking in Spanish at all times, even though I speak it at home. [Today] I was tasting how words felt on my tongue and how the rhythm in Spanish affected me."
>
> —*Afro-Caribeña actress*

Other actors said that certain arguments made more sense in Spanish than in English. To me, this was particularly evident in Act I, scene vii, when Lady Macbeth asks,

> "*Qué bestia entonces*
> *fue la que te hizo revelarme a mí esta empresa?*
> *Cuando a ello te atrevías fuiste entonces hombre.*"[19]

In Spanish, this argument had a layered meaning. An Argentinian actress said that she could hear and feel the fluidity of the thought in Spanish. Another Puerto Rican actress said, "*era como si las palabras solas hacieran toda la acción*" (as if the words alone made all the action).

Although the course was scheduled for three hours per week for four weeks, Varon and I tutored students outside of class. We both coached the actors in acting and text work; additionally, I coached them in embodying more articulatory fluency with their Spanish pronunciation. We encouraged actors to work through the text in their own Spanish idiolects, which fostered a direct connection to their sounds of home. We wanted to cultivate a space for exploration without the pressure of outside observation or judgment. Therefore, we agreed to hold the class solely for participating actors and not open it up to auditing.

Working in Spanish allowed actors to hear and feel the text's percussive qualities—the power of each word. The actors directly connected to the meaning of the thought: They were not translating in their heads as they did when working with Shakespeare in English. In examining the text in translation, actors challenged the conflicting meanings in unfamiliar word usages and expanded their rhetorical skills using new verse forms.

A Nigerian-American, Spanish-proficient actor acknowledged the challenges in trying to think in a language he does not fully own. He empathized with how his native Spanish-speaking classmates felt, trying to make sense of text in English. Hearing his native Spanish-speaking classmates maneuver through the text helped him feel the sense of heightened emotion inherent in Spanish.

We explored identity in rehearsals through the vehicle of Shakespeare's language in translation, tapping into something visceral, immediate, and personal that seemed to grant actors permission to access a broader palette of expression. We understood how our multilingual selves may be affected in one language versus another, as our experiences in each language differed. Through this language-embodied exploration, the actors who were raised multilingual blossomed and found new levels of depth, richness, and familiarity in Spanish. For one Cuban-American, non-Spanish-speaking actor, the process helped him begin to claim the Spanish he had never learned growing up. He said he felt not only greater confidence speaking the language, but was also more connected with his identity. Language researchers, Ana Sánchez-Muñoz and Angélica Amezcua, argue that "it is fundamental to recognize the importance language has on the development of a person's identity because this understanding can lead to language equality in educational institutions and the deconstruction of hegemonic language ideologies."[20] Therefore, by exploring language as part of the training, we were also helping actors affirm identity.

At the end of the class module, we shared the work with the rest of the acting faculty, who witnessed the importance of language and identity in the Shakespeare performances. Their responses were tremendously positive. One colleague remarked that the project may influence how we offer text classes in the future; another commented she heard the play in a new way. Others remarked that they had never seen certain actors work at such a high level.

We also had an opportunity to share the work-in-progress publicly. Rebecca Goodhart at Elm Shakespeare Company in New Haven, Conn., invited us to present the work on Zoom as part of its Building a New Brave Theatre series. The event, *Dándole Voz: An Exploration of Shakespeare in Spanish/Una Exploración de Shakespeare en Español*,[21] began with a conversation about the inspirations for the course. Dr. Chantal Rodriguez, Associate Professor of Dramaturgy and Dramatic Criticism and Associate Dean at the Drama School, moderated. The actors performed scenes from *Macbeth* in sequential order. This was followed by an audience-inclusive question-and-answer session, led by Dr. Rodriguez, in which the actors investigated the use of bilingual Shakespeare.

> My biggest discovery was the visceral connection between language and experience and how much information and truth can be conveyed through the musicality of language. It shifted how I approach Shakespeare in English. I have more sound and language tools to play with the poetry of heightened language.
> —*Afro-Caribeña actress*[22]

## Más Español at Yale—Translanguaging *Bodas de Sangre*

Shakespeare in Spanish sparked a hunger in all who participated to continue to explore performing in Spanish. As a result, we considered Federico Garcia Lorca's *Bodas de Sangre (Blood Wedding)* as a production for fall 2021. Building on my prior experience in adapting and directing Lorca's *Yerma* at California State University, Stanislaus, in 2017, I urged our chair, Walton Wilson, and incoming chair, Tamilla Woodard, to present *Bodas* bilingually at Yale. In her article, "Staging Bilingual Classical Theatre,"[23] Della Gatta outlines many of the "considerations" in working bilingually, especially in the adaptation of languages. With that in mind, I proposed creating a production in which the language was fluid and the characters would speak in Lorca's original Spanish text, interwoven with an English translation.

In addition to co-adapting *Bodas*, I was the vocal and dialect coach. Our department chair selected Columbia University-trained Argentinian director Tatiana Pandiani to take on the project. Woodard assured us from the outset that one of the project's key aims was to "privilege the native Spanish-speaking actors" and to honor the actors' emotional impulses with their home language.

Pandiani and I, meeting via Zoom throughout the late summer, developed a three-column version of the script: the original Spanish-language, the chosen English translation,[24] and our bilingual adaptation. We were excited by how language could communicate formality versus intimacy among the characters. Working with our dramaturg, Madeline Pages, we created a language map that allowed us to make textual decisions and track which characters would speak entirely in Spanish, which would code-switch, and which would speak only English. For example, La Luna's text remained entirely in Spanish, retaining the language and structure of Lorca's poetry. Spanish further served as the language of intimacy between Leonardo and La Novia; they mostly spoke Spanish in the first two acts and solely spoke Spanish in Act Three when alone in the woods. By contrast, Leonardo spoke to his wife exclusively in English, even though Leonardo's wife spoke to him in Spanish as a way to symbolize his marital disconnection. La Madre spoke in both languages, and El Novio spoke in English but with some Spanish. We wanted the language choices to make sense as part of the larger scope of the American experience, in which many multigenerational households communicate multilingually.

Nearly all the actors who took part in the Shakespeare-in-Spanish class were cast in *Bodas*, along with several other non-Spanish-speaking actors who rounded out a decidedly multicultural cast. My having previously taught the actors in the program helped me to tailor the adaptation on each actor's level of fluency in Spanish. One of the first decisions we made in pre-production was that the rehearsal room would be run bilingually. This allowed all of the players, actors and designers alike—many of them Latinx—to bring Spanish into the room and to model how we can coexist in training while realizing our full cultural and linguistic selves. Our active Spanish-speaking and bilingualism in rehearsal also invited those with an elementary knowledge or no experience with Spanish to listen, and speak, with a profound level of awareness and care. Speaking Spanish became the norm in the rehearsal room, not the exception.

As the vocal and dialect coach, I encouraged the actors to bring their linguistic and cultural selves into creating their characters. I was careful not to impose a "standard" accent in Spanish; instead, I helped them fill the capacity of the language with full linguistic detail, expanding the space of vowels and feeling the power of consonants. Working with Lorca's elevated language demanded that the actors engage their voices fully in both Spanish and English; hence, I offered a vocal warm-up in both languages to support expanding breath and articulation.

Our work was unprecedented in the Drama school. Pandiani, for example, also had never worked in this manner in a university setting:

> Often times in English dominant spaces, predominantly white spaces, there is this idea of the Latino identity and a Latino relationship to language but

that's actually so general that it doesn't actually represent the personal history and the family history with language. I think that for simplicity's sake everyone gets lumped up together in one box linguistically. Actors' relationships with language are very unique and personal, and I thought that in *Bodas* our actors were allowed to use that to their advantage. I thought you were very smart in tailoring to each of them—specific to who they were and the [place] where those two languages live inside of them.[25]

I equate this mode of working—inviting language and culture as part of the linguistic storytelling—to what Patricia Herrera and Marci R. McMahon call "sonic latinidades."[26] This concept supports creation of sonic performances as expressions of identity to forge new understandings of belonging. Pandiani and I agreed that, because the actors brought with them different relationships with the language, the work felt authentic and grounded. Although the actors shared Spanish, they brought their unique cultural knowledge and history with the language into the work; however, they were invited to do so without the expectation that they meet in the middle in some common representation of the language. Instead, they created a "sonic Latinidad."

Individually, the actors employed a new way of "translanguaging" on stage—that is, blending language, thought, culture, and performance, in what Ofelia Garcia and Wei Li refer to as "bringing together different dimensions of their personal history, experience and environment, their attitude, belief and ideology, their cognitive and physical capacity into one coordinated and meaningful performance."[27] In essence, they created a new code in which language hybridity can live without compartmentalization. Pandiani explained:

> If you are a bilingual or multilingual person, you basically have these versions of yourself that are coexisting at all times, and so I can imagine for actors that there are other parts of themselves, of their psychology, their way of being, that never get to come to the surface when they are always performing in a foreign language.[28]

Because we had the script formatted with the translation side by side, every time a question about meaning arose, we could refer to the Spanish version to clarify our understanding. For the actors, this way of working allowed them to look at the text and length of the thought in Spanish and its meaning in English. Actors also had agency to play with the lines in both languages and choose to revert the text to Spanish; thus, we continued to tailor the adaptation based on each actor's level of fluency in Spanish, while honoring their acting and linguistic impulses.

One noted challenge of working with two languages is that the process takes longer for actors to embody their characters. The generous rehearsal process allowed the actors to embody characters at their own tempos. The actress playing La Madre, who had the most Spanish and English interwoven text, said she first had to understand the structure of each language with the character to make it her own before she could inhabit the role. She employed both languages in performance, not simply by code-switching but ultimately by utilizing mode of translanguaging, in which "all users of language select and deploy particular features from a unitary linguistic repertoire to make meaning and to negotiate particular communicative contexts."[29] This process of integrating two languages is akin to what we refer to in actor training as "embodied communication."

*Bodas de Sangre* was the first fully bilingual Spanish-English production in the School of Drama's history. Close to 70 percent of the text on stage was in Spanish. The performances were strong, emotional, invested, and transcended language. No super-titles were needed.

*Bodas* provides a template for staging linguistically diverse and heightened text classics. Together with the Shakespeare in Spanish, we are working toward a more identity-conscious theatre making, and I hope we will continue to employ more ways of culture and language inclusivity.

In actor training, we need to champion the linguistic skills of bilingual actors, as more professional productions will seek actors to meet the demands of bilingual storytelling. As a trainer working in a predominantly white institution, I will continue to advocate for opportunities that allow actors to bring their language and *cultura* into training.

## Notes

1 Bill Rauch, theatre director and inaugural artistic director of the Ronald O. Perelman Performing Arts Center. Prior to that he was the artistic director of The Oregon Shakespeare Festival (2007–2019) and Cornerstone Theatre (1986 to 2006).
2 Lydia Garcia is the Executive Director of Equity and Organization Culture at the Denver Center for the Performing Arts. A dramaturg, educator, and facilitator, she was a founding member of artEquity. She was the Resident Dramaturg at the Oregon Shakespeare Festival (2012–2019).
3 Susan Knudson, "Tradaptation Dans Le Sens Québécois: A Word for the Future," in *Translation, Adaptation and Transformation* (London: Bloomsbury Publishing Plc, 2014), 112–122, 114.
4 The Play On series can be purchased at the Arizona Center for Medieval and Renaissance Studies Press, https://acmrspress.com/series/play-on-shakespeare/; https://playonshakespeare.org/about/about-us/.
5 Trevor Boffone, "Creating a Canon of Latinx Shakespeares: The Oregon Shakespeare Festival's Play On!" in *Shakespeare and Latinidad*, ed. Della Carla Gatta (Edinburgh: Edinburgh University Press Ltd., 2021), 181–195, 186.
6 For more information, see The Comedy of Errors was produced at ASU in 2017 by Ocampo-Guzman. Antonio Ocampo-Guzman, "Blinders Off, Please: Creating a Color-Sighted Comedy of Errors," *Borrowers and Lenders* IV, no. 1 (2009): 2.
7 Lydia Garcia, "Talkback with the Creatives of La Comedia of Errors," Lecture, Arizona State University, Tempe, AZ, February 20, 2022.
8 Roberto Gómez Bolaños (21 February 1929–28 November 2014) aka Chespirito also known as "Little Shakespeare" is an iconic Mexican comedian.
9 Micha Espinosa and Ruben Garcia. Interview post-production. Personal interview. Phoenix, March 2, 2022.

10 Espinosa, Micha, and Mexican-American female-identifying student. Interview post production. Personal interview. Phoenix, March 4, 2022.
11 Gloria Anzaldúa, *Borderlands = La Frontera* (San Francisco: Aunt Lute Books, 1999), 85.
12 In the fall of 2021, the Yale School of Drama underwent a name change to the David Geffen School of Drama at Yale.
13 Cynthia Santos DeCure, "La Voz De Shakespeare: Empowering Latinx Communities to Speak, Own and Embody the Text," in *Shakespeare and Latinidad*, eds. Trevor Boffone and Della Carla Gatta (Edinburgh: Edinburgh University Press Ltd, 2021), 90–96.
14 Cynthia Santos DeCure and Daniela Varon. Shakespeare in Spanish Reflection. Personal Interview, February 16, 2022.
15 Carla Della Gatta, "From West Side Story to Hamlet, Prince of Cuba: Shakespeare and Latinidad in the United States," *Shakespeare Studies* 44 (2016): 151–56, 154.
16 William Shakespeare, *Macbeth*, trans. Jorge Plata (Bogotá: Panamericana Editorial, 1997).
17 William Shakespeare, "Macbeth," in *Tragedias*, trans. Agustin Garcia Calvo (Barcelona: Penguin Clásicos, 2016), pp. 678–766.
18 Acting students' reflections from Shakespeare in Spanish. Personal Interview from class, March 3, 2021.
19 Shakespeare, "Macbeth," 697.
20 Ana Sánchez-Muñoz and Angélica Amezcua, "Spanish as a Tool of Latinx Resistance Against Repression in a Hostile Political Climate," *Chiricú Journal: Latina/o Literatures, Arts, and Cultures* 3, no. 2 (2019): 59, https://doi.org/10.2979/chiricu.3.2.05, 61.
21 "Dándole Voz—Elm Shakespeare Company: Bringing People Together Through Shakespeare," *Elm Shakespeare Company | Bringing People Together Through Shakespeare*, April 2021, www.elmshakespeare.org/dandole-voz.
22 "Email -Reflection on Process from Afro-Caribeña Student," *Email-Reflection on Process*, February 2, 2020.
23 Carla Della Gatta, "Staging Bilingual Classical Theatre," *HowlRound Theatre Commons*, September 15, 2020, https://howlround.com/staging-bilingual-classical-theatre.
24 Lorca García Federico, *Three Plays: Blood Wedding, Yerma, the House of Bernarda Alba*, trans. Michael Dewell and Carmen Zapata (New York: Farrar, Straus, and Giroux, 2001).
25 Cynthia Santos DeCure and Tatiana Pandiani. Reflection on Bodas de Sangre. Personal Interview, February 21, 2022.
26 Patricia Herrera and Marci R. McMahon, "¡Oye, Oye!: A Manifesto for Listening to Latinx Theater," *Aztlan: A Journal of Chicano Studies* 44, no. 1 (2019): 239–48, 242.
27 Ofelia García and Li Wei, *Translanguaging: Language, Bilingualism and Education* (Basingstoke: Palgrave Macmillan, 2018), 24.
28 Cynthia Santos DeCure and Tatiana Pandiani. Reflection on Bodas de Sangre Interview with Tatiana Pandiani. Personal Interview, February 21, 2022.
29 Sara Vogel and Ofelia García, "Translanguaging," *Oxford Research Encyclopedia of Education*, 2017, https://doi.org/10.1093/acrefore/9780190264093.013.181.

# 15

# NAVIGATING THE MUSICAL THEATRE INDUSTRY FOR LATINX ACTORS

*Julio Agustin*

Getting to coach young artists of Latinx descent who are passionate about changing the industry with all of its flaws and failures is one of the best parts of my career. As a working director and audition coach, the challenge becomes shifting the narrative and creating work that does not perpetuate negative stereotypes while also preparing young people to navigate the industry *as it is*. A working professional understands that undoing white supremacy in the musical theatre industry means shifting the ground upon which it was built, *pero you have to get into the room to change it!* This chapter is about getting into the room where it's all happening.[1]

My own career trajectory has been similar to many who have come before me. Artists of Latinx descent have almost always brought the duality of technical proficiency and activism to the musical theatre landscape in the quest to make space and create greater visibility for those coming behind us. Prior to transitioning into the dual career of stage director and university educator, I was fortunate to have enjoyed a 17-year career as a stage performer in musicals that included featured roles in the Broadway revival of *Bells Are Ringing*, *Chicago the Musical*, and Pedro Almodóvar's *Women on the Verge of a Nervous Breakdown*. Yet as many of us are often called to do, my success was in part due to my ability to shift and morph as per the needs of those behind the table. Given that acting roles for Latino male-identifying actors in musical theatre were sparse, I worked extensively as a dancer in the chorus, sang whatever vocal parts were needed when in the swing track, and spoke the lines of both English and Spanish-speaking characters wherever possible. I also worked in commercials and commercial print as well as in Spanish-language voiceovers continuing to almost mutate as per the requirements of our slowly evolving industry. My early piano education and undergraduate degree in music afforded me the ability to create a parallel career as a vocal and audition

DOI: 10.4324/9781003021520-18

coach, and my training in dance gave me options when the increased need for choreographers of Latinx descent began to expand. I also earned an advanced degree in directing, thereby increasing my qualifications as a skilled collaborator and leader with the ability to speak the language of designers, historians, and dramaturgs. And after several years expanding my profile as an audition coach, I worked to put all of my research into one book, *The Professional Actor's Handbook: From Casting Call to Curtain Call*, as a way of reaching a wider audience of young people seeking to make a successful transition from student to professional. As many of my contemporaries know from experience, Latinx musical theatre artists must first substantiate their credentials prior to being fully welcomed into the room where it's happening. Thus, I made sure that I was never lacking in education, connections, mentorship, and tenacity—all important characteristics of the successful musical theatre artist.

In brief, a few of the basic tools required to work in the musical theatre industry are the headshot, resumé, and some form of an online presence, which could include a personal website, access to performance reels, or one of the many social media sites. For those performers of Latinx descent who are not white presenting, it is useful to seek out a headshot photographer who is skilled at lighting skin tones of black, brown, olive, and tan hues. As to the resumé, it is crucial that the performer include specific and detailed information regarding their special skills. Examples of this could include specific languages such as "bilingual English-Spanish" or "native Spanish speaker" as well as the level of proficiency in both their speech and dialect work. Specificity with regard to dialects might include "South Bronx Puerto Rican" or "Mexico City dialect in Spanish." Additionally, for those who are also skilled dancers, making sure to include proficiency in such social dance styles as bachata and salsa, or formalized ballroom training and ability to partner dance, is incredibly important information for today's choreographers to know. This detailed breakdown of skills will be immensely impactful in helping their resumé to stand out from the crowd. And finally, having some sort of online presence is indispensable; unfortunately, performers of all ages often neglect this aspect of their career. Remember that, if they cannot find the performer, they cannot hire the performer. The actor's comfort level in their online exposure is a personal one; however, it is crucial for directors who are interested in knowing a bit more about the actor's work to locate this without too much difficulty.

In considering audition repertoire for the Latinx musical theatre performer, it is immensely useful to include material that showcases the actor in both Latinx characters and non-Latinx roles. Regrettably, source books of songs from musicals with Latinx characters often include stereotypical examples of exoticism which have "little or nothing in the way of Latin subject matter or setting."[2] A few of the more well-known examples of early 20th-century musicals with songs containing Latinx rhythms or characters of supposed Latinx descent include *Knickerbocker Holiday*, *My Fair Lady*, and *Damn Yankees*. A performer of Latinx descent might also consider researching selections from *West Side Story*, *Man of La Mancha*, *Evita*,

*Kiss of the Spider Woman*, and *The Capeman* given that these contain material written for communities of Argentinian, Spanish, and Puerto Rican descent. However, the performer would do well to consider the background of the writing teams as well as their frequent lack of knowledge of, and exposure to, people from the selfsame nationalities about which they were writing. Fortunately, at the time of this writing, there are a few musicals that feature Latinx characters in mostly non-stereotypical circumstances and written by people of the diaspora. These include the musicals *In the Heights* by Lin-Manuel Miranda and Quiara Alegría Hudes, *On Your Feet!* by Gloria and Emilio Estefan, and the off-Broadway offering of *Four Guys Named Jose and Una Mujer Named Maria* originally directed by Susana Tubert containing songs by a variety of Latinx composers and lyricists including Dolores Prida.[3] This last one, however, does play on some tropes of Spanish-speaking communities so performing the material out of context might be necessary in order to avoid playing into those stereotypes. Still, these can be excellent resources given that the actor of Latinx descent can usually identify with at least one of the characters from these musicals, thereby selecting audition material that showcases their abilities. The obvious dearth of material is why Latinx communities are called not only to be onstage telling their stories, but also, like composer-arranger Jaime Lozano,[4] to inspire and cultivate each other's gifts in writing the next generation of stories about their experiences. There are a growing number of grants seeking to encourage and support this endeavor including The Miranda Family Foundation Voces Latinx National Playwriting Competition[5] and The Sol Project under Jacob G. Padrón.[6] Thus, through one's selection and preparation of appropriate audition material, actors of Latinx descent can increase their chances of getting into the room where it's all happening while also preparing to shift the industry from within.

As actors of Latinx descent continue to expand their audition repertoire so as to make the greatest impact in the audition room, they must first identify (1) *who they are in this industry* and (2) *what is unique about what they are bringing into the audition space*. That "thing" that they are marketing is typically referred to as *the actor's essence*. Terms such as "type," "brand," and "unique selling points" may be provocative and potentially hurtful; still, it is imperative to recognize that these terms continue to be used by those running auditions.[7] By defining their actor's essence, they will make the strongest impression from the moment they walk into the audition room or begin their audition reel, even prior to saying their first word or singing their first note. Where others are trying to guess what the auditors are looking for, those who have clearly defined their actor's essence are able to bring their fullness into the audition space, thereby propelling themselves beyond those who are relying on guess work or luck.

For musical theatre performers, the actor's essence is the sum of three distinct parts: (1) their reputation/work ethic/training; (2) their type/essence; and (3) their personality trait. In other words, it is a combination of what directors say about their work, the type of roles that they tend to play, and what it is that their friends say about them as a person. For example, my reputation in the industry is "detail-oriented," my essence is "educated working-class dad," and my friends say that I am "compassionate." Therefore, the *detail-oriented, educated working class dad who is compassionate* is my actor's essence. This means that everything that I sing, what I choose to wear, how I walk and talk in the audition space—all of these have to support how I am marketing myself in the musical theatre industry.

Now does this mean that I cannot play an upscale businessman or a witty demented neighbor (my favorite!)? No, it just means that I am going to get *hired* by most musical theatre directors to portray the "experienced working-class dad who is compassionate" (think "Kevin Rosario" in *In the Heights*) but will get *rehired* because I am a trained actor who can play a variety of characters! As a further example of how this works, let us consider the actor Omar Lopez-Cepero who, at the time of this writing, is best known for his work portraying "Emilio Estefan" in the Broadway musical *On Your Feet!* People in the industry know Lopez-Cepero to be superiorly dependable given that he first started the show as an understudy. Additionally, he usually portrays the sensual leading man roles—typically, the love interest which tends to be very serious. And yet, for those who have worked with him, they would say that he is incredibly playful in his approach to his work, in both the rehearsal process and his real life. And thus, one might say that Omar Lopez-Cepero's actor's essence is "The Dependable, Sensual Leading Man Who Is Playful." Is it beginning to make sense how the actor's essence for the musical theatre performer works? Take a moment to create yours right now. And fight the urge to get it perfectly at first; you just need a starting point that will continue to evolve as you work to define who you are in this industry. In my book, I talk about putting ourselves into a box to book the first gig; then, by demonstrating our talent and reliability on that project, we have greatly improved our chances of being hired to play roles that they may not have envisioned us portraying our first time around. The more we can get a handle on this basic fact of the business, the better our chances of getting into the room and changing the industry from within. Thus, we are being intentional in first creating specificity for ourselves in the quest to later expand our opportunities. Understanding that we must first get into the room, and creating a strategy for doing so, is part of navigating the current industry while also shifting the perception of what it means to be a musical theatre artist of Latinx descent.

Among the more well-known legends who have made an impact as both musical theatre artists and change makers include Rita Moreno, Raúl Julia, and Graciela Daniele—artists who have dedicated their entire lives to shattering the glass ceiling of what is available to Latin performers. Moreno's seven decades in the industry inspired choreographers like Jerome Robbins and is an example of a chameleon who has fought for racial and gender equality, childhood education, and immigrant rights.[8] Julia's career spanned stage, screen, and even classical theatre and advocated for the Hispanic Organization of Latino Actors as he fought to end the portrayal of Latinos as stereotypes: "There's great ignorance in this country about what a Hispanic person is."[9] And despite her 54-year career and over 20 Broadway musicals,[10] Daniele was only recently awarded a Tony Award for lifetime achievement.[11]

To say that the industry continues to struggle with inclusivity when it comes to members of the Latin diaspora living in the United States is an understatement. At the time of this writing, the younger generation of Latinx artist-activists—Eva Noblezada, Robin De Jesús, Bianca Marroquín, Lindsay Mendez, and Karen Olivo (KO)—are some of the most outspoken professionals bringing to light such issues as equality for LGBTQ communities, body positivity, economic transparency, and, of course, Latinx representation and visibility in the commercial industry.[12] Still, until there are more Lin-Manuel Mirandas and John Leguizamos writing the kind of theatre that shows the fullness of our various nationalities of the Latin- and Caribbean-American experience, I advocate for creating our own spaces while also navigating the industry from within. For unless we are in the room where it's happening, we will continue to struggle to have our voices heard and stories told. Being a musical theatre performer has always been about living a dual life of dedication to the craft and visibility of what it means to be a professional in the musical theatre industry.

As actors of Latinx descent continue to build up the community by encouraging and making space for these stories and voices, it is imperative that they work with accountability partners to help them to show up for auditions. There are many reasons Latinx performers get discouraged from showing up to auditions; this is especially true when their experience has been that, unless the casting notice states explicitly "actively seeking Latinx talent," the casting tends to be white—understood. However, I advocate for shifting the actor's mental state to one of empowerment. For me, I have always told myself that, although they may not have considered someone like me for this role, I am *exactly* what the role calls for! Very rarely was I, as a young musical theatre artist, what they *thought* they were looking for but almost always who they were forced to hire. What we do is, in large part, a mental game and we have to prepare ourselves for success. Remember that we book 0 percent of the jobs we do not show up for—so actors of Latinx descent must show up despite everything that may stand in the way. They are creating a reputation, and reliability is an important trait of those who work professionally. Thus, they must hold themselves, and each other, accountable by showing up regardless of lack of representation, imposter syndrome, or other potential challenges.

Finally, actors of Latinx descent must call upon their six-degrees-of-separation connections as they move through the industry. Actor and dialect coach Cynthia Santos DeCure stated in an interview, "My work as dialect coach is mostly based on referrals; and when I was acting full-time, referrals and professional reputation were also important."[13] I always tell my students who are submitting for a project to include either in the subject line of the e-mail or somewhere in the body of their submission, "referred by Julio Agustin." This name recognition will help to build trust between themselves and the person to whom they are submitting. They must remember that casting directors receive hundreds of unsolicited e-mails a day so creating a way for theirs to stand out by including a connection in the subject line or body of the e-mail will go a long way to helping them create the career that they want and deserve!

As musical theatre artists of Latinx descent, we are charged to navigate the industry with the same level of education and training, connections, and drive as our non-Latin counterparts while also taking our uniqueness and specializations into consideration. Making sure that we are able to articulate who we are and where we fit into this industry, as well as what our goals for shifting the narrative might be, will help to get us into the room where it's happening while also execute the changes that we want to see in our lifetime.

*Adelante y presente!*

## Notes

1 The phrase, "room where it's happening," is repeated throughout this essay and refers to the popular song title Room Where It Happens, from Act 2 of the musical Hamilton. The musical written by Lin Manuel Miranda premiered on Broadway in 2015. There is also a Hamilton fan podcast titled, The Room Where It's Happening.
2 John David Cockerill, "A Little Rumba Numba: Latin American Music in Musical Theatre" (Dissertation, New Haven, 2012).
3 "4 Guys Named José . . . and Una Mujer Named Maria," *The Guide to Musical Theatre*, accessed November 25, 2021, www.guidetomusicaltheatre.com/shows_f/4guysjose.html.
4 "Jamie Lozano," *New Musical Theatre*, accessed November 25, 2021, https://newmusicaltheatre.com/collections/jaime-lozano.
5 "The Miranda Family Foundation Voces Latinx National Playwriting Competition," *NYCplaywrights*, accessed January 21, 2021, www.nycplaywrights.org/2020/10/the-miranda-family-foundation-voces.html.
6 Olivia Clement, "12 Theatres Join New Initiative for Latina and Latino Writers," accessed May 26, 2016, www.playbill.com/article/12-theatres-join-new-initiative-for-latina-and-latino-writers.
7 Julio Agustin and Kathleen Potts, *The Professional Actor's Handbook From Casting Call to Curtain Call* (New York: Rowman & Littlefield Publishers, 2017).
8 "How Rita Moreno Inspired Young Women: From Movies to TV," *Harper Collins Publishers*, accessed November 25, 2021, www.harpercollins.com/blogs/harperkids/how-rita-moreno-inspired-young-women
9 Monica Castillo, "Top 7 Things to Know About Raúl Juliá," *PBS SoCal*, accessed September 13, 2019, www.pbssocal.org/shows/voces/top-7-things-know-raul-julia.
10 Julio Agustin, "From Mu-Cha-Cha to Ay-Ay-Ay! A Critical Explication of the Use of 'Latin' Dance Styles and the Absence of Latinx Creatives in the Broadway Musical," *Johns Hopkins University Press* 31, no. 1 (2021): 43–54, https://doi.org/10.1353/tt.2021.0011.
11 Daryl H. Miller, "A Special Tony Award, a New Musical About Her: At 81, Graciela Daniele Finds Life Abloom," accessed September 17, 2021, www.latimes.com/entertainment-arts/story/2021-09-17/graciela-daniele-gardens-of-anuncia-lifetime-achievement-tony.
12 Clayton Davis, "'Tick, Tick . . . Boom!' Star Robin de Jesús on Latinos in Hollywood and Working with Lin-Manuel Miranda," accessed November 19, 2021, https://variety.com/2021/film/awards/robin-de-jesus-tick-tick-boom-lin-manuel-miranda-1235116184/.
13 Cynthia Santos DeCure, Zoom interview, October 18, 2021.

## Bibliography

Agustin, Julio. "From Mu-Cha-Cha to Ay-Ay-Ay! A Critical Explication of the Use of 'Latin' Dance Styles and the Absence of Latinx Creatives in the Broadway Musical." *Johns Hopkins University Press* 31, no. 1 (2021): 43–54. https://doi.org/10.1353/tt.2021.0011.

Agustin, Julio, and Kathleen Potts. *The Professional Actor's Handbook From Casting Call to Curtain Call*. New York: Rowman & Littlefield Publishers, 2017.

Castillo, Monica. "Top 7 Things to Know About Raúl Juliá." *PBS SoCal*. Accessed September 13, 2019. www.pbssocal.org/shows/voces/top-7-things-know-raul-julia.

Clement, Olivia. "12 Theatres Join New Initiative for Latina and Latino Writers." Accessed May 26, 2016. www.playbill.com/article/12-theatres-join-new-initiative-for-latina-and-latino-writers.

Cockerill, John David. "A Little Rumba Numba: Latin American Music in Musical Theatre." MSc diss. University of Nebraska—Lincoln, 2012. https://digitalcommons.unl.edu/musicstudent/50/.

Davis, Clayton. "'Tick, Tick...Boom!' Star Robin de Jesús on Latinos in Hollywood and Working with Lin-Manuel Miranda." Accessed November 19, 2021. https://variety.com/2021/film/awards/robin-de-jesus-tick-tick-boom-lin-manuel-miranda-1235116184/.

The Guide to Musical Theatre. "4 Guys Named José . . . and Una Mujer Named Maria." Accessed November 25, 2021. www.guidetomusicaltheatre.com/shows_f/4guysjose.html.

Harper Collins Publishers. "How Rita Moreno Inspired Young Women: From Movies to TV." Accessed November 25, 2021. www.harpercollins.com/blogs/harperkids/how-rita-moreno-inspired-young-women

Miller, Daryl H. "A Special Tony Award, a New Musical About Her: At 81, Graciela Daniele Finds Life Abloom." Accessed September 17, 2021. www.latimes.com/entertainment-arts/story/2021-09-17/graciela-daniele-gardens-of-anuncia-lifetime-achievement-tony.

New Musical Theatre. "Jamie Lozano." Accessed November 25, 2021. https://newmusicaltheatre.com/collections/jaime-lozano.

NYC playwrights. "The Miranda Family Foundation Voces Latinx National Playwriting Competition." Accessed January 21, 2021. www.nycplaywrights.org/2020/10/the-miranda-family-foundation-voces.html.

# 16
## SCHOOL OF AUTODIDACTS

*Mónica Sánchez*

There is no formula, no operating manual, and no clearly blazed trail for "how to be an actor."

There is no one right way to train. Indeed, there are as many paths as there are artists. It is a singular journey, but not a solitary path. Ultimately, we each must find our own way, whether it be our training, the preparation for an audition, fulfilling the demands of a particular production, and perhaps most importantly, our role in the world as artist-citizen. The actor's journey is a continual evolution of making choices, taking risks, honing skills and technique, and *cultivating presence*. It is a constant process of becoming.

"School of Autodidacts" is a deliberate oxymoron hinting at the theme of this chapter wherein we illuminate the course of training on one's own. No one succeeds or fails alone. Likewise, the auto-didact does not, and cannot learn in isolation. For our purposes, the self-taught actor is one who seeks out and gleans knowledge (training) from sources other than an institutional model. The following is excerpted from a conversation among three Latina actors who have been navigating our own professional journeys for over 30 years without any of the potential benefits or hindrances of M.F.A. or conservatory training. We, Lisa Ramirez,[1] Zilah Mendoza,[2] and myself,[3] have approached our craft as auto-didacts.

I met Lisa Ramirez in San Francisco in the early 1990s during a thriving, creative environment ripe with new work in performance art, dance, music, the plastic arts, installation, and of course, Theatre. The pre-dot com economy made it possible to afford to live and make things in a diverse city of kindred creatives. Among so many others, this place and time delivered the work of Culture Clash, The Latina Theatre Lab, El Teatro de la Esperanza, Brava for Women in the Arts, Campo Santo, Marga Gomez, Mónica Palacios, Cherie Moraga, and I would be remiss if I didn't mention the prolific work of Octavio Solís at that time. The numerous opportunities I had to work with Solís on new work account for some of my most formative training and experience as an actor. I never had the opportunity to work with Lisa, but I followed her memorable performances in the Bay Area without an inkling that 30 years later we would be looking down the other end of the pike together.

I also have never been in a production with Zilah Mendoza. We met shortly after I moved to Los Angeles in 1999. At that time, there was a palpable level of developmental support for new work. The Hispanic Playwrights Project (HPP) at South Coast Repertory with Juliette Carrillo and José Cruz González at the helm, and The Latino Initiative at the Mark Taper Forum (under the inspired and indefatigable leadership of Luís Alfaro, and the late Diane Rodriguez) were two robust resources for playwrights and actors alike. It was at these venues that I got to know Zilah as we workshopped and presented many staged readings of new work, including *Electricidad* by Luís Alfaro, which Zilah would go on to author the title role of the world premiere.

Over a two-hour Zoom conversation from which the following has been extracted, the three of us mused, remembered, confessed, cracked up, and teared up. I have loosely organized the conversation into the following sections that only begin to scratch the surface of our plática: "Beginnings," where we share our stories of origin in the Theatre; "Cast Away," how we have been cast and have maneuvered as self-propelled Latina actors; "On Latinx Methodology," how we identify and how do we approach a Latinx play, and finally, our "Despedida," a closing reflection with consejos. My friendship and deep admiration for these artists run exponentially deeper than what I have gleaned here. I long for the opportunity to one day share the stage with them, and in the meantime, I hope you are fortunate to be in the rooms when and where they happen.

## Beginnings

LISA: From the time I was born I've had what I call "chronic rebellion disorder"; somebody tells me I can't do something, and I'm like, "Okay, motherfucking watch me." I decided I was going to be an actor because I saw a movie and I couldn't stop crying. I began taking classes at the Jean Shelton Acting School where I got a scholarship in exchange for cleaning the theater. She, Jean, taught her own method and really taught me how to analyze and personalize a script. She was heavily influenced by Stella Adler, having studied with her in NYC as a young woman.

Later, I remember feeling dumb because somebody asked me about a playwright I didn't know. So, I went to the Berkeley library. I went from A to Z and over the course of a year, I read every play so I would never feel that way again. I'd take a Shakespeare class here and there. There was a part of me that wanted to be the

Latin Meryl Streep or De Niro, and maybe try to get into Yale. But then, I just started working! Somebody said I couldn't do Shakespeare, but I thought about Raul Julia, so I continued to study on my own. If I wasn't in a play, I might work with the director, or I would do costumes or I would inspire myself in any way that I could. When I was in my 20s, somebody told me my voice was too high, and I went home and cried. The next day I decided, "Okay, I'm just going to take a voice class. I'm going to lower this motherfucking voice." And I did. It's always been about the possibility for me. I think that, eventually, especially now, that society rewards rebellion, I feel like that's what we've done; how we've trained is a rebellious act.

MÓNICA: My own rebellion was not as self-possessed! I've had a serpentine educational trajectory beginning when I dropped out of kindergarten; practice for dropping out of High School later on. Eventually, I eked my way through an undergraduate degree, and 30 years later, an MFA in Playwriting. My initial artistic impulse, since childhood, was to draw and paint. It wasn't until my early 20's that I met my destiny when my father took me to see a play in Albuquerque by a local bilingual company that had just returned from the Edinburgh Fringe Festival. I joined the La Compañia, and began my on-the-job training. The company had been founded by José Rodriguez, a charismatic, RADA-trained, Puerto Rican artist who was a lead actor with El Repetorio Español, at the helm of René Buch, (who would become the spiritual godfather of La Compañia). During that time, I was pursuing a liberal arts degree and because I was already working in the theater, I didn't take theatre classes. I strategized that I would be a better actor if I knew something about literature, anthropology, sociology, history, etc., and Spanish which I'll come back to. The time working with La Compañía was invaluable. This was during the late 1980's and we brought in the likes of (the late) Rubén Sierra, Jorge Huerta, René Buch and Rubén Pagauga-Sandoval (MX) to direct and devise. In 1990, I moved to California and spent a year in residence at El Teatro Campesino gleaning from el maestro Luís Valdez and the other veteran company members. And so went the next another iteration of my OJT (on-the-job training).

I had a cassette recording of a Flamenco class I took at University of New Mexico. I'd come in early every day to use the mirrors and train with that tape. In truth, I'm a frustrated dancer—maybe that's why I've always valued and strived for a strong gestural vocabulary and robust physicality on-stage. After Teatro, I moved to San Francisco, then to LA.

ZILAH: I had this really wild mother whose eccentricities brought us into situations that we probably wouldn't have gotten into otherwise. She was doing Danza Azteca, and Baile Folklorico, she was very interested in performing, and so was I as it turned out! A company of New York-based actors, very much into the Method[4] came to the desert to start a theatre company working with Native Americans at Pima Community College, which is right on the Pima Reservation in Tucson. My mother wanted to take that course and the only way my dad who was working all day long said okay, was if she took me with her. She asked the instructor if she could bring me, and he said yes. She was the only Chicana to show up, nobody straight off the reservation came, and no Mexicans came; she was the only one, and I got to go with her. And that's where my love for the type of theatre they introduced us to started. I was eight years old when I was in *The Caucasian Chalk Circle*. We did these wonderful exercises. They introduced all sorts of different things from the Method and we learned to break down a script in a linear way. I loved the Sense Memory work, at that age it was great fun. My mother played three characters, and I played two. There were two directors, so I learned to work with two different styles right off the bat. I remember getting in trouble for calling them out because they weren't on the same page. I learned early on: "Oh, you have to wait and be patient. You're an actor and they're working it out, you don't get to tell them that they don't know what they're doing, and that they better get it together." I got that lesson at a very young age!

We got bit by the bug right away. My mom wanted to try out LA, so we came out, and she joined up with Ralph Wade and everyone at Los Angeles Actors Theatre, back then it was the Los Angeles Actors Theatre on Santa Monica Blvd. and Western. At that time, they were doing all new work. Miguel Piñero and artists from all over the world were there. It was fun and a little scary because it was the late 1970s; everybody was partying like crazy!

The hardest thing about not having a formal education was not having the vocabulary to relay what I've learned throughout all of these years. It's not that I didn't learn different techniques and methods to pick and choose from; it's that I didn't have the vocabulary to communicate them. I'd have to show that I can do all the work that more collegiate minds need to see. I know how to do the deed! I know what my objective is. I know how to look at different perspectives of how to get what I want. I can break down a script, break down all the beats. I know how to do a psychological profile of the character, I know impulse control, I know Alexander technique. I know Meisner. I know all of this because I've studied since I was eight years old.

## Cast Aways

LISA: I came up in the Bay Area when I could be cast in a Tennessee Williams play, an Arthur Miller play, a Shakespeare play, or a world premiere. It might not be race-specific, maybe it was a character named Ella who was 25 and lived in a trailer park. "Oh well, Lisa could do that."

MÓNICA: Now that you mention it, most of the only non-specified Latino roles I've played were in San Francisco: *The Trojan Women, Etta Jenks, Thru the Leaves*.

LISA: When I got to New York, 20-something years ago, I got sent out to audition for hookers and maids. It was quite jarring to me to experience that kind of racism, having acted for 10 years, now in my early 30s, and now suddenly experiencing extreme racism from casting directors. It was devastating. I think I will actually take it so far as to say that that began the beginning of my heavy drinking. I've been sober 20 years now—it was almost like I was taking out on myself how they were seeing me—out of sobriety, I became a writer; to show all the things that we are.

ZILAH: It's difficult to think back on going to New York with a play—

MÓNICA: *Living Out* by Lisa Loomer, for which you won an Obie! The 1st Chicana to be awarded an Obie for a leading role, to date!

ZILAH: I was an anomaly as one of the only Mexican Americans/Chicanas out there. This was the early 2000's, I'd be interviewed by journalists, who'd ask: "Well, there's no theatre in LA. how did you learn to act like this?" They marketed it as if: "You're our discovery! New York has discovered you!" There it was, systemic racism right there, embedded into their marketing strategy. And I'd respond with, "That's actually a total misconception. You're here, looking at my work with admiration. I didn't just like dream up the ability to act. I worked on it. I worked on it with mentors, there's a strong lineage of wonderful theatre-makers in California who I learned from. How can you say there's no theatre in California? I'm proof that there is!"

MÓNICA: The irony is not lost on me how your experience parallels the obstacles of racism that the character goes through. I have to wonder if in addition to their regional bias, how they might have received your performance if you had had a high-powered grad school or conservatory credit on your resume? The truth is, we are not un-trained. As you've said, you've studied. You've done the work!

I think back to one of the first plays I was ever in, and not being connected during the rehearsal. The director and fellow actor bombarded me with the questions, "What is your objective?! What action are you playing?!" I had no idea what they were talking about, and in a way, I still don't! I mean, yes, I understand action/objective, and will sometimes utilize it when troubleshooting a problem I'm having with the text, but it has never been organic to me—as human beings, we operate at a much more subconscious level—I'm rarely aware of what it is I want in the immediate moment unless it's a biological impulse. I think the deeper existential longings, that is, "objectives" are so much more sub-consciously driven.

LISA: That actually reminds me of what Susan Peretz said to me one day: "Lisa, the Method was created for people who need it." The Method was created for people who *sometimes* need it. Jean (Shelton) and Stella's (Adler) method was almost anti-Strasberg. It was more about your own personal imagination, how you observed the world and a script.

ZILAH: It helps me have a bigger palette, but it's not something that I go to all the time because it's about being present, and listening, and responding. That's what acting is. It's being vulnerable, it's being open.

## On Latinx Actor Methodology

So far in this chapter, we have not addressed the *elefante* in the room: what is Latinx? Who "makes up" *la comunidad Latina*? We Latinos/a/e, are comprised of a myriad of cultures, countries, customs, and dialects. Arguably the most obvious common denominator is the Spanish language. Whether or not we are Spanish speakers or bilingual, our experience as Latinx/Latino/a/e is informed by the culture of the language, artifact, and commodity of the less apparent and more profound shared legacies of colonialism. The Spanish Crown, followed by the settler colonialism under which we still exist both imposed their own foreign languages as means of subjugation. As we conclude this interlude, we three weird *hermanas* talk about how we identify, what Latinx work might demand from the actor that is distinct from non-Latinx work, and what we might offer from this particular perspective in our still-evolving odysseys.

ZILAH: I don't relate to "Latinx" and "Latino" is also problematic in its erasure of our Native American roots. It does not speak to the totality of who I am. I'm a Chicana. It's taken a long time to even be able to use that term because it's so politicized. But if I look at the trajectory of my life and career as an actress, it is very Chicano/Chicana.

MÓNICA: I also identify as Chicana. Unlike "Latinx," "Chicano" is a term of self-identification vs. an academic, top-down moniker. I also say tongue in cheek though it is perhaps the most precise, that I am a NEW Mexican: a new version of Mexican, who also happens to be from New Mexico.

LISA: I'm mixed race my mother is Irish, my father Salvadoreño. I consider myself a Latina actress, and I identify as she/her/hers. I don't identify as Latinx because people that I know from other countries, especially those that I work with in grassroots organizing are very confused by the "X."

ZILAH: One thing that occurs to me that is prominent in so many Latino plays is a quality of timelessness, not writing in linear time. In a social drama or living room drama, it's a sequential, predictable beginning, middle, and end. So much Latino work requires you to make these giant leaps of faith in regard to time, it's a whole different way of coming into it for me as an actor.

MÓNICA: Yes! So much contemporary Latinx work invites us to cultivate the nonlinear, the non-literal, a poetic lyricism as preparation for the plays. I often find that missing when I go to the theater. I can tell when an actor doesn't entertain that dimensionality in their life because they're not able to bring it, the poetry, the poetics to the performance, either vocally or gesturally.

ZILAH: Also, language. Having to learn a second language or having to learn different dialects of Spanish, which is intimidating and exciting. I don't know Spanish very well, but I'm a really good parrot, I just need the time to be able to study and prepare the rhythms.

MÓNICA: Yes, Spanish. Even a script in English by a Latinx playwright will likely include proper names, often some level of code-switching, and various degrees of bilingualism. It completely takes me out of a performance when I hear a mispronunciation in English or Spanish.

LISA: The first Latina role that I was cast in, in the Bay Area was at a time when I was reintegrating with my father. I lost that part of myself because it was not allowed in the house, So, when I was cast, I almost didn't want to do it because I was afraid. I remember being in rehearsal and having to throw a tantrum in Spanish toward my sister (played by Wilma Bonet). She corrected my Spanish in front of everybody, and I had a complete meltdown. I mean, everybody was there, and I felt like such a fucking Gringa. Afterward, I pulled Wilma aside and I told her that I was left by my father, and there's some pretty major scars and some shame, and if you will be so kind to help me, we can build together. And then she gave me nothing but love.

MÓNICA: As it should be. Language is so primal, and many of us have a very complicated relationship to Spanish, either because of our parentage, our education, or ancestral/colonial trauma. And yet speaking as someone who did not grow up bilingual and is now fluent—in the context of Latinx actor training, learning a language, or at the very least, learning the phonetics of a language is a skill not unlike juggling; stage combat or a musical instrument that can be learned! Not to mention the exponential benefits of knowing another language.

## La Despedida

MÓNICA: Looking back through the years of rehearsals, studios, stages what are the things that have served you most in honing your craft and lives as actors? What consejos would you offer to our fellow travelers on this beautiful, creative journey?

LISA: I studied with Susan Peretz at the Actors Studio in LA. I just couldn't understand her class. I cried through every class. And then, finally, I did a scene after studying with her for a year. I was like, "Fuck it. I'm not gonna do any preparation; I'm just gonna lie down on the floor before it's my turn and fucking breathe!" I presented the scene with my partner. It was just Lisa listening deeply and responding. Peretz said: "What did you do differently this time?!" I told her, "I just breathed and listened to my body." At that point, I decided that I'm never taking an acting class again. Trust your talent and trust yourself. The thing that you're most embarrassed by, the thing that you think is your weak spot is actually your artistic gold.

ZILAH: Breath work. Breathe. As long as you are in your body and responding authentically, you're going to have a performance that moves people. Remember, there is time. Be patient with yourself. Love yourself. It's not a competition, it's an art form. Be honest to that art form, which means bring your truth. Find your truth. Tell your story.

MÓNICA: My consejos: 1) Travel. 2) Learn to partner dance. 3) Learn to cook. There will likely be lean times on this path. It's cheaper, healthier, and often tastier to prepare your own food. Preparing and sharing food will sustain your body, your spirit, and often your community.

LISA: That's funny, the cooking. I remember being with Naomi Izuka, and she taught me how to make soup. I wasn't a writer yet, but she would say, "If you ever become a writer, you got to learn how to make soup." It's like a meditation, But it's the same with acting, right?

MÓNICA: Yes! Initially, the Theatre called to me as a vehicle to explore cultural identity, political expression, and social change. As my own self-taught methodology developed, I began to see acting as a spiritual act—the ability to focus, to cultivate presence onstage, became for me, the rehearsal for mindfulness offstage.

One of the attributes often touted of graduate programs or conservatory training is the access to relationships with instructors and cohorts, and yet, here we are, the three of us connected directly to each other and by a vast network of collaborators with whom we've cultivated and celebrated relationships with for over 30 years. I take this to heart more than ever, the value of our relationships.

We spoke earlier about the "action/objective" model from The Method. I'd like to entertain the notion of intention (vs. objective) as fundamental to the work: Why do we, the actor before the character, do what we do? For me, it is a desire to connect, to follow an inherent impulse toward community. It was Luís Valdez and El Teatro Compassion who introduced me to the Mayan concept of "In Lak'ech," "you are my other self." The "Golden Rule" tells us to "do unto others as we would have them do unto us," but the Mayans tell us *why*: Because you are me and I am you! Zilah said earlier that an authentic performance is about being vulnerable and open. This is the charge and gift of our work as actors, to reflect and reveal "the other" as us. I believe our best work as theatre artists transcends the illusion of self. Perhaps this is the fundamental pedagogy from the School of Autodidacts: breath, presence, compassion.

In Lak'ech.

## Notes

1. Lisa Ramirez is an accomplished actor and playwright whose work has been produced by the Working Theater, 3-Legged Dog, and Cherry Lane Theatre in NYC, and well as The Workshop Theatre and the Oakland Theater Project. As an actor she has performed extensively Off-Broadway and Regionally. Credits include THE CONVENT at Rising Phoenix/Rattle stick Theater; GOOD GRIEF at the Vineyard Theatre, ANGELS IN AMERICA at Berkeley Rep and A STREETCAR NAMED DESIRE at Oakland Theater Project, and a solo rendition of T.S. Eliot's THE WASTE LAND.
2. Zilah Mendoza's acting awards include the OBIE, a Garland, and a Lotrel nod, in addition to numerous Backstage awards. She has originated lead roles in the many world premieres including *Living Out* by Lisa Loomer, Sara Rhul's Pulitzer nominated *The Clean House, Electricidad* by Luís Alfaro, Jose Rivera's *Untranslatable Secrets* and Billy Corbin's *Confessions of a Cocaine Cowboy*. Television credits include: The King of Queens, MAD TV, Law and Order, Medium, Curb Your Enthusiasm, Grey's Anatomy, 24, Nip/Tuck, and The Closer and Modern Family.
3. Mónica Sánchez is an actor, playwright, and educator. Select credits: *Oedipus El Rey* by Luís Alfaro; *Conjunto* by Oliver Mayer; *Earthquake Sun* by Luís Valdez; *Marisol* by José Rivera; *Prospect; Santos & Santos; El Paso Blue;* and *El Otro* by Octavio Solís Film and television credits include *Whiskey Tango Foxtrot; Frontera; House of Cards; Dexter; The Closer; Grey's Anatomy; When You Finish Saving the World; Trigger Warning;* and the role of Dolores Huerta in *The Glorias: My Life on the Road*. She is Assistant Professor of Playwriting and Performance at Colorado College. dramatista.com.
4. The Method is the system for approaching the craft of acting developed by Konstantin Stanislavski, later adapted by Lee Strasberg, Stella Adler, and Sanford Meisner.

# 17
# THE FIVE ELEMENTS

*Caridad Svich*

**The Practice Hall**

I am sitting in a practice hall. We are working on a new play. The actors are parsing through the complex and sharp interior to exterior turns in the play-text. They are riding the music of the work, applying their physical and emotional instruments to the material. I have not asked any of them where they have trained as actors. It is clear to me that some of them perhaps have worked on classical texts before because of the way they handle phrasing and understand breath control. But they could have equally trained in spoken word and hip-hop, which also require a sensitive and deft understanding of these same things.

As a playwright, I am a language architect. My languages are vocal, physical, and visual, and weaving throughout them is a strong and intentional aural dramaturgy. On the vocal end, sometimes the work mixes languages. On the more overt side this could be interpreted in the way I wield English (in its many variants) and Spanish and sometimes Spanglish. But I also work with the languages of texting, slang, and even invented words. Actors who work with me on a regular basis know my "vocabularies" and can swoop and glide and move through my texts with precision, boldness, vulnerability, dexterity, and grace. But I often ask myself: What is at the heart of what actors do? Or are asked to do?

The histories of acting and its training tend to be impacted by the histories of playwriting and production. Acting and playwriting go hand in hand. Writers write for actors. Actors develop their instruments through the range and variety of the many materials upon which they work. For instance, the history of the poetic realistic playwriting of 1950s US dramatists cannot be divorced from the rise of US training approaches to interpreting Stanislavski's "Method." Similarly, the work of dramatists in the United States between the late 1990s and into the first decade of the 21st century has been greatly impacted by elements of the Suzuki Method and more specifically, Anne Bogart's interpretation of Mary Overlie's Viewpoints. So, when one is looking at and thinking through the works of Latine/Latinx dramatists from the United States, perhaps it is useful to consider what acting "methods" imprinted themselves upon their works.

## Forebears

Luis Valdez and Maria Irene Fornés are often considered the "parents" of US Latine/Latinx playwriting, and thus one could argue of US Latine/Latinx acting. The work that Valdez did with el Teatro Campesino in the Central Valley of California and later through his collaborations with Anglo-dominant, cis-het patriarchal, hierarchical institutions like the Mark Taper Theatre in Los Angeles that premiered his legendary play *Zoot Suit* with an all Latine cast influenced the movement of Latine West Coast theatrical writing and production. Among the more significant playwrights and theatre makers who can trace their "lineage" to Valdez are Luis Alfaro, Culture Clash, Jose Luis Valenzuela, and Evelina Fernandez. Fornés' initially downtown NY-centered but geographically and temporally expansive work on both the east coast and the west coast of the United States in the late 1960s through 1990s impacted, of course, not only a generation or two of playwrights who trained with her and/or saw and read her works, but also Latine and non-Latine actors who worked with her (as director) on her fiercely individual, formally adventurous, rigorous plays. It is useful to note, however, that Fornés was deeply influenced by acting guru Lee Strasberg, whose classes on his interpretation of Stanislavski's Method, she attended for a time at the Actors Studio. She borrowed and adapted these techniques into writing exercises that became the foundation of her own pedagogical work with playwrights. In other words, what is important to consider is the fact that Latine/Latinx actors and writers are not merely drawing from one cultural and aesthetic well. How could they when Latine/Latinx is in and of itself a term that encompasses a vast range of people who trace their origins and heritages from different countries in the Americas and their specific micro- and macro-cultures, ethnicities, castes (and the political construction of race), languages, and more.

Identifying and/or locating a singular Latine/Latinx acting "method," thus, is something of a minefield and one prone to the following kinds of stereotypical generalizations:

> Latine/Latinx actors (light skinned, Indigenous and Afro-Latinx both) are hotter, more expressive of their sensuality on stage.

They are more "in their bodies" than Anglo or other POC actors.

They are more connected to ritual and ritualistic modes of articulation than Anglo actors.

They are all bilingual and therefore can code-switch easily.
They are steeped in the stylistic modes of telenovela.

Obviously, there is some exaggeration here but not much. I have been in casting sessions where all five of the above have been said and not just by Anglo, politically white creative types, but also by Latine/Latinx ones. How to break these stereotypes and the violence they cause actors and creative teams in both training academies and institutions as well as the industry?

It is not easy. But one way to begin is to think about the kinds of works that Latine/Latinx playwrights have been making for the last 30 years in the United States—years that have seen not only the rise of Lin-Manuel Miranda, Quiara Alegria Hudes, and Tanya Saracho, but also, among many others, Nilo Cruz, Eduardo Machado, Migdalia Cruz, John Leguizamo, Cherrie Moraga, Jose Rivera, Naomi Iizuka, Kristoffer Diaz, Octavio Solis, Luis Alfaro, and Karen Zacarias. Distinguishing factors of the very wide range of works by this extremely eclectic group of writers are a buoyant, swaggering use of languages, a delight in the musicality of speech, a highly visual, conceptual approach to examining the plasticity of the stage, an often raucous, raw sense of humor, an emphasis on earthy realism touched with elements of the fantastical and supernatural, a strong commitment to social justice, and a mischievous and sometimes feverish syncretization of trans-cultural and/or interdisciplinary theatrical elements. Drawing on the energies, say, of professional wrestling signifiers in Kristoffer Diaz's *The Elaborate Entrance of Chad Deity* or the hip-hop inflections and structures in *Hamilton* requires different skill sets and approaches from performers than, say, working on one of Annie Baker's plays, which often demand that actors work in a minutely rendered realistic register. Let us consider, then, how the five stereotypical elements listed earlier can be dealt with in casting sessions, practice halls, and in performance.

## Hotness

There is a joke among US Latine/Latinx playwrights that goes something like this:

> "Did you hear the one about the magic realist play?"
> "Oh. You mean how *all* Latinx plays are described?"

While it is true that some US Latine/Latinx playwrights openly embrace the modes and tenets of the kind of magic realism associated with the works of Gabriel Garcia Marquez, Isabel Allende, Laura Esquivel, and Alejo Carpentier, many do not. Yet, the assumption, or should I say, "labeling" by the theatre industry and sometimes its audiences as well is that this mode of writing applies to all Latinx playwrights regardless of the kind of work they are making. Interesting to note here that authors like Salman Rushdie, Haruki Murakami, Angela

Carter, Octavia Butler, Mark Helprin, Neil Gaiman, and Toni Morrison, all of whom also write and/or wrote magic realist works, often do not get mentioned as influences on US Latinx playwrights. There is a curious Latinx-only authorial lineage leveled at Latinx playwrights, as if writers only read and are influenced by works made by other Latinx authors. The narrow focus aimed at many Latinx playwrights affects, in turn, Latinx actors.

The expression of sensuality is not obviously a unique trait exclusive to Latinx actors, but often in practice halls and especially in casting sessions the word is bandied about when describing the Latinx affect needed for a role, especially a role in a play written by a Latinx playwright—a play that may or may not be magic realist or demand an intellectual and corporeal understanding of playing inside a story world that breaks the divide between material and spiritual realms and/or has elements of the fantastical co-existing alongside those that are mundane. Headshots are placed upon a table or screened online, and video reels are browsed through, searching for the "hot" (read: sensual) Latinx performer. This kind of labeling stems from a settler colonialist Othering of Latinx roles in the history of US theatre and, especially, Hollywood films. The high-profile "Latine cis-female and cis-male bombshells" embodied by Rita Hayworth, Maria Montez, Dolores del Rio, Ricardo Montalban, and Fernando Lamas in the 1940s and 1950s and the current "bombshells" of the last 20 years—Jennifer Lopez, Salma Hayek, Antonio Banderas, and Ricky Martin—have marked the imaginations of the casting industry in the United States, which has tended to be white-figured and centered, and have forced Latine/x actors to be placed in a position where they are perceived as either conforming to or as rebelling against this stereotype. In casting for the theatre and/or in training actors for the stage and live performance, this heavy marker has often meant that Latine/x actors are judged not for their abilities at the outset but rather for their "hotness." Now, this is not always true, and yes, blockbuster shows like *In the Heights* have helped dispel some of the loaded expectations with which Latine/x actors walk into casting and training situations. But curiously, the "hot factor" lingers as an instant label that Latine/x actors need live up to. Even America Ferrara, whose first starring role on film was in Josefina Lopez's *Real Women Have Curves*—a film that placed a plus-size Latina at the center of the narrative—has had to deal with being applauded in the industry for slimming down, and therefore "more viable" as a leading actor. Think of "hotness," then as the X factor that many Latine/Latinx actors must deal with when they walk into auditions and practice halls.

Breaking the X factor of hotness as a value ascribed to Latinx actors is as necessary as breaking the magic realist label ascribed to Latinx playwrights. Neither is useful pedagogically or within the industry and does not allow Latinx actors and writers from being seen fully on their own terms. Latinx actors do not have a sixth sense or special skill they bring to material that makes them more expressive of sensuality than other performers. What some actors may be able to do is replay or reinscribe the hot mama or Latin heartthrob stereotype that casting directors are looking for. A knowingly ironic and complicit playing with the stereotype is different from being locked into a stereotype. Yet, both from acting and writing perspectives, it is important to contest and obliterate the damaging restrictions that this stereotype holds.

## In the Body

Culture lives in the body. Who you are, how you grew up, and what your origins and heritages are affect how you speak, move, and behave on stage and in real life. You carry culture with you. As your body is always in evolution and undergoing change, so is how you manifest and radiate as a performer. Owning up to and being free to own up to the cultures from which you spring is crucial for actors as well as writers in the arts. There is no "white default" or "standard" American accent that need be lived up to, even if for many years in the industry these seemed to be the case. Respecting and honoring the many "you's" that exist within you means you will have more to offer the work you encounter on the page and stage as a performer. Being a Latinx actor means being someone that contains multitudes. Being an actor means being someone that contains multitudes. Thus, being "allowed" to express all of them, given the roles or projects you are working on, means that you are on the path toward artistic and spiritual fulfillment. But just as Latinx actors are not de-facto "hot" just because they are Latinx neither are they de-facto "in their body" because they are Latinx. Each actor who walks into a room is different. They may share cultural references and even know how to code-switch in similar ways, but their life experiences are different. Actors are actors. Some are more expressive with their bodies than others. When actors are training, assumptions made by teachers about someone's "innate" cultural ability to be expressive are micro-aggressions that can not only stop an actor from being seen in a practice room but can also damage their evolution as an artist.

## Ritual

What makes a Latinx actor a Latinx actor? I ask this in all earnestness. Is a Latinx actor someone who is born into or descendent of Latinx people? The answer to this would be "yes." Is a Latinx actor always signifying what a collectively agreed-upon meaning of Latinx-ness is? Uh. No. Because there is no one meaning to being Latinx in the world. How, then, to contend with the role that ritual plays in theatre in many Latinx cultures?

Let us consider oppression and more specifically Eurocentric, three-act, rising action-centered theatrical narratives. By all accounts, many training programs and conservatories in the United States (the focus of this essay) still tend to privilege in their syllabi the study of works from the canon. An acting student can spend four years without hardly ever encountering or working on material that is Latinx. Still. In this country. *Hamilton, In the Heights,* and *Water by the Spoonful* notwithstanding, it is relatively rare—though this is changing slowly—for actors in training to work on plays by authors from South America, the Caribbean, Mexico, and Central America. One could walk out of a conventional and even highly regarded training program in the United States with barely a smattering of knowledge of and appreciation for the work of major artists from the Americas. This is, of course, due to white supremacy. But these same training programs tend to funnel artists into producing mechanisms in the industry that also replicate this same supremacy. It is a vicious cycle and one that needs to be broken. And this is as true of the world of theatre as it is of film. The replication of three-act Hollywood screenwriting "rules" affects what projects get read, greenlit, and recognized in and by the industry, and what, in turn, is deemed "viable." White supremacy, structural racism, and settler colonialism are at the heart of the tenets of most acting training programs in the United States. As I said earlier in this essay, acting and writing movements go hand in hand. If you train as an actor and all you are trained in and for are in works that fit into the canon with occasional "detours" into maybe Boal or Suzuki or perhaps Noh and Butoh theatre, then the lens by which you see the world and which your instrument is prepared for is limited.

Curiously enough, though, often Latinx actors may find themselves cast in and/or working on devised pieces or scripted works by writers Latinx that are built along different lines and conceptual matrixes. Indeed, some of the so-called "magic realist" work that US Latinx writers make are drawing upon or influenced by structures that are Indigenous and/or West African in origin: Plays that are steeped in circular or spiraling structures and that place a collective protagonist at the center and that often employ speech-song, dance, and call-and-response as central navigating modes rather than character-driven and plot-driven ones. Syncretic and hybrid works are these. Works that reflect the mestizaje (with all the complexities of how the mestizaje came to be) of being Latinx tend to run counter to most of the work in which US actors are trained. Yet, Latinx actors are often cast in such pieces and expected to know the "ritualized" nature of much of this kind of work simply because they are Latinx. Troubling this further is the fact that a lot of contemporary text-based work from Latin America and experimental US Latinx writing for live performance, specifically, are also influenced, in turn, by the German post-dramatic tradition—work that emphasizes "narra-turgy" as one of the chief manners in which the theatricality of the work is deployed, and what results perhaps is a total (to use the crude term) mind fuck for an actor to have to walk through.

It could be posited that if only Latinx actors connected with their respective levels of cultural mestizaje, they would then be able to be more fully able to dive into the kinds of works that ask of them to tap into so-called alternative structures, which are not alternative at all, but simply another way of thinking about and making theatre. However, what complicates this supposition is that on a daily basis, Latinx actors are being asked to usually do several things at once—play a version of Latinidad for white-dominant culture, read "ethnically ambiguous" enough to be cast in a wide variety of roles, sublimate their own unique relationship to being Latinx against cultural expectations of what being Latine means (both within and outside Latinx theatre and film circles), and seek white-adjacent status in order to obtain enough industry credentials to greenlight, author, or power their own projects into existence.

It is, uh, a lot.

## Bilingualism and Telenovelas

Not all Latinx actors are bilingual (Spanish-English). In fact, many Latinx actors in the United States grew up in non-Spanish-speaking households and/or in environments where spoken Spanish was penalized in the school system. For that matter, not all Latinx playwrights in the United States write in Spanglish or choose to do so, yet often the stereotype is that a "typical" sentence by a Latinx writer will look something like this (and bear in mind that I am exaggerating to make a point): "mi abuela walked to the tienda and she bought some arepas for the fiesta because she prayed to Santa Barbara to give her the mojo to get through the dia in one piece."

Okay. Nothing complicated necessarily about this sentence. Other than a cadence is expected? A certain kind of Latinx rhythmic delivery?

Let me flip this another way. I was in a rehearsal room once with a British theatre director working a piece about Latinx characters and the first thing he told the cast—all white British from various places in Britain—is that they had to play my text with a Latine accent because clearly, even though my text was written entirely in English, if they did not do so, the rhythm would be off. Whose rhythm? Is there a specific identifiable Latinx rhythm? Does it sound like congas and cowbells? You get my meaning.

Blanket assumptions are often levelled at Latinx actors that will easily act between and intra languages when this is not always the case or should be. The assumptions also include what I like to call tacking an easy "ese-ness" to Latinx speech in plays. "Hey, mi ese, como va?" An ese-ness that may or may not have anything to do with the play at hand. Just like when actors are asked to perform their Latinidad through gestural vocabulary and behaviors on stage and on film, so too they are often asked to perform actual languages with which they may not be fluent (and fluency in Spanish opens the can of worms that is the many kinds of Spanish that are spoken in the Americas) and "rhythms" that may not be organic to the material or even to them as performers.

This leads us to the problematic semiotics of the telenovela, which seems to haunt Latinx writing and dramaturgy as much as magic realism does. Now obviously the telenovela is a contemporary iteration of melodrama. Latine telenovelas, especially the ones filmed in Mexico City, in their heyday had a studied, heightened, knowingly cheesy kind of acting for the camera that was easily parodied and conveniently used as a short cut when describing Latinx theatrical work as a whole. Somehow the ubiquity of this marker extended to an assumption that all Latinx actors know "in their bones" (excuse me?) how to play "telenovela" and lean into those tropes.

Nothing can be further from the truth, and it is high time to stop asking Latinx actors to be "experts" in something other than what they bring to the table as individual performers—be it language or a specific form of drama—simply because they are Latinx.

## The Playground

There are many acting methods, among them those attributed to Stanislavski, Adler, Strasberg, Meisner, Grotowski, Boal, and Suzuki. Actors train in a variety of methods to strengthen their physical and emotional instruments, deepen their skill sets, and expand their sensibilities as creative people. Training programs at the college, university, and conservatory level focus, to varying degrees, on preparing actors for careers in theatre, film, and television. At root, the goal is to encourage actors to be ready to play. But what is the act of play?

Legendary game designer and fun theorist Bernie de Koven centered the act of play in the imagination. A game was always understood to be an act of engagement between the player and the game. Neurotypical and neurodivergent children embrace and experience play in different ways. The playground, though, to cite de Koven is "infinite" not only because the realm of play has infinite variables and approaches but also because the imagination in the playground—in the room of play which is the theatre—is unbounded and free.

Here is my utopian proposition: actor and writing training programs need re-center their pedagogy around the infinite, while acknowledging the truths and varied, complex experiences of every individual that is in the practice room or hall, and thus enable true liberation for all.

# 18
# AFRO-LATINAS IN CONVERSATION

Interview With Debra Ann Byrd, Founder of Harlem Shakespeare and Creator of Becoming Othello

*Christin Eve Cato*

On August 4, 2021, in New York City at Lincoln Center, I witnessed drumming that filled the space as Debra Ann Byrd called for her ancestors, performing her solo show *Becoming Othello*. It was Harlem Week at Lincoln Center, and Debra Ann Byrd gave a riveting performance at The Isabel and Peter Malkin Stage at Hearst Plaza. Watching Byrd explain why she has a right to perform and adapt Shakespeare was like observing a master class. Her proclamation shook the foundation of the entire space:

> Recently, I had my DNA done: 37% is from the Congo. Not surprising as approximately 2 million of the stolen Africans came from there; another 29% is from Benin/Togo. Again, not surprising as another 2 million came from there. Now I have 6% Portuguese blood, so obviously I carry the marks of the leading slavers. The Portuguese were the first Europeans to explore West Africa. Do you know in the late 16th century many Portuguese settled in Angola and took over the kingships of various tribes? They took African wives: This caused all kinds of problems about who should inherit the tribe. The mulattoes from the tribe, or the legitimate children from Portugal? . . . I am 6% Spanish. (Pause). Well, my daddy comes from Puerto Rico, which used to be one of the chief markets to disperse slaves to the Portuguese and Spanish new worlds. This includes Brazil (with its sugar cane and coffee plantations); Southern and Central America (with its gold and silver mines). Besides earning money from transporting the slaves themselves, the English loved to raid the Spanish ships. It made England rich. And 10% of my ancestry is from England, Whales, and Northern Europe.—I can hear them calling. Calling to help me TRANSCEND and PUSH PASS my inherited pain. Calling![1]

DOI: 10.4324/9781003021520-21

Everyone in the audience laughed with her, wept with her, and celebrated with her. I was inspired because her story spoke to me and made me feel seen. I am an Afro-Latina playwright and performing artist, who was born and raised in the Bronx. My identity is important to me because it is the basis of my personal mythology. My artistic expression is Puerto Rican and Jamaican heritage, Caribbean culture, the Afro-Latina diaspora, and urban life. My aesthetic is the world that has nurtured me: the sounds of the city, the smells of *arroz con gandules* and jerk chicken, the ballads of family dramas, the cries of neighborhood tragedies, the colors of adolescent curiosities, first-love joys, and the struggles of poverty. As I grew up witnessing the world on television and the stage, I longed to see myself portrayed. I longed to see stories that were like mine. When I saw Debra's work, it was a testimony that there is a world where we have agency over our work.

Interviewing Debra Ann Byrd for this chapter was an honor. I first met Debra Ann Byrd at a diversity panel sponsored by Theatre Resources Unlimited (TRU). She is the Founder of the Harlem Shakespeare Festival and Take Wing And Soar Productions, where she currently serves as Chief Executive and Producing Artistic Director. Since her company's birth in 1999, her organization has supported women, youth, classical artists of color, and theatre arts groups throughout New York. Debra Ann Byrd was the recipient of the 2009 LPTW Lucille Lortel Award and the 2006 Josephine Abady Award for Excellence in "Producing Works That Foster Diversity" At the TRU Diversity Panel, Byrd spoke frankly about the disparities of Afro-Latinx stories in the Theatre industry. Her fearlessness about claiming her identity in her work and pedagogy impacted me at the beginning of my career. It was a pivotal moment that taught me the importance of embracing who we are in our creative lives.

Debra Ann received a B.F.A. degree in Acting from Marymount Manhattan College and graduated from the New York Shakespeare Festival Lab at The Public Theater. She also completed her training with the Arts Leadership Institute, at Teachers College/Columbia University, and with The Broadway League at the Commercial Theatre Institute. She is the Artistic Director of the Southwest Shakespeare Company.

Our conversation went many ways, but we kept circling back to two subjects, Afro-Latinidad identity and our mutual experience of attending predominantly white institutions (PWIs).

Afro-Latinidad represents those who identify with the African Diaspora in Latin America and the Caribbean. The term reclaims African heritage in a society that continually erases Blackness from Latino culture. Black Latinos must contend with an image of *Latinidad* (Latino identity) that often does not include people who resemble them while also living with the stigma of Blackness perpetuated by other Latino and ethnic groups.[2] The history of "Latino" and "Black" as homogenous groups has made studies on Afro-Latinos and their identity extremely limited. During my interview with Debra Ann Byrd, we discussed the lack of understanding of Afro-Latinx[3] identity and how that limited lens creates unequal experiences for Afro-Latinx students in actor training and the theatre industry. She expressed how *knowing thyself* is imperative to having a strong sense of identity to combat these limitations:

> If you are an artist, and you're truthful about looking at yourself with a lot of reflection, human spiritual development, and growth you will see that since childhood, your parents, your grandparents, and even the ones you never met, have been communicating with you. If we look into our lives and our cultures, and our personal life as an artist, you will see that not only were your living people talking to you, but the Spirit and Self were talking to you as well. Your ancestral people were always talking to you. If you are not afraid and are willing to listen, you can talk back sometimes.

To claim Afro-Latinidad means to reckon with the past, which also includes understanding the history of Black erasure and colorism in the Latino culture. Politically, the concept of Latinidad has grouped all Latinos into one category regardless of our unique differences. Debra Ann and I discussed the importance of investigating our identities and the value of being grounded in our history. Understanding the complexities of our Afro-Latinidad was affirming for both of us when we were in theatre training. Debra and I attended PWIs where we were the only Afro-Latinx creatives in our departments. We experienced feelings of isolation, imposter syndrome, and microaggressions. We laughed during the interview when I asked the question: Why did we chose our training in PWIs that are often notorious for upholding systemic racism in education?

Debra Ann and I grew up with similar socioeconomic backgrounds in New York City, in a household that believed education was liberation from poverty. Where we come from, attending a private or Ivy League university, is frequently the tried and tested path to success. This is most likely because graduates from these institutions fare overwhelmingly well compared to graduates of other less prestigious schools. According to the US Department of Education Scorecard from 2015, the median annual earnings for an Ivy League graduate ten years after starting amount to well over $70,000 a year, whereas for graduates of all other schools, the median is around $34,000.[4] For us, the track records of these PWIs spoke for themselves. Debra and I wanted to ensure that our futures would be full of promise. We could not afford to pass over an opportunity that could offer security and financial stability.

The first opportunity to come my way was LaGuardia High School for Music and Art and the Performing Arts (LaG). Attending LaG was one of the best creative experiences of my life. I was a Vocal Major and wrote a new song every day, whether during class, after school with friends, or quietly in my room. I was immersed in Art and learned about all its possibilities. At LaG, I auditioned for my first musical, *West Side Story.* At this audition, I sat in a room with all the stellar Latina students who were called back for the role of *Maria,* to then later learn that an Italian American girl would get the part. Although this was a devastating moment, it was also a redefining one. I realized that the only way I would feel autonomy in my future career would be to create my own work. The idea of writing became crucial to me. The second opportunity was Fordham University. However, when I attended Fordham for my undergraduate studies, I majored in political science and philosophy because my family insisted that I have something to "fall back on." This idea of a "plan B" is not uncommon in households that depend on education as means for achievement. No matter, as an undergrad, I found ways to incorporate my artistic life during those years. After I graduated from Fordham University, I was able to find well-paid entry-level positions. I knew I was qualified, but I am also sure that the name of the institution I attended played a part in my credibility. Opportunities often come because of who we know, but if we do not have the privileged background of *knowing* people in high positions, we must rely on other ways to get a seat at the table. Being a member of a prestigious institution is one way to find the opportunities you need for success.

After graduating from Fordham, I plunged right back into the performing arts scene. I became a UNIT 52 ensemble member at INTAR Theater and later joined the Pregones/Puerto Rican Traveling Theatre (PRTT) team. I became a member of these theatre communities by *showing up*. One of the greatest lessons I've learned is that if we want to become a part of something, we must make it our duty to be present there. These two infamous Latino theaters in New York City are the places that have housed me as an actor. I was finally performing on New York City stages! Conversely, these experiences on stage only created a stronger thirst for writing. So, I started writing plays and self-producing them. I would submit tons of applications to have my work developed only to receive rejection letters. My professional writing career finally took off in 2018 when I started grad school at Indiana University to pursue an M.F.A. in Playwriting. Although I had been a writer all my life, attending grad school was the catalyst that forced the rest of the world to recognize me as a writer. Since then, I've developed my plays with many renowned institutions. My writing improved at this graduate program because of the time and work I dedicated to my craft. However, I cannot deny that as I sought out opportunities, being an M.F.A. candidate most likely played a role in my credibility as a writer.

Debra Ann Byrd's journey began quite differently. When Byrd decided she wanted to study Shakespeare and the classics, she insisted that she go to college to learn these disciplines because she wanted to be *excellent*. She had already been an actress in the Black theatre industry, doing mainly Gospel plays. At this point of her life, she was 33 years old, grappling with the decision of becoming a preacher, and was taking care of her daughter who was diagnosed with cerebral palsy. Her mind shifted when she saw a troop of Black actresses performing Shakespeare at Harlem's Victoria 5 Theatre:

> When I saw that troop of Black actresses performing Shakespeare, I said, "Oh my god, I want to learn that. I want to do that." But my

daughter was sick, and I was in a terrible spiritual state. How was I going to start a whole new career? That's when I fought with God. I asked God, "Why am I on this planet? And what am I here to do? And if I'm going to be here on this planet, then I have to be excellent. I have to make a difference in this world. That's when I decided, "Well, if I'm going to learn Shakespeare and work in the theatre, then I need to go to school." I didn't want to be ordinary. A few weeks passed, and I was on the bus with my daughter, leaving an appointment with her doctor. To my surprise, there was an advertisement on the bus that read: "MMC (Marymount Manhattan College) Theatre Program at the Center of Excellence." And then I thought,—that's where I want to be, at the center of excellence.

Debra described the advertisement which caught her attention. She believed that becoming an alumna of MMC would advance her career and understood that attending a prestigious institution that offers showcases and networking opportunities was one of the best ways. Our connection grew as we thought about the triumphs and tribulations we faced during our educational experiences. For instance, when I attended Indiana University, I experienced imposter syndrome because my colleagues had formal training in theatre, whereas most of my knowledge came from the work I did on stage. Therefore, I spent a lot of time "catching up" on Theatre Academia. There were many moments when I had to teach my colleagues about my culture and background. There were also times when I felt disrespected because my name was misspelled on a program. These microaggressions are common, not just because of historical systemic racist practices but also due to the demographical construction of these institutions. According to a 2017 New York Times analysis, Black and Latino students were more underrepresented at the nation's top colleges and universities than they were 35 years ago.[5] This underrepresentation often isolates minorities at these institutions.

Debra Ann recalled a similar experience during her time at MMC, where she was discriminated against because she was cast as the lead role in *The Importance of Being Earnest*:

> I was cast in the very coveted role of Lady Bracknell. Now, here's where the world started shifting. Some of my colleagues were not happy that the director decided Debra Ann will take the final bow. Some of my cohort members said, "If she's taking the final bow, I'm quitting the show." When it was time to act on the stage, my scene partner wouldn't look me in my face. He would look all around the theater so that the audience wouldn't notice that he wasn't looking at me. I'm doing all my scenes and delivering them to him while he was delivering his lines to the wings.
>
> I decided, "I'm going to be brilliant, no matter what." Why? Because at this point, I realized that there had never been a Black Lady Bracknell on the entire planet. And if classically trained Debra Ann does not get this

right, then maybe they won't let us do it again. And so, I felt the weight of all the future generations of Black and Brown classically trained actors on my shoulders. And I felt the weight of the Black people who were watching me on my shoulders. Because now, if I don't get this right, I'll mess it up for everybody. I also felt the weight of trying to be a British woman with this high British attitude. No matter, I fully became Lady Bracknell, and there was no one to deny that because I fully encompassed her. I made sure that nobody could mistake the fact that this Black girl is extremely British, and extremely high class. I made sure to let the world know that I belonged on that stage.

I had no other choice but to be brilliant. I told myself: "I'm not White. I'm not Black. I'm not Asian. I'm not Hispanic. I am brilliant. And I'm well-studied and well-trained and well-practiced. And can I play this role? Absolutely." When it comes to the classics, race and culture go out the window because what I'm bringing to the table is this story. I was determined to have the audience see this story and not think that something was off kilter. That a classical play can feature Black actors and not be off kilter. The stage did not break down and explode, other than my performance that made your heart go pitter, patter, patter, patter. I was resolute in having my audience say, "Oh my God, look at this." It's undeniable that this performance is right.

As Debra Ann faced these microaggressions, she became more determined to improve her experience at MMC. There were times when Debra Ann Byrd was pigeon-holed into playing stereotypical roles because of her Blackness. The MMC department often cast her in Black plays, when she was clear about attending their institution to work on classical European plays. She argued that the entire trajectory of her career up until that moment was playing Black roles, that she didn't decide to attend a program to continue playing the same kind of characters. "*I had lived those lives, I had lived the rhythms of those plays my entire life, and I wanted to do something different.*" Debra Ann overcame her obstacles by changing the narrative. I asked her what the action steps were when seeking out opportunities in classical theatre:

> There was a scholarship available offering money to artists who wanted to do something in their community. I applied because I knew exactly what I wanted to do for my community. I said, "I'm going to start a theatre company where classically trained actors of color who graduate with BFAs and MFAs are going to have some way to practice their craft." That's when I formed Take Wing And Soar Productions for Asians, Latinos, and Black actors. I also included White folks, because I wanted to demonstrate how to not be exclusive. However, the aim was to always have artists of color be at the center of the stage. At these predominantly White institutions, when someone tries to box you in because of your Blackness or culture, turn their

no into a yes, and always aim for success. Remember, nobody can tell you who you're supposed to be.

Debra knew that by becoming an actor-playwright she could uplift and represent Afro-Latinx culture, tradition, and history in her storytelling. I agree with her philosophy because making space for Afro-Latinx actors in this industry is accomplished by deconstructing the traditional casting practices and creating stories that center Afro-Latinidad. I asked Debra Ann about any advice she would offer to Afro-Latinx actors planning to attend a PWI to further their education. Her response was:

> People need to know who you are and what you're bringing to the table. I say use your platform to help inform the world of who you are. As an Afro-Latinx person entering these predominantly White institutions, we're not there to become like them. You need to tell yourself that: "I'm here to better myself. This place is promising me the kind of education that I need to change myself and the people around me. To be better for my family and to get my papers in order. And while I'm here, I understand that I might run into someone who will say, 'Don't touch me. Get away from me.' But I'm going to keep it moving because I can't allow you to run me away from my own destiny." Go in there and talk to one person at a time. Tell them about who you are and why you're there.
>
> I decided that, in my bio, I was going to identify as an Afro Latina. That way when a person asks, "What is that?", it would open up a conversation. These conversations are important to have because you want to spread the word! You want to debunk the myths and declare that you cannot be placed in a box. I am both Afro and Latina. I am of African descent, and I'm of Hispanic descent. If you look at my real DNA, I am native, I am European, and I am Black. I'm all these things, which means I'm GLOBAL. Therefore, YES, people need to know who you are, what you're bringing to the table, what you are capable of, and what knowledge you might have to add to the pot.

At the end of the interview, Debra's words echoed in my mind. I will never forget our time together and her powerful play, *Becoming Othello*. Her words reminded me that one needs to stand up and speak out when they experience any injustice or microaggression and to choose the path of solidarity. Debra Ann Byrd's brilliant journey taught me that embracing your identity often requires courage and leadership. That amid marginalization, pushing to interculturalize our spaces is a must. As a fellow Afro-Latina, she inspires me to define and appreciate my global self, reclaim my narrative, and continue telling my stories as an act of resistance.

> "I turn my pain into power and decide to fight back."
>
> —*Becoming Othello*

## Notes

1. *Becoming Othello: A Black Girl's Journey,* produced and playwright by Debra Ann Byrd, dir. Tina Parker, The Isabel and Peter Malkin Stage at Hearst Plaza, New York, NY, August 4, 2021.
2. Elizabeth Hordge-Freeman and Edlin Veras, "Out of the Shadows, Into the Dark: Ethnoracial Dissonance and Identity Formation among Afro-Latinxs," *Sociology of Race & Ethnicity* 6, no. 2 (2019): 146–60, https://doi.org/10.1177/2332649219829784.
3. Although we used the term *Latinx* during our interview, it does not exclude the recognition that *Latiné* is how many LGBTQ and non-binary people of the diaspora prefer to identify. The "e" in *Latiné* derives from the Spanish language as a representation of gender neutrality. The "x" in *Latinx* serves the same purpose of gender neutrality but is not necessarily rooted in the Spanish language since the "x" is pronounced differently than in English. We chose to use *Latinx* because it is the term most widely used in the United States; it does not reflect our preferred way of identifying our community.
4. Paul R. Lowe, "Why Your Child Should Apply to an Ivy League College or University?" accessed February 13, 2018, https://drpaulloweadmissionsexpert.blog/2018/02/13/why-your-child-should-apply-to-an-ivy-league-college-or-university/
5. Jeremy Ashkenas, Haeyoun Park, and Adam Pearce, "Even with Affirmative Action, Blacks and Hispanics Are More Underrepresented at Top Colleges Than 35 Years Ago," accessed August 24, 2017, www.nytimes.com/interactive/2017/08/24/us/affirmative-action.html.

## Bibliography

Ashkenas, Jeremy, Haeyoun Park, and Adam Pearce. "Even With Affirmative Action, Blacks and Hispanics Are More Underrepresented at Top Colleges Than 35 Years Ago." Accessed August 24, 2017. www.nytimes.com/interactive/2017/08/24/us/affirmative-action.html.

Hordge-Freeman, Elizabeth, and Edlin Veras. "Out of the Shadows, Into the Dark: Ethnoracial Dissonance and Identity Formation among Afro-Latinxs." *Sociology of Race & Ethnicity* 6, no. 2 (2019): 146–60. https://doi.org/10.1177/2332649219829784.

Lowe, Paul R. "Why Your Child Should Apply to an Ivy League College or University?" Accessed February 13, 2018. https://drpaulloweadmissionsexpert.blog/2018/02/13/why-your-child-should-apply-to-an-ivy-league-college-or-university/.

# 19
## ON LATINX CASTING

Interview With Peter Murrieta, Emmy Award-Winning Writer and Producer

*Micha Espinosa*

On April 3, 2021, I interviewed Peter Murrieta, an actor and seasoned improv artist-turned two-time Emmy award-winning writer and producer. He contributed to many television network shows that feature Latinx characters and narratives, including *Welcome to Tucson*, *The Wizards of Waverly Place*, *Cristela*, *Lopez*, *One Day at a Time*, and *Mr. Inglesias*. Originally from Tucson, Murrieta, now a Professor of Practice and Deputy Director at the Sidney Poitier New American Film School at Arizona State University (ASU), continues as a working professional in Los Angeles.

Our conversation focused on casting and his origin story as a theatre and improv artist, the lessons he has learned, and the teachers and mentors who encouraged him. We also discussed his and my shared geographical, cultural, and artistic backgrounds. We both were born in the late 1960s and lived in Mexican-American households. We even graduated from the same high school in Tucson, Arizona, and in the same year. Both of us think Sabino High School, Eegees (crushed ice drink), and, possibly, Carlos Murphy's cheese crisps and chimichangas had something to do with this coincidence. Murrieta and I, now colleagues at ASU, share a dedication to lifting up Latinx narratives and to improving Latinx representation.

Murrieta attended the University of Arizona, where his humanities professor, Donna Swain, responding to his hilarious, albeit ungradable, paper on existentialism, introduced him to the campus improv group, Comedy Corner. After writing and performing with Comedy Corner, Murrieta realized he needed training, so he took acting classes at the University of Arizona. Then, he found his way into the local theatre scene, where he gained experience playing bit parts in shows like Lanford Wilson's *Balm in Gilead*.

After seeing the legendary Chicago-based improvisational company Second City on tour, Murrieta realized that he could make a living doing improv. He

DOI: 10.4324/9781003021520-22

moved to Chicago, with one duffle bag and a desire to see snow. Eventually, training with, then joining the Second City company, he developed improv skills that informed his writing. Hungry to make a difference, Murrieta moved on to Los Angeles.

Our conversation covered migration of the Irish-Mexican communities of Tucson, the complexity of the border, bi-national and bi-cultural identities, racial justice and social inequality, and the psychological navigation required to resist the cultural imprinting of our parents' belief systems. We discussed his 20-year history of casting Latinx actors for network television, the challenges of being at the forefront of what many hoped would be the Latino wave, the lack of mobility for Latinx actors, the dynamics of casting, the resilience required when working for change, and the disturbing narratives of trauma he has encountered. We concluded the interview by discussing techniques for combating ignorance and negativity for today's identity-conscious[1] actors, producers, writers, and audiences.

As I reflect on my conversation with Murrieta and the shifts in casting that have happened in theatre, television, and film, I am reminded of Princeton professor Brian Herrera's 2015 manuscript, "Latin Numbers: Playing Latino in 20th-century U.S. popular performance,"[2] which offers an excellent examination of the history of Latinx casting and how that casting has influenced US perspectives on race and ethnicity.[3]

I am also brought back to the August 9, 2016, town hall entitled "The Color Game: Whitewashing Latinx Stories." The standing-room-only gathering was hosted by the Association of Latinx Theatre Artists (ALTA) of Chicago at the Victory Gardens' Biograph Theatre in Chicago, Illinois.[4] I was in Chicago for the Voice and Speech Trainers Association's 30th Anniversary Conference, held at De Paul University, when I attended the convocation. The town hall primarily focused on casting a non-Latinx actor in the lead of Lin-Manuel Miranda's and Quiara Alegría Hudes' production of "In the Heights" at Porchlight Theatre. The town hall's conversations on authenticity and representation, race, and ethnicity led to numerous essays by noted scholars,[5] articles in leading newspapers,[6] and online blogs[7]—each publication calling for a more identity-conscious approach and a vigorous expansion of the casting process itself.

That same month, I was cast—along with a primarily Mexican-American cast—in Phoenix Theatre's "In the Heights." Our show was not without controversy: Usnavi (the male lead) was of Iranian-Canadian descent—not Latino.[8] Since many of us had limited exposure to Nuyorican culture, that is, the Puerto Rican immigrant culture in New York City, the theatre had the foresight to bring in a voice and text coach/cultural advisor, my co-editor Cynthia Santos DeCure, originally from Puerto Rico and New York. Santos DeCure made sure that she equipped us with the linguistic authenticity worthy of the show. I knew that Pasha Yamotahari was a skilled actor, who understood and respected the immigrant experience (being an immigrant himself), and we Chicanos/Mexican-Americans also understood the immigrant experience. Still, our Latinidad did not mean we didn't have to do the work to understand the world of the play. I also knew that Phoenix Theatre, a community theatre with limited budgets and a tight production schedule, had a myriad of reasons to cast Yamotahari. Budgets and schedules aside, I believe that the controversies and subsequent conversation and policy building have moved Phoenix Theatre and others toward more transparency, inclusion, and authenticity in casting.[9]

The battle to improve hiring practices is one Murrieta has been fighting for 20 years. In our interview, we glimpse how the industry is shifting and how his work has significantly made an impact addressing underrepresentation of Latinx actors in television. Murrieta is not the only one seeking change: Quiara Alegría Hudes and her sister, Gabriela Sanchez, created a Tumblr blog called The Latinx Casting Manifesto,[10] which examines the ethics of casting from a feminist point of view. At the end of the 2020 Hispanic Heritage month, 270 leading Latinx feature writers, showrunners, and producers, with Murrieta among them, signed a letter that proclaimed: "We are tired and we demand action." *La Letter* produced by Las Hermanas (a group of Latina activist writers) and known as "The Untitled Latinx Project"[11] calls for more inclusivity and representation across the industry and demands systemic change. There has also been a rise in talented, activist Latinx casting directors—like Victor Élan Vázquez,[12] Alan Luna, and Carmen Cuba—who celebrate their Latinidad and advocate for identity-conscious casting.

Like Peter Murrieta, these job creators hold themselves and others accountable for our future, embrace the complexity of Latinx identity across the diaspora, and value authenticity in storytelling.

## The Interview

### *Peter*

I grew up in a household that was Mexican-American. My dad had worked very hard to move us to a rising, middle-class neighborhood. We were the only Mexican-Americans that I knew of in the entire community. My dad raised us to be aware of our culture and to be proud of it. Gustavo Arellano,[13] a writer for the *L.A. Times*, and I were talking about our fathers. My friend admitted: "It took me years to realize that my father was always putting up with racist behavior but saying it was cool because he was personally about letting it roll off his back in order to keep moving." Our fathers were involved in their personal struggles, but what they were doing at the time is they were making it okay for people to behave that way because they were "letting it roll off."

When I got to Chicago, to my mind, no one who was Latino had been there before me. I don't remember any other name on that wall [Second City's photo wall archives the company's members]. Horatio Sanz and I were contemporaries, and the two of us were kind of "it." I don't think I understood the oppression or the racism of it until last year [2020].[14]

However, last year, an alumna of Second City reached out to me to sign onto a letter about all the institutional racist tendencies of Second City. When I got on the phone with her, she's like, "It would mean so much to us if people like you and Horatio would sign because you're the only Latinos we see in the archives."

So, when she started talking to me about the racist tendencies and microaggressions, I was like, "Yeah, they were like that" and "Yep, somebody said that and that." I think Horatio and I were just going along like our fathers, just letting it roll off our backs, because we were there. I think it was when I moved to Los Angeles that I decided "Enough was enough." Improving Latinx representation has been my mission, and I'm very proud of what I've accomplished while knowing what the struggles are.

## Micha

As a producer and writer, you have been present in the casting room when decisions are made about Latinx identity. What can you share about your experience there?

## Peter

The best lens to look through takes you from 2003 to 2019. In 2003, when *Greetings From Tucson* was picked up and green-lit to a pilot, we were ready to cast five or six regular parts for Mexican-American characters. That number would have *tripled* the roles for Mexican-American characters on a network. At the time, it was gigantic—a game changer. And you would always hear from executives and studio people "that the pool was really thin"—and this and that. One was automatically being asked to compromise. The compromise wasn't exactly them saying, "Let's cast white people," but the tone was very much like "We will see."

Lupe Ontiveros played my grandmother on the show. She was so incredible! She was the first one cast. She was "*offer only*," meaning that when an actor creates a body of work to the point that they do not read, they no longer audition. You know who they are, and if you want what they have, you offer them the part. She had earned that.

The network I was on was WB—all about *Dawson's Creek* at the time, very pretty, gorgeous people. I remember the casting director saying "The first role you are going to cast is this 70-year-old grandmother on the WB." That's the first role! I was like "Well, Lupe is *offer only*, and we are reading [auditioning] everyone else." Lupe requested to have a conversation with the executive producer. So, I called her. She said, "Peter, you're not going to make me play a maid, are you?" I said, "No, you're a grandma." She replied, "Yeah, and what do I do?" I go, "She's retired," and Lupe goes, "from what?" and I go, "Whatever you want to retire from. It doesn't matter to me. We can do this backstory together." She goes, "Well, I want to be tough," and I said, "All right, how about if you were a mechanic in the Korean War, so you're a veteran." She liked that! So, we worked that backstory in. She was amazing, a legend.

Then, the other parts became harder to cast. We were looking for the two adult brothers—the uncle and the dad. Jacob Vargas, an incredibly talented actor known for dramatic roles, came in and gave the best audition I've ever seen. The network was like "He does drama," but I said, "Look at what you just saw." We went back and forth this way. He "destroyed" that part, but I had to go to bat for him.

Then casting the dad was even harder because the dad had to be rough, he had to be mean, he had to have cutting wit. In 2003—when I don't think we did what we do in 2020—we saw a lot of people, but we kept coming back to Julio Oscar Machosa. Julio is Cuban and sounds Cuban. We wanted Julio not to sound Cuban. We had him come back, and we're like, "Julio, do it the best as you can. I'm not asking for a Mexican-American accent, but give me something."

Of course, when he did it, it sounded okay, but it wasn't funny, mean, or sarcastic. We were all just left with a decision, in 2003, of what to do. I was the only Latino in the room. We've got producers, directors, and executives. There ain't nobody but me there. I said, "Let's cast Julio because he's the best for the part." They said, "What happens if you get asked about his heritage?" I said, "I'm going to say, the win in 2003 is that we have six Latino actors in one show, every week. They're not guest stars. They're here in that house.

Now, flash forward to 2019: when we were casting *Mr. Iglesias*, and I had to go to the mat for Jacob Vargas again because after, *Greetings From Tucson*, he kind of went back to guest starring and to hour-long dramas and movies. He's so good, but there just weren't parts for him in the comedy world. So, all those years later, we had to cast Gabriel Iglesias' best friend. I brought Jacob in, but I got some resistance. I had to dig up some clips from *Tucson*, and he won the part. He's a superstar.

Then we cast the villain part. He was originally going to be another Mexican-American; however, Oscar Nuñez of Cuban descent comes in, reads. We cast him. The best actor for the job gets the part. We create a story line that clarifies a reason for this Mexican-American and this Cuban-American to talk. We are doing things differently now. Resistance is always there, and you need people like me in those rooms. We need more executives; we need more producers; we need more directors because it's hard to fight that fight by yourself.

## *Micha*

I bet it has been. You have already alluded to the perception that "there are not enough trained Latinx actors," but does that perception still exist?

## *Peter*

Yes. Because it's a self-replicating cycle. I believe this phenomenon exists because Latinx actors aren't given opportunities to be on shows for years when they don't have to carry the whole weight of the show. The easiest way to explain it is to talk about a Black actor who is super successful, Donald Glover.

When Donald Glover was hired to be a writer on *30 Rock* and a featured performer as a writer, he didn't have to carry that show. He could be around all those incredible actors and writers for a few years and learn what was up. After six seasons of *Community*, three seasons of being at *30 Rock*, he's doing his music and movies. Now he's ready to do *Atlanta*. We need someone to let Latinx actors be No. 4 on a call sheet for six years on a show where they are allowed to grow into superstars without the pressure of carrying a show.

What happens instead is a stand-up comic will break out. I've seen this happen a bunch, and you're like, "Well, wouldn't it be better if Gabriel were on *Cristela* for a year," which he was, and he did 13 shows. He didn't have to carry the show, and now he knows what he's going to do. That is why I think we got two seasons out of *Mr. Inglesia*.

## Micha

That makes so much sense. When Latinx actors—the green ones and the seasoned ones—are in the room, what do you view as winning strategies to use as they navigate the White gaze and the White imagination?

## Peter

I'm going to speak to my experience, and then I'm going to speak to what I think goes on in other rooms. When I'm in the casting room with casting directors whom I love, Ruth Lambert and Sandy Logan, they know I don't want any "spice it up." I don't want any performative adjustments to make it seem more Chicano or more "this." I like that actor to stand before me and give me the best interpretation of the part. I know that because, in a lot of rooms, many actors are navigating the room where someone is like, "We wrote this in English, but if you want to make it Spanglish and play with it, then do it." I think that it's tough because the green actor wants the job. I would say when you have those questions asked, even if you're green and fearful, try to have enough of your feet on the ground that you can ask some questions back—in a friendly way.

Now once you reach the level of, say, Jacob Nuñez, who is not a superstar but should be, he and I have conversations all the time about him not going to read for a part because he just doesn't want to play a druggie, and that makes sense. But in the meantime, someone has to do that, someone needs to get their health insurance, and someone needs to work.

I think there's nothing wrong with an actor coming in and saying, "I'm Dominican, and this is my speaking voice, and I'm going to read for you, and this is what I think this guy would be." If they ask for Tony Montoya, then I think you are allowed to say, "I was doing this for this reason, but if I do it that way, it might feel a little cartoony. Do you want me to try it?" It is okay to ask those questions. You might not win the part, but it's the kindest way possible to tell people what is not acceptable.

## Micha

I was just looking at your page on Internet Movie Database (IMDb). I'm excited to see all the projects you have worked on and the ones about to happen. What are the trends in Latinx storytelling?

## Peter

I think I'm going to be a little sad, but I want to be hopeful. I'll talk about when I'm selling a show. I took out a show to shop it around. There are no perfect laboratory conditions where I could say this is why a show doesn't sell or why it is selling. Many factors go into a pitch: What else have they bought? What did their bosses say right before they met with me?

There are no perfect conditions. I say this as a disclaimer. Last summer, I took out a show with a partner, a Latina writer. I worked with her on *Iglesias* as her mentor. We did a show about female mentorship based on a famous sportscaster. The idea was two women in a man's world, sort of a cross between *30 Rock* and *Sports Night* [Aaron Sorkin's 1998 sitcom]. We thought about this concept, and at the core of it was the idea that you break down doors, but you don't always get to pick who comes in after you. We based the older female mentor on me, and we based the younger lead actor on her. We used our history, our sometimes contentious but always loving conversations about her particular Latina writers' group. It's this generational and gender conversation, right? Each has a valid viewpoint. We take it out and pitch it.

The lead is 25, a Latina, an "Influencer," someone with 25 million followers who does these cute little sports videos. She then gets hired by this giant company, like ESPN, to be a co-anchor, and this older character who has done 25 years of journalism is flabbergasted, like, "What have you handed me?" We go out and pitch it, and we get *nada* from all the networks. We get nothing, which happens all the time.

Then a few months later, someone said to me privately, "One of those networks was looking for me because they had a concept that they were working on." The agent calls me and says,

> I got a call from such and such network. They got this idea of a workplace comedy set at a customer call-center south of the border that is staffed by undocumented people, who have been kicked out of the United States. They are great at the Mexican call center because they've been in the United States so long that they speak good English. Kind of like *Superstore* meets *The Office*.

My agent, whom I love dearly, told me this only in the aftermath without checking with me. When they asked, "Would Peter be interested?" she responded, "That sounds really racist, so I don't think he would."

When you hear this story, your mind reels. You aren't going to understand the super successful, non-traumatic 25-year-old female with 25 million followers, who is over her head at a new job. But you do understand the Dreamer kicked out of the United States, who works at a call center. That's the kind of mindset we are up against. They want to buy our trauma and don't understand why we won't watch it.

## Micha

Latinx actors often face another form of identity politics in casting. Are conversations about colorism blatant in the room?

## Peter

No, I've never been a part of them, but people know who I am walking into a room. The only time I can think about color organically coming up in conversation is if you are casting a mother and daughter or father and son. I can easily see a producer saying, "We booked so and so, and now we're casting the daughter. We're bringing in people, and we've got our final four candidates." I feel you would do that casting any family, to some degree. You'd want to put people up, look at their headshots and go, "Do they look like a family?" I don't find fault with that, but I've never heard anybody say somebody is too light or too dark.

## Micha

But maybe not Latino enough?

## Peter

For sure, I've heard that all the time, but nobody talks about it. It's a good point. You go anywhere else in the whole world, and nobody has that problem.

## Micha

Because Latinos have a variety of phenotypes. And there are immigrants all over the world.

## Peter

I saw this online video. Someone had a last name like Frizarri (I'm making up the name). He was a chef, and he's talking, and some interviewer is like, "It's so crazy you've got the last name Frizarri and you're Mexican." Poor Carlos Frizarri has got a huge, sardonic smile because he's talking to an American, who is making television, and the American just can't get it in his head that Italians live in Mexico.

### Micha

That limited mentality does exist and reinforces the stereotypes. How do you think future actors' training can undo this stereotype?

### Peter

It's a good question. I'm going to talk about ways to navigate an audition. One of the ways to combat the stereotype is not to be afraid to be yourself before you slate. Don't get out of your car and decide that you have to code-switch once you go through the studio gate. It's ok to use a little bit of Spanish—and then slate. Then do whatever accent they want. I believe that's a way to combat it.

I think another way is to have a conversation with your agent. Say, "I've spent money. I'm trained; you can send me in for all kinds of things. I don't want to just go in on Latino/a/x parts. I'd rather go in for a wider range of parts so send me in on ones that I feel I could nail in the Latinx spaces. I think it's essential to have that kind of open relationship with an agent.

### Micha

I saw the article by Fidel Martinez in the L.A. Times, "Latinx Files: What will the future of Latinx television look like?"[15] You are quoted in that piece. As you are writing and dreaming, what will the future of Latinx television look like?

### Peter

Much of the press coverage is negative about us. It's focused on what is not being done. I can only describe the "Future of Latinx Television" as part of my mission. When I got my first show on the air in 2003, I thought we were about to have a Latinx wave of the likes we had never seen. *George Lopez* came on the air the same month I did. *Culture Clash* had done a sketch show for Fox, and there was a one-hour drama on N.B.C. called *Kingpin,* a forerunner of *Narcos.* I thought, we are here! Five or six years before that, we had James Olmos on *Miami Vice* and Jimmy Smits on *L.A. Law.* Then the Latin wave just didn't happen.

Back then, I thought I would be around 12 people, all versions of me. Male/female, showrunners, comedy writers. There wasn't. As the years went on, it became this bigger mission. I need to hire Latinx writers. I need to support them and coach them. I need to hire those actors that can be No. 5 on the call sheet. I think about soon-to-be superstars Cree Cicchino and Fabrizio Zacharee Guido [they played Marisol and Mickie, on *Mr. Iglesias* for two years]. They didn't have to carry the show, and they are advancing. They are growing, and they are fantastic.

Finally, this appointment at ASU was a perfect fit for my mission. I'm going to overwhelm them with numbers. There will be no denying it. I feel the future of Latinx Television is for us to play—<u>all the parts.</u>

Remember that show I told you about, the one I couldn't sell about the hip Latina journalist? Someone is going to sell a show like that. Someone will sell a show about a kick-ass lawyer, who is raising a daughter by herself—only because we want to have more conflict for the lead, not because of some stereotypes about Latinas. It's going to be a female lead who's a kick-ass Latina, and that's just going to be it. Just like Queen Latifah in *The Equalizer*. No one is going to have any questions about it. I think that the future is going to be awesome. I feel driven to make sure I see the wave.

### Micha

We are coming out of some really rough years where the narrative around Latinos couldn't have been worse, right?

### Peter

And you know that perception hurts. Another thing that hurts me is when younger press-savvy colleagues talk about their shows. They lament, "Growing up, I never knew I could be represented on TV. I knew it was going to be up to me to do it because we are not represented." And I think, "Well, did you watch *Wizard*? Did you watch *Tucson*? Did you watch *George Lopez*? Did you watch *Ugly Betty*? We've been doing it. Don't diminish the past that we did have."

Last year, I tried to behave in a way that would be exemplary. If there is a show about us, I watch it. I don't want to feel later that a show got canceled because I didn't support it. If there is a movie about us, I go to it. I want to do the behavior we should all be doing, and so I started a group that's an advocacy group for each other. We have three rules:

- You can't show up and talk *chisme (gossip)* about anybody.
- This group is here to support you; if you want something from the group, ask for it. When you ask for something from the group, then you have to give something to the group.
- We show up.

It's a multi-gender group, multi-ethnic group. It's not just writers or actors; there are comics and executives in it. Our other fourth rule (which we don't talk about) is:

- We don't publicize it.
- We don't care about the selfie. We care about action, about doing things.

## Micha

Thank you so much for being an agent of change. Your journey and your mission provide me with a lot of hope for the future of Latinx representation.

## Notes

1 Identity conscious ideologies have been adopted by directors, casting agents, and vocal coaches (myself included) to improve intergroup communication and representation. For studies of diversity ideologies, see Lisa M. Leslie, "On Melting Pots and Salad Bowls: A Meta-Analysis of the Effects of Identity-Blind and Identity-Conscious Diversity Ideologies," *Journal of Applied Psychology* 105, no. 5 (2020): 453–71, https://doi.org/10.1037/apl0000446; Hector Y. Adames, Nayeli Y. Chavez-Dueñas, and Maryam M. Jernigan, "The Fallacy of a Raceless Latinidad: Action Guidelines for Centering Blackness in Latinx Psychology," *Journal of Latinx Psychology* 9, no.1 (2021): 26–44, https://doi.org/10.1037/lat0000179. For understanding of diversity ideologies and their applications to theatre, see Lavina Jadwahni and Victor Vazquez, "Identity-Conscious Casting: Moving Beyond Color-Blind and Color-Conscious Casting," *Howlround*, accessed February 2, 2021, https://howlround.com/identity-conscious-casting; Claire Syler and Daniel Banks, *Casting a Movement: The Welcome Table Initiative* (London: Routledge, 2019).
2 Brian E. Herrera, *Latin Numbers: Playing Latino in Twentieth-Century U.S. Popular Performance* (Ann Arbor: University of Michigan Press, 2015).
3 For a further research on the history of casting and what it means to be casting as a Latinx individual, explore David Mendizábal and Joey Reyes, "The Casting Room with Brian Herrera & Victor Vazquez," *SolTalk*, July 17, 2019, Podcast, MP3 audio, 53:38, https://soltalk.podbean.com/e/soltalk-episode-four-feat-brian-herrera-victor-vazquez/.
4 Howlround, "Conversation: The Color Game: Whitewashing Latinx Stories," accessed August 9, 2016, https://howlround.com/happenings/conversation.
5 Trevor Boffone, "Whitewashed Usnavi: Race, Power and Representation in In the Heights," *Studies in Musical Theatre* 13, no. 3 (2019): 235–50, https://doi.org/10.1386/smt_00003_1; Brian E. Herrera, "'But Do We Have the Actors for That?' Some Principles of Practice for Staging Latinx Plays in a University Theatre Context," *Theatre Topics* 27, no. 1 (2017): 23–35, https://doi.org/10.1353/tt.2017.0004; Brandon Johnson, "Whitewashing Expression: Using Copyright Law to Protect Racial Identity in Casting," *Northwestern University Law Review* 112, no. 5 (2018): 1137–69.
6 Raul A. Reyes, "Chicago: 'In the Heights' Non-Latino Lead Stirs Controversy," *NBC News*, accessed August 25, 2016, www.nbcnews.com/news/latino/chicago-heights-non-latino-lead-stirs-controversy-n637266; Jessica Gelt, "Authenticity in Casting: From 'Colorblind' to 'Color Conscious,' New Rules Are Anything But Black and White," *Los Angeles Times*, accessed July 13, 2017, www.latimes.com/entertainment/arts/la-ca-cm-authenticity-in-casting-20170713-htmlstory.html.
7 Aja Romano, "Lin-Manuel Miranda's 'in the Heights' is the Latest Battleground in the Theater Community's Fight Against Whitewashing," *Vox*, accessed July 28, 2016, www.vox.com/2016/7/28/12297480/in-the-heights-casting-controversy-chicago; Michael Lueger and Brian Herrera, "Theatre History Podcast # 11: 'You Don't Read Latino': Discussing the History of Latinx Casting with Brian Eugenio Herrera," *Howlround*, October 31, 2016, Podcast, MP3, 39:42, https://howlround.com/theatre-history-podcast-11; Trevor Boffone, "Casting an 'Authentic' in the Heights," accessed July 20, 2016, https://trevorboffone.com/2016/07/20/casting-an-authentic-in-the-heights/; Sherman Howard, "Intricacies and Intent Surrounding Race and Ethnicity in Casting," *Arts Integrity*, accessed July 27, 2016, www.artsintegrity.org/intricacies-and-intent-surrounding-race-and-ethnicity-in-casting/.

8 Kerry Lengel, "'In the Heights' Casting Controversy Comes to Phoenix," *Azcentral*, accessed July 15, 2021, www.azcentral.com/story/entertainment/arts/2016/08/19/phoenix-theatre-in-the-heights-casting/88877340/.
9 Lin Manuel Miranda's and Quiara Alegría Hudes' film *In the Heights* opened on June 10, 2021. The film's opening was complicated by criticism around colorism and the casting of light skinned Latin actors which did not reflect the majority dark skinned population of Washington Heights. Apologies were issued by Miranda for his casting decisions. The exclusion of Blackness from Latinidad is painful reality of racism within the Latinx community, for further understanding of how colonial and anti-blackness ideology is rooted in Latinx psychology, see Hector Y. Adames, Nayeli Y. Chavez-Dueñas, and Maryam M. Jernigan, "The Fallacy of a Raceless Latinidad: Action Guidelines for Centering Blackness in Latinx Psychology," *Journal of Latinx Psychology* 9, no. 1 (2021): 26–44, https://doi.org/10.1037/lat0000179; Monica Castillo, "The Limitations Of 'Latinidad': How Colorism Haunts 'in The Heights'," *NPR*, accessed June 15, 2021, www.npr.org/2021/06/15/1006728781/in-the-heights-latinidad-colorism-casting-lin-manuel-miranda
10 Quiara, "Latinx Casting Manifesto," accessed July 15, 2021, www.quiara.com/latinx-casting-manifesto.
11 Untitled Latinx Project, "LA Letter," accessed July 15, 2021, https://untitledlatinxproject.com/la-letter.
12 X Casting, "About," accessed July 15, 2021, www.xcastingnyc.com/about.
13 Los Angeles Times, "People: Gustavo Arellano," accessed July 15, 2021, www.latimes.com/people/gustavo-arellano.
14 In the summer of 2020, after a series of open letters, the Second City theaters and training institutions committed to re-envision and reform the organization's 60-year history of racial disparities. See Melena Ryzik and Jake Malooley, "Second City Is Trying Not to Be Racist. Will It Work This Time?" *New York Times*, accessed August 13, 2020, www.nytimes.com/2020/08/12/movies/second-city-black-lives-matter.html.
15 Fidel Martinez, "Latinx Files: What will the future of Latinx Television Look Like?" *Los Angeles Times*, accessed February 4, 2021, www.latimes.com/world-nation/newsletter/2021-02-04/latinx-files-future-of-television-latinx-files.

## Bibliography

Adames, Hector Y., Nayeli Y. Chavez-Dueñas, and Maryam M. Jernigan. "The Fallacy of a Raceless Latinidad: Action Guidelines for Centering Blackness in Latinx Psychology." *Journal of Latinx Psychology* 9, no.1 (2021): 26–44. https://doi.org/10.1037/lat0000179.
Boffone, Trevor. "Whitewashed Usnavi: Race, Power and Representation in In the Heights." *Studies in Musical Theatre* 13, no. 3 (2019): 235–50. https://doi.org/10.1386/smt_00003_1.
Castillo, Monica. "The Limitations Of 'Latinidad': How Colorism Haunts 'In The Heights'." *NPR*. Accessed June 15, 2021. www.npr.org/2021/06/15/1006728781/in-the-heights-latinidad-colorism-casting-lin-manuel-miranda
Gelt, Jessica. "Authenticity in Casting: From 'Colorblind' to 'Color Conscious,' New Rules Are Anything But Black and White." *Los Angeles Times*. Accessed July 13, 2017. www.latimes.com/entertainment/arts/la-ca-cm-authenticity-in-casting-20170713-html story.html.
Herrera, Brian E. *Latin Numbers: Playing Latino in Twentieth-Century U.S. Popular Performance*. Ann Arbor: University of Michigan Press, 2015.

———. "'But Do We Have the Actors for That?' Some Principles of Practice for Staging Latinx Plays in a University Theatre Context." *Theatre Topics* 27, no. 1 (2017): 23–35. https://doi.org/10.1353/tt.2017.0004.

Howard, Sherman. "Intricacies and Intent Surrounding Race and Ethnicity in Casting." *Arts Integrity*. Accessed July 27, 2016. www.artsintegrity.org/intricacies-and-intent-surrounding-race-and-ethnicity-in-casting/

Howlround. "Conversation: The Color Game: Whitewashing Latinx Stories." Accessed August 9, 2016. https://howlround.com/happenings/conversation.

Hudes, Quiara Alegria. "Latinx Casting Manifesto." Accessed July 15, 2021. www.quiara.com/latinx-casting-manifesto.

Jadwahni, Lavina, and Victor Vazquez. "Identity-Conscious Casting: Moving Beyond Color-Blind and Color-Conscious Casting." *Howlround*. Accessed February 2, 2021. https://howlround.com/identity-conscious-casting.

Johnson, Brandon. "Whitewashing Expression: Using Copyright Law to Protect Racial Identity in Casting." *Northwestern University Law Review* 112, no. 5 (2018): 1137–69.

Lengel, Kerry. "'In the Heights' Casting Controversy Comes to Phoenix." *Azcentral*. Accessed July 15, 2021. www.azcentral.com/story/entertainment/arts/2016/08/19/phoenix-theatre-in-the-heights-casting/88877340/.

Leslie, Lisa M., Joyce E. Bono, Yeonka S. Kim, and Gregory R. Beaver. "On Melting Pots and Salad Bowls: A Meta-Analysis of the Effects of Identity-Blind and Identity-Conscious Diversity Ideologies." *Journal of Applied Psychology* 105, no. 5 (2020): 453–71. https://doi.org/10.1037/apl0000446.

Los Angeles Times. "People: Gustavo Arellano." Accessed July 15, 2021. www.latimes.com/people/gustavo-arellano.

Lueger, Michael, and Brian Herrera. "Theatre History Podcast # 11: 'You Don't Read Latino': Discussing the History of Latinx Casting with Brian Eugenio Herrera." *Howlround*. October 31, 2016. Podcast, MP3, 39:42. https://howlround.com/theatre-history-podcast-11.

Martinez, Fidel. "Latinx Files: What Will the Future of Latinx Television Look Like?" *Los Angeles Times*. Accessed February 4, 2021. www.latimes.com/world-nation/newsletter/2021-02-04/latinx-files-future-of-television-latinx-files.

Mendizábal, David, and Joey Reyes. "The Casting Room With Brian Herrera & Victor Vazquez." *SolTalk*. July 17, 2019. Podcast, MP3 audio, 53:38. https://soltalk.podbean.com/e/soltalk-episode-four-feat-brian-herrera-victor-vazquez/.

Reyes, Raul A. "Chicago: 'In the Heights' Non-Latino Lead Stirs Controversy." *NBC News*. Accessed August 25, 2016. www.nbcnews.com/news/latino/chicago-heights-non-latino-lead-stirs-controversy-n637266.

Romano, Aja. "Lin-Manuel Miranda's 'In the Heights' Is the Latest Battleground in the Theater Community's Fight Against Whitewashing." *Vox*. Accessed July 28, 2016. www.vox.com/2016/7/28/12297480/in-the-heights-casting-controversy-chicago.

Ryzik, Melena, and Jake Malooley. "Second City Is Trying Not to Be Racist. Will it Work This Time?" *New York Times*. Accessed August 13, 2020. www.nytimes.com/2020/08/12/movies/second-city-black-lives-matter.html.

Trevor Boffone. "Casting an 'Authentic' in the Heights." Accessed July 20, 2016. https://trevorboffone.com/2016/07/20/casting-an-authentic-in-the-heights/.

Untitled Latinx Project. "LA Letter." Accessed July 15, 2021. https://untitledlatinxproject.com/la-letter.

X Casting. "About." Accessed July 15, 2021. www.xcastingnyc.com/about.

# 20
# CHAMPIONING UNHEARD VOICES
Developing the Civic Voice Through Story

*Michelle Lopez-Rios*

Augusto Boal spoke of the human being as a unity, "an indivisible whole." The mind and body are inseparable. We think and absorb the world with our whole body.[1] Our experiences in our cultures and communities are part of that "whole." As a Latina theatre maker and voice teacher, I invite actors to bring all of themselves and their experiences into their training. In voice classes, we critically discuss whose voices are heard in the stories we witness in our communities and in the media. We identify what ignites their passion and how they use their civic voice in their community. As we explore ways to nurture a healthy and powerful voice, we celebrate the whole of the individual. Finally, I challenge actors to take the knowledge they gain in training back into their community.

## Conservatory Training of the Past

Growing up in Texas, the rhythms and customs of my Mexican-American culture surrounded me. Every gathering started with *saludos* (heartfelt greetings to find out how each person is doing). The latest *chisme* (life's latest stories or gossip) could be heard rolling off the tongue in Spanglish while delicious food was passed around. As cumbias played on the Tejano radio station, everyone from babies to my great-grandmother danced through the room. However, I quickly learned to hide or subdue these rhythms in my body and voice when I entered undergraduate acting conservatory training. I limited my tongue to the sounds of Standard English. I reduced my caloric intake on the advice of my teachers and focused on ballet class and British characters. It was not until I left training that I would invite my beloved community and culture back into my artistic work.

After a decade of acting in theaters around the country, I returned to school in 2004 to pursue my M.F.A. in Theatre at the University of Houston. My focus on

DOI: 10.4324/9781003021520-23

the teaching of voice, speech, and dialects was met with the typical opportunities of exploring the texts of Aeschylus, Shakespeare, Chekhov, and other European names I had encountered in my undergraduate theatre training. But these were not the Latin American and US Latina roles I had been performing professionally. As I began to articulate my teaching pedagogy, I became specifically interested in how the individual's community and culture could not only be invited, but also actually flourish in a performance training environment. In this chapter, I will examine how techniques used by The Royal Mexican Players and subsequent community projects directly shaped my teaching pedagogy.

## The Latinx Voice

As I designed my path as a teacher, I thought deeply on who this performance work was for and who these stories were about. I studied Fitzmaurice Voicework® and embraced the concept of "destructuring" not only my breath, but also the traditional ways of approaching actor training that focused on white European stories. The rebuilding or "structuring" aspect of the work empowers the individual to take space and communicate with ease and precision.[2] I was drawn to the work of Dudley Knight who had written about "standards" of speech and championed vigorous voice and speech work that did not hold white Eurocentric speech as the standard.[3] The work focused on allowing the individual to find their most authentic sound, not replicate the sounds of others. These are powerful tools for the individual in society.

At the same time, I began working with playwright Alvaro Saar Rios on a piece called *The Crazy Mexican Show*.[4] The Spanglish scenes in the show were influenced by sketch comedy and other traditional theatre pedagogy and spoke to the heart of the Latinx community. We performed at the Cultural Center M.E.C.A. (Multicultural Education and Counseling through the Arts) to sold-out audiences. Much of the predominately Latinx audience had attended few, if any, plays. Dubbing ourselves as "Houston's brownest performance troupe," The RMP was born.

RMP continued to work on new material, performing in Houston, San Antonio, and even Potsdam, New York. Instead of working within the parameters of predominately white theatres, we produced shows written, directed, performed, and attended by the Latinx community. Taking inspiration from Boal and his community-engaged work,[5] we also shared our process of creating work by offering performance workshops. In these workshops, we used discussions, voice exercises, and writing prompts to tell stories. We embraced our Mexican-American customs to create spaces to actively nurture new voices to tell stories.

### *Nuestra Voz, Nuestra Historia*

In 2006, I was hired to create and teach the voice curriculum in the University of Wisconsin-Milwaukee B.F.A. Acting Program. My goal from the start was to create a space where artists were comfortable to fully be themselves. I would not teach a standard way to speak, but invite many beautiful ways to speak. I believed this approach could simultaneously celebrate the sounds of the individual and introduce new ways to strengthen the individual's voice. I was also interested in continuing the community-engaged work we had started in Houston.

Being new to Milwaukee, I did not know the Latinx community. UWM is a predominately white institution and did not have the diversity in students, staff, or faculty I experienced in Houston. The Latinx representation in the department was shockingly small. The first thought that came to mind was the call to action from Luis Valdez, "If the Raza won't come to the theater, then the theater must go to the Raza."[6] I turned to community for the answer.

Funded by a grant from the UWM Roberto Hernandez Center, RMP devised and directed a two-part project. Part one was a six-week voice and writing workshop open to Latinx students, staff, faculty, and members of the Milwaukee community. The second part included performances of the pieces created in the workshop at UW-Milwaukee and at Walker Point Center for the Arts, located in a Latinx neighborhood of Milwaukee.

We gathered the diverse group with intention. Flyers were hand-delivered to various local Latinx community centers, arts organizations, grocery stores, and Spanish immersion schools in the community. We sent out e-mails to UWM student groups, faculty, and staff. We offered in-person gatherings to answer questions and/or concerns. The successful result was a mix of 16 Latinx students, staff, and community members, who created a space to share stories.

We created a working environment nourished by our culture. We took time to listen, talk, and share food before diving into the work. We began the workshop discussing goals and thoughts about how we could share the space, support each other, and meet the needs of the folks in the room. Each Saturday began with time for *saludos*. We would pass around the *pan dulce* (Mexican sweet bread) while discussing the events that transpired over the previous week. These little check-ins with each person allowed the group to support those who had a tough week or lift those who had news to celebrate. It was essential time to build community and create a space to share personal stories. We took our time to listen, to engage, and to reflect. We spent the first half of the day exploring voice and freeing sound in the body with exercised based in Fitzmaurice Voicework®. Then, we explored stories through discussions and writing prompts. There were also group exercises to build community influenced by Boal exercises.[7]

Most of the workshop participants continued on to perform their original pieces in a show that would be called *Nuestra Voz, Nuestra Historia* (Our Voice, Our Story). We headed into rehearsal and continued to focus on creating a brave space where individuals strengthened their voice. The performers shared stories about family, being mixed race, being undocumented, being American, and even what one performer dubbed "un-fairy tales" to sold-out audiences. Latinx community members from all over Milwaukee showed up in the audience, some of whom had never been to a play.

Participant Veronica Sotelo auditioned and enrolled as a student in the UW-Milwaukee B.F.A. Acting program after the experience, sharing that while working on the project she "was also inspired by storytelling, performance and how theatre can bring a voice to those who are often underrepresented in society."[8] Sotelo went on to organize and direct *The Latina Monologues*. This collection of poetry and monologues became an annual event that was performed at the university and in the Milwaukee and Madison communities. Poet and performer, Angela C. Trudell Vasquez reflected on her journey as a part of *The Latina Monologues*, "This is us telling our own stories, not someone else writing them for us. We are defining ourselves, and not being defined by someone else. We are creating our own history."[9]

It became clear to me after working on *Nuestra Voz* that nurturing and supporting an individual's voice was essential in the training of voice. The histories and complex sounds that live within individuals are the essence of their unique voice. The traditional pedagogy for training performers was shifting; there was more attention to finding material that spoke to different cultures. There were more discussions about how to be more inclusive in training. It was not enough. I began to incorporate writing into the voice classes. Sharing original poetry and stories became part of developing the individual voice.

## *Precious Lives*

In 2014, the horrific news story of five-year-old Laylah Peterson being shot by a stray bullet while sitting on her grandfather's lap in her home gripped the hearts of Milwaukee residents. The tragic event on the heels of the Sandy Hook shooting inspired a 100-part weekly radio series/podcast produced by 371 Productions called "Precious Lives."[10] Through storytelling, the series focused on understanding what was causing the gun violence and how it affected the youth in the city. I was brought onboard to devise and direct a live performance of the show.

The hope was to create a live performance to spark intimate community conversations about gun violence in Milwaukee and how to stop that violence. Together with composer and musician Kiran Vee, we offered a four-week performance workshop at a COA Youth and Family Center for youth affected by gun violence. We used music, voice, and storytelling exercises to explore their stories through rap, song, and poetry. Much like *Nuestra Voz*, we took time to create a supportive space where the participants felt comfortable sharing their stories and strengthening their voices. *Saludos* and snacks provided nourishment and an opportunity to build community. Dr. Earl Bracey, a local psychologist, joined us as a resource to the youth as we crafted the stories around their painful experiences. Laughter and tears flowed from the room as participants shared their most vulnerable memories. While some participants shared their voice immediately, others were hesitant to be so vulnerable. After weeks of listening to others share stories, one young woman told her story about the loss of a sibling to gun violence. She was deeply struck by the group's attentive listening and powerful reaction to her story. In her reflection she shared that until that experience of sharing her story, she never thought her story was important.

Four of the young participants in the workshop (the youngest age 13) continued on to the live performance. They were joined by two local young spoken word artists and three adult community activists. We crafted three 15-minute pop-up shows, each composed of three personal stories of gun violence with live underscoring followed by a live conversation.

The Pabst Theater in downtown Milwaukee hosted a kickoff performance and community discussion to an audience of over 1,000 people. Community organizations set up tables in the lobby to share information on how they were working to end gun violence or offering services to those affected by gun violence. The voices of the performers were strong and filled the huge theater. Audience members both reacted on social media and gave powerful feedback during the community discussion. They commented on how deeply affected they were by the stories and expressed being moved to take action to end gun violence. The audience asked many questions about the process and offered much praise to the performers. During the talkback, performer Nicole Newsom offered that she shared her powerful spoken word poetry knowing, "If I get through to somebody, maybe it will change the lives of others."[11] Audience members who had previously seen gun violence as someone else's problem began to see it as a community issue.[12]

The work I do in the studio with actors is the same work I do in the community. Everyone has a story and that story matters. *Nuestra Voz* and *Precious Lives* are two examples of how the power of the individual voice strengthens the community. The needs of the individual and the needs of the community demand training that supports the individual to use their voice to its absolute fullest on stage and in life.

## Community in Training

In 2017, I joined the voice faculty at The Theatre School at DePaul (TTS) to teach voice in the M.F.A. and B.F.A. Acting Programs. The space we build is vital to the work. The guidelines or agreements we establish together create a space for individuals to be fully seen and heard. *Saludos* or check-ins at the beginning of class allow us to see what outside forces are affecting the people in the space on a particular day. Sometimes the simplest bit of shared information can completely change the trajectory of how the group interacts. We can take the time to nourish and support individual needs with kind words or simply by listening to their worries or fears. We take time to listen and acknowledge the challenges facing different communities. We can be fully present with each other.

The exercises we do in performance are gifts that are useful beyond the stage or camera. We practice being fully present with each other, listening deeply and taking time to care for each other and ourselves. As my students say these are practices that "lead us to be better human beings," voice students will sit with a stressed-out non-theatre roommate and teach them how to breathe slowly and deeply to help calm their nervous system. Sometimes, after a break, a student will share that they went home and taught a parent how to tremor[13] or structure and support their voice so that they could be heard on important issues. The students share the practices with their own communities to release stress, build presence, and strengthen communication. In turn, the communities directly benefit from the work we do in the classroom.

The *Precious Lives* production used the power of storytelling to ignite discussion about gun violence in the Milwaukee community. At The Theatre School at DePaul, first-year actors present "Passion Speeches" in voice class. They research and present a persuasive argument to change a policy, law, or social norm that is oppressive. The speeches raise awareness about needs and experiences of different communities and inspire conversation. It is an exercise that Boal might call "rehearsal for life." Students take the knowledge of how to use their healthy and powerful voice to articulate social justice and equity in their community.

In voice classes, we nurture and strengthen the voice. This begins by inviting the whole of the individual and their unique journey. The goal of our work together is not to change the rhythms or sounds of the individual, but to allow them to be fully embodied and expressed as we explore the endless sounds and possibilities in our voices and bodies. Our individual communities and cultures nourish and ground our voices to express ourselves fully and actively engage our voice. We reciprocate this nourishment by giving our civic voices back to our communities. Creating this circle can start very simply. One of my favorite prompts asks the individual to complete the sentence, "I am . . ." The possibilities are infinite. It is the beginning of your story and what you have to say. Everyone has a story, and every story is important.

## Notes

1 Augusto Boal, *Games for Actors and Non-Actors* (New York: Routledge, 2002), 59.
2 "About Fitzmaurice Voicework," The Fitzmaurice Institute, accessed June 6, 2021, www.fitzmauriceinstitute.org/fitzmaurice-voicework.
3 Dudley Knight, "Standards," *The Voice & Speech Review* 1, no. 1 (2000): 1–17.
4 *The Crazy Mexican Show,* performed by Alvaro Rios, Lupe Mendez, Chris Rivera, and Michelle Lopez, MECA, Houston, Texas, April 2004.
5 The exercises developed by Augusto Boal target muscular, sensory, memory, imagination, and emotion systems. These techniques are excellent stimuli for storytelling. See Boal, *Games for Actors and Non-Actors*.
6 Luis Valdez and El Teatro Campesino, *Actos El Teatro Campesino*, 1st ed. (Fresno: Cucaracha Press, 1971), 10.
7 See Note 5.

8. Jennifer Morales, "UWM's Michelle Lopez-Rios Champions Unheard Voices," *UWM Report*, accessed October 9, 2015, https://uwm.edu/news/uwms-michelle-lopez-rios-champions-unheard-voices/.
9. Angela C. Trudell Vasquez, "The Making of the Latina Monologues," *Verse Wisconsin Online*, accessed May 12, 2021, https://versewisconsin.org/Issue108/prose/trudell_vasquez.html.
10. Precious Lives, accessed 15 May 2021, https://preciouslivesproject.org.
11. Michelle Maternowski, "#075 Precious Lives: Stories, Songs and Poems Highlight Gun Violence's Impact on Milwaukee," *WUWM*, June 21, 2016, MP3 audio, 57:08, www.wuwm.com/2016-06-21/075-precious-lives-stories-songs-and-poems-highlight-gun-violences-impact-on-milwaukee.
12. Sarah Hauer, "Precious Lives Show Features Those Touched by Violence," *Milwaukee Journal Sentinel*, accessed June 16, 2016, https://archive.jsonline.com/news/crime/precious-lives-show-features-those-touched-by-violence-b99743872z1-383293111.html/.
13. Tremor exercises are part of Fitzmaurice Voicework® and are used to release tension in the body.

## Bibliography

Boal, Augusto. *Games for Actors and Non-Actors*. New York: Routledge, 2002.

The Fitzmaurice Institute. "About Fitzmaurice Voicework." Accessed June 6, 2021. www.fitzmauriceinstitute.org/fitzmaurice-voicework.

Hauer, Sarah. "Precious Lives Show Features Those Touched by Violence." *Milwaukee Journal Sentinel*. Accessed June 16, 2016. https://archive.jsonline.com/news/crime/precious-lives-show-features-those-touched-by-violence-b99743872z1-383293111.html/.

Knight, Dudley. "Standards." *The Voice & Speech Review* 1, no. 1 (2000): 1–17.

Maternowski, Michelle. "#075 Precious Lives: Stories, Songs and Poems Highlight Gun Violence's Impact on Milwaukee." *WUWM*, June 21, 2016. MP3 audio, 57:08. www.wuwm.com/2016-06-21/075-precious-lives-stories-songs-and-poems-highlight-gun-violences-impact-on-milwaukee.

Morales, Jennifer. "UWM's Michelle Lopez-Rios Champions Unheard Voices." *UWM Report*. Accessed October 9, 2015. https://uwm.edu/news/uwms-michelle-lopez-rios-champions-unheard-voices/.

Valdez, Luis, and Teatro Campesino. *Actos El Teatro Campesino*. 1st ed. Fresno: Cucaracha Press, 1971.

Vasquez, Angela C. Trudell. "The Making of the Latina Monologues." *Verse Wisconsin Online*. Accessed May 12, 2021. https://versewisconsin.org/Issue108/prose/trudell_vasquez.html.

# 21
# THEATRE WHERE YOU ARE

*Emilio Rodriguez*

"You must not be from here."

I heard these words from a stage manager when I auditioned for a small theatre company in Los Angeles. I attended the audition without an appointment; I explained that I had submitted my headshot and resume but that I had not received a time. The stage manager further explained: "If you sent your headshot and resume and didn't hear back, it means we don't need to see you."

Having just graduated with my bachelor's degree in theatre from the University of California at Irvine (UCI), I had never experienced restrictions at auditions. In my small university-theatre world, everyone had been given the opportunity to at least try out. The bare minimum was that actors were given a chance to show what they had prepared. My mentality was, "If I do the work, someone will see it!" But, here, I was being told that I was not even allowed to audition because of my headshot.

This audition incident in Los Angeles made me flash back to my "Intro to Acting" course at UC Irvine. At my end-of-year debrief, my teacher, a graduate student, had told me that my look was "too unconventional for mainstream theatre" and that I should "consider doing improv instead." Once again, I was being pre-judged by my looks but not by my talent. I began to question whether I had chosen the wrong career and whether I was even meant to be a theatre actor.

On my drive home, I saw a billboard for John Leguizamo's one-man show, which became known as "Ghetto Klown." I went to see the show and was enamored with the way Leguizamo used his personal experiences to prove he was not only the perfect person to play the role but also the only person who could play it. The day after seeing the show, I enrolled in a playwriting class at South Coast Repertory. In this Orange County professional theater, I took acting classes while simultaneously studying at UC Irvine. The class gave me the tools and structure

DOI: 10.4324/9781003021520-24

to craft a narrative, so I took the full progression of three courses before moving to Detroit to teach high school English for the program called Teach for America (TFA).

I remember talking to my TFA recruiter about moving to Detroit. "I don't know if I want to leave Los Angeles. There isn't a theatre scene outside of LA or New York." I now know how wrong I was. However, this points to a more significant issue of universities and textbooks: uplifting New York- and Los Angeles-based companies, making students believe that those are the only places where theatre exists.

My recruiter told me, "You can make theatre wherever you are."

Who knew that my best piece of theatre advice would come from someone completely unrelated to theatre? So simple, almost ignorant, yet it was better than any advice I had received in my four years of university education. Although Detroit had a robust theatre scene in 2012 (and still does), I was not able to find a lot of spaces for playwrights or theatre artists of color. I could see 50 theaters doing *Death of a Salesman* or *Pippin*, but I could not find a place to develop my voice as a writer or share a space with other actors of color. However, that recruiter's voice played in my head again and again: "make theatre wherever you are."

In 2015, I hosted a Fringe festival in Detroit after rewatching season two of the future cult classic, *Smash*.[1] My threefold, original intentions were selfish: I wanted to write and direct an original play starring me as a dynamic character; I resolved to show that opinionated U.C. Irvine undergraduate acting teacher that my "look" was not an impediment; and I was determined to show that L.A. stage manager that I needed to be seen. However, as I started collecting submissions for the festival, opening acts, and transition pieces, I realized that so many other theatre makers felt unconventional and so many others also felt unseen. So I ended up cutting my plans for a two-hour play to a ten-minute scene, thus creating room for more artists to share the stage.

Little did I know that we were also creating a community.

My connection with artists strengthened the following year when I co-founded Black and Brown Theatre with a group of Detroit artists who wanted to see more diverse actors and creatives on Detroit stages. That fall, we produced a showcase of scenes written by writers of color starring local actors of color.

Our message was simple: We. Are. Here.

We invited local directors, artistic directors, casting directors, and producers to this performance. Our production sent a clear message to them that Detroit was replete with actors of color to cast and writers of color to produce.

Initially, we developed the tagline, "The goal is to fail." We meant that in five to ten years, we would disband because we thought, if we were truly successful, a theatre company for artists of color would no longer be necessary because all theatres would cast and hire equitably. We even formed a database of headshots and resumes from actors of color in the southeast Michigan area, which helped us bring in ally companies in the beginning to establish that Black and Brown Theatre was not a threat. Having a database was important as the Michigan theatre scene is extremely competitive due to limited funding for new theatres.

According to Encore Michigan,[2] more than 100 professional theatre companies exist in the State of Michigan (for this article, I define "professional" as theatre companies that compensate theatre artists for shows). In addition to the professional companies, Michigan also has community theaters that either do not pay their talent or charge their talent a fee to participate. Of the more than 100 professional theatres listed on Encore Michigan,[3] only 11 are credited as receiving operational support from the 2020 Michigan Council for Arts and Cultural Affairs. With this plethora of companies competing for a relatively low pool for grants, many artists justifiably felt that the funding disparities create an environment of gate-keeping and power hoarding.

While our initial strategy successfully alleviated the competitive nature of starting a new theatre company, it also made theatre companies and their artistic directors view us as a resource rather than a theatre company. We were disappointed to receive e-mails from artistic directors looking to cast their upcoming season but, then, not see the directors in the audience at our performances. Nevertheless, we were committed to creating meaningful work that reflected who we are and the theatre we wanted. This strategy also meant that we purposefully avoided plays about trauma and explicit racism because we live those realities every day; instead, on stage, we wanted to see ourselves as heroes, as leaders, as people falling in love, building families, and developing meaningful friendships. Consequently, when directors refused to see our work and continued to e-mail us only to cast another play, say, about segregation in the 1960s, we had to rethink our plan. We had to strategize.

The tagline and focus of the company went from "the goal is to fail" to "the goal is to change." We wanted to make sure that our programming was making a change in as many ways as possible, so we started questioning our work: How is it changing the representation of Black and Latinx artists on stage? How is it bringing positive change to the Black and Latinx communities? How is it transforming the career and leadership trajectories of the Black and Latinx artists with whom we work, collaborate, and create?

With these questions at the forefront of our new strategy, we asked ourselves a new question: "For whom are we creating theatre?"

A brilliant librarian friend of mine proffered a question in turn: "If you write the most widely-regarded dissertation or journal entry, but your own family can't understand what you wrote, is it meaningful?" This thought-provoking question brought about an internal dilemma for me. Was I judging my artistic merit based only on accolades created by and for white people who were not a part of my community? Had I defined my idea of success and my career goals in the theatre based on performances and awards that had no value to my community or my family?

Originally, Black and Brown Theatre's intent was for our work to be seen by artistic directors; however, although local artistic directors failed to see our work, our community did. Thus, we shifted our focus to create for our community; we started asking our audiences what they and their families wanted to see and what would entertain them. We learned from this informal data that audiences were excited to see more positive stories, stories that they were familiar with, and stories that their whole families—adults and children alike—could enjoy. Consequently, by rethinking our programming to meet the needs of our audience, we shifted our offerings to create meaningful family programming.

I had seen children's theatre during my undergraduate education at the UC Irvine, but the programs were haphazardly thrown together and relegated to actors who were not cast in mainstage shows. The scripts were poorly written, rarely revised, and conceived with a biased narrative only for preschool children. However, I did experience high-quality children's theatre back in 2009: Cynthia Santos DeCure cast me in a show that she directed for Long Beach Shakespeare Company. The production was an abridged version of *The Tempest*, using the actual Shakespearean text and intended for children to watch with their families. We performed in a park. I remember when Cynthia first told me about it, I thought, "Shakespeare . . . for kids? Are they going to get it?" However, she reassured me that, if we played the emotions truly, children would understand. They did!

I decided to bring that positive experience I had had with Long Beach Shakeskespeare Company back to my creative team at Black and Brown Theatre as we envisioned making high-quality, engaging, yet still age-appropriate scripts. That is also when we started drawing inspiration from classic coming-of-age 1990's television sitcoms like *Fresh Prince*, *Sister Sister*, and *Family Matters*. These shows had become cultural staples for their ability to bring the whole family together to watch a story unfold, thanks to the topical and emotional plots that the parents could relate to, the catchy music and flashy fashion that hooked the teenagers, and the silly gags and daring stunts that held kids' attentions.

We re-launched the program with an original adaptation of *The Frog Prince*, telling the story in rhyming couplets. I told the story in verse so that the actors would experience a complexity of language not always found in a children's show. I also liked the idea of the verses being composed of rhyming couplets because they made the story more engaging to listen to and because they bridged between theatre plays and children's literature, often told in rhymes. Lastly, the fairy tale element presented familiarity and fantasy, which helped us hook the interests of children and their families alike.

We often conversed about how to ensure that casting was not simply color blind but also color conscious.[4] We were not trying to say, "We do not see race" but rather, "We <u>see</u> race, and we see the beauty in diversity." We are Black AND Brown Theatre. Therefore, we need to see Black AND Brown people sharing the stage and working together backstage to tell stories. Our stages are richer because of the diversity of races, skin tones, accents, ages, and experiences. We wanted to have a multiplicity of backgrounds and identities in a fantastic, dream-like fairy tale. I also wanted to see people who never had an opportunity to play a principal role play the lead. The message to our company members was that we all deserve to be center stage.

The first show was filled with uncertainties: Would anyone attend? How would people react? Did we make the right decisions? These thoughts looped in my head like a techno beat during the pre-show set-up of our first performance, a test launch of our *Frog Prince* adaptation at a local library in Ann Arbor, Michigan, home of the University of Michigan, a Big Ten football school. We forgot that last part. Somehow, when scheduling the performance, both the librarian and I had overlooked that the play would occur during one of UM's fanatical football games. UM football culture demands no other events on game day. I also had not anticipated that the library and its parking lot would be under construction that day.

On the day of the show, I set up a craft booth for children who arrived early. None arrived. Devastated and defeated, I made a frog mask for myself as the actors got to their places. I had let everyone down. Maybe I was not cut out to lead. Was my "Intro to Acting" teacher right?

As I finished gluing beady eyes on my frog mask, Justino, the actor playing the Prince, asked me to move the table back.

"Why?" I asked bluntly and obliviously.

He pointed to the door. "Look!" he commanded.

While I was gluing and doubting, about 30 children and their parents had entered the library's tiny community room. More followed behind them. Justino and I quickly shoved the table against the wall. In my best leader's voice, I ordered him to get in place for the show. I ran to ask the librarian for more chairs. By the time the show had started, we had more than 120 people crammed into a library-community center under construction to watch our little play. On a UM game day! However, we had something different: We had a story people wanted to see and told by people who had never told the story before. We had a story filled with heart and messages that parents approved of, alongside playful gags and bold, bright costumes. That day, we made theatre in a library community room.

We had made theatre where we were!

The success of that initial show led to more adaptations and original stories, but we kept one goal in mind: Make it something that the whole family can watch together. As artists, many of the company members of Black and Brown Theatre had never made "children's theatre" before, so we were "building the car as we drove it" and developing it to our own rules. Many companies producing children's theatre in the area comprised all-white performing shows that did neither reflect our community nor invite us or our aesthetic. We set out to create worlds where both parents and children, Black and Latinx, could see themselves.

Hearing parents tell us how they loved the positive messages that we were embedding in the show moved us. Seeing tiny children hug actors whom they had never met before because they were so deeply connected with the actors' characters moved us. The genuine reaction of a child is immediate—and honest—feedback. There's nothing like it! Their joyful and positive responses let us know that they valued our work.

This shift in programming for the company was uncharted. This was a measurable risk because we were amalgamating inspirations to lay a new path. But, truthfully, we had already been incorporating this new path. We differentiated ourselves by making theatre that defied stereotypes. So we officially modified our motto to "Make theatre wherever you are that the Black and Brown communities want to see."

As we were relishing the joy of our success, COVID-19 slammed our collective world. All our operations immediately shut down. To thrive, we had to innovate again.

Thus, we crafted a new series of digital programming, including a series called All the Web's a STAGE, where aspiring writers from all over the world could write and submit a monologue for one of our actors. But instead of a panel of artistic curators deciding which pieces would be performed, we chose to empower the actors to select them.

From the All the Web's a STAGE programming, we created another series called Our Voices, where we offer free writing classes to students and community members. Our company's actors perform pieces the student and community members write; then the student and community writers become directors, selecting who acts in the playlets and how they bring the pieces to life. This series was exciting for our youth programming because Youth Theatre Programs often involves an adult director and adult writer telling children how to perform. Staying true to our mission of creating change, we flipped the script: "What if children wrote a script and told adults how to bring it to life?" This program has been one of our most popular programs, and one that we've been able to continue in person with masks and social distancing as we adhere to ever-shifting COVID-19 restrictions. We've also been able to film many of the Our Voices series, enabling performances to be preserved and to be shared in the world of social media.

The Once Upon a Rhyme Series has also grown from an original performance in a library with a $2,000 budget to a small series of five shows accumulating more than $100,000 in grant funding and performance fees. This December, we performed one of the latest Once Upon a Rhyme shows to more than 4,000 Detroit first-grade students, thanks to a partnership with the Detroit Public Schools Community District.

Our goal at Black and Brown Theatre is to continue to transform, to take lessons we have learned from the pandemic with us into the future. We will continue our roles as storytellers. We will not limit ourselves to traditional boundaries of theatre narratives and performance locations.

Black and Brown Theatre will create new programs for our community that will enable us to change how we make and define theatre for a new generation.

## Notes

1. *Smash* is an American musical television series created by Theresa Rebeck; it played 32 episodes on NBC from 2012 to 2013.
2. EncoreMichigan.com is web-based publication focused on Michigan's professional theatre industry. It describes itself as the state's premier source for free, up-to-the-minute news and information about Michigan's professional theatre community and industry.
3. "Theaters," *Encore Michigan*, accessed November 16, 2021, www.encoremichigan.com/theaters/.
4. For more information about color-blind and color-conscious casting, see Kristin Bria Hopkins, "There's no Business Like Show Business: Abandoning Color-Blind Casting and Embracing Color-Conscious Casting in American Theatre," *Harvard Journal of Sports and Entertainment Law* 9, no. 2 (Spring 2018): 131–56.

## Bibliography

"Theaters." *Encore Michigan*. Accessed November 16, 2021. www.encoremichigan.com/theaters/.

Black and Brown Theatre. Accessed November 16, 2021. www.blackandbrowntheatre.org/.

Hopkins, Kristin Bria. "There's no Business Like Show Business: Abandoning Color-Blind Casting and Embracing Color-Conscious Casting in American Theatre." *Harvard Journal of Sports and Entertainment Law* 9, no. 2 (Spring 2018): 131–56.

# 22
# STRATEGIES FOR DIRECTING LATINX PLAYS

*Jerry Ruiz*

Latinx plays have enjoyed a long history of being produced in American *teatros*, going back to the mid-1960s, with companies such as Teatro Campesino and INTAR Theatre leading the way on the west and east coasts, respectively.[1] Over the last three decades, however, Latinx plays have been produced more and more frequently by primarily white institutions such as regional and off-Broadway theaters, as well as in university theatre departments. Each of these contexts presents directors with opportunities to bridge cultural divides and illuminate misunderstandings and misconceptions about the Latinx experience, if the material is handled deftly.

From the beginning of my professional career in 2008, I have largely directed Latinx plays at mainstream theatre companies in New York City as well as regionally, and in academic settings. In other words, I have mostly directed Latinx plays at primarily white institutions. After graduating from UCSD's M.F.A. Directing program in 2007, my professional directorial debut was a bilingual adaptation of the Argentinean comedy *Esperando La Carroza*, by Jacobo Langsner, for Mixed Blood Theatre in Minneapolis in 2008. Following a Van Lier Directing Fellowship at Second Stage Theater in New York City in 2009, I began frequently collaborating with contemporary Latinx playwrights such as Tanya Saracho and Mando Alvarado.

Working on the NYC and world premieres of their plays allowed me to direct for well-regarded companies such as Clubbed Thumb (2011), SummerStage (2011, 2012), Rattlestick Playwrights Theater (2013), Second Stage Theater (2014), Denver Center for the Performing Arts (2016), and Primary Stages (2017). During that time, I also directed academic productions of several of Quiara Alegría Hudes' plays, as well as *In the Heights*, for which she wrote the book. In 2019 and 2020, I directed Marisela Treviño Orta's *The River Bride* and Hudes'

*Water by the Spoonful* at Stages (Houston), one of the larger professional theaters in the region. As early as 2010, it became clear to me that while I might occasionally collaborate with non-Latinx playwrights or even direct Shakespeare, helming Latinx plays would provide me a path through the profession. In 2018, I joined the faculty of Texas State University, where I am now the Head of Directing. This position at a Hispanic Serving Institution (HSI) allows me the opportunity to frequently mentor Latinx actors and directors, and listen to their concerns.

Mainstream producing companies and academic theatre departments continue to bolster their efforts to program seasons that reflect increasingly diverse audiences and constituencies. Meanwhile, Latinx playwrights are gaining national prominence and recognition. As such, I would like to offer strategies for directors, both Latinx and non-Latinx, in approaching these plays. For example, perhaps an academic theatre department will want to produce a play with roles for their Latinx students but not have a Latinx director on faculty or available locally. Maybe a regional theater will want to assign one of their non-Latinx artistic staff members as a director for a play by Saracho or Hudes. Or perhaps a Mexican-American director raised on the US/Mexico border will be hired to direct a play by a Puerto Rican playwright from the East Coast. This essay will propose approaches that will allow directors to navigate the complexities of making Latinx theatre in a way that is empowering for actors, whether in the professional or educational setting.

How do we create a space that can empower Latinx artists, professionally and in academic contexts, while successfully relaying these stories to largely non-Latinx audiences? Three fundamental approaches can yield successful processes for directors: Assembling a culturally competent creative team; empowering Latinx actors to bring their perspectives and cultural experiences into the process; and deepening our knowledge of the various Latinx cultures experiences depicted in Latinx plays, illuminating their specific nuances through careful directorial interpretation of the text.

I always urge producers, departments, and directors to build culturally competent creative teams to deal with challenges inherent in producing Latinx works inside primarily white institutions. One additional team member to consider is an EDI (Equity, Diversity, and Inclusion) advocate, especially when staging Latinx and other culturally specific plays. In her January 28, 2019 article for *American Theatre Magazine*, "How an EDI Advocate Can Improve Your Rehearsal," New Orleans-based theatre maker Amelia Parenteau writes about her experiences as an EDI Advocate on the People's Light production of *Such Things as Vampires*.[2] Following some "tone-setting work" at the beginning of the process, Parenteau writes that from her perspective as a neutral observer, she could

> foster a rehearsal environment so that everyone in the room—actors, co-creators, stage management, designers, institutional and production staff—could feel safe in sharing concerns and thoughts, to feel ownership over the generative process, and to be present with their whole identities.[3]

The overall effect of Parenteau's work in that process, it seems, was to foster a space where the creative team and cast members alike could feel able to broach difficult conversations. Given the "baked-in power dynamics" Parenteau identifies in the rehearsal room, this work strikes me as valuable to the rehearsal process.[4]

EDI advocacy begins to get to the heart of what directors need to do in order to have a successful process. Ultimately, we must foster spaces where creativity, risk-taking, honesty, and collaboration flourish. As directors, we need to do this proactively and consciously, especially when working with Latinx actors in primarily white institutions.

I'll never forget my experience assisting Bill Rauch on *Measure for Measure* at Oregon Shakespeare Festival 2013. This production of a Shakespearean work through a Latinx lens featured Latinx actors in the critical roles of Isabella, Angelo, and Claudio. Additionally, there were Black, Middle Eastern, and Asian American actors cast in key supporting roles. The Duke of Venice, however, was played by an older white actor. As written, this character "solves" everyone's problems at the end of the play. The actress playing Isabella rightfully expressed concerns about the paternalistic message this would send given the casting and modern-day setting. Rauch, probably the most collaborative director I ever assisted, had the cast and company sit in a circle for over an hour and hash out possible ways of dealing with this issue onstage. Everyone received an opportunity to voice concerns and ideas, as Rauch worked his way around the circle, gathering input from the cast and artistic staff. This discussion ended up leading to a powerful solution for staging the final moments of the play which ultimately restored Isabella's agency after the Duke's sudden marriage proposal. Rauch's readiness to engage with the concerns of his Latinx actors proved instrumental to the success of the process and product alike.

Self-advocacy and cultural collaboration, such as that seen in Rauch's process for *Measure for Measure*, can be an important tool for Latinx actors and their directors in rehearsal, and during the design process. For instance, I served as a directing advisor on an academic production where an interesting design challenge arose. A Mexican-American actress from suburban Dallas was playing a Nuyorican character from the Bronx. She had done extensive work on her dialect, wanting to ground the performance, primarily because of the character's explicit language. However, at her costume fitting, she was dismayed to find that the costume did not feel specific at all to her character's background. I advised this student actor to alert her director to the situation, and provide him with research images of Latinas from the Bronx in the 1990s, who often took fashion cues from trends in hip-hop. Eventually, the director and actor negotiated some crucial adjustments with the costume designer.

This example was an instance of an actor navigating a situation where a designer lacked cultural fluency. At the same time, it points to the importance of assembling a diverse design team with specific cultural knowledge. I strongly advocate for diverse creative teams regardless of whether one is directing a Latinx play or not, but it is essential when approaching culturally specific material. Probably the most cohesive, successful design team I have worked with professionally was the team for *Fade* in New York City at Primary Stages and Hartford TheaterWorks in Connecticut.

As a director, I usually have a significant amount of input in hiring the creative team, although that can vary from theater to theater. Indeed there are different considerations at play for academic productions. For the Primary Stages production in NYC, I was able to shape the team precisely as I wanted, as the theater agreed to hire my first choices. It was probably the first time in my directing career that the design team was not predominantly white. Taking this culturally competent approach paid off handsomely. These designers were incredibly attentive to the story being told, and created a visual and sonic vocabulary that allowed for the nuances of the play to become clear. A team not as attuned to the cultural context might inadvertently flatten out those nuances or make my job more challenging because of their lack of specificity.

The importance of having a Latino stage manager in creating a safe space for the actors and myself during *Fade* should not be underestimated. The stage manager did an incredible job of stewarding the rehearsal and tech process for high-stakes New York City premiere production. For instance, he brought in culturally specific rehearsal props that he happened to own, such as the Catrina doll mentioned as one of Lucia's personal effects. When the eventual "show" version of the doll made its way into the room, the rehearsal version sat on his table and later on the tech table. These gestures, while seemingly minor, felt significant in terms of giving the cast and creatives ownership of a usually primarily white space. In addition, the stage manager was fluently bilingual, which allowed him to call a show with significant swaths of Spanish in it with ease.

The team a director assembles extends beyond designers and stage managers. These collaborators can also make a huge impact toward the success of a production or even of a particular acting performance. Such as early on in my career when I directed a production of Hudes' play *26 Miles* for Arizona State University. Professor Micha Espinosa served as our voice and dialect coach. She proved absolutely instrumental to the process. Given the demographics of the theatre department, the Latinx students who auditioned were primarily Mexican-American, and I cast a Mexican-American student in the lead role of Beatriz, a Cuban mother reconnecting with her teenage daughter on a road trip. With Espinosa's guidance, the young woman playing Beatriz was eventually able to land on a believable Cuban accent. In turn, finding that accent helped her transform into the character and craft a compelling depiction of a character with a different Latinx identity and experience than her own.

This kind of specificity and sensitivity is crucial when depicting Latinx experiences that differ from our own. For instance, I identify primarily as a Mexican-American, and my family has a long history in Matamoros and Brownsville, two towns on the Texas/Mexico border. Taking my own experiences as an example,

I can illustrate the complexity and uniqueness of these identities. I grew up in South Texas on the US–Mexico border in a city that was 90 percent Hispanic. My father identified as a Mexican-American. He was US-born, but his family lineage in the area now known as South Texas traces back hundreds of years to when Spanish settlers first colonized it. My mother grew up across the border in Matamoros and was a Mexican national until the 1990s, although she has now lived in Texas for three-quarters of her life. Her ancestors emigrated to Mexico in the 1800s from Germany and Italy, but by the time my grandparents grew up in the early 1900s, their families spoke only Spanish and identified as Mexican.

When I direct plays set in South Texas by writers like Tanya Saracho or Mando Alvarado, I benefit from coming into the rehearsal process armed with a certain amount of first-hand experience about our unique border culture. That knowledge equips me as a director to navigate the terrain of those plays. Because Alvarado and Saracho grew up in Texas' Rio Grande Valley, we share a specific cultural context. But if I am directing a play by Quiara Alegría Hudes, a Puerto Rican playwright who grew up in Philadelphia and sets many of her plays there, in that case, it behooves me to prepare differently. I should approach this situation as carefully as I might prepare for a play by a Black or an Asian-American playwright. I should acknowledge that I have a great deal to learn about Puerto Rican history and culture, and the Puerto Rican communities in the United States.

A play like *Water by the Spoonful*, frequently produced by university theatre departments and primarily white institutions at the regional level, benefits from its universal themes, broad scope, and diverse ensemble cast. Nevertheless, the play is also full of culturally specific Latinx content. For example, the play culminates with the protagonist Elliot, a veteran of the Marine Corps, and his cousin Yazmin scattering the ashes of their beloved grandmother Mami Ginny, the family matriarch who immigrated from Puerto Rico to the United States, over a waterfall in El Yunque, the Puerto Rican rain forest. While in Puerto Rico, Elliot cathartically confronts the ghosts of PTSD and addiction that have been haunting him throughout the play. Yazmin, meanwhile, decides to buy her grandmother's old house and move back to North Philadelphia following her divorce. That these breakthroughs happen during a visit to Puerto Rico is no coincidence. In her essay "How to Read a Latinx Play," Patricia Ybarra writes, "time on the island provides revelations for both Yaz and Elliot. While there, Yaz decides to . . . buy Ginny's house; it is also where Elliot decides to go to Los Angeles."[5] *Water by the Spoonful* can be understood as an immigrant story, or a story of the grandchildren of immigrants struggling with legacy and returning to a cultural homeland when in need of spiritual guidance. That legacy is one of community building as represented by Ginny, but also of poverty, addiction, and trauma as represented by Elliot's biological mother Odessa. Elliot and his family, including his more acculturated, college-educated cousin Yazmin, have paid a price for their lives in the United States. These characters may find redemption, but only by returning to Puerto Rico, albeit temporarily. Although the play contains themes that have given it crossover appeal, this specific cultural content makes it a Latinx play, primarily dealing with the Puerto Rican experience.

My knowledge of Puerto Rican history and culture is quite limited compared to my knowledge of the Southwestern borderlands. Each Latin American country and community is unique, partially because the Spanish colonizers encountered very distinct Indigenous peoples as they colonized the new world, leading to highly differentiated cultures and resulting in distinct Spanish dialects across the Americas. Additionally, the countries of the Caribbean have also been deeply influenced by the cultures of the African diaspora. Therefore, I need to recognize my knowledge deficit when telling stories from these diverse Latinx cultures that are not my own, and prepare myself appropriately by assembling a team of experts to assist me with the linguistic and cultural context.

It is crucial for any director—Latinx or not—approaching the plays of, say, Tanya Saracho to bear the complicated and nuanced history of colonialism in Mexico in mind. Saracho's plays often deal with classism and colorism. Her oft-produced two-hander *Fade* largely deals with the privileges afforded to Lucia, a white-passing novice television writer originally from Mexico City and college-educated in the United States, as opposed to the harsh realities facing the working-class custodian, Abel, who she befriends. Through her dialogue, Saracho makes it unmistakably, though subtly, clear that Abel and Lucia come from different worlds. Not only that, but they *look* like they come from different worlds. In an early interaction, Lucia apologizes to Abel for assuming earlier on that he only spoke Spanish. She attempts to amuse him by telling him about a similar interaction she had with a waitress, explaining, "She looked like she spoke Spanish." Abel replies, "Like I look," Lucia clarifies, "Like . . . we look." To which Abel tersely replies, "Right." Lucia's attempts to align herself with him and his experiences are met with clear skepticism from the more realistic, less sheltered Abel. This interaction is Saracho's razor-sharp commentary on the effects of colorism in Latin American cultures. In an *Americas Quarterly* article titled "The Effects of Skin Color in the Americas," Edward Telles and Liza Steele write that

> racial identification in Latin America—where the categories themselves are often situational, context-dependent, and have fuzzy boundaries—is often more ambiguous and fluid than in the United States . . . [but] varieties in skin tone among those who identify in the same ethno-racial category may lead to different socioeconomic opportunities and overall life outcomes.[6]

Indeed, while Lucia and Abel might both consider themselves as Latinx, Hispanic, or of Mexican descent, the difference in their skin colors means they are destined to be viewed and treated differently in Mexico as well as in the United States.

For instance, although Lucia initially confronts racist and sexist microaggressions from the all-white, all-male staffers who go out of their way to remind her that she is the diversity hire, her color and class privilege eventually enable her to succeed and move up in the show staff's hierarchy. Her self-stated authenticity fades as she curries favor with her boss and ultimately appropriates significant parts of Abel's life story into a character and plotline for the show. However, he's explicitly asked her not to reference certain events which he shared with her. Essentially, the play recreates the system of exploitation and appropriation that people like Lucia have long benefited from in Mexico, whereas mestizo or Indigenous people fade into invisibility. The last image of the play is Abel vacuuming the hallway after Lucia exits her impressive new office. In this way, the two characters unwittingly fulfill their class destinies.

Considering the layers of history here is crucial to understanding the charged relationship between these two characters; and why it fails to transcend all the obstacles to becoming a true friendship or even a successful romance. In order to succeed at the "white man's game," Lucia betrays her friendship with Abel and her own hopes to tell authentic Latinx stories. It's part of Saracho's mission to show how white, upper-class Mexicans can use and abuse their privilege—and their fellow Mexicans—to advance. Through the dialogue, and even in the character breakdown which precedes the play, Saracho has given directors subtle but unmistakable clues about the cultural context and how her characters fit into it.

Like many of the best contemporary Latinx plays, Saracho's and Hudes' works illuminate the rich variety and complexities of the Latinx experience in the United States. Their plays brim with nuance and cultural specificity, requiring directors, creative team members, and actors, to prepare themselves assiduously, especially when depicting cultural experiences that may differ from their own. To equip themselves to succeed when staging these plays in primarily white institutions, directors must:

- Build a culturally competent team that can respond to these unique challenges.
- Empower their Latinx actors to bring their own cultural experience and expertise to the process.
- Prepare themselves through in-depth cultural research and analysis of the script, working to understand, uncover, and highlight highly charged issues such as colorism.

A director, Latinx or not, fully prepared to navigate these complexities will be able to succeed in using the theatrical experience to illuminate the audience's understanding of Latinx cultures.

## Notes

1. INTAR Theatre was founded in NYC in 1966 by Cuban and Puerto-Rican theatre makers and was led by Max Ferrá from its founding until his retirement in 2004. It continues producing new Latinx plays today under the leadership of Artistic Director Lou Moreno. Luis Valdez founded Teatro Campesino in 1965 during the Delano Grape

Strike as a wing of Cesar Chavez's United Farm Workers before relocating to San Juan Bautista in central California in 1971.
2. Amelia Parenteau, "How an EDI Advocate Can Improve Your Rehearsal," *American Theatre*, accessed January 28, 2019, www.americantheatre.org/2019/01/28/trigger-warnings-are-not-enough-why-you-need-an-edi-advocate/.
3. Ibid.
4. Ibid.
5. Patricia Ybarra, "How to Read a Latinx Play in the Twenty-first Century: Learning From Quiara Hudes," *Theatre Topics* 27, no. 1 (March 2017): 53, https://doi.org/10.1353/tt.2017.0001.
6. Edward Telles and Liza Steele, "The Effects of Skin Color in the Americas," *Americas Quarterly*, accessed February 21, 2012, www.americasquarterly.org/article/the-effects-of-skin-color-in-the-americas/.

## Bibliography

Parenteau, Amelia. "How an EDI Advocate Can Improve Your Rehearsal." *American Theatre*. Accessed January 28, 2019. www.americantheatre.org/2019/01/28/trigger-warnings-are-not-enough-why-you-need-an-edi-advocate/.

Telles, Edward, and Liza Steele. "The Effects of Skin Color in the Americas." *Americas Quarterly*. Accessed February 21, 2012. www.americasquarterly.org/article/the-effects-of-skin-color-in-the-americas/.

Ybarra, Patricia. "How to Read a Latinx Play in the Twenty-first Century: Learning From Quiara Hudes." *Theatre Topics* 27, no. 1 (March 2017): 49–59. https://doi.org/10.1353/tt.2017.0001.

# 23
# TEACHING ACTING USING THE FOUR AGREEMENTS AS A FRAMEWORK FOR SELF-ACCEPTANCE AND CULTURAL CONNECTION

*Christina Marín*

### Flashback

I was ten years old and living in Queens, New York. Even though we had moved into our new home more than two years earlier, I didn't know many young people in our neighborhood because I still went to the elementary school closer to my old house. But one afternoon, all that would change. Several kids from the apartment building next to our house came to my front door and rang the bell. One of the girls held out a book and an audio cassette tape (yes, this was 1980!). "Hi! We got this book out from the library, and it came with this cassette tape, and we want to put on a play. Do you want to do theatre with us?" I reached out my hands, took the book and the tape, and said, "Come back in a few days and I will let you know." Several days later, the would-be thespians returned for my decision. When they rang the doorbell this time, I had my answer prepared, "Sure, I'll do theatre with you, but I'm going to be the director, and I'm going to be playing the role of Rosie." The play was *Really Rosie* by Maurice Sendak with music by Carole King. I wasn't messing around. I was ten years old when I decided to make theatre my life.

### Fast Forward #1

As a junior, I was cast as one of the leads in my high school's musical production of *Guys and Dolls*.[1] It didn't seem like a natural fit; I was brunette, 4′ 11″, and a Latina, and Miss Adelaide was traditionally a blonde, leggy Hot Box performer and white. A few weeks before we went into tech rehearsals, my director told me that we would need to go to midtown to fit my blonde wig. I wasn't aware that I would be wearing a wig. I then learned the two costume designers would be using light

DOI: 10.4324/9781003021520-26

pancake makeup before every performance to balance the coloring of my arms and legs and lighten my full body complexion to match my new blonde countenance. I was perplexed, but my 17-year-old self was afraid to ask questions. It did not occur to me that I was being asked to play the role of Miss Adelaide in whiteface. At best, this young Latina actress was naive, believing this was "normal." After all, didn't I play Baby John's girlfriend, a Jet, in the previous year's production of *West Side Story* while my white friends had their hair dyed darker to play Maria and Anita?

## Fast Forward #2

The following summer, I attended the pre-college summer theatre program at Carnegie Mellon University School of Drama as a high school junior. We took Acting, Dance & Movement, Voice, and Dramatic Literature classes. In my acting class, I was cast as Babe Botrelle in a scene from Beth Henley's *Crimes of the Heart*, and in the Dramatic Literature course, we were introduced to traditional script analysis using plays from the canon of Eurocentric-Western theatre. We read Ibsen, Chekhov, Miller, and O'Neill. There were no playwrights of color. And no roles in the acting class, or songs in my Voice class that could lend themselves to me exploring my cultural identity through theatre. Still, I was young, and again, wasn't theatre all about playing roles that are different from ourselves? It never occurred to me that I was possibly the only Latina student in the program. It never crossed my mind that most of the other students completely identified with the roles they were asked to interpret and the plays we were analyzing. When I got home after that summer, I told my mom that I wanted to go to Northwestern University and apply for Early Decision. She asked me what my backup schools were and I told her I would go to Northwestern or I would not be going to college. Luckily, this naive young thespian got into Northwestern University Early Decision to study theatre in 1988. Unfortunately, this predominantly white institution (PWI) would not only be costly (30 years later I'm still paying off my student loans from my undergraduate degree), but it would also perpetuate the notion that theatre was mainly an art form produced and consumed by white people.

My acting classes followed traditional canons from the Greeks to Chekhov and then Shakespeare to Mamet. We studied acting through the teachings of Constantin Stanislavski, Michael Chekhov, Sanford Meisner, Uta Hagen, and Stella Adler, and, because we were near Chicago, Viola Spolin, and Paul Sills. There were no Latino/a professors to take classes with or visit during their office hours. We were not reading Latino plays or using scenes from them for acting exercises. I learned a lot during my four years at Northwestern. Many of my pedagogical approaches in the acting classroom are rooted in theories of the aforementioned masters. I value and teach everything from substitution to psychological gestures, emotional preparation, repetition to transference, and specificity. I guide my students through detailed text analysis and still revel in theatre games and improvisation. But something was always missing.

## Today

As the Program Director for Theatre & Film at Phoenix College, a Hispanic Serving Institution (HSI) in the Maricopa County Community College District, my history impacts how I interact with all of my students. When I finished my doctoral program in Theatre at Arizona State University, I was hired at New York University in the Educational Theatre Program (five years) and then Emerson College (six years). For 11 years, I sat on the other side of the fence in private higher education at PWIs where the majority of my students came from the dominant culture. According to Community College Review, one of Phoenix College's school highlights is that "Minority enrollment is 75% of the student body (majority Hispanic). The total percentage of Hispanic students at Phoenix College is 36%, which is higher than the state's community college average."[2]

The diverse population that I now have the privilege to serve at Phoenix College comes from all over the world. Many of them are immigrants who maintain strong ties to their countries. English is often their second, third, or even fourth language. They are often from nations steeped in centuries, if not millennia of history, and have deep connections to their cultural roots. I kept thinking of the void I felt all those years ago when I studied acting in college. I knew there had to be a connection to theories and teachings beyond the dominant ideology. In graduate school, I was introduced to the work of Augusto Boal and the Theatre of the Oppressed. Within this arsenal, there are theatre techniques that certainly lent themselves to help acting students with character development. Later, while working at Emerson College, I was introduced to the theatrical concept of the Rasaboxes developed by theorist and educator Richard Schechner and rooted in the Bharata Natyashastra, an Indian drama text encompassing a "detailed treatise and handbook on dramatic art that deals with all aspects of classical Sanskrit theatre."[3] This practice was something beyond the traditional canon of approaches to the study of acting that I found truly appealing. Focused more on the physical manifestations and breathing connections to the character, Rasaboxes' work gives students opportunities to flesh out roles beyond the text they are speaking. And then, there is the practice of mindfulness. While teaching at NYU, I was introduced to the writings of the Vietnamese Buddhist monk Thich Nhat Hanh. Since then, I have been interested in the connections people make between mindfulness and the teaching of acting around the world. In an article on the British website *The Stage*, Samantha Marsden explains, "Psychotherapist Barry Smale runs sessions with RADA's (Royal Academy of Dramatic Arts) acting students and faculty on resilience and creativity, using mindfulness and meditation techniques."[4] She quotes him as saying:

> Mindfulness is helpful to anyone. It helps you to become more aware of your own brain's thinking processes and to be released from spirals of negative thoughts. This can be particularly helpful for actors, who are under a

lot of scrutiny in their profession and may struggle to separate the work they produce—and any assessment or criticism of it—from who they are as people.[5]

Several years ago, I was introduced to the writings of Don Miguel Ruiz through his book *The Four Agreements*.[6] I instinctively felt this writing could be tied to my acting pedagogy, specifically for my community college students. While I am not suggesting that this be considered an acting textbook, its principles have given me a framework to shape how my students approach their study of the craft, including feedback sessions, research into given circumstances, objectives, and character development.

## The Four Agreements

*The Four Agreements* is also known as *A Toltec Wisdom Book*. According to Ruiz, by way of the briefest of introductions,

> Thousands of years ago, the Toltec were known throughout southern Mexico as "women and men of knowledge." . . . They came together as masters (naguals) and students at Teotihuacan, the ancient city of pyramids outside Mexico City known as the place where "Man Becomes God."[7]

The importance of this cultural history is that in using these agreements as a framework in the study of acting, my students, many of whom claim ancestry in Mexico and Guatemala, are finally tapping into the wisdom of their ancestors. They can identify with the deep roots of their heritage, while still respecting the theories and teachings of the Russians, the Germans, and the Americans. It means something to them to see the name Miguel Ruiz because it proves that they have cultural ties to the literature being used in their college courses. In the classes and workshops that I have used this framework in, I preface the sessions with the fact that I do not wish to provide a formula but a roadmap, one that will lead them on an individual journey. There have even been moments in these classes when a student makes a new connection with an agreement that I had never made before. These authentic discoveries are what make use of the agreements dynamic.

Before delving into each one of the separate Agreements and drawing the connections I have made with my acting students in classes and workshops, I will outline all four for the reader here:

- Be impeccable with your word.
- Don't take anything personally.
- Don't make assumptions.
- Always do your best.

While these may sound like, and indeed are in some contexts, the tenets of a self-help book, I would argue that many acting students could use a good self-help text. *The Four Agreements* is subtitled *A Practical Guide to Personal Freedom*.[8] I believe this is truly indicative of what these four agreements have the potential to provide our students with as they develop their craft of acting.

The following short blurbs are not my summaries; they appear on inspirational posters you can buy all over the Internet—Amazon, Etsy, etc.[9]

## Be Impeccable With Your Word

*Speak with integrity. Say only what you mean. Avoid using the word to speak against yourself or to gossip about others. Use the power of your word in the direction of truth and love.*

According to Don Miguel Ruiz, "The first agreement is the most important one and also the most difficult one to honor. . . . It sounds very simple, but it is very, very powerful."[10] In any acting class or workshop, our words are among the most important tools we have. At a basic level, we use the words of playwrights to create the worlds we portray for our audience. Another important way in which we utilize our written or spoken word is in giving feedback to one another. An unfortunate way in which words are used in any social context is through gossip. The acting class and theatrical productions are no exceptions. Finally, as actors, we need to learn boundaries of when our words are appropriate and when they are not.

## *The Words of the Playwright*

As both an acting teacher and a director, I have always tried to impress upon my students the importance of fidelity to the playwright's words. I find that, too often, young actors (and even some not so young) try and take shortcuts when memorizing their lines. They make excuses about how hard it is and claim to be paraphrasing to the best of their ability. My usual response is, "Try writing the entire script." When we pair student actors and student playwrights, they begin to have these conversations about the importance of words. I often do an exercise with actors when they are having trouble learning their lines. We take the script we are working on, sentence by sentence, and I have them write three to five variations of what the character could have said that would mean "roughly" the same thing. We compare this to choosing our own words in every conversation we have. Uncovering these different versions of what the playwright could have written often gives the actors more respect for the actual lines in the text and it helps them remember them. Recently, when we layer this idea of being impeccable with their word onto the memorization process and the importance of telling the story in the playwright's words, students have expressed a deeper understanding of paying the respect that is due to the writing.

## Giving and Receiving Feedback

Ruiz reminds us that

> We have learned to live our lives trying to satisfy other people's demands. We have learned to live by other people's points of view because of the fear of not being accepted and not being good enough for someone else.[11]

As a collaborative practice, acting can set us up for some of the most vulnerable moments in our lives. Every time we take the stage, we expose ourselves, whether in a class or in a production. We work for the applause and the reviews, and we hope that our work moves people, either to tears or fits of laughter—or to think critically about the world. We yearn for approval. When giving feedback to their peers, I remind my students how crucial it is to use their words to build each other up and not tear one another down. That is not to say I encourage only rainbows and butterflies in my classroom. However, there are ways to express how a fellow actor might work further on a monologue or scene, make different choices, or deepen their character development that do not have to make the person feel worthless. For this reason, in class, I appreciate and use the Critical Response Process developed by choreographer Liz Lerman, which focuses more on the student's work in progress and encourages respondents to ask questions rather than pass judgment.[12]

In addition, this agreement applies to when we speak about ourselves and our work. Too often, young actors fall into a pattern of self-deprecation. Perhaps they believe that if they criticize themselves first, it will be easier to accept the criticisms of others in the feedback process. As a result, they tear down their performance before anyone else has the chance to, or they make excuses about why they did it better in rehearsal.

> Being impeccable with your word is the correct use of your energy; it means to use your energy in the direction of truth and love for yourself. If you make an agreement with yourself to be impeccable with your word, just with that intention, the truth will manifest through you and clean all the emotional poison that exists within you.[13]

I remind my students to never speak against themselves using this agreement.

## Gossip

Ruiz reminds us that this all too common social problem is not new to us:

> We learned how to gossip by agreement. When we were children, we heard the adults around us gossiping all the time, openly giving their

opinions about other people. They even had opinions about people they didn't know. Emotional poison was transferred along with the opinions, and we learned this as the normal way to communicate.[14]

I began to proactively address this problem in acting classes and during the first table read for productions. I share the agreements, and we unpack how insidious gossip can be among classmates or a cast, and for the most part, I have had success in preventing incidents.

## *Finding Our Boundaries*

As actors, we need to learn the boundaries of when our words are appropriate and when they are not. I use this agreement to reiterate with my student actors that they should never presume to give another actor notes; that is the director's job (or the musical director, choreographer, dialect coach, etc.). As an actor, they must work to interpret their own role. They can be in dialogue with a scene partner about choices; however, all of those choices should be run by the director during rehearsals. This agreement goes a long way in resolving issues some actors might have perceiving that there are too many people offering feedback. As with the gossip issue, we address this potential problem at our first rehearsal.

Next, we move to the second agreement. While it is the one that gets the most initial pushback, it can often become an anchor for students in their acting work.

## **Never Take Anything Personally**

*Nothing others do is because of you. What others say and do is a projection of their own reality, their own dream. When you are immune to the opinions and actions of others, you won't be the victim of needless suffering.*

Discussions about this agreement often begin with students arguing that theatre is a personal art form because it comes from their creation, and they are constantly being judged. They ask, "How can I not take it personally?" When we navigate this agreement, I remind them,

> Even when a situation seems so personal, even if others insult you directly, it has nothing to do with you. What they say, what they do, and the opinions they give are according to the agreements they have in their own minds.[15]

Ruiz also encourages us in his writings:

> *Don't take anything personally* because by taking things personally, you set yourself up to suffer for nothing. Humans are addicted to suffering at different levels and to different degrees, and we support each other in maintaining these addictions.[16]

Now, I am not advocating for the allowance of other people to say whatever they want about you in derogatory or demeaning ways. However, another element to this agreement is to reflect on how we also treat other people and their potential to take things personally. While we would all prefer not to have anyone say anything negative about us, that is not always realistic. With the help of this agreement, we can take that experience and learn how not to treat others with our words. We can turn the potentially negative experience into one of life's important lessons. The following are just a few topics that I have explored with students and other educators through this agreement in classes and workshops.

## Casting

One of the most important things for young actors to learn and hold onto is that casting decisions should never be personal. Through this agreement, I ask my students to realize that many casting choices are not just about them. Often, directors and casting directors try endless combinations before landing on the perfect fit. Actors need to develop resiliency. Is it hard? No one ever said it was going to be easy. As Don Miguel Ruiz puts it, "When you make it a strong habit not to take anything personally, you avoid many upsets in your life. Your anger, jealousy, and envy will disappear and even your sadness will simply disappear if you don't take things personally."[17]

## Feedback From Your Director

The director has a central artistic vision, and it is their job to give feedback. An actor's job is to take the feedback and incorporate it into their interpretation of the director's vision. They need to learn to distinguish between criticism and feedback. When criticism is given negatively, one of the essential parts of communication is to let the director know how it was perceived. If feedback is given constructively, the actor should be able to see how the changes they are being asked to make will work for the good of the production. If one takes everything the director says personally, it will cause endless suffering. Every note should be seen as a chance to try something new and develop acting skills. Again, constructive criticism has the potential to help the actor learn. Microaggressions, however, have no place in a constructive artistic environment. I had a Latina student share with me that she attended an audition outside of school, and the director told her that the most he could do was give her a chorus role because she was just too ethnic to play any of the leads. She politely thanked him and left the audition. Not because she wouldn't have been willing to play a chorus role, but because she felt his attitude toward her during the audition would only continue throughout the production. She simply did not want to put herself in that position. When the student told me this story, she admitted that these experiences could sting initially, but she walked away prouder to be Latina. She chose not to take it personally because that would have been defeatist. Reframing negative experiences like this one can help our students advocate for themselves.

## *The Playwright's Words*

Finally, and in line with the previous section, some of the plays I am referring to depict hostile environments in which the language chosen by the playwrights can be jarring, disrespectful, and insulting. However, they are simply holding that proverbial mirror up to the world's injustices. Therefore, actors must separate the world of the play from the real world and not take personally any of the language that they speak or others speak to them in the course of the scene or the play. One of my students at Phoenix College, Hamblet Lemus, illustrated this agreement when he took on the role of Pablo Picasso in a production that I directed of *Picasso at the Lapin Agile*. At our table read, Hamblet, Guatemalan by heritage, asked the cast always to leave rehearsals looking at him as Hamblet and not the womanizing character he would be portraying. He owned that he would not be treating some of his fellow scene partners as he would in the real world and apologized, reminding them that nothing he did or said while playing this role should be taken personally.

Next, the third agreement can help students deepen their acting choices through research and asking questions.

## Don't Make Assumptions

*Find the courage to ask questions and to express what you really want. Communicate with others as clearly as you can to avoid misunderstandings, sadness, and drama. With just this one agreement, you can completely transform your life.*

According to Ruiz:

> We have the tendency to make assumptions about everything. The problem with making assumptions is that we *believe* they are the truth. We could swear they are real. We make assumptions about what others are doing or thinking—we take it personally—then we blame them and react by sending emotional poison with our word. That is why whenever we make assumptions, we're asking for problems. We make assumptions, we misunderstand, we take it personally, and we end up creating a whole big drama for nothing.[18]

Now while we are in the business of "creating a whole big drama," I often say, "let's leave the drama on the stage where it belongs, shall we?" The following are a few ways we can apply this agreement to our actors' work, from the monologues and scenes we interpret in class to entire productions.

## *Do Your Research*

As actors, research is one of our key tools in character development. In a sense, we each need to do the research of a dramaturg on our characters and the context of the world we inhabit through the play. Without this research, actors risk portraying one-dimensional characters with no depth. I believe it is the responsibility of all the creatives involved in the production to do their research and bring that knowledge to the table in the rehearsal hall and every production meeting. Research habits like these begin in our acting classes.

## *Ask Questions*

"Ask questions" are two powerful words for our work as theatre artists. Questioning is essential to the actor's research and fosters curiosity. Actors need to cultivate the desire and fearlessly and respectfully ask questions of their directors, designers, scene partners, class members, and the playwright if accessible. The danger lies in making assumptions. We work in an art form that is rooted in communication. The theatre's foundation is collaboration. Use these tools, ask these questions, and you will uncover limitless possibilities in your work as an actor. Discoveries are not fixed but open the actor to even more options and ways of thinking.

Too often, we make a breakthrough in a scene we are working on, and then we repeat it endlessly because we feel that we found the correct choice. This fixed mindset is a terrible assumption that leaves the actor unable to play and unaware of the discoveries they might make if they open themselves to try something different. Actors rob themselves of the most crucial part of the work when they close themselves off from digging deeper into the possibilities. Choices, once made, should not remain static. We call it a rehearsal because we "re-hear" our work, we might find something new just below the surface.

The fourth and final agreement draws from all the previous agreements and is the most straightforward. As Ruiz puts it, "it's the one that allows the other three to become deeply ingrained habits."[19]

## **Always Do Your Best**

*Your best is going to change from moment to moment; it will be different when you are healthy as opposed to sick. Under any circumstance, simply do your best, and you will avoid self-judgment, self-abuse, and regret.*

This final agreement is perhaps both the easiest and the hardest for students to apply in their acting work. Because students might still be trapped in that cycle of self-deprecation, they may not be able to let go of self-judgment so easily. I make every attempt to encourage students to see every opportunity to get up on stage and perform as a chance to do their best. When we layer this agreement into our work, students begin to accept that acting is a living, breathing, physical experience that requires our instruments (our voice, our mind, and our body) to be healthy. We must take care of ourselves to do our best. In approaching the work through the lens of this agreement, students have also brought up the fact that as a collaborative art, the best work happens when all scene partners bring their very best to the rehearsal and performance space. In the acting class, I am currently teaching at Phoenix College, every one of the students is Latinx. While I certainly believe that this agreement applies to them, I steadfastly maintain that this final agreement applies to all of my students, no matter what their heritage and culture. Always do your best.

The four agreements pay homage to ancient Toltec wisdom that plays a large part in the history and culture of our Latinx students. They have helped some of my students make connections beyond the Western-centric theories and teachings of modern theatre to see their ancestors in the work they do. I hope they can help your students too.

## Notes

1 "Guys and Dolls: A Musical Fable of Broadway," Internet Broadway Database, accessed June 17, 2021, www.ibdb.com/broadway-production/guys-and-dolls-1892.
2 "Phoenix College," *Community College Review*, accessed January 12, 2022, www.communitycollegereview.com/phoenix-college-profile.
3 Virginia Gorlinski, "Natyashastra: Indian Drama Treatise," *Britannica*, accessed April 12, 2011, www.britannica.com/topic/Natyashastra.
4 Samantha Marsden, "Can Mindfulness Help You Improve Your Actor Training?" *The Stage*, accessed March 10, 2020, www.thestage.co.uk/advice/can-mindfulness-help-improve-your-actor-training.
5 Ibid.
6 Don Miguel Ruiz, *The Four Agreements: A Practical Guide to Personal Freedom* (San Rafael: Amber-Allen Publishing, Inc., 1997).
7 Ibid., xiii.
8 Ruiz, *The Four Agreements*.
9 To download a free poster and learn more about the teachings of Don Miguel Ruiz and his sons, see "The Four Agreements Poster," The Four Agreements for a Better Life, accessed December 14, 2021, https://amber-allen-publishing.mykajabi.com/store/MCu2LnCK.
10 Ruiz, *The Four Agreements*, 25.
11 Ibid., 17.
12 Liz Lerman and John Borstel, *Liz Lerman's Critical Response Process: A Method for Getting Useful Feedback on Anything You Make, From Dance to Dessert* (Takoma Park: Dance Exchange, Inc., 2003).
13 Ruiz, *The Four Agreements*, 32–33.
14 Ibid., 37–38.
15 Ibid., 49.
16 Ibid., 56–57.
17 Ibid., 58–59.
18 Ibid., 63–64.
19 Ibid., 75.

## Bibliography

Community College Review. "Phoenix College." Accessed January 12, 2022. www.communitycollegereview.com/phoenix-college-profile.

The Four Agreements for a Better Life. "The Four Agreements Poster." Accessed December 14, 2021. https://amber-allen-publishing.mykajabi.com/store/MCu2LnCK.

Gorlinski, Virginia. "Natyashastra: Indian Drama Treatise." *Britannica*. Accessed April 12, 2011. www.britannica.com/topic/Natyashastra.

Internet Broadway Database. "Guys and Dolls: A Musical Fable of Broadway." Accessed June 17, 2021. www.ibdb.com/broadway-production/guys-and-dolls-1892.

Lerman, Liz, and John Borstel. *Liz Lerman's Critical Response Process: A method for getting useful feedback on anything you make, from dance to dessert*. Takoma Park: Dance Exchange, Inc., 2003.

Marsden, Samantha. "Can Mindfulness Help You Improve Your Actor Training?" *The Stage*. Accessed March 10, 2020. www.thestage.co.uk/advice/can-mindfulness-help-improve-your-actor-training.

Ruiz, Don Miguel. *The Four Agreements: A Practical Guide to Personal Freedom*. San Rafael: Amber-Allen Publishing, Inc., 1997.

# 24
# PERFORMANCE OF IDENTITY —A PRACTICE

*Marie Ramirez Downing*

For many years, Performance of Identity (PI) practice has centered my work as an actor, educator, and creator of theatre. My practice continues to evolve and find new life through the courses I teach and the projects I create. This essay outlines what PI practice is, who I am, and why I am inspired to make this subject the focus of my creative research. I will also share PI exercises and detail a workshop, a larger summer PI project, and students' PI creative research. These formats in the PI practice give actors many approaches and means to enliven how they tell their stories and choose to perform their identities for the stage.

I envisioned and developed PI to celebrate the voices of all. In this practice, actors and artists construct performance pieces inspired by their own identities, including heritage, ethnicity, gender identification, and political, social, and cultural aspects. The PI practice also engages audiences by awakening them to the many identities that populate our diverse world. Lastly, Performing Identity practice moves performers away from exploiting theatre as an "escape" and submerges them in "revelation" of self. The PI practice may express challenges and triumphs of identity through, for example, dance, song, spoken word, poetry, lyrical, and heightened text. How people define their individuality for the stage does not have one definitive formula. Philosopher Charles Taylor, author of *Sources of the Self: The Making of the Modern Identity,* explains his view on human identity:

> Our identities, as defined by whatever gives us our fundamental orientation, are in fact complex and many-tiered. We are all framed by what we see as universally valid commitment (being a Catholic or an anarchist) and also by what we understand as particular identifications (being an Armenian or a Quebeçois). We often declare our identity as defined by only one of these, because this is what is salient in our lives, or what is put in

DOI: 10.4324/9781003021520-27

question. But in fact our identity is deeper and more many-sided than any of our possible articulations of it.[1]

Thus, there are no limitations to how actors perform identity as it is an art form that represents the authentic self in whatever version, iteration, or space.

PI practice is particularly potent for Latinx actors, who are susceptible to systemic and institutionalized racism and to the sting of identity politics. Identity Politics plays a role in the PI. According to Cressida Heyes, Professor of Political Science and Philosophy at the University of Alberta, "Identity politics is a tendency for people of a particular religion, race, social background, etc., to form exclusive political alliances. Identity politics is the idea that some social groups are oppressed."[2] Latinx actors have historically been a part of an oppressed group because limited representation in the performing arts means Latinx actors have been subjected to racial stereotypes. According to socio-linguist, Rosina Lippi-Green,

> Historians see the Treaty of Guadalupe Hidalgo as the beginning of systemic racism and discrimination toward Mexican and Spanish speakers more generally. The many bicultural and Spanish dominant communities around the border can document a long history of discrimination in every aspect of daily life.[3]

Through my experiences with Latinx actors in classrooms and professional workshops, I have seen many create the PI practices as calls to action—their cries to be seen.

My identity as a Mexican and an American informs my work and explains why I teach PI. I confronted my bicultural identity at a very young age as a California native raised by two bilingual parents. Spanish being their first language, they spoke Spanish to each other and English or Spanglish to my four siblings and me. My father was punished in school for speaking Spanish, so he felt that he was protecting his children from physical and mental harm by encouraging us to assimilate to the American culture through language. Even though we did not speak Spanish, we still grew up with Mexican culture in music, food, and family legacy. As a result, at times, I felt as if I could not identify with Spanish-speaking Mexicans or with white Americans. I lived in a liminal space.

As a theatre major in the mid-1990s, I was taught standard stage speech, meaning that I was prescribed particular sounds in American English to sound more "general." I flattened out and shifted my speaking. The result? My cultural identity was erased. For me, this meant my accent no longer reflected the inflections of my Chicano father or the rhythms of my mother's Mexican accent. The cadence in which I spoke became the cookie-cutter stage actor I thought people wanted to hear. My own community thought I sounded "white" and that is because I no longer sounded like where I grew up and abandoned my family's linguistic imprint.

When I entered grad school and the world of acting, I sometimes felt shame around my stage voice. It did not reflect my colorful background, that is, the rich roots of the Ramirez family of Jalisco or the vibrant sounds of the Perez family of San Luis Potosi, Mexico. Directors and teachers further complicated my struggle over my identity by telling me I needed to sound more Latina to be cast. One grad school professor told me that if I did not find an accent, casting directors would not know what to do with me. I lived with this restriction for many years. I tried to fit into those molds, but I never felt as if I were doing enough. I questioned whether I could find authenticity in my acting and life if I did not speak the language of my heritage—Spanish—fluently.

My confidence in my identity shifted when I started training to be a Linklater voice teacher. Kristin Linklater, a luminary in the field of voice, taught me to bring my identity into the classroom. She valued my voice and story. She taught me that being seen and respected for being simply and fully "you" changes lives. As of today, I am the only self-identifying Mexican-American Linklater voice teacher of over 300 worldwide.

In 2015, I taught my first PI course at California State University—Chico, a Hispanic Serving Institution.[4] Although participants included a mix of theatre majors and non-majors, it was not a performance course; instead, it was a theatre studies course incorporating scholarly articles, plays, and popular performances. I selected readings and plays by writers of the global majority and I picked articles that addressed identity politics, cultural appropriation, and queer and drag theory.

My objectives for students in PI were to:

- learn the historical and theoretical moments, which form the bases of studies in marginalized populations of diversity, including race, gender, and sexuality in relation to performance;
- understand the role of identity in performance while examining theatre and other live performing arts;
- analyze and criticize identity performances via media and live performances that illustrate and stimulate well-formed critical responses; to develop skills to identify labeling race, gender, and/or sexuality in performance, media, and text;
- study and explore notable theatre artists and other performance artists whose works and theories are the bases for Performance Studies with a focus on identity in relation to issues of gender, race, and sexuality;
- explore and understand their own identities, including how to express them through creative projects.

This course succeeded grandly as students saw how they could work from themselves or, as Cressida Heyes refers to it, from "the possibility of a more authentic or self-determined alternative."[5]

I yearned to explore these identity practices with actors and other theatre artists, so I presented my creative research on PI practice at the 2016 Association for

Theatre in Higher Education Theatre Conference (ATHE) in Chicago. I titled my presentation, "Performance of Identity: How much labor does it take to be you?" My objective during the presentation was for theatre artists to explore and express their identities by strengthening their focus on performance using imagery, voice, and movement. I led participants through a series of activities inspired by their own intersectionality, including heritage, culture, or socioeconomic background. I interpret intersectionality as Kimberly Crenshaw defines it as, "a metaphor for understanding the way the multiple forms of inequality or disadvantage sometimes compound themselves and they create obstacles that often are not understood within conventional ways of thinking."[6] Intersectionality helps us understand that identity is complex and there could be many factors within a given social structure (race, gender anti-racist politics) that influence how these performers are seen in our American society and unfairly treated. They then engaged with other attendees to learn about each person's various backgrounds, cultural experiences, and barriers to understanding different identities. The exercises were followed by a discussion on the subtitle of the practice. "Labor to be you" often includes emotionally draining code-switching to fit in with particular communities, groups, and in various situations and places, including the institutionalized racism of academia. Hearty discussion revealed the social, political, and cultural complexity of identity for all the participants; however, participants who self-identified as Latinx further shared that the lack of representation on and off stage and the presence of damaging stereotypes diminished their mental and physical energy. That means that the taxing emotional labor affects tension in the body. As per Kristin Linklater: "blocked emotions are a fundamental obstacle to a free voice."[7] Through Linklater's teachings, I knew that holding in unexpressed anger or sadness can manifest in shoulders, neck, and belly muscles and in the jaw and tongue. So I led participants through embodied voice and movement exercises to free their breath and expression.

Inspired by Kristin Linklater's Voice Poem, I guided participants to see their identity from three points of view by drawing their identities in either abstract or literal interpretations: "My identity as I see it," "My identity as others see it," and "What's stopping people from seeing my identity as I see it?" While they drew, I offered prompts to carefully guide participants to look at themselves from multiple perspectives.

In the next part of the exercise, I separated participants into small groups so they could share their images. Next, they recorded on the backs of their drawings anything that surprised them, excited them, or impacted them. Afterward, each participant wrote an 8 to 10-line poem entitled, "An Ode to my Identity," and then presented the poem to the group. To conclude, the participants explored their poems a second time with a focus on sound and movement.

The workshop participants shared not only that they now had a greater understanding of the weight of the emotional labor but also how that burden manifests into physical tension. I told the students about the emotional labor I've endured through my own struggles in social situations when I have to explain where I am from and that I don't speak fluent Spanish but that I am deeply connected to my Mexican roots.

With the success of the PI practice workshop, I created an expanded format for the California State University Summer Arts[8] program. The course, "Performance of Identity: Past and Present Voices Meet," was an exciting collaboration among Latinx playwright Octavio Solis; designated-Linklater voice teacher and theatre professor of practice, Natsuko Ohama; actor and director Lisa Wolpe, creator of the all-female, multi-cultural Los Angeles Women's Shakespeare Company; and Sheila Bandyopadhyay, an Alexander Movement-certified teacher and movement specialist in Trish Arnold Swings.

Sheila's work aimed to free the actors from limited notions of themselves, that is, from their habituated mode of physical expressions to open new pathways and to gain a larger sense of their identity. The Trish Arnold Swings method supports performers because it studies the body's release, momentum, and reorganization, thus stimulating students' imagination. Next, Natsuko used Linklater's progression of exercises to support the imagery, language, and text the actors created. The range of activities helps actors free their bodies of tension and release breath to keep the voice strong when expressing personal and intimate imagery. Next, Octavio used exercises to develop the actors' personal stories and perspectives in order to find a sense of lyrical and heightened language as well as to illuminate their voices for the stage.

Finally, Lisa shared her solo performance, "Shakespeare and the Alchemy of Gender," as an example of PI process in performance. The students profited from a deep, eye-opening conversation about the creation, her family history, Shakespeare's becoming both a vessel and bridge to her coping with tragedy in her life, and the connection to expressing her identity in the present time. Lisa's work was invaluable as the actors grasped how sharing narrative in a heightened and embodied performance can serve as vehicle for healing and reflecting. The workshop succeeded in aiding all 14 actors to experience growth in their own powerful, rich, and heartfelt stories.

PI practice is the basis of my creative research projects with students at Sonoma State University. In 2021, I received a grant from The Koret Foundation to develop a project that studied identity in under-represented communities. The project offered funding to Mexican and Chicanx students to research and collect samples of dialects to contribute to the International Dialects of English Archive (IDEA).[9] The project expanded under-represented samples of Mexican and Mexican-American dialects in California. Students developed their connections to the projects. They learned the stories hidden within the samples—survival stories during COVID-19 lockdowns and during California wildfires as well as stories of family life growing up as non-native English speakers in California. Then, students used the Performance Identity process to create performance projects: they learned to embody and embrace the community members they had interviewed, honoring each donor's humanity while finding physical and vocal authenticity in their stories.

I encourage educators to use the tools and techniques outlined in this essay, including the PI exercises, workshop format, and continued creative research in the classroom. The PI process offers awareness, acknowledgment, and freedom. Through the PI process, the experience and narratives of oppressed and under-represented identities are empowered and envisioned.

I have benefited from this work's vocal and physical empowerment and witnessed the transformative power of identity practice when working with Latinx students. Expanding their sense of self makes them more prepared to enter into transformation and the performance industry. PI is a foundational practice in actor training.

## Notes

1. Charles Taylor, *Sources of The Self: The Maker of The Modern Identity* (Cambridge: Harvard University Press, 2001), 28–29.
2. Cressida Heyes, "Identity Politics," in *Stanford Encyclopedia of Philosophy* (Stanford: Metaphysic Research Lab, Stanford University, 2020), https://plato.stanford.edu/entries/identity-politics/.
3. Rosina Lippi Green, *English With an Accent* (New York: Routledge, 2012), 256.
4. Hispanic Serving Institution (HSI) defined under the Higher Education Act (HEA) as colleges or universities where at least 25 percent of the undergraduate, full-time enrollment is Hispanic; and at least half of the institution's degree-seeking students must be low-income.
5. Heyes, "Identity Politics."
6. *Kimberlé Crenshaw: What Is Intersectionality? YouTube* (National Association of Independent Schools (NAIS), 2018), www.youtube.com/watch?v=ViDtnfQ9FHc.
7. Kristin Linklater, *Freeing the Natural Voice: Imagery and Art in the Practice of Voice and Language* (London: Nick Hern Books, 2006), 25.
8. California State University (CSU) Summer Arts is a multidisciplinary, systemwide program offering academic credit plus a festival in the visual, performing, and literary arts. Summer Arts runs for four weeks in July, and consists of two, two-week sessions. The most distinguished CSU faculty, exemplary professionals, and hundreds of talented students in the visual and performing arts participate each year.
9. IDEA is a worldwide database of accents and dialects digitally recorded and studied by actors, teachers, and directors in theatre, film, and television to accurately represent and perform them.

## Bibliography

Crenshaw, Kimberle. "Demarginalizing the Intersection of Race and Sex: A Black Feminist Critique of Antidiscrimination Doctrine, Feminist Theory, and Antiracist Politics [1989]." *Feminist Legal Theory* (2018): 57–80. https://doi.org/10.4324/9780429500480-5.

Delgado, Richard. "Rodrigo's Reconsideration: Intersectionality and the Future of Critical Race Theory." *96 IOWA Law Review* 1247 (2011).

Heyes, Cressida. "Identity Politics." In *Stanford Encyclopedia of Philosophy*. Stanford: Metaphysic Research Lab, Stanford University, 2020. https://plato.stanford.edu/entries/identity-politics/.

Linklater, Kristin. *Freeing the Natural Voice: Imagery and Art in the Practice of Voice and Language*. London: Nick Hern Books, 2006.
Lippi-Green, Rosina. *English with an Accent: Language, Ideology and Discrimination in the United States*. New York: Routledge, 2012.
Taylor, Charles. *Sources of the Self: The Making of the Modern Identity*. Cambridge: Harvard University, 1989.

# 25
# FITZMAURICE VOICEWORK® AS A CONTEMPLATIVE PRACTICE AND A DECOLONIZING AGENT IN ACTOR TRAINING

*Lorenzo González Fontes*

The phenomenon of actor training, born in the 20th century and now seeing its way into the 21st, has turned into a labyrinth of avenues of apprenticeship. Among others' dicta, Stanislavski[1] declared: "Love the art in yourself, not yourself in the art."[2] That dictum launched a myriad of training methods, techniques, and approaches in preparing actors to survive on stage to deliver "The Truth." But to be truthful on stage, Stanislavski advises us to adopt an ethic as performing artists, that is: prepare. In the end actors develop their own methods, yet acting still remains a mystery; however, no actor can work without practice and enquiry. It is important for actors to be students of literature, science, philosophy, and other arts, as much as it is for them to train their bodies, voices, imaginations, and sense of complicity.

The hunt for integrity in the art of acting has brought Contemplative Practice into the province of our training methods. On the surface, one of its features, meditation,[3] is a good antidote to actor anxiety, that is, to tame the ego and alleviate neurosis. As a Latino/Latinx/Mexican-American/immigrant actor, I have found that Contemplative Practice has acted as a decolonizing agent. The practice helps calm my disquietude that results from imperialism and cultural subjugation; the practice allows me to endlessly create myself so as to not lock myself into an eternal circle of self-doubt. I have learned not to let this circumstance weigh me down and to instead be driven by my creative awareness. Simply put, Contemplative Practice trains the mind to get out of the way of the mind.

As the director of Naropa's Performance program and as a teacher in my acting classroom, I have learned to recognize my students' disconnection and displacement caused by the violence of colonialism that is stored in their somatic memories. I think it's important to offer them a transformative experience that will quiet the turmoil to let their creative possibilities flourish.

DOI: 10.4324/9781003021520-28

Fitzmaurice Voicework® approaches the well-being of the artist holistically and fosters greater creativity, attunement, and compassion toward the self. As such, it is among the Contemplative Practices available for actors to train today. In this essay, I share my understanding of Fitzmaurice Voicework® as a contemplative practice, offer historical background for the method, its function, and process, and analyze how it can serve Latinx actors as preparation for performance and a decolonizing agent.

As an actor/theatre maker/educator, I have been very fortunate to work and practice with some of the leading engineers of Contemplative Education in actor/performer training, including Barbara Dilley,[4] Lee Worley,[5] and Mary Overlie.[6] Wendell Beavers[7] who laid on to me the mantle of chair of the M.F.A. in Theatre: Contemporary Performance at Naropa University—a radical program Beavers co-founded with Erika Berland[8] that is grounded in Contemplative Practices. "El Maestro" Luis Valdez would chide me for classifying his work as "Contemplative Practice Training for the Actor" because he is in a category all of his own, but he did say, after I told him of my involvement with contemplative education, "Well, you're an alum of the Theatre of the Sphere. Don't you remember *los veinte pasos* (the 20 steps)?" At that point, we both said in quick unison, "*IMIX, IK, AKBAL, KAAN, CHICCHAN, CIMI, MAN-IK, LAMAT, MULUC, OC, CHUEN, EB, BEN, IX, MEN, CIB, C'HABAN, EDZNAB, CAUAC, AHAU*,"[9] and he concluded, "That's contemplative."

I owe a debt of gratitude to all these masterful practitioners, but my initiation in Contemplative Practices for Actor training first came when I was a student at Los Angeles City College, where I studied under my out-and-out mentor, Catherine Fitzmaurice, creator of Fitzmaurice Voicework®[10] (FV®).

## Fitzmaurice Voicework®

By profession an actor, Catherine Fitzmaurice, initially undertook the search for a method to supply honesty, authenticity, strength, flexibility, and health to the voice of theatre performers. Of course, theatre performers, or singers, do not hold exclusive rights to the living voice; therefore, this practice serves every human being. Its scope goes well beyond obtaining a sonorous and functional voice for the stage. The voice mirrors our being. The honesty and vitality of the voice also attest to our health and reveal the integrity of our being. The purpose of FV® is to free up that pathway and that resounding nexus of connection.

FV® has a simple and elegant formula composed of two phases: Destructuring and Restructuring. Each of these stages includes interludes, such as the Tremwork™,[11] during the Destructuring phase, or the Focus Line[12] during the Restructuring phase. Nevertheless, it is important to perceive these two as a single succession or process.

Among the multiple and rigorous studies that Catherine Fitzmaurice has developed for her practice, most significant to the foundation of the practice is her education at the Royal Central School of Speech and Drama in London, England. Next in importance to the foundation of the practice is the fusion of two currents of thought: Buddhism and Reichism, that is, the research of Wilhelm Reich, a forerunner and revolutionary figure in the history of psychoanalysis. Of course, these are not the only thought paradigms that have nurtured the practice of FV®. Yoga, chakra theories, Gestalt psychology, chaos theory, various studies in neurology, as well as extensive studies in linguistics, anatomy, acupuncture, and shiatsu massage have also influenced it. The practice is ever evolving as certified teachers continue to deepen and build it worldwide.[13] But these two models of thought—the secular spirit of Buddhism as a practice[14] and the physical psychology of Wilhelm Reich—stand like two pillars that require special attention. They provide an ideological framework for understanding the reasoning behind the phases of Destructuring and Restructuring that constitute Fitzmaurice Voicework® to make it a Contemplative Practice.

Buddhism in FV® is not only secular but also pluralistic and influenced by various traditions and multiple exponents and schools. In a way, syncretism, the amalgamation of religions, weaves into the practice of FV® to reconcile idiosyncrasies.

## Main Inspirational Points of Buddhism in FV®

### First Pillar—Buddhism

Buddha is the state of creative awareness, of enlightenment for the benefit of one's well-being. A state of harmony, available and present in everyone, needs only to be awakened. Similarly, in FV® our brilliant voice—full of meaning, full of our being, something we all possess—can be awakened. Buddha, like a doctor, initially diagnoses suffering. Then he examines the causes of suffering: our desires or cravings and our drives toward the pleasant and away from the unpleasant. He then recognizes that the origin of desire is to be found in greed, or grasping; hatred, or feelings of violence; and ignorance, mistaken notions, or delusion. After analyzing the ailment and its cause, he gives his prognosis: To recover from suffering it is necessary to dilute desire. Then, says the Buddha, healing is possible!

Not all desires lead to suffering; some needs are essential. Therefore, we must carefully observe; we must study what our likes and dislikes are and how these can cause our pain; we must make friends with yearnings that imprison us in order to work through them so we can trade them for kindness, compassion, and wisdom.

This attitude is basic to FV®. One of the purposes of the Destructuring phase is to find the knots that bind our vocal production and prevent our enlightened or awakened voice to shine. Finding these obstacles broadcasts excellent news because working through them means that we will achieve the integrity of our voice. Favoring an outcome differs from working against something.

Finally, Buddha[15] prescribes the medicine to treat the complexities of the world. He gives us a multiple method: Follow the eightfold path:

(1) Right View
(2) Right Resolve (Intention)
(3) Right Speech
(4) Right Action
(5) Right Livelihood
(6) Right Effort
(7) Right Mindfulness
(8) Right Concentration

The word "right," sometimes translated as "perfect" or "correct," implies a judgmental, fault-finding doctrine, but that is not the spirit behind the eightfold path. I prefer the word "sensible" because it denotes adequacy in following the path, that is, we adapt and adjust to the measure of the circumstances of time and space in which we find ourselves. Buddhism is a view, not a mandate. The paths, viable and flexible, are recommended: They are paths, not laws, orders, or traditions that must be followed to the letter. Taking one path can illuminate the others. The objective of the eightfold path is to find our wisdom. Therefore, we are following a sensible path. The purpose of these paths is to place us in the "now" where we create, not mitigate, qualify, criticize, or judge. This concept of temporality is crucial for the FV®. We want to use our voice in the "now." Plant it in the now, free from complaints and self-judgment; keep it spontaneous, created in the moment, full of joy and vitality even if the text or song is well known. We want to bring our voice into the presence of our creative action. The fact that I address only two paths, Mindfulness and Concentration, does not imply that the other paths are not related to the FV®, but emphasizes their special connections.

## Mindfulness

Buddha prescribes the path of sensible mindfulness, or "right" mindfulness, which can be summarized as the act of contemplating the nature of the body, the mind, the feelings, and other phenomena in existence, or keeping an alert mind to everything that affects the body and mind. A crucial point here is that when we talk about the body and the mind, we must abandon our Western concept of duality. Instead, we must adopt the paradox offered by the Zen master Shunryu Suzuki: "Our body and our mind are not two and not one."[16] The body/mind also includes the heart; embodiment, a buzzword in actor training, is not only a central idea in Buddhist practice but also preeminent to FV®.

Also prominent is the concept of the mind as one of our senses. We can say that FV® is one of several contemplative practices that render lucidity, helping us to recognize our being, in order to better cultivate and train the body/mind/

heart. The sounds we produce, including speaking and singing, are the product of the actions of our organism, mainly the breathing and phonation system, which is a somatic action. All our systems act together, not just the muscles or the skeleton, which support us, but also the blood and all the organs that keep us alive. Breathing is a bio-mechanical act. This physical act of producing sound accompanies our mental and emotional intention. Sound partners with our thoughts and ideas—be they logical, analogical, abstract, linear, or circular—and with all sensory images. For example, memories and other cognitive processes are mental sensations. Loose and unfettered, the sounds of our voice fill with meaning, feeling, and transformative power—they are acts of absolute mindfulness.

## *Right Concentration*

Right Concentration gives clarity to the mind. In this path, we find meditation as the means to gain sensible concentration. In essence, we are always meditating because something always occupies the spaces of our minds with a tumult of thoughts. An automatic mechanism keeps the mind busy with all sorts of cravings and rejections, so we tend to dwell on them and keep them fixed. Training our concentration allows us to detect things when they start to arise and see them for what they are, allowing us to respond creatively and choose to follow them or not. Mindful meditation frees us from the automatic mechanism of our desires, recognizing feelings, perceptions, and thoughts as they arise, become present, then disappear.

The practice of Destructuring and Restructuring serves as a meditation that loosens the power of thoughts that trap and burden us with all kinds of confusion and that placate and slow us down. Buddha suggests concentrating on the breath while meditating.[17] The breath anchors us in the "now." Breathing brings us back to the totality of the moment. Breathing keeps us alive. When we stop breathing, we stop being.

For this reason, using the breath as an object of meditation is an ideal instrument to achieve total concentration. I consider FV® a school of meditation in which we learn to uncover the full capacity of our breathing with technique and dexterity. The methodology then allows us to concentrate and imbue the sounds we make with the imagery and poetry begotten in our own being.

However, mastering the breath in FV® goes beyond that. Manifesting the whole dimension of the body/mind/heart imbues integrity in our voice, but also the breath awakens the inner teacher. As a Latinx actor in the United States, it meant I had to reeducate my being to let go of the defenses I had built around letting my culture manifest itself. De-anglicizing the pronunciation of my name seems undemanding, but the level of aliveness that comes from taking the breath to produce the sound of one or the other makes a big difference in who shows up in the room.

## Second Pillar—Reich

Open, free, and deep breathing is essential for the voice and, at the same time, gives us access to plumb the complexities of our being. But what if our breathing is limited and shallow or the support for our voice is inadequate so that our voice is full of tensions that obstruct its resonance? Some discomforts require the attention of a professional doctor, but we ourselves can heal some obstacles. The resplendent voice already exists in our being. We just have to unleash it.

Early in the 1970s, Catherine was introduced to the writings of Wilhelm Reich.[18] Reich's most significant contribution lies in his development of somatic, psychology. Toward the turn of the 20th century, Reich, together with Don Segismundo Freud[19] and Carl Gustav Jung,[20] studied therapeutic techniques and theories of the unconscious, those mental processes that occur automatically or are not readily reached through introspection. In contrast to Freud and Jung, Reich proposed that a person's psychological make-up is not purely mental but also physical. Reich explains that, through our development, we forge a muscular armor, that is, the accumulation of frustrations that prevent circulation of life energy, which Reich calls the "orgone."[21] Anna Freud then called this process the defense mechanism. We also now know, thanks to the work of Alexander Lowen[22] and others, that the armor is not only muscular but also somatic. No human being exists without armor whose very purpose is to protect. The degree of rigidity or flexibility of the armor determines our character and our level of frustrations, or physical/mental tensions.

The armor is responsible for many of our habits and body postures. In the voice, armoring causes shallow breathing and excessive effort in supporting the voice, and blocks emission of resonant sounds. We erect this armor during injurious and harmful moments as well as in innocuous and innocent ones. The seemingly harmless admonition to "*Say it in English*" (a frequent demand during a bi-cultural upbringing along with similar contradictions in the acculturation process) brings split seconds of bewilderment and surprise that impress on our body/mind/heart. These impressions become part of our reflexive arcs, some of which bring unwanted tension.

At its core, FV®, allows us to locate these nodules of tension and, furthermore, to soften them as well as to disarm them to re-establish the organic, efficient, biological, and ergonomic production of our primordial breath and sound. A free breath brings authentic life to acting.

## Natural Breath and Sound Production

In childhood, we have not yet formed an armor. We can see ease of movement in babies whose wide and deep breaths lightly expand the rib cage as well as the abdomen, efficiently supporting the voice that allows the baby to roar resoundingly. Thanks to the flexibility of the intercostal muscles and the unencumbered muscles of our core, our lungs fill with air from the base to their top edges. The lungs are conical, like an isosceles triangle, with an elongated broad base and a pointed top. As the lungs fill with air, the base expands to the sides and downward, and then as they fill further, the top expands.

Generally, when an adult breathes deeply, the top of the lungs expands, but there is little movement at the base because deep breathing naturally expands the abdomen. As the lungs inflate at the wide base where there is more volume, the lungs need more space. The diaphragm, which creates this space, is a dome-shaped muscle that pushes the stomach and other organs outwards. Dilation of the abdomen is a stigma in the global society that admires a flat belly. Thus, the origin of many an armor, an aesthetic posture imposed by society that is also a somewhat distorted idea because it forces a change in the natural function of the organism, altering our somatic physiology.

Vocal support is essential to create the necessary pressure to oscillate the vocal folds that bring about the vibrations that are then amplified by resonating throughout our body. Correct and effective support for the controlled expulsion of air in sound production is provided by the abdominal transverse muscle in synergy, in conjunction, with the diaphragm muscle. The transversus muscle is the deepest of the abdomen; it is wide like a girdle wrapping the abdominal area from the last ribs and the pelvis to the lumbar area of the spine and the iliac crest. The transverses are located below the rectus abdominis muscle and the internal and external obliques. The transversus is the ideal and appropriate muscle for vocal support. So often, our vocal support is excessive because we use too many muscles and expel air uncontrollably, damaging our vocal cords. FV® not only frees the breath but also cultivates adequate use of the abdominal transverse for vocal support.

## Destructuring and Restructuring

During the Destructuring phase, Tremwork™ is used to gain full awareness of our body/mind/heart. Tremwork™ is a series of poses or psychosomatic exercises involving our psyche and soma, which bring the central nervous system (CNS)[23] in communication with the autonomic nervous system (ANS).[24] This instigates a tremor that flows through the entire body. The tremor is our natural health-giving mechanism. Intersecting the transmissions of these two lines of the nervous system—the CNS and ANS—brings on spontaneous, free, open breathing and helps restore the task, balance, and harmony among the unconscious, automatic functions of the body with the conscious, deliberate ones. This phase is one of inquiry where biology and biography meet. The tremor work allows us to find and locate our armor, re-patterning our systems to improve bio-ergonomic function.[25]

During the Restructuring phase, we anchor in deep breathing and healthy vocal support, expanding the ribs on inhalation and training the transverse abdominal muscle to act in concert with the diaphragm so it can control the speed and force with which we drive air through the vocal folds, thereby making sounds. Intentionality (mentally directing thoughts, images, or ideas) marries sound through the use of the "focus line." In this phase, we concentrate on "structured breathing," which involves the physiological aspects of making sound and the psychological compound of breath/sound/meaning.

## Practice in Actor Training

My students often ask, "is Contemplative Practice a therapy or an acting technique?" Although I may consider them both because FV® can mend some strains, the answer is that this is an acting technique that urges you to ask questions in the "now." It is not a spiritual by-pass practice to avoid facing unresolved issues; it is meant as a positive force in life in the arts. One essential attribute of Contemplative Practice in Actor Training is that it makes possible and contributes to the artist's well-being. Therapy is treatment for circumstances that require special care and attention. Therapeutic needs—health giving tools—need not always conflate with therapy. Any pathology, physical or mental, needs to be treated by a medical doctor or certified counselor/psychiatrist. Caring for the instrument—body/mind/heart—is the actor's responsibility.

Contemplative Practice and, for that matter, FV® and Valdez's 21 steps also have provided a decolonizing tool for my Latinx students and me. Radical and transformative, I have witnessed my Latinx students develop capacities for deep concentration in the midst of theatrical action, opening them up to their creative possibilities. As one of my former students described, "contemplative and mindfulness practice in my actor training has decolonized my Latinx identity which is integral to my technique and artistry, and opened me to a world of choices which are not bound by mainstream expectations."[26] These new possibilities do not mean students need to esconse, compartmentalize or ignore the effects of oppressive privilege and power. Today, mending racialized trauma is part of our collective consciousness, as are conversations about diversity and inclusion; but 40 years ago, we had not recognized that racism affects not just our heads but also our bodies. That was not part of the greater discourse. We shift the conversation: from having to assimilate to a dominant culture to freeing our human possibilities from it and inventing a culture of equality where we shatter the delusion of race.

As artists, we cannot miss this occasion. We are obliged to recognize the trauma embedded in our bodies and to open our hearts to share the wisdom of our wounds. As far as I am concerned, Contemplative Practice in Actor/Performer Training takes head on the wordless stories stored in our body/mind/heart. Our historical bodies, and those of the elders who are still with us, have so many stories to tell, and we have so many splendid voices to tell them with that all we need to do is help ourselves. It does not take much to become a good actor if we train thoroughly; on the other hand, a great actor is a generous one. Opening our hearts to an audience, our fellow actors, and technicians starts with being compassionate with ourselves. Only then may we, sometimes, release all limiting boundaries.

## Notes

1 Konstantin Sergeyevich Stanislavski (1863–1938) was the groundbreaking Soviet and Russian theatre practitioner to whom we owe the proposal of a system of actor training and preparation, along with the inception of modern rehearsal techniques.
2 Konstantin Stanislavski, *My Life in Art,* trans. Jean Benedetti (London and New York: Routledge, 2008).
3 Chögyam Trungpa, *Meditation in Action* (Boston: Shambhala Publications, 2004).
4 Barbara Dilley (1938–) is an American dancer, performance artist, improvisor, choreographer, and educator. She was a prominent member of the Merce Cunningham Dance Company and of many ground-breaking companies. See Barbara Dilley, *This Very Moment: Teaching Thinking Dancing* (Boulder: Naropa University Press, 2015).
5 Lee Worley (1941–) is an American theater artist who trained as an actor in the Neighborhood Playhouse and was a member of Joseph Chaikin's Open Theater. See Lee Worley, *Coming from Nothing: The Sacred Art of Acting* (Boulder: Turquoise Dragon Press, 2001).
6 Mary Overlie (1946–2020) was an American choreographer, dancer, theatre artist, professor, author, and the originator of the Six Viewpoints technique for theatre and dance.
7 Wendell Beavers, teacher, dancer, choreographer, and director, was a founding faculty member of New York University's Experimental Theatre Wing (ETW), where he was involved in developing the Viewpoints in collaboration with originator Mary Overlie. He is the creator of Developmental Technique™ based on extensive study with Bonnie Bainbridge Cohen, developer of Body-Mind Centering®.
8 Erika Berland is a Certified Practitioner of Body-Mind Centering® and is pioneer in the field of somatic education creating new techniques and applications of Bonnie Cohen's groundbreaking work.
9 Luis Valdez (1940–), father of Chicano Film and theater, is best known for his play *Zoot Suit,* his movie *La Bamba,* and his creation El Teatro Campesino. The Theatre of the Sphere is Valdez's approach to theatre making and actor training. Los veinte pasos—the 20 steps of the creator—are found in the sacred Mayan calendar and represent not only the Mayan cosmology but also its psychology. Each one of the steps denotes a particular charge, or undertaking, a point of focus in training that brings awareness of the body-heart-mind-spirit union. With five steps dedicated to each one of the essences of the whole.
10 For more information and resources concerning FV®, please visit The Fitzmaurice Institute website. See The Fitzmaurice Institute, www.fitzmauriceinstitute.org/.
11 Tremwork™ is the cornerstone of FV®. It consists in activating the nervous system in order bring in concert its *voluntary* and *involuntary* functions for a healthy and vibrant production of the voice.
12 The "focus line" is a mental image used during the production of sound, channeling the breath and the communication through the length of the spine, in and out to capture the full compass of the listening audience.
13 All certified associate teachers of FV® strive to uphold the "Eight Values of the Fitzmaurice Institute." See "Eight Values of the Fitzmaurice Institute," The Fitzmaurice Institute, www.fitzmauriceinstitute.org/eightvaluesfi.
14 Stephen Batchelor, *Buddhism Without Beliefs* (New York: Riverhead Books, 1997).
15 Martine Batchelor, *The Spirit of the Buddha* (New Haven: Yale University Press, 2010).
16 Shunryu Suzuki, *Zen Mind, Beginner's Mind* (Boston: Shambhala Publications, 2010).

17 John Welwood, *Toward a Psychology of Awakening: Buddhism, Psychotherapy and the Path of Personal and Spiritual Transformation* (Boston: Shambhala, 2000).
18 Wilhelm Reich (1897–1957) his system of psychoanalysis concentrated on overall character structure rather than on individual neurotic symptoms.
19 Sigmund Freud (1856–1939) is considered as the founder of psychoanalysis. For Freud the libido, or sexualized energy, along with the death drive, was the source of compulsive or neurotic behavior.
20 Carl Gustav Jung (1875–1961), founder of analytic psychology, in response to Sigmund Freud's psychoanalysis. Jung postulated a process of psychological integration he called "individuation," which is largely dependent on the dynamics between the mythic images of the "shadow" and the "archetype."
21 See Wilhelm Reich, *The Function of the Orgasm,* trans. by Vincent R. Carfagno (New York: Farrar, Straus and Giroux, 1973). Reich calls our animating energy "orgone," coupling the words orgasm and organism, because he discovers the energy follows the pattern of expansion and contraction of the orgasm. Referring to orgasm as a way to heal neurosis was taboo during the time, so Reich was expelled from Freud's group. Alexander Lowen, a disciple of Reich, later calls it Bioenergetics. See Alexander Lowen, *Bioenergetics* (New York: Penguin Books, 1976).
22 Alexander Lowen (1910–2008) was an American physician and psychotherapist disciple of Wilhelm Reich during the 1940s and early 1950s. Lowen developed bioenergetic analysis and body-oriented psychotherapy. See Lowen, *Bioenergetics*.
23 CNS consists of the brain and spinal cord. It combines information from the entire body and coordinates activity across the whole organism. It controls everything the body does and feels.
24 ANS is the control system that acts largely unconsciously and regulates our involuntary bodily functions, such as the heart rate, digestion, and breathing. It divides into the sympathetic and parasympathetic. The sympathetic nervous system is responsible for *"fight or flight"* response.
25 For deeper understanding of bio-ergonomic function see Alexander Lowen, *Way to Vibrant Health: A Manual of Bioenergetic Exercises* (Shelbourne, VT: The Alexander Lowen Foundation, 2012); Michael Morgan, *Constructing the Holistic Actor: Fitzmaurice Voicework* (Lexington, KY: Michael Keith Morgan, 2012).
26 González Fontes, Lorenzo. Interview with former student, Maria Luisa Meza-Burgos. Personal, July 29, 2022.

## Bibliography

Batchelor, Martine. *The Spirit of the Buddha*. New Haven: Yale University Press, 2010.
Batchelor, Stephen. *Buddhism Without Beliefs*. New York: Riverhead Books, 1997.
The Fitzmaurice Institute. www.fitzmauriceinstitute.org/.
———. "Eight Values of the Fitzmaurice Institute." www.fitzmauriceinstitute.org/eightvaluesfi.
Dilley, Barbara. *This Very Moment: Teaching Thinking Dancing*. Boulder: Naropa University Press 2015.
Lowen, Alexander. *Bioenergetics*. New York: Penguin Books, 1976.
———. *Way to Vibrant Health: A Manual of Bioenergetic Exercises*. Shelbourne, VT: The Alexander Lowen Foundation, 2012.
Morgan, Michael. *Constructing the Holistic Actor: Fitzmaurice Voicework*. Lexington, KY: Michael Keith Morgan, 2012.
Reich, Wilhelm. *The Function of the Orgasm*. Translated by Vincent R. Carfagno. New York: Farrar, Straus and Giroux, 1973.

Stanislavski, Konstantin. *My Life in Art*. Translated by Jean Benedetti. London and New York: Routledge, 2008.
Suzuki, Shunryu. *Zen Mind, Beginner's Mind*. Boston: Shambhala Publications, 2010.
Trungpa, Chögyam. *Meditation in Action*. Boston: Shambhala Publications, 2004.
Welwood, John. *Toward a Psychology of Awakening: Buddhism, Psychotherapy and the Path of Personal and Spiritual Transformation*. Boston: Shambhala, 2000.
Worley, Lee. *Coming From Nothing: The Sacred Art of Acting*. Boulder: Turquoise Dragon Press, 2001.

# BENDICIONES

*Bendiciones* are blessings that our elders, mentors have bestowed on us throughout the generations.

*Para ustedes*, for you, *nuestra comunidad*: Whether you identify as Latinx, Latino, Latina, Latine, Hispanic, by your family's country of ancestry, bicultural or simply as a human—

May your imagination and determination allow you to able to pursue your artistic dreams.

By lifting each other up, we will grow in our craft, expand our scholarship and understanding, reshape the industry, prosper and most importantly thrive in our art.

*Muchas bendiciones.*

# INDEX

Note: Page numbers in *italics* indicate a figure and page numbers in **bold** indicate a table on the corresponding page.

accent 45, 46, 52, 57, 98, 102, 122, 124–126; standard American 118–119, 123
accent and dialect training 118, 127n6, 132–133, 142n1–3; importance of understanding Latinx 142; state of affairs in 133–135; suggestions for the Latinx actor 139–141, 143n19; teaching and coaching Latinx accents and dialects in 135–139
acting activism: acting technique of listening to the body of an actor and collaboration 36–37; *Las Mujeres Del Mar* and 29, 33–34; legacy and impact of Rodríguez on 37–38; physical embodiment of storytelling and 34–36
*Acting in the Academy* 14
African diaspora and dancing body 156–157
Afro-Caribbean, Afro-Caribeña, 132, 157
Afro-Cuban 55
Afro-Dominican 55
Afro-Latina 200–201, 206–207
Afro-Latinidad 201–202, 206
Afro-Latinx 138, 193, 202
Aguijón Theater 11
Agustin, Julio 176–177, 180
Aíza, Llever 150
A Laboratory for Actor Training (ALAT) 51

Albee, Edward 45
Alfaro, Luis 32, 137, 184, 193, 194
Ali, Muhammad 55
Almodóvar, Pedro 176
Alvarado, Elisa Marina 11
Alvarado, Mando 235, 239
*America Hurrah* 61
American actor training, traditional 118
*American Theatre Magazine* 236
Amezcua, Angélica 170–171
Anamú group 43
Anderson, Christina 164
Anthony, Adelina 11
Anzaldúa, Gloria 106, 121, 168
Araiza, J. Ed 21
Arias, Orlando 53
Ariaza, Ricky 165
Arizona State University 22–23, 74, 98, 164, 174, 208, 238, 245
Arreola, Dora 22
Asian American Performers Action Coalition (AAPAC) 20
Association of Theatre in Higher Education (ATHE) 133
assumptions, not making 251–252
*Atlanta* 213
auditions 228–229
autodidacts 183–190
autonomic nervous system (ANS) 268, 271n24

Baker, Annie 194
Balmaseda, Pedro 53, 54, 59
*Balm in Gilead* 208
Banda, Víctor Hugo Rascón 151
Bandyopadhyay, Sheila 259
Barba, Eugenio 51
Beavers, Wendell 263
Beckman, Brad 56
*Becoming Othello* 200
*Bells Are Ringing* 176
Belluso, John 32
Berland, Erika 263
best, doing one's 252–253
bilingualism 198–199
Billingslea, Aldo 8
Black, Indigenous, and People of Color (BIPOC) persons 1, 14, 20, 76
*Black Acting Methods* 1
Black and Brown Theatre 228–233
*Blade to the Heat* 55
Blau, Herbert 47
Boal, Augusto 44, 47, 87, 153, 199, 221, 222
*Bodas de Sangre* 23, 171–174
Boffone, Trevor 164–165
Bogart, Anne 193
*Bomba* dance 157
border aesthetics 85
*Border Brujo* 73, 75–76
Bouly, Julio 53
boundaries, finding one's 249
Bracey, Earl 224
Brando, Marlon 112
Brava! For Women in the Arts 11, 183
breathing 266, 267
Brecht, Bertolt 32, 46
Brewer, Nicole 120, 122
Briceño, Neher Jacqueline 53, 59
British Received Pronunciation 119
Brody, Alan 47
Brooke, Peter 31
Broyles-González, Yolanda 9
Buch, René 11, 23–24, 185
Buddhism in Fitzmaurice Voicework® 264–266
Buenaventura, Enrique 17
Byrd, Debra Ann 200–206

Cabrera, Pablo 44
Cacheiro, Jorge Luis 22
California Institute of the Arts 19–20, 21
Calvo, Agustin Garcia 169
Calzadilla, Fernando 53–54
Campo Santo 183

*Capeman, The* 178
Capoeira dance 156–157
Cara Mía 11
Carballido, Emilio 64
Cardenás, Nancy 7
Cardona, Cora 11
Cardona, Javier 48
Carreri, Roberta 51
Carrero, Jaime 46
Carrillo, Juliette 184
*Casa de Los Flores* 167
Castellanos, Zaida 53
casting, Latinx 208–218; resiliency and 250
Castro, Fidel 52
Castro, Robert 21
Castro, Vicente 45
Castro Smith, Charise 137
*Caucasian Chalk Circle, The* 186
Cedano, Carlos 53, 54
central nervous system (CNS) 268, 271n23
Centro Universitario de Teatro (CUT) 66–67
Chávez, César 99
*Chejov vs. Chejov* 59
Chekhov, Anton 59
Chibás, Marissa 19, 21, 110, 138; see also Mythic Imagination and the Actor
*Chicago the Musical* 176
Chicana, Chicano
Chicano/Latinx theatre companies 8–14, 24n3
*Chicano Theater: Themes and Forms* 20
Chicanx 11, 30, 33, 65–71, 75–76, 99, 259
Cicchino, Cree 216
Cieslak, Ryszard 67
Cisneros, Sandra 33
civic voice 225–226; conservatory training of the past and 221–222; Latinx voice and 222–226; *Nuestra Voz, Nuestra Historia* and 222–224; *Precious Lives* and 224–225
Colaianni, Louis 120
Colio, Bárbara 151
Colón, Alvan 48
Colón, Miriam 43, 45–46
*Comedy of Errors, The* 164–168
*Commedia dell'arte* 52, 66, 153, 156
*Community* 213
*Conduct of Life, The* 16
*Conference of the Birds* 31

Contemplative Practices 262–263, 269–270
Corazza, Juan Carlos 146
*Couple in the Cage: Two Undiscovered Amerindians Visit the West* 73
COVID-19 pandemic 151, 259
*Crazy Mexican Show, The* 222
Crenshaw, Kimberly 258
*Crimes of the Heart* 244
*Cristela* 208, 213
critical consciousness 99–100
*Cruci-fiction Project, The* 73
Cruz, CarlosAlexis 153
Cruz, Migdalia 194
Cruz, Nilo 137, 194
Cuba, Carmen 210
culturally competent (cultural competency) 3, 20, 125, 134, 236, 238, 241
cultural context in accent and dialect training 135–136
culturally inclusive pedagogy 124–127, 138
Culturally Relevant Pedagogy 88, 91n20
Culture Clash 183, 193, 216
Curiel, Tony 16–19

*Damn Yankees* 177
*Dándole Voz: An Exploration of Shakespeare in Spanish/Una Exploración de Shakespeare en Español* 171
Daniele, Graciela 179–180
Darío, Rubén 51
*Dawson's Creek* 211
*Dear White American Theater* 20
*De Cero Al Extremo* 157–159, *158*
de-colonizing 88
De Jesús, Robin 180
de Koven, Bernie 199
de la Barca, Calderón 151
de Lima, Ana Maria 53
Della Gatta, Carla 169, 171
Demos, Mickey 55
Destructuring in Fitzmaurice Voicework® 268–269
de Vega, Lope 23, 151
dialect *see* accent and dialect training
Dias Gomes, Alfredo de Freitas 46
Diaz, Kristoffer 194
*dignidad* 12, 24
Dilley, Barbara 263
directing of Latinx plays 235–241; feedback and 250–251; *see also* playwriting, Latinx

Dolan, Jill 142
*Domestic Negotiations* 30
Domingo, Coleman 21
*Doña Rosita la Soltera* 58–59
Douglas, Timothy 32
Downing, Marie Ramirez *see* Performance of Identity (PI) practice
Dragún, Osvaldo 43, 46
Dubatti, Jorge 44
Dunn, Kaja 120
Duprey, Jacqueline 22

*Elaborate Entrance of Chad Deity, The* 194
*Electricidad* 184
*El Gallo de La Habana* 48
*El Huracán* 137
Eliade, Mircea 75
El Teatro Campesino (ETC) 9, 29, 30–33, 66, 154; Alma Martinez at 67–70, *69*; Micha Espinosa and 99
El Teatro de la Esperanza 183
El Teatro Nacional de Aztlán (TENAZ) 13
*El Testamento del Perro* 64
English as a Second Language (ESL) classes 121
*Equalizer, The* 217
Equity, Diversity, and Inclusion (EDI) advocacy 236–237
*Esperando al Zurdo* 64
*Esperando La Carroza* 235
Espinosa, Micha 22, 74, 106–107, 118, 164–168; academic background of 97–99; on anti-immigration/anti-Latino/a/x/ sentiment 104; on cultural myths and Latinx actor training 99–103; on current state of Latinx students in the classroom 101–102; on danger of clumping Latinos together 102–103; on Mayan concept of In Lak'ech in actor training 105–106; MEChA and 98–99; *Not Barrio Enough* 97; on role of family in Latinx student's lives 104–105; at UCSD 98–99; on voz cultural 98
Espinosa, Victoria 44
Estefan, Emilio 178, 179
Estefan, Gloria 178
*Etta Jenks* 187
Eugenio, Olga de Martin 53
Eurocentric performance techniques 87–88
Eustis, Oscar 110

*Evita* 177
*Exploring Learning, Identity, and Power Through Life History and Narrative Research* 100

*Fade* 238, 240
*Family Matters* 231
feedback, giving and receiving 248, 250–251
Fernandez, Evelina 193
Ferrá, Max 10
festivals, Chicano/Latinx theatre 13
*Filo al Fuego* 55
Finlay, Bill 51–52, 55
Fitzmaurice, Catherine 98, 99, 107n2, 262–270
Fitzmaurice Voicework® 126, 143n21, 222, 262–270; destructuring and restructuring in 268–269; development of 263–264; main inspirational points of Buddhism in 264–266; natural breath and sound production in 267–268; Practice in Actor Training and 269–270; right concentration in 266
Flaten, David 66
*Floating Island Plays, The* 110
Floyd, George 20
Fornés, María Irene 8, 16, 193
Fought, Carmen 138
*Four Agreements* framework 246–253; always doing your best in 252–253; never taking anything personally in 249–251; not making assumptions in 251–252; speaking with integrity in 247–249
*Four Guys Names Jose and Una Mujer Named Maria* 178
"Freeing the Natural Voice" method 145, 151–152; applied to Spanish 146–147; bilingüe teacher and 148; finding a better educational framework for 149–150; Kristin Linklater and 145–146; new generation of maestros using 150–151
Freeman, Brian 32
Freire, Paulo 99–100, 149
*Fresh Prince* 231
Freud, Anna 267
Freud, Sigmund 267
*Frog Prince, The* 231–232
*Fuenteovejuna* 23

GALA Hispanic Theatre 12
García, Edgar M. 22
Garcia, Lydia 164–168
Garcia, Maria 53, 54
Garcia, Tony 9
García-López, Saúl 74; on arriving at experiential, philosophical, and epistemological shift 88; early stages in Mexico City 82–83; as indigenous queer, brown, and *Puto-Prieto-Chacal* artist and pedagogue 88–89; La Pocha Nostra and 84–87; on Latin embodiment and Eurocentric performance techniques 87–88; as radical nomad 84
Garneau, Michael 164
Gatica, Esther Banegas 56–58
*George Lopez* 216, 217
Global Majority 1, 98, 117, 120–121, 257
Glover, Donald 213
Godinez, Henry 11, 13, 21
Goldsmith, Barclay 9
Gómez, Balitrónica 74
Gomez, Marga 183
Gómez-Pena, Guillermo 73, 84; exercises employed by 76–78; La Pocha Nostra (LPN) and 74–75, 76; *Performance for Innocents* and 73, 78–81; seminal performances of 73–74, 75–76
González, Aníbal 42
Gonzalez, Eliberto 11
Gonzalez, Humberto 53
González, José Cruz 184
González, José Eduardo 10
González, Tania 150
"Good American Speech" 118–121
Goodhart, Rebecca 171
Goodman Theatre Latino Festival 13
*Good Person of Setzuan, The* 32
gossip 248–249
*Greetings From Tucson* 211, 212, 217
Grotowski, Jerzy 63–67, 71, 199; Poor Theatre 67–70, *69*
Guido, Fabrizio Zacharee 216–217
*Guys and Dolls* 45, 243

*Hamilton* 194, 196
Harlem Shakespeare Festival 200–206
Harnett, Penelope 100
Hauck, Rachel 32
hegemonic whiteness 86, 89n7
Henley, Beth 244
*Henry V* 45
Hernandez, Jorge 53
Hernández, Teresa 48
Herrera, Brian 209

Herrera, Patricia 173
Heyes, Cressida 256, 257
*Hij@s de la Bernarda* 48
Hispanic Playwrights Project (HPP) 184
Hoffman, Dustin 112
*House on Mango Street* 33
*How to Succeed in Business Without Really Trying* 61
Hudes, Quiara Alegría 178, 194, 209–210, 219n9, 235–236, 238–239, 241
Huerta, Delores 99
Huerta, Jorge 2, 9, 44, 98, 134, 185; *Chicano Theater: Themes and Forms* 20; at University of California San Diego 14–19
Huertas, Luisa 150
Hurst, Jeff 11

Ibargüengoitia, Jorge 151
identity 1–2, 63–64, 78–79, 82, 132, 146, 147, 168, 170–174, 201, 206, 244, 256–258; African culture and Hispanic 111; bilingual 145, 148; borderlands 73; Chicanx 70–71, 98–102; cultural 15, 54–55, 59, 106–107, 170; linguistic 117–127, 167; oppressive forces on 83–84, 88; poetry of 97; psychosocial 105; self-determinations of 86–87; stages of consciousness toward 103
idiolect 118, 125, 134, 135, 136, 137, 138, 170
Iizuka, Naomi 194
Inclán, Valle 43
indigenous 3, 14, 20, 64, 69–70, 88–91, 111, 135, 153, 158–159, 162, 193, 197
indigenous-Mestizx ethnicity *see* García-López, Saúl
In Lak'ech 105, 190
*In Search of Duende* 111
institutional training programs 14–20, 16–18
INTAR 10
*Intercultural Acting and Performance Training* 1
Interián, Alina 51
International Hispanic Theatre Festival of Miami 13
International Phonetic Alphabet (IPA) 125–126
intersectionality 2, 142, 258, 260n6
*In the Heights* 178, 196, 219n9, 235
Iriarte, Sonia de Martin 53
Ishii, Leslie 120

Jiménez, Livia Esther 145
Jodorowsky, Alejandro 78
*Joy of Phonetics and Accents, The* 120
Juliá, Raúl 46, 180
Jung, Carl Gustav 267
Justiniano, Nathaniel 22

Kanelos, Nicolás 8, 44
King, Carole 243
*Kingpin* 216
*Kiss of the Spider Woman* 178
*Knickerbocker Holiday* 177
Knight, Dudley 119–120, 222
Knight-Thompson Speechwork (KTS) 120, 125, 143n20
Knutson, Susan 164
*Korean Approach to Actor Training, A* 1
Kushner, Tony 31–32

Laboratorio de Acrobacia Indígena 154–155
LAByrinth Theater Company 10
*La carreta* 45–46
*La casa de Bernarda Alba* 45, 48
*La Comedia of Errors* 23, 164–168
Ladson-Billings, Gloria 124
*La Gran Carpa de los Rasquachis* 66, 68
*L.A. Law* 216
*La Letter* 210
*La Liberación de la Voz Natural: el Método Linklater* 147
*La Maestra* 17
*La Mancha* 23
*La Máscara Popular* 155–156
Lambert, Ruth 213
*La muerte no entrará en palacio* 46
Langsner, Jacobo 235
*La pasión según Antígona Pérez* 45
La Pocha Nostra (LPN) 74–78; Saúl García-López and 84–87
*La Pocha Nostra: A Handbook for the Rebel Artist in a Post-Democratic Society* 76, 84
La Saula *see* García-López, Saúl
*Las Mujeres Del Mar* 29, 33–34, 37–38; physical embodiment of storytelling in 34–36
Latifah, Queen 217
*Latina Monologues, The* 224
Latina Theatre Lab 183
Latin embodiment and Eurocentric performance techniques 87–88
*Latinidad* 2, 93, 101–102, 173, 174n5, 175n13, n15, 201–202, 209–210, 218n1, 219n8

# Index

Latino Actors Base 10
Latino Theater Company, Los Angeles 8, 10
Latino Theatre Initiative (LTI) 32–33
Latins Anonymous 31, 40n22
Latinx actor training 1–3; accent and dialect training in (*see* accent and dialect training); Afro-Latinas 200–206; Alma Martinez on (*see* Martinez, Alma); casting and 208–218; in Chicano/Latinx theatre companies 8–14, 24n3; civic voice and 221–226; critical consciousness in 99–100; current state of 20–23; *dignidad* and 12, 24; directing of Latinx plays and 235–241; Fitzmaurice Voicework® in 126, 143n21, 222, 262–270; Guillermo Gómez-Pena and (*see* Gómez-Pena, Guillermo); incomplete archives on 7–8; institutional programs for 14–20, *16–18*; Latin embodiment and Eurocentric performance techniques and 87–88; Latinx faculty and 21–22, 52–54; linguistic identity and (*see* linguistic identity, Latinx); for musical theatre 176–181; the mythic and 111–116; Performance of Identity (PI) practice and 255–260; for physical theatre (*see* physical theatre pedagogy, Latinx-driven); playwriting and (*see* playwriting, Latinx); in Puerto Rican theatre 42–48; Saúl García-López on (*see* García-López, Saúl); self-taught 183–190; at Teatro Prometeo (*see* Teatro Prometeo); using the *Four Agreements* framework 243–253
Latinx community: diversity of 111, 118; growth in the United States 2, 118, 127n4; as part of Global Majority 1, 98, 117
Latinx Theatre Alliance/Los Angeles (LTA/LA) 28
Latinx Theatre Commons (LTC) 2
*La zapatera prodigiosa* 46
Lechuga, Susy 53
Leguizamo, John 180, 194, 228
Lerman, Liz 248
Lewis, Vicky 32
LGBTQIA community 11, 14, 180
linguistic identity, Latinx 117–118; reclaiming and reaffirming *Nuestras Voces* and building a culturally and language inclusive pedagogy for 124–127; speech training or linguistic bias and 121–124;

standard accent and the legacy of "Good American Speech" 118–121
Linklater, Kristin 145–146, 151–152, 257–259; *see also* "Freeing the Natural Voice" method
Lippi-Green, Rosina 118–119, 256
listening, deep 36–37
*Little Engine That Could, The* 45
*Living Museum of Fetishized Identities, The* 73
*Living Out* 187
Logan, Sandy 213
Loomer, Lisa 187
*Lopez* 208
López, Josefina 10
Lopez-Cepero, Omar 179
Lopez-Rios, Michelle 22, 221–226
Lorca, Federico García 19, 23, 43, 46, 58–59, 111, 151, 171–172
Los Angeles Theatre Center (LATC) 10
Lozano, Jaime 178
Luna, Alan 210

*Macbeth* 169, 171
Machado, Eduardo 110–111, 137, 194
Machosa, Julio Oscar 212
Macomber, Annie Weisman 32
Malán, Dañel 10
*Man of La Mancha* 177
Margolis, Ellen 1
Mariano, Nola 74
Marín, Christina 243–246
Marín, Gerard Paul 45
Marqués, René 8, 45–46
Márquez, Rosa Luisa 42–48
Marquez, Sandra 21–22
Marquez, Willie 110
Marroquín, Bianca 180
Marsden, Samantha 245
Martinez, Alma 21; birth through high school, 1954–1971 60–61; at Centro Universitario de Teatro (CUT), 1976–1977 66–67; as Chicana academic of acting methodologies 71; at El Teatro Campesino's Theatre of the Sphere and Grotowski's Poor Theatre 67–70, *69*; at Universidad de Guadalajara, 1972– 1973 63–64; at USC Department of Drama, 1971– 1972 61–63; at Whittier College, 1974– 1976 64–66; and *Zoot Suit* and Chicanx identity, 1979– 1980 70
Martinez, Fidel 216
Mártinez Álvarez, Alicia 156

Martorell, Antonio 46–47, 48
Mastache, Carmen 150
Matos, Julio Jr. 22
Mayer, Oliver 55
McCranie, Sara 53
McLean, Margaret 119
McMahon, Marci R. 173
*Measure for Measure* 237
Medrano, Hugo 12
Meléndez, Priscilla 42
Mendez, Lindsay 180
Mendoza, Héctor 65, 67
Mendoza, Zilah 183–190
Messulam, Melissa 53, 54
Method acting 83, 89n1, 113, 192, 193
*Mexterminator Project, The* 73
*Miami Vice* 216
Miller, Vernice 51
mindfulness 265–266
Miranda, Lin-Manuel 178, 180, 194, 209, 219n9
Mirecka, Rena 67
Mirren, Helen 31
Molik, Zygmunt 67
*Monologues for Latino Actors: A Resource Guide to Contemporary Latino/a Playwrights for Actors and Teachers* 22
Montoya, Tony 213–214
Moraga, Cherie 183, 194
Moreno, Rita 179
Morín, Francisco 52
Moser, Joshua Feliciano-Sánchez 22
*Mr. Inglesias* 208, 212, 213, 214, 217
Munoz, José Esteban 76
Murphy, Carlos 208
Murrieta, Peter 208–218
musical theatre 176–181
Mustelier, Maria Christina 54
*My Fair Lady* 177
*Mythic Imagination and the Actor* 21, 111–113

*Narcos* 216
Newsom, Nicole 225
Noa, Jorge 53, 54, 59
Noblezada, Eva 180
*Not Barrio Enough* 97
*Nuestra Voz, Nuestra Historia* 222–224
*Nuevos Pasos: Chicano and Puerto Rican Drama* 44
Nuñez, Oscar 212

Obama, Barack 33
Ocampo-Guzman, Antonio 22, 118, 145
Odets, Clifford 64
Odin Teatret 51
*Office, The* 214
Ohama, Natsuko 259
Olivo, Karen 180
Olmos, James 216
*One Day at a Time* 208
Ontiveros, Lupe 211
*On Your Feet!* 178, 179
*O pagador de promessas* 46
Orellana, Tanya 35–36
Oropeza, Luz 73, 78–79
Orta, Marisela Trevino 235
Ortega, Gabriela 35
Ortiz, Johnny 10
Othering 87–88
*Our Town/Nuestro Pueblo* 23
Overlie, Mary 193, 263

Pacheco, Ferdie 55
Padrón, Eduardo 51
Padrón, Jacob G. 178
Pagauga-Sandoval, Rubén 185
Pages, Madeline 172
Palacios, Mónica 183
Pandiani, Tatiana 23, 171–172
*Papeles* 56
*Paradise Now* 43
Parenteau, Amelia 236, 237
Paz, Coya 11
Pensado, Indira 150
Peretz, Susan 187, 189–190
Pereyra, Melisa 22
Perez, Jesse 21
*Performance for Innocents* 73, 78–81
Performance of Identity (PI) practice 255–260
*Performance Theory* 75
Peterson, Laylah 224–225
Peterson, Lisa 32
phonology 136, 143n11–13
physical embodiment of storytelling 34–36
physical theatre pedagogy, Latinx-driven 153–154, 159–160; African diaspora and dancing body 156–157; *De Cero Al Extremo* 157–159, *158*; Laboratorio de Acrobacia Indígena 154–155; La Máscara Popular 155–156; Voladores de Papantla 155; warm-up exercises 160–161
Picasso, Pablo 251
*Picasso at the Lapin Agile* 251
Picket, Manuel José 13
Pinero, Miguel 186

Piñero, Yarani del Valle 53
Pino, Hector 56
*Pipo Subway no sabe reír* 46, 48
Plata, Jorge 169
playwriting, Latinx 192–193; acting methods and 199; bilingualism and telenovelas and 198–199; culture living in the body and 196; Latinx stereotypes and 194–196; major figures in 193–194; ritual and 196–198; speaking with integrity in 247; *see also* directing of Latinx plays
*Politics of Actor Training, The* 1
Practice in Actor Training 269–270
Pradera, Carlota 53
*Precious Lives* 224–225, 226
predominantly white institutions (PWI) (also, primarily white institutions) 201, 202, 206, 236–237, 239, 244–245,
Pregones Theater 42, 48
Prida, Dolores 8, 178
*Professional Actor's Handbook: From Casting Call to Curtain Call* 177
prosody 135, 137
*Psychomagic: The Transformative Power of Shamanic Psychotherapy* 78
Puerto Rican theatre 42–48
Puerto Rican Traveling Theatre (PRTT) 9–10, 42–43, 45–46
puppet theater 46–47

Queen's English 119
Quesada, Claudia 56–57
questioning 252

Ramirez, Lisa 183–190
Ramirez, Robert 21
*rasquache* 9, 70, 72n9
Rauch, Bill 164–168, 237
Raúl Julia Training Unit 10
Read, Rebecca 12
*Really Rosie* 243
Rebull, Cristina 53, 59
Reich, Wilhelm 264, 267
Renaud, Lissa Tyler 1
Repertorio Español 12, 23–24
research by actors 252
resiliency 249–250
Restructuring in Fitzmaurice Voicework® 268–269
R. Evolución Latina 10
Right Concentration 266
Rios, Alvaro Saar 222
Rivera, Jose 194

Rivera, Sonia Sofia 36
River Bride, The 235
Rizk, Beatriz 53
Robbins, Jerome 178
Rodriguez, Chantal 7, 171
Rodríguez, Diane 28–30, 38–39n9, 184; on acting activism 29; acting philosophies from El Teatro Campesino to the White House 30–33, 40n24; acting technique of listening to the body of an actor and collaboration 36–37; cultivating the physical embodiment of storytelling 34–36; *Las Mujeres Del Mar* and 29, 33–34; Latino Theatre Initiative (LTI) and 32–33; Latins Anonymous and 31, 40n22; legacy and impact of 37–38; on Socorro Valdez 28–29
Rodriguez, Emilio 228–233
Rodriguez, Gonzalo 55, 59
Rodriguez, José 185
Rojas, Teresa María 13, 51, 52
Rolón, Rosalba 48
*Roosters* 16
*Rosa Luisa Márquez, memorias de una teatrera del Caribe: Conversaciones con Miguel Rubio* 48
Rosenberg, Joseph 13
Ruiz, Don Miguel 246–253
Ruiz, Jerry *see* directing of Latinx plays
Ruiz, Vivian 53, 59

Salinas Schoenberg, Janine 29, 33, 34–35, 37, 38n6
Sanchez, Gabriela 210
Sánchez, Luis Rafael 45
Sánchez, Mario Ernest 13, 52
Sánchez, Mónica 183–190
Sánchez-Muñoz, Ana 170–171
Sanchez-Scott, Milcha 16
San Diego Repertory Theatre Annual Latinx New Play Festival 13
Sandoval, Rafael 63
Santaliz, Pedrito 44
Santos DeCure, Cynthia 22, 23, 180, 209, 231; *Bodas de Sangre* and 171–174; Shakespeare en Español at Yale and 168–171; *see also* accent and dialect training; linguistic identity, Latinx; Shakespeare works
Saracho, Tanya 11, 194, 235, 239, 241
*Scenes for Latinx Actors* 2, 22, 129n47
Schechner, Richard 43, 75, 76
Schirle, Joan 153

*Seascape* 45
self-taught actors 183–190
Sendak, Maurice 243
Sevan, Adriana 29, 32, 34–35, 36–37, 38
Shakespeare 57, 83, 103, 148, 151, 222, 231, 259: acting courses in 22, 23; festivals 17, 237; Harlem 200–206
Shakespeare works: tradaptations en La Frontera with Micha Espinosa 164–168; translanguaging *Bodas de Sangre* 171–174; at Yale with Cynthia Santos DeCure 168–171
Shakira 100–101
Shank, Adele 15, 19
*Shelter* 138
Sierra, Ruben 185
Sifuentes, Roberto 74
Simpson, Dwayne 55
*Sister Sister* 231
SITI Company 10
Skinner, Edith 119–120
*Smash* 229
Smith, Betty Franklin 100
Smits, Jimmy 216
Solís, Octavio 184, 194, 259
Sotelo, Veronica 224
*Sources of the Self: The Making of the Modern Identity* 255
Spanish vowel shaping warm-up exercise 139–141, 143n19
speaking with integrity 247–249
*Speak with Distinction* 119
*Spoon River Anthology* 61
*Sports Night* 214
*Stage, The* 245
standard American accent 118–121
*Standard Speech: The Ongoing Debate* 119
Stanislavski, Konstantin 61, 64, 65, 192, 193, 199, 262
Steele, Liza 240
stereotype 3, 31–32, 39, 53, 76, 98–100, 102–103, 106, 122–123, 127, 132, 169, 176, 178–179, 194–196, 198, 216–217, 233, 256, 258
Stoever, Jennifer 122
Strasberg, Lee 193, 199
Suasunna, Arianna 64
*Such Things as Vampires* 236
*Superstore* 214
Suzuki, Shunryu 197, 199, 265
Suzuki Method 21, 22, 76, 193
Svich, Caridad *see* playwriting, Latinx
Swain, Donna 208
*Sweetheart Deal, The* 30, 32

Talenti, Pier Carlo 32
Taylor, Charles 255
Taylor, Diana 22–23, 48
Teach for America (TFA) 229
Teatro Avante 13
Teatro Bilingüe 13
*Teatro Campesino* 44
Teatro Dallas 11
*teatro de guiñol* (puppet theater) 46
Teatro Espejo 13–14
*Teatro La Barraca* 43
Teatro Libertad 9
Teatro Luna 11
Teatro Milagro 10
Teatro Prometeo 13, 50; cultural identity of shows produced by 54–57; curriculum of 52, 57–58; development of 51–52; faculty of 52–54; founding of 51; legacy of 58–59; programming and culture of 54
teatro tradition 9–12
Teatro Vista 11
Teatro Vivo Austin Latinx New Play Festival 13
telenovelas 198–199
television and film 2, 3n3, n4, 10, 21, 29, 53, 60, 66, 123, 133, 199, 208
Telles, Edward 240
*Tempest, The* 231
*Temple of Confessions* 73, 76
*Theatre of the Oppressed* 47, 100
*Theatre of the Sphere: The Vibrant Being* 9, 105
*30 Rock* 213, 214
*Threepenny Opera* 46
*Thru the Leaves* 187
Tilly, William 119
Torres, Edward 11
tradaptations of Shakespeare 164–168
Tramposch, Emma 74
transforming from self 124–125
translanguaging *Bodas de Sangre* 171–174
Tremwork 263, 268, 270
Treser, Robert 65
*Trojan Women, The* 187
Tubert, Susana 178
*26 Miles* 238
Two River Theater Crossing Borders Festival 13

*Ugly Betty* 217
United Farm Workers (UFW) Movement 30, 70
Universidad de Guadalajara 63–64

University of California Los Angeles 21
University of California San Diego 14–19, *16–18*, 21, 98–99
University of La Verne 21
USC Department of Drama 61–63

Valdéz, Luis 8, 9, 44, 71, 105, 154, 185, 263; Alma Martinez and 66–68; on critical consciousness 99–100; as parent of Latinx playwriting 193
Valdez, Socorro 28–29, 31, 68
Valenzuela, José Luis 10, 193
Vargas, Jacob 212
Vargas, Rosario 11
Vargas, Sebastián Eddowes 7
Varon, Daniela 23
Vasquez, Angela C. Trudell 224
Vázquez, Victor Élan 210
Vázquez, Viveca 48
Vee, Kiran 224
Vega, Liliam 53
*veinte pasos* 263
Villafañe, Miguel 42
Voice and Speech Trainers Association (VASTA) 120–121, 133, 209
Voladores de Papantla 155
*voz cultural* 98

Wade, Ralph 186
*Waiting for Godot* 47
Warren, Iris 145–146
*Water by the Spoonful* 196, 236, 239

*Welcome to Tucson* 208
We See You White American Theatre 1
*West Side Story* 177, 202, 244
White, Bill 62–63
Whittier College 64–66
Wilder, Thornton 23
Wilson, August 8
Wilson, Lanford 208
Wilson, Walton 171
*Wizards of Waverly Place, The* 208, 217
Wolpe, Lisa 259
*Women on the Verge of a Nervous Breakdown* 176
Woodard, Tamilla 171
Worley, Lee 263

Yale School of Drama 2, 22, 23; *Bodas de Sangre* at 171–174; Shakespeare en Español at 168–171
Yarrow, Joann *see* Teatro Prometeo
Ybarra, Patricia 239
Yew, Chay 32
*Yo Tambien Hablo de las Rosas* 64

Zacarias, Karen 194
Zaldívar, Gilberto 11–12
Zamora, Romulus 13
Zayas, Dean 153
Zayas, José 13
Zazzali, Peter 14
Zentella, Ana Celia 122–123
*Zoot Suit* 67, 68, 70, 193

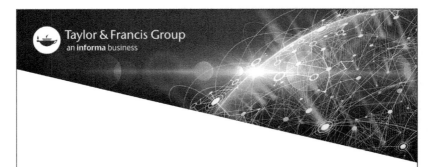